# GLOBAL PERSPECTIVES ON CRIME PREVENTION AND COMMUNITY RESILIENCE

# International Police Executive Symposium Co-Publications

**Dilip K. Das, *Founding President – IPES***

**PUBLISHED**

**Global Perspectives on Crime Prevention and Community Resilience**
Edited by Diana Scharff Peterson and Dilip K. Das, ISBN: 978-1-4987-4897-1

**Global Issues in Contemporary Policing**
Edited by John A. Eterno, Arvind Verma, Aiedeo Mintie Das, and Dilip K. Das, ISBN: 978-1-4822-4852-4

**Change and Reform in Law Enforcement**
Edited by Scott W. Phillips and Dilip K. Das, ISBN: 978-1-4987-4168-2

**Economic Development, Crime, and Policing: Global Perspectives**
Edited by David Lowe, Austin T. Turk, and Dilip K. Das, ISBN: 978-1-482-20456-8

**Policing Major Events: Perspectives from Around the World**
Edited by James F. Albrecht, Martha Christine Dow, Darryl Plecas, and Dilip K. Das, ISBN: 978-1-466-58805-9

**Examining Political Violence: Studies of Terrorism, Counterterrorism, and Internal War**
Edited by Frederic Lemieux, Garth den Heyer, Dilip K. Das, ISBN: 978-1-466-58820-2

**The Evolution of Policing: Worldwide Innovations and Invites**
Edited by Melchor C. Guzman, Aiedeo Mintie Das, and Dilip K. Das, ISBN: 978-1-4665-6715-3

**Policing Global Movement: Tourism, Migration, Human Trafficking, & Terrorism**
Edited by S. Caroline Taylor, Daniel Joseph Torpy, and Dilip K. Das, ISBN: 978-1-466-50726-5

**Global Community Policing: Problems and Challenges**
Edited by Arvind Verma, Dilip K. Das, and Manoj Abraham, ISBN: 978-1-439-88416-4

**Global Environment of Policing**
Edited by Dilip K. Das, Darren Palmer, Clifford D. Shearing and Anthony L. Sciarabba, ISBN: 978-1-4200-6590-9

**Strategies and Responses to Crime: Thinking Locally, Acting Globally**
Edited by Dilip K. Das, Mintie Das, and Larry French, ISBN: 978-1-4200-7669-1

**Effective Crime Reduction Strategies: International Perspectives**
Edited by James F. Albrecht and Dilip K. Das, ISBN: 978-1-4200-7838-1

**Police Without Borders: The Fading Distinction between Local and Global**
Edited by Cliff Roberson and Dilip K. Das, ISBN: 978-1-4398-0501-5

**Urbanization, Policing, and Security: Global Perspectives**
Edited by Gary Cordner, Dilip K. Das, and AnnMarie Cordner, ISBN: 978-1-4200-8557-0

**Criminal Abuse of Women and Children: An International Perspective**
Edited by Obi N. I. Ebbe and Dilip K. Das, ISBN: 978-1-4200-8803-8

**Contemporary Issues in Law Enforcement and Policing**
Edited by Andrew Millie, PhD and Dilip K. Das, ISBN: 978-1-4200-7215-0

# GLOBAL PERSPECTIVES ON CRIME PREVENTION AND COMMUNITY RESILIENCE

Edited by
Diana Scharff Peterson
Dilip K. Das

International Police Executive Symposium Co-Publications

Routledge
Taylor & Francis Group
LONDON AND NEW YORK

First published 2018
by Routledge

2 Park Square, Milton Park, Abingdon, Oxfordshire OX14 4RN
52 Vanderbilt Avenue, New York, NY 10017

*Routledge is an imprint of the Taylor & Francis Group, an informa business*

First issued in paperback 2019



*Library of Congress Cataloging in Publication Data*
Names: Scharff Peterson, Diana, editor. | Das, Dilip K., 1941– editor.
Title: Global perspectives on crime prevention and community resilience / edited by Diana Scharff Peterson and Dilip K. Das.
Description: 1 Edition. | New York : Routledge, 2018. |
Series: International police executive symposium co-publications | Includes index.
Identifiers: LCCN 2017023110| ISBN 9781498748971 (hardback) | ISBN 9781315368481 (ebk)
Subjects: LCSH: Crime prevention. | Communities.
Classification: LCC HV7431 .G444 2018 | DDC 364.4–dc23
LC record available at https://lccn.loc.gov/2017023110

ISBN: 978-1-4987-4897-1 (hbk)
ISBN: 978-0-367-87550-3 (pbk)

Typeset in Minion Pro
by Wearset Ltd, Boldon, Tyne and Wear

This book is dedicated to Ana Das – we love you. Your perseverance and strength following our Sofia meeting has inspired all of us. Jimmy Albrecht – this large effort is also dedicated to you, so that you will continue to build a better world and come back to perfect health, as the world needs you. Sedat Mülayim – now you are truly a guiding light in heaven and beyond – you are greatly loved and missed. We are certain that you are now one of the brightest stars in the nighttime sky, and gratefully dedicate this book to you.

# Contents

# Foreword

## STAN STOJKOVIC AND HELEN BADER

It was the sociologist Egon Bittner (1970) who understood the conundrum that democracies face when they attempt to apply coercive power. The instrument of this coercive power is typically presented through the police, at least in Bittner's understanding, yet the application of coercive power in democracies as evidenced by the entire criminal justice system is also somewhat apparent and potentially controversial and problematic. The disjuncture between state sponsored coercive power, on the one hand, and the legitimate functioning of a democracy where an appreciation of diversity of opinion is valued, on the other hand, is the essence of what Bittner recognized as a problem for democracies.

Bittner recognized something that even to this day we still struggle with in democracies: the expression of coercive force in a democracy must always be monitored, assessed, and questioned if we are ever to sustain democratic thinking and its concomitant principles of justice, equity, fairness, and the rule of law. Yet, the struggle to maintain criminal justice practices under a democratic political system is often times very difficult. Maybe this is as it should be. Democracy and its attendant criminal justice systems are evolving projects; they require constant vigilance and work to remain vibrant and receptive to the needs of the polity.

In early twenty-first-century democracies, we are seeing disturbing trends and calls for action and change in criminal justice practices. Take, for example, police violence in America. It has seemed to escalate, at least the appearance is the police are acting arbitrarily in many of their encounters with ordinary citizens, most of whom are poor and come from communities of color. Whether it is Ferguson, Missouri, Miami, Florida, Chicago, Illinois, or any other community with a high profile racially based encounter, and in some cases, confrontations with the police, the outcomes are being questioned. This, again, may not be a bad thing, as it represents the responsiveness of criminal justice officials and political leaders to minimize the appearance of problems and in some cases clear and convincing evidence of criminal justice practices gone awry.

This volume begins a conversation that highlights the tensions of criminal justice responses to crime in both democracies and other developing nations across the world. What editor Peterson has put together is a treasure-trove of articles and research findings that highlight global perspectives on crime prevention and community resilience. As you read these articles, take note of what is being employed across America and the rest of the world to address crime and how community resilience is an interesting proposition put forward by many authors in this volume.

Yet, being community resilient is often times not enough. We have had for many years, for example, the principles and practices of "target hardening" to prevent crime and disorder as a community resilience strategy. Since the early 1990s, we have seen urban communities across the country embrace community policing ideals and practices in response to crime and criminals. The community policing rubric is fairly broad and encompassing and can mean different things to different communities. We know community policing efforts in one city are not the same community policing efforts in another city. This is why policing has and is such a community phenomenon. As noted by the historian Sam Walker (1980), American criminal justice has always had a uniquely local and community bend to it, or in his words, "popular justice has always been influenced by the norms and values of the community." Centralized operations of criminal justice functions really are not an American phenomenon or ideal and never have been.

What is uniquely American is the diversity of responses to crime across this country and the almost bizarre ways in which Americans accept this diversity as normal but only to a point. The tipping point seems to be when criminal justice practices run counter to another American value: the rule of law. The twentieth century has seen a plethora of laws passed at all levels of government – federal, state, and local – to guide and direct criminal justice practices. As we unfold the twenty-first century, we now are seeing the advent of new issues, laws, and expectations in our evolving democracy that raise many questions regarding the responsiveness of local criminal justice systems to the communities they serve. No other issue is as paramount now than how criminal justice actors are viewed by their respective communities. The reasserting principle of democracy in action is ever present in communities across America. In fact, we see the yearning for more democracy across the world. The struggles of countries in the Middle East, for example, such as Egypt and Syria, to mention a few, are daily reminders of the search for democracy and the price that must be paid to earn it and to sustain it over time. America only reflects a democracy that has reinvented itself many times over roughly 200 plus years.

The twenty-first century must be understood as a time where there is much upheaval and unrest across the world. The world does seem less safe to many, especially to Americans who have now experienced terrorism first hand in the 1990s and on 9/11. The question is how do we best respond to this changing world? This volume attempts to address this question by examining specifically police practices in the new world order. Some of the articles offer specific advice surrounding certain crimes, e.g., burglary suppression, while others focus more on community resilience across the world. Regardless of focus, the volume begins an inquiry into what are the various global perspectives on crime prevention and community resilience.

This inquiry will take many forms and expressions. Some of the articles have a research focus or are based on a research strategy; other articles will be more prescriptive. What is important is that all 18 pieces in this volume provide either a conceptual roadmap on how to understand a community resilient plan to address crime or offer invaluable practical advice to communities on how best to address crime. The challenge for communities will be how to operationalize the ideas and strategies put forward here into action plans that make sense for their communities.

As one of the articles in this collection states, there is no "one size fits all" approach to neighborhood policing strategies. As neighborhoods vary within a community, so do communities and countries vary tremendously, and as such, there is no panacea solution to crime. As you go forward and read the articles in this volume, we would ask the following fundamental questions: how is what the author is conveying relevant to my community? What hurdles or obstacles exist in my community that make the adoption of any ideas or action plans presented here likely or unlikely? Is there political consensus on how best to address crime problems in my community? Do we have examples of resiliency in my community that we can learn from in addressing and managing crime? What special populations exist within the community that would require innovative or minimally different approaches to criminal justice practices?

Providing initial answers to these questions will be useful as you read the articles and assess their relevance to individual communities. Additionally, there are larger contextual issues that require the attention of the reader. These issues typically reflect some realities of criminal justice practices that must be addressed or some larger contextual issues that require your examination. Take, for example, the burden that is often times felt by local criminal justice officials when they are asked to address and even manage large institutional failures, yet criminal justice practices will never sufficiently address the ills of society: a failing school system, chronic unemployment or underemployment, fractured families, or non-responsive churches. Criminal justice practices operate within the realm of governmental rules, regulations, political differences, and infinite expectations for stellar performance in a reality of finite resources. We know of no police executive who believes he or she is adequately funded, but we can show you police organizations that are expected to provide miracles to the communities they serve.

Moreover, criminal justice agencies operate in a world of political processes and clear realities. We mean the importance of the political process to successful criminal justice operations cannot be overstated. We often times state to our students that politics does not have to be a dirty word; politics is a process by which things either get done or they do not get done. Successful criminal justice administrators are those who understand politics as a process and work to influence that process toward positive outcomes for their people and agencies. As you read the articles, please consider how what is being discussed or advocated could be operationalized through the political process or not. Remember, the road to hell is paved with good intentions. Similarly, great criminal justice ideas are meaningless if they cannot be operationalized in the real world. This is food for thought as you read these articles and consider the ideas presented within the community context in which you reside.

Additionally, as you read the articles in this volume, it is necessary for you to place the findings, ideas, and discussions in the broader context of some realities that define and direct criminal justice organizations. We have already mentioned, for example, that all criminal justice agencies operate under limited resources and infinite expectations. This is an important consideration, but there are other equally important considerations that need to be understood as you read the articles offered here. These considerations are by no means an exhaustive list of important concerns for those interested in pursuing crime reduction strategies, but they do assist in laying out the broader context within which criminal justice agencies function. By comprehending these considerations you will have a more complete understanding of what can be accomplished and what cannot be accomplished to reduce crime. The articles serve as knowledge resources regarding effective crime management strategies and the considerations lay the larger context. These crime reduction prescriptions, however, become meaningless unless they are placed in the larger context of considerations discussed here. There have been many great ideas to reduce crime, but very few become part of criminal justice practices because they ignored contextual realities within communities. As considerations, they should be assessed within the community context, and as we suggested earlier, criminal justice practices in America have always been influenced by a strong local character. Taken together – research findings and their prescriptions in concert with the considerations presented here – offer us reasonable hope and a methodology to address crime.

The first contextual consideration is the chaotic and almost unpredictable nature of the political process. Since the political process dictates largely how criminal justice organizations will respond to crime, it is imperative that knowledge of localized political processes and persons are critical to developing and implementing effective crime reduction strategies. Many of the descriptions and subsequent crime reduction prescriptions from the articles presented in this volume implicitly or explicitly state the necessity of political agreement and support in order to get a crime reduction strategy in place and implemented by local criminal justice officials. The down side is that often times political figures change or their expectations change, or worse yet there is very little scientific evidence to support the views they are extolling or pitching. No criminal justice policy change occurs in a vacuum; political support is the most important thing in order for any crime related legislation to move forward. This reality is not only an American phenomenon, but can be found in any country in which a democracy operates or wishes to operate (developing democracies, for example).

The primary problem with the political process is its uncertainty in both program outcomes and program implementation and also the sheer arbitrariness that permeates political discussions surrounding tax payer supported initiatives. It is very common for politicians to advocate for crime reduction approaches that have very little support in any science. The best example of this phenomenon is project DARE (Drug Abuse Resistance Education) as a criminal justice effort directed toward reducing drug abuse among young people. Project DARE has been one of the most expensive and implemented criminal justice initiatives in the history of the country, yet the scientific evidence, again, is clear: it does very little to nothing to reduce drug usage among its participants. So, why does it still exist? It has political support among police chiefs, politicians, the general citizenry, and crime reduction advocates. They are a political coalition that has been very effective promoting DARE programs across the country. It is tough to buck their political message: who does not want kids to get off of drugs!

A second consideration is the lay of the land regarding stakeholders and crime reduction efforts. All crime reduction strategies have both supporters and critics; this is a given in the political process, but the diversity of stakeholders is almost mind boggling. Ask any police chief about the people who come out to express either their support or displeasure with any specific crime reduction strategy. While we expect both supporters and critics of our efforts, what we often do not realize is the differential levels of power and influence stakeholders have. In other words, not all stakeholders have the same level of resources or the degree of influence to affect the political process. This second consideration highlights the importance of recognizing differential levels of influence regarding resources and political clout as an important consideration. Many of the articles show what works and does not work to address crime, but what they do not provide is the knowledge of degrees of resource acquisition and political influence among community stakeholders. In this process, quite simply, some stakeholders are more influential than others. So, who are they and how are they enlisted to assist in the development and/or implementation of specific crime reduction strategies?

Performance expectations for criminal justice organizations are robust, but public funding to achieve these expectations are being severely reduced or coming to an end. Criminal justice administrators are similar to other publicly funded agencies and organizations. The funding streams for publicly funded enterprises, such as schools, highways, health care, and criminal justice, are drying up. Whether it is due to different political choices or the lack of tax revenue, we think it is fair to say "public" funding for these endeavors is under extreme scrutiny, probably greater than any other time in the nation's history. More and more communities are consolidating police services, for example, as a way to cut administrative and operational costs. As anyone in the public sector knows, it is not clear such measures actually save communities monies, and more importantly, if savings are evidenced through such measures how does that affect the provision of important criminal justice services and ultimately their impact on crime rates? There are no immediate and sufficient answers to this question, yet this is still a question of value for criminal justice agencies as they compete with other public and private agencies for limited public dollars.

Improving technologies will have a direct impact on the administration and operations of criminal justice organizations. Criminal justice administration and operations are going through revolutionary changes as it relates to the application of newer technologies to suppress crime. Criminal justice employees are more versed in these technologies and their use should be a concern for criminal justice administrators and communities alike. How far, for example, do we allow surveillance technologies into our lives, sometimes in an unwitting and unknowing way? Who controls the access to information stored by surveillance devices? Will the technologies be overwhelming to criminal justice agencies and overwhelming not only regarding costs of the technologies and how to use and maintain them, but also how to satisfactorily train and supervise employees with newer technologies?

A final consideration for criminal justice organizations around the world is the growing globalization of crime and the varied responses to it by countries. No longer is crime just a local community issue. In America, the response to crime has always been uniquely local, and we stated this point earlier, but more importantly, crime now reaches to all parts of the world. Whether it is organized crime, computer hacking of corporations and governments, or child pornography, we are seeing crime as part of a global reach strategy that encompasses the entire world. Much of this is due to the newer technologies available to both cops and crooks, e.g., child pornography and the internet. The technology is upon us and the need to coordinate efforts across countries is both essential and critical but also problematic at the same time. How we address this challenge may be the defining moment for countries and their systems of social control as we proceed further into the twenty-first century.

This small collection of articles provides the requisite information across a myriad of topics and issues. The book is designed to both inform but also educate lay people and communities to respond to crime in not only newer ways but also recognize the impact of globalization on crime. To talk about crime is no longer just an American discussion. Crime is now and into the future everyone's problem. Learning how other communities across the globe deal with crime is both informative and practical. This volume attempts to fill the void regarding the knowledge about crime control and community resilience, but in addition, asks the reader to move beyond basic descriptions of criminal justice responses to crime around the world.

After reading this collection of essays the reader should be better informed about crime and community resilience, but more importantly, should have a sense of how little we actually know about the varied criminal justice systems in the world. We can truly know and do more. This book provides the foundation for continued conversations and research efforts that integrate knowledge with actual practice, something that is sorely needed around the world when addressing crime. Editor Peterson and the authors in this volume are to be commended for their efforts. It is now the obligation of the reader to take the discussion regarding crime and community resilience to the next level. This means more research collaborations between criminal justice organizations and researchers with the aim of producing research that both informs and builds knowledge and provides concrete solutions to the problems crime presents to communities around the world.

## References

Bittner, E. (1970). *The functions of the police in modern society.* Chevy Chase, MD: The National Institute of Mental Health. Center for Studies of Crime and Delinquency.

Walker, S. (1980). *Popular justice: The history of American criminal justice.* Oxford, England: Oxford University Press.

# International Police Executive Symposium Co-Publication Preface

The *International Police Executive Symposium* (IPES) was founded in 1994 to address one major challenge, i.e., the two worlds of research and practice remain disconnected even though cooperation between the two is growing. A major reason is that the two groups speak in different languages. The research is published in hard to access journals and presented in a manner that is difficult for some to comprehend. On the other hand police practitioners tend not to mix with researchers and remain secretive about their work. Consequently there is little dialog between the two and almost no attempt to learn from one another. The global dialog among police researchers and practitioners is limited. True, the literature on the police is growing exponentially. But its impact upon day-to-day policing, however, is negligible.

The aims and objectives of the IPES are to provide a forum to foster closer relationships among police researchers and practitioners on a global scale, to facilitate cross-cultural, international, and interdisciplinary exchanges for the enrichment of the law enforcement profession, to encourage discussion, and to publish research on challenging and contemporary problems facing the policing profession. One of the most important activities of the IPES is the organization of an annual meeting under the auspices of a police agency or an educational institution. Now in its 17th year the annual meeting, a five-day initiative on specific issues relevant to the policing profession, brings together ministers of interior and justice, police commissioners and chiefs, members of academia representing world-renowned institutions, and many more criminal justice elite from over 60 countries. It facilitates interaction and the exchange of ideas and opinions on all aspects of policing. The agenda is structured to encourage dialog in both formal and informal settings.

Another important aspect of the meeting is the publication of the best papers presented edited by well-known criminal justice scholars and police professionals who attend the meetings. The best papers are selected, thoroughly revised, fully updated, meticulously edited, and published as books based upon the theme of each meeting. This repository of knowledge under the co-publication imprint of IPES and CRC Press–Taylor & Francis Group chronicles the important contributions of the International Police Executive Symposium over the last two decades. As a result in 2011 the United Nations awarded IPES a Special Consultative Status for the Economic and Social Council (ECSOC) honoring its importance in the global security community.

In addition to this book series, the IPES also has a research journal, *Police Practices and Research: An International Journal* (PPR). The PPR contains research articles on police issues from practitioners and researchers. It is an international journal in the true sense of the term and is distributed worldwide. For more information on the PPR visit www.tandf.co.uk/journals/GPPR.

The 25th meeting in Sofia, Bulgaria, marked not only an anniversary year for the International Police Symposium, but yet another endeavor for police leaders, scholars, and practitioners to emerge together to address current global challenges and strategies for change and best practices. Delegates from 43 countries were present in Sofia, honoring our commitment to lay groundwork for building a bridge to both build and restore resilience and safety from crime and violence to communities around the world.

IPES advocates, promotes, and propagates that POLICING is one of the most basic and essential avenues for improving the quality of life in all nations; rich and poor; modern and traditional; large and small; as well as peaceful and strife-ridden. IPES actively works to drive home to all its office bearers, supporters, and admirers that, in order to reach its full potential as an instrument of service to humanity, POLICING must be fully and enthusiastically open to collaboration between research and practice, global exchange of information between police practitioners and academics, universal disseminations and sharing of best practices, generating thinking police leaders and followers, as well as reflecting and writing on the issues challenging to the profession.

Through its annual meetings, hosts, institutional supporters, and publications, IPES reaffirms that POLICING is a moral profession with unflinching adherence to the rule of law and human rights as the embodiment of humane values.

**Dilip K. Das**
*Founding President,*
*International Police Executive Symposium,*
*www.ipes.info*

*Book Series Editor for Advances in Police Theory and Practice*
*CRC Press, Taylor & Francis Group*

*Book Series Editor for Interviews with Global Leaders in Criminal Justice*
*CRC Press, Taylor & Francis Group*

*Book Series Editor*
*IPES/CRC Press Co-Production Series*

*Founding Editor-in-Chief, Police Practice and Research: An International Journal, PPR,*
*www.tandf.co.uk/journals/GPPR*

# Acknowledgments

This special volume is a collection of presentations from IPES' 25th meeting in Sofia, Bulgaria, co-hosted by the Bulgarian Ministry of Interior, entitled, *Crime Prevention and Community Resilience.* We met as a group of 43 concerned countries on the first day of our meeting on Sunday, July 27, 2014. This was ten days following the tragic fated Malaysian Airlines Flight 17 from Amsterdam to Kuala Lumpur, which was shot down in Ukraine by a surface-to-air missile near the Ukraine-Russian border and nearly 300 deaths resulted. Our participants were highly concerned to travel to Bulgaria, with recent memories of ill-fated Malaysian Airlines Flight 370 from Kuala Lumpur to Beijing last making radio contact less than an hour after take off on March 8, 2014. March 8, 2014 was also a unique date for IPES, as it coincided with our 24th IPES meeting in Trivandrum, India. Our tensions were high, as were our worries for our global family, all different in kind, but alike in motives and intentions to make the world less violent and communities more resilient. Our team of scholars and practitioners have gathered global ideas and proven practices to better our world, especially in turbulent times of today and in memory of lives lost in Istanbul, Turkey; Baton Rouge, Louisiana; Sagamihara, Japan; Dallas, Texas; Orlando, Florida; Brussels, Belgium; Ft. Hood, Texas; Las Vegas, Nevada; Isla Vista, California; Paris, France; Garland, Texas; Charleston, South Carolina; Chattanooga, Tennessee; Pas-de-Calais, France; Rosenberg, Oregon; Ankara, Turkey; Saint-Denis, France; Colorado Springs, Colorado; San Bernardino, California; Kalamazoo, Michigan; Newton, Kansas; Hesston, Kansas; Nice, France; and Austin, Texas. Our prayers and thoughts reach out across the globe to better our world, while honoring lives lost.

It is our intention to build a bridge of hope and better practices for guidelines for police leaders to follow to build a safer and more resilient world. Moreover, building stronger communities is a key component that not only practitioners and scholars can solve alone, as we are all responsible for protecting and caring for each other. The International Police Executive Symposium brings many different races, cultures, religions, colors, and creeds together for a common goal to build a safer world. We are stronger than any team on the Olympics in our efforts to save the world from crime and violence. Due to our ties with the United Nations as Non-Governmental Organizations, we can make true change. Please consider joining our network enforcing efforts to find strategies to build a better world for our children and our children's children. This volume is a collection of chapters written by 38 authors, scholars, and practitioners in a global challenge to better our world. Thank you my Sofia participants and chairs! This is dedicated to all of your hard work and dedication to making our communities more resilient. In times of turbulence and stress in 2016–2017, please continue to fight the fight and bring new ideas, strategies, and practices to a global stage, as the world is listening.

This was truly a global effort. Thank you to Dilip and Ana Das, who started my international adventures with the International Police Executive Symposium. Lastly, the

Criminal Justice/Criminology and Social Work undergraduate and graduate students at the University of Texas, Permian Basin, Southeast Missouri State University – your help with this project has been priceless to us. May you all be guiding lights in the future of violence prevention and building paths to more resilient communities. Thank you to Ellen Boyne, Eve Strillacci, and Carolyn Spence at Taylor & Francis and Routledge – you were fantastic supporters of this global effort. We are very grateful for your insight. Thank you for believing our global effort to fight crime and violence, while building more resilient communities, and for your everlasting patience with our progress to the finish line. Adam Mortimer – thank you for help and efforts, as without you, this project could not have been completed. I would like to thank my wonderful and patient children Landon, Colten, and Madison Peterson, and Hayden and Arolsen Bruns. I could not have done this without your support. Therefore, thank you for giving up your time with me from the beginning of the preparation for the Sofia meeting to this book's completion.

Diana Scharff Peterson

# Editors

**Diana Scharff Peterson**, PhD, has nearly 20 years of experience in higher education teaching in the areas of research methods; comparative criminal justice systems; race, gender, class, and crime; statistics; criminology; sociology; and drugs and behavior at seven different institutions of higher education. Dr. Peterson has been the chairperson of three different criminal justice programs over the past 15 years and has published in the areas of criminal justice, social work, higher education, sociology, business, and management. Her research interests include issues in policing (training and education) and community policing, assessment and leadership in higher education, family violence, and evaluation research and program development. Dr. Peterson is a Professor of Criminology and Graduate Program Director at the University of Texas, Permian Basin. Currently, she has taken temporary leave from the University of Texas to attend graduate school at Arizona State University, concentrating on the disciplines of Public Affairs (Emergency Management) and Social Justice and Human Rights. She will graduate in May 2018. She has published over 30 articles in the areas of criminal justice, sociology, social work, business, management, and higher education and is the Liaison and Representative for the International Police Executive Symposium (consultative status) for quarterly annual meetings at the United Nations meetings in New York City, Geneva, and Vienna including the Commission on the Status of Women in New York. Dr. Peterson chaired and organized the 25th Annual Meeting of the International Police Executive Symposium, entitled *Crime Prevention & Community Resilience: Police Role with Victims, Youth, Ethnic Minorities and Other Partners*, in Sofia, Bulgaria, July 27–August 1, 2014 (27 countries and 43 presenters). She formerly served as the Managing Editor of *Police Practice and Research: An International Journal.*

**Dilip K. Das**, PhD, is the President, International Police Executive Symposium (IPES) (www.ipes.info) and Editor-in-Chief, *Police Practice and Research: An International Journal.* After his Master's degree in English literature, Dr. Das joined the Indian Police Service, an elite national service with a glorious tradition. After 14 years in the service as a Police Executive including Chief of Police he moved to the USA in 1979 where he achieved another Master's degree in Criminal Justice as well as a doctorate in the same discipline. Dr. Das has authored, edited, and co-edited more than 40 books, and numerous articles. He is the Series Editor to *Advances in Police Theory and Practice* and *Interviews with Global Leaders in Policing, Courts and Prisons.* He has traveled extensively throughout the world in comparative police research, as a visiting professor in various universities, including organizing annual conferences of the IPES, and as a Human Rights Consultant to the United Nations. Dr. Das has received several faculty excellence awards and was a Distinguished Faculty Lecturer.

# Contributors

**Tiffiney Barfield-Cottledge** is currently Assistant Professor of Criminology at the University of Houston-Clear Lake. She received her PhD in Juvenile Justice and has a comprehensive background in teaching, counseling, and criminal justice. Dr. Cottledge began her career in criminal justice as a State Parole Officer for the Texas Department of Criminal Justice and since that time has published book chapters on the topics of corrections and prison privatization based on her practitioner experience. In addition, Dr. Cottledge has published several scholarly journal articles that examine criminological theories as explanations of crime and delinquency. While her research is largely honed in the areas of female gangs, adolescent substance abuse, and juvenile sex offenders, Dr. Cottledge has also researched human trafficking and transportation and their relationship to organized crime.

**Christiaan Bezuidenhout** is a Professor in the Department of Social Work and Criminology, University of Pretoria. He teaches psychocriminology, criminal justice, and contemporary criminology at undergraduate and postgraduate level. Research methodology and ethics, psychocriminology, policing issues as well as youth misbehaviour are some of his research foci. He recently completed a cross cultural study with an American colleague. The focus of the study is on the legal and policing dilemmas of trafficking in humans. During his academic career he has published numerous scientific articles in peer reviewed journals and chapters in books. Professor Bezuidenhout has also acted as editor-in-chief for different scholarly books. He is the program coordinator of the Criminology Honors degree program at the University of Pretoria. He has also supervised several postgraduate studies (MA and DPhil students). He has participated in national and international conferences and has been actively involved in various community projects focusing on crime prevention and has assisted the South African Government in the development of different crime prevention initiatives. Professor Bezuidenhout also does court work as an expert witness. He is currently the president of the Criminological and Victimological Society of South Africa (CRIMSA). He holds the following degrees: BA (Criminology), BA Honors (Criminology), MA (Criminology), DPhil (Criminology). He also holds an MSc degree in Criminology and Criminal Justice from the University of Oxford.

**Octavia S. Bolton** is a current clinical psychology graduate student at Texas Southern University, with a BA in Psychology from the University of Houston.

**Jose Cervantes** earned his MA in Criminology and his BS in Psychology from the University of Houston-Clear Lake.

**Kyung-Shick Choi**, PhD, is an Associate Professor who holds a dual appointment in the Department of Criminal Justice at Bridgewater State University and the Department of Applied Social Sciences at Boston University. As the cybercrime program coordinator at Boston University, Dr. Choi oversees the graduate certificate program in Cybercrime Investigation and Cybersecurity. In 2009, the Korean Institute of Criminology, in cooperation with the United Nations Office on Drugs and Crime, invited Dr. Choi to facilitate the UN's Virtual Forum against Cybercrime as an instructor. Dr. Choi's research focuses on the intersection of human behavior and technology – and how criminal justice can respond effectively to the challenges of cybercrime. In 2008, he proposed his Cyber-Routine Activities Theory, which has become a predominant theory of computer crime victimization. Dr. Choi's work has appeared in numerous peer reviewed journals. He published the books *Risk Factors in Computer Crime* (LFB Scholarly, 2010) and *Cybercriminology and Digital Investigation* (LFB Scholarly, 2015). His scholarly interests focus on the study of transnational crimes including bullying, cybercrime, police information technology, and human trafficking topics.

**Heather Correia** received a graduate degree in criminal justice with a concentration in victimology. Her graduate thesis focuses on bullying victimization in the school environment. Ms. Correia is currently working as a full-time public safety dispatcher for Raynham Police Department and also as a special police officer for the Town of Raynham in MA.

**Jay Corzine**, PhD, has had an academic career which has spanned two universities in the USA: the University of Nebraska-Lincoln from 1978 to 1996 and the University of Central Florida (UCF) since 1996. His research focuses on violent crime, with specific interests including the impact of transportation routes on homicide and robbery, human trafficking, mass victimization incidents, the lethality of types of firearms, risk factors for assaults on police officers, and the influences of medical resources on lethality. He has published in numerous journals, including *Criminology*, *American Journal of Sociology*, *Violence and Victims*, *Victims and Offenders*, *Homicide Studies*, *Deviant Behavior*, *Justice Research and Policy*, and *Journal of Contemporary Criminal Justice*.

**Shea Cronin** is an Assistant Professor of Criminal Justice and a Program Coordinator at Boston University's Metropolitan College. He received his PhD in Justice, Law, and Society from American University, School of Public Affairs. His research interests include the administration of criminal justice, communities and crime, policing, and issues of democratic accountability. His research has been published in *Crime and Delinquency*, *Justice Quarterly*, *Policing*, and other academic journals. Dr. Cronin teaches in the graduate and undergraduate criminal justice programs at BU, including courses in criminology, criminal justice, policing, communities and crime, and analytic methods.

**Joshua Ofori Essiam** is a Lecturer/Researcher at the University of Professional studies, Accra and a PhD candidate reading Adult Education and Human Resource studies at the School of Continuing and Distance Education at the University of Ghana. He is adept at fostering strong working relationships with his students, peers, and superiors. His areas of research interest include but are not limited to human resource development, education for sustainable development, entrepreneurship development, risk management, operations management, and quality management.

**Doraval Govender**, PhD, Criminology (Security Sciences), is currently an associate professor at the University of South Africa (UNISA). Dr. Govender had a 36-year safety and security career in the South African Police Service (SAPS), where he served operationally and at different management levels both in the uniform and detective divisions until the rank of Assistant Commissioner (Major General). He underwent many educational, training, and development programs both internationally and nationally including the FBI program for international students in Quantico, USA (199th session). He also served as the President of the FBI Middle East, Africa Chapter for the FBI retrainer session from 2001 to 2005. In 2009, he joined UNISA as a lecturer in the Department of Security Management. Since 2009, he has published several articles in accredited journals. He is also the subeditor of the *Acta Criminologica* journal. He has chaired several sessions at different conferences and has presented papers both internationally and nationally on safety and security related issues. Dr. Govender also has an Mtech degree in Forensic Investigations and an honors and a bachelor's degree in Policing.

**Johan van Graan** is currently an Associate Professor at the Department of Police Practice at the University of South Africa. He was a member of the South African Police Service for 17 years before joining academia in 2011. He resigned from the police as a Warrant Officer with a collection of commendations for his involvement in the covert investigation of various high profile national and international crime investigations. He has successfully completed courses, among others, in specialized and unconventional methods and techniques in the gathering of covert crime intelligence. He is also actively involved in community policing and initiatives that communities can implement to mitigate property crimes in their neighborhoods. Professor van Graan's research interests include the dynamic fields of community policing, the prevention and investigation of crime against women and children, and intelligence led policing. He has published widely in these fields.

**Gerald Dapaah Gyamfi** has a PhD in Higher Education Administration from the University of Phoenix, USA; an MSc in Human Resource Development from the University of Manchester, UK; and is a Fellow of the Institute of Chartered Secretaries and Administrators (ICSA), UK. Dr. Gyamfi has authored articles published in internationally recognized refereed journals and written many chapters of books published by Routledge, Taylor & Francis Group/CRC Press and others. He has attended and presented papers at many international conferences including Police Stress presented at the IPES meeting hosted by the United Nations in New York City; Commitment and Retention of Police Officers presented at the IPES/Bulgarian Police meeting; Human Trafficking Menace presented at the IPES/Thai Police meeting; and Domestic Violence presented at the IPES/

George Washington University meeting. On behalf of IPES, Dr. Gyamfi organized and presented a paper on Trans-National Organized Crime at the Side Event of the 7th Conference of the Parties to the United Nations Convention against Trans-National Organized Crime at the UN Headquarters in Vienna, Austria. He is IPES Director of Publicity and Public Relations for Africa. He is a Faculty Dean at the University of Professional Studies in Ghana; a member of the National Accreditation Board, representing all Recognized Professional Bodies in Ghana; the CEO of Geraldo Travel & Tours Ltd, based in Accra; and the proprietor of the ICSA Study Center, Ghana. He is a philanthropist and loves serving in the vineyard of God.

**Robert Hanser**, PhD, is the Coordinator of the Department of Criminal Justice, and the Director of the Institute of Law Enforcement at the University of Louisiana at Monroe. He is also a past administrator of North Delta Regional Training Academy (NDTRA) where he provided leadership and oversight for police officer and jailer training throughout the northeast region of Louisiana. He is the Past-President on the Board of Directors for the Louisiana Coalition Against Domestic Violence (LCADV) for the State of Louisiana. Dr. Hanser is also a Certified Title IX Coordinator and a Certified Title IX Investigator; he has processed numerous complaints related to gender based mistreatment. He has dual licensure as a professional counselor in Texas and Louisiana, is a certified anger resolution therapist, and has a specialty license in addictions counseling. He is also the Lead Facilitator for the 4th Judicial District's Batterer Intervention Program (BIP).

**Cynthia Hernandez** earned her MA in Criminology from the University of Houston-Clear Lake, and her BA in Latin American Studies from the University of Texas at Austin.

**René Hesseling** has been a Senior Researcher at The Hague Police Service for the past nine years. After his study in the discipline of sociology, he has worked from 1985 at the Research and Documentation Centre of the Ministry of Justice as a researcher, at the Immigration and Naturalization Service as head of the Human Smuggling Information Unit, as policy advisor on organized crime at the Ministry of Justice, and as analyst in the field of radicalization and counterterrorism. For The Hague Police Service, his main research topics are high impact crime and organized crime.

**Lin Huff-Corzine**, PhD, is a professor and co-director of the University of Central Florida (UCF) Crime Lab in the Department of Sociology at UCF in Orlando, Florida, USA. Professor Huff-Corzine's research primarily focuses on violent crime. She is currently the Vice President of the Homicide Research Working Group, an international organization focusing on homicide and any violence that may lead to homicide. She is co-author of the research monograph, *The Currents of Lethal Violence* (SUNY Press, 1994), and her articles appear in numerous journals, including but not limited to *Criminology, Deviant Behavior, Homicide Studies, Justice Quarterly*, the *Journal of Contemporary Criminal Justice*, the *Journal of Research on Crime and Delinquency, Social Forces, Victims and Offenders*, and *Violence and Victims*.

**Attapol Kuanliang** is an Associate Professor of Criminology and Criminal Justice at Midwestern State University, Texas, where he serves as the director of the juvenile justice institute. His primary interests include juvenile justice and delinquency, correction, drug abuse and treatment, victimology, quantitative methods and analysis, program evaluation, and minority issues. He has published several book chapters and articles in reference journals. He also serves as advisory and consultant in numerous agencies such as The Department of Juvenile Observation and Protection, Ministry of Justice, Thailand; the 4th Judicial District Youth Service Planning Board; and Children's Coalition of Northeast Louisiana. Dr. Kuanliang received a BA with honor in Political Science which focuses on Administration of Justice from Kasetsart University, an MA in Criminal Justice and an MS in Psychology from the University of Louisiana at Monroe, and a PhD in Juvenile Justice from Prairie View A&M University.

**Miranda Lai** is a Lecturer and trainer in interpreting and translating at RMIT University, Melbourne, Australia. She is undertaking her PhD research into the PEACE police interviewing model mediated by interpreters. Her research interests include investigative interviewing in multilingual settings, public service translation and interpreting, and intersection of security and communication.

**Bruno Meini**, PhD, holds a doctorate in Criminology from the University of Bologna, a master of arts in criminal justice from the School of Criminal Justice at Rutgers University, and a master's degree in research methods in the social sciences from the University of Florence. His research interest lies in the areas of policing, crime prevention, penology, the social dimensions of HIV, and crime and security related issues. He formerly served as the Executive Assistant to the International Police Executive Symposium President and as the Production Editor for *Police Practice and Research: An International Journal.*

**Sedat Mülayim**, PhD, was the Discipline Head of the Translating and Interpreting programs at RMIT University in Melbourne, Australia. Dr. Sedat taught Translating and Interpreting Skills, Translation and Technology, and Professional Ethics courses. He also designed and delivered numerous training workshops in Australia and internationally in police and court interpreting, and professional ethics for interpreters and translators. Dr. Sedat published widely in investigative interviewing mediated by interpreters, training interpreters in refugee languages, and pedagogy of online interpreting training. He was the lead author of *Police Investigative Interviews and Interpreting – Context, Challenges, and Strategies.* Dr. Sedat, our dear friend and scholar, passed away on June 30, 2016.

**Paul van Musscher** is the Police Chief of The Hague region of the National Police in The Netherlands. In 1984, he began his career as a beat officer and found his way to the higher levels of the police organization by working on several executive functions in different areas. During his career, he attended the required educations and training courses to become the Executive Master of Police Management. Next to police chief of one of the largest regions of the National Police, he is also National Coordinator of

Migrants and Migrant Related Crime and National Coordinator of Diversity, Equality and Unity.

**Mike Perkins**, PhD, is a Lecturer in Management at the British University Vietnam, based in Hanoi, where he leads a wide variety of management modules. He carried out his undergraduate and PhD studies in Management at the University of York, UK and his thesis explored the factors underlying public confidence in policing. His primary research interests include performance management in public and private organizations, and how local law enforcement can influence public perceptions of police forces. He is also expanding his research into issues of gender equality, and transparency and integrity within emerging markets.

**Judy Putt** is Senior Research Fellow at the University of Tasmania, with postgraduate degrees in Anthropology and Criminology. Dr. Putt has undertaken and published research on a wide range of subjects, including violence against women, missing persons, community policing, crime in the fishing industry, people trafficking, and substance misuse in Australia. Having worked in drug and crime prevention policy and as a community worker, she has a strong commitment to practice and policy relevant research. In recent years, she has focused primarily on evaluations of initiatives and programs in remote Aboriginal communities and regional areas. Dr. Putt is currently working as an official visitor of prisons and on a national research project with women's specialist domestic and family violence services.

**Blake M. Randol** is an Assistant Professor in the Department of Criminal Justice at the University of Wisconsin-Milwaukee. His primary area of research involves the application of organizational theory to the study of police organizations. He holds a PhD in Criminal Justice and Criminology from Washington State University.

**Harold Rankin** is a 20-year veteran with the Mesa Police Department (Arizona). He is currently assigned to the Organized Crime Section, which is responsible for the investigation of organized criminal structures within the City of Mesa and throughout the metropolitan area. He has also served as a Division Criminal Investigations Lieutenant where he supervised detectives, analyzed emerging crime trends, developed response plans, and coordinated with other departmental assets to achieve significant reductions in crime. He has been instrumental as the on-body camera system program manager for the City of Mesa. He was responsible for the supervision and implementation of a year-long evaluation of the Axon Flex camera system to determine the impact on civil liability, departmental complaints, and organizational transparency. He partnered with the Arizona State University School of Criminology and Criminal Justice to plan, monitor, and evaluate the deployment of the camera systems through the use of line officer surveys and field contact reports. Evaluation revealed a 40 percent decrease in departmental complaints and a 75 percent decrease in use of force complaints. Prior to this assignment he served as the Budget and Finance Lieutenant responsible for overseeing and coordinating the budgeting and fiscal planning for the Mesa Police Department, which operates on a $142 million budget. He also served as the Communications Lieutenant and exercised management of the emergency 9–1–1 and dispatching services for both police and fire for five Arizona agencies with an annual call volume of 1.1 million calls.

**Rick Sarre**, PhD, is Professor of Law and Criminal Justice in the School of Law, University of South Australia where he teaches criminology, sports law, commercial law, and media law. He currently serves as the President of the Australian and New Zealand Society of Criminology (ANZSOC) and sits on the Board of the International Police Executive Symposium. For the past six years he has been the Chair of the Academic Board of the University, and a member of the University Council. He received an Australian Learning and Teaching Council citation as a nationally recognized tertiary teacher in 2008. His research is focused on the legal regulation of private security, and the law and social justice more generally.

**Zora Sukabdi** is a PhD Candidate at the Swinburne University of Technology, Melbourne, Australia. Her approach in rehabilitating former perpetrators inside and outside prisons in Indonesia and their families is viewed to be holistic which include psychosocial, vocational, spiritual-ideology, and cultural aspects. Her works also include identifying parameters of successful rehabilitation and after care programs for terrorism convicts as well as bombing victims. Her dedication underlines her outstanding achievements and promoted her to receive the Allison Sudrajat Prize and be nominated as a representative of Swinburne University of Technology at the International Women's Day. She is currently acting as the Head of Re-Education and Re-Integration Department in the Indonesian Institute for Society Empowerment (INSEP) and as the Director and Founder of Global Center of Well-Being (GeoWB), Indonesia.

**Adki Surender**, PhD, the Principal of Vivek Vardhini College of Arts and Commerce, Jambagh, Hyderabad, completed his MA, Mphil, and PhD in Public Administration at Osmania University, Hyderabad. Since 1990, he has been working as a Lecturer in Public Administration at Vivek Vardhini College. Presently, he is the Associate Professor in Public Administration and Research Supervisor for PhD scholars. His area of research is Police Administration with the specific area of "Traffic Control and Police Enforcement." He is the Principal Investigator for the major research project on "Urban Traffic and Transportation – Role Traffic Police Enforcement," sponsored by the University Grants Commission (UGC), New Delhi. His other research areas of interest include women police, human trafficking, and crime against women (he received a national award on this subject in 2013). He has contributed a number of research articles/papers for various international and national journals and books. He participated and presented a number of research papers at international and national workshops/symposia and conferences on various aspects of Police and Public Administration. He serves as a peer reviewer to *Police Practice and Research: An International Journal.* He is a member of various professional bodies like

Indian Institute of Public Administration (IIPA), New Delhi, New Public Administration Society of India (NEPASI), New Delhi, and International Road Safety Partnership (IRSP), USA, and a regular participant of International Police Executive Symposium, USA.

**Peter Versteegh** has worked for the past 42 years for The Hague Police Service. In 1974, he started his career as a beat officer. After his police studies, Mr. Versteegh studied Sociology at the University of Leiden. In the 1990s, he became head of the unit for Crime Analyses and Research, which is the scientific division of the police department. His main research objectives are evidence based policing, problem oriented policing, (youth) delinquency, repeat offending, gang related crime, violence, and high impact crime. At present, he is the safety advisor of the police chief.

# Introduction: Executive Summary of Crime Prevention and Community Resilience

## Police Role with Victims, Youth, Ethnic Minorities and Other Partners

LIN HUFF-CORZINE

### Contents

## Abstract

This summary focuses on the primary discussion points of the 25th International Police Executive Symposium meeting held in Sofia, Bulgaria, in 2014. Co-hosted by the Republic of Bulgaria Ministry of Interior and the Bulgarian National Police, the symposium's theme was "Crime Prevention and Community Resilience: Police Role with Victims, Youth, Ethnic Minorities and Other Partners." Daily sub-themes included (1) strategies for crime and violence prevention and reduction; (2) community initiatives for crime reduction; and (3) promoting best practices for police effectiveness, safety, and professionalism. Attendees left this conference with numerous ideas to prevent or reduce crime in their communities.

## Introduction

The 26th International Police Executive Symposium (IPES) was held in Sofia, Bulgaria, from July 27 through July 31, 2014 at the Balkan Sofia Hotel. Co-hosted by the Republic of Bulgaria Ministry of Interior and the Bulgarian National Police, the symposium's theme was "Crime Prevention and Community Resilience: Police Role with Victims, Youth, Ethnic Minorities and Other Partners." The IPES Organizing Committee led by Dr. Dilip Das was comprised, in alphabetical order, of Mintie Das Koivisto, Bruno Meini, Dr. Snezana (Ana) Mijovic-Das, Paul Moore, and Dusan Sipovac. Dr. Diana L. Bruns served as Chair for this conference. IPES Sponsors included the Republic of Bulgaria Ministry of Interior, the George Washington University (Frederic Lemieux), Starosel Winery, PAE (Mark Kroeker), the University of Louisiana at Monroe (Robert Hanser), and Liverpool John Moores University (David Lowe).

One evening was spent enjoying a traditional Bulgarian dinner and folk dancing show hosted by the Bulgarian Ministry of Interior at the Vodenitsata Restaurant on top of Vitosha Mountain. Escorted by the Bulgarian National Police, the afternoon following the close of the symposium was spent having lunch at a traditional restaurant, touring two of Sofia's historical sites, and taking a guided walking tour of Sofia's central city. The Boyana Church, a medieval Bulgarian Orthodox church, was constructed wing-by-wing between the late 10th and 19th centuries. A total of 89 fragile scenes with 240 human images are portrayed on the church walls. The National Historical Museum, Bulgaria's largest museum, was the second stop on the tour where we learned that the earliest human remains from 44,000 BC were found in what is now Bulgaria. In addition, a history of Bulgaria was presented by the tour guide and ancient pottery, jewelry, and other artifacts were admired.

Sixty-eight delegates representing 25 countries, from the continents of Africa, Asia, Australia, Europe, North America, and South America, attended the four-day symposium at which over 40 papers were presented. Focusing on crime prevention and reduction, the symposium presentations and discussions centered around:

- strategies for crime and violence prevention and reduction;
- community initiatives for crime reduction; and
- promoting best practices for police effectiveness, safety, and professionalism.

## Inauguration of the Conference, Opening Ceremony, and Theme for July 28: Strategies for Crime and Violence Prevention and Reduction

The first full day of IPES began with an inauguration of the conference and an opening ceremony. Progress being made in Bulgaria under the Minister of Interior to prevent and reduce crime was shared followed by Dr. Das' presentation of IPES' unique global perspective.

## Keynote Address: Treatment of Drug Offenders – What Works and How to Make it Work (Dr. Igor Koutsenok, United Nations)

The Keynote Address given by Dr. Igor Koutsenok from the United Nations in Vienna focused on what works when treating drug offenders. Dr. Koutsenok provided a valuable paradigm for determining the time and financial cost effectiveness for treating drug offenders. On a continuum of substance-related offenders, best practice efforts to reduce recidivism need to be identified and approached proactively.

## Panel Session 1: Global Approaches to Crime/Violence Prevention (Chair: Owen Hortz, Australia)

This session, chaired by Owen Hortz, Australia, focused on crime and violence reduction programs. Overarching the message of each presentation is the need for communication among the various agencies and their respective populations.

Professor Juan Salgado, Mexico, analyzed the scope and limitations of three police reform programs in place between 2002 and 2013 to reduce crime and violence in Brazil, Colombia, and Mexico. Then, he identified ways to enroll local strengths to reduce crime, especially violence. Consideration was given to duties of citizen security decision makers and police in regard to citizen civil rights and conclusions were drawn for the differing styles of government; centralized administration in Colombia and federal administration in Brazil and Mexico. Police reform was also the topic introduced by Odd Malme from Norway. His work examined the four "Ds" – depoliticization, decentralization, decriminalization, and demilitarization; overarching challenges to police reform efforts in Serbia. Related to local community opinion and behavior, Sedat Mülayim and Miranda Lai from Australia studied the views of ethnic residents about police communication methods employed with their community members. Their findings show that the ethnic communities considered preferred direct contact with police over other methods of communication.

Turning attention to particular types of crime, Peter Versteegh and René Hesseling from The Netherlands explained their B3W Matrix, which has been in place since 2005. Their study explored how residential burglaries are currently dealt with in each of the 31 police teams of the Hague Police Service and compared them with their Police Services' safety strategy, The Best of Three Worlds or B3W, which combines Problem-Oriented Policing, Intelligence-Led Policing, and Community-Led Policing. Results were mixed contingent upon the seriousness with which B3W was applied. Based on the findings, Versteegh and Hesseling recommend strengthening the B3W approach where application seriousness was questionable. Like Versteegh and Hesseling, Doraval Govender, Sr. Lecturer, from South Africa also focused his research on residential burglaries and added house robberies as well. Arguing that as long as there are large sections of the population who experience unemployment, poverty, and relative deprivation, burglary and robbery will exist, he suggests promoting effective, efficient Physical Protection Systems (PPS). When Govender discovered that PPS was not providing the protection needed, he completed in-depth interviews with burglary and home robbery victims and found that PPS were not designed well and were not being evaluated regularly. Coordination between police and homeowners is required for PPS to be effective. Finally, Shrino Sasaki, Lecturer, from Japan examined specialized fraud, which is currently a major problem in Japan. Using a variety of community-based methods, including having cell phone service providers reinforce customer ID checks and financial institutions warn customers about specialized fraud, Japanese Police are appealing to the public to help reduce their risk of victimization.

## Panel Session 2: Global Examinations/Strategies to Combat Crimes Against Women (Chair: Erica-Maria Unbricht, Switzerland)

This session focused on crimes against women across the globe and offered suggestions for reducing these events. Two presentations focused on crimes against women in India, one by Dr. Karine Bates from Canada and the second by Dr. Adki Surender from India. Using various anthropological and legal perspectives, Dr. Bates viewed women's access to justice as a dynamic set of interactions among social actors and community members. Dr. Surender reviewed the complex cultural, social, and economic factors and statistics related to women's victimization in India. Then, he examined government strategies to reduce crimes against women and concluded with suggestions to strengthen the government's actions to reduce, hopefully eradicate, crimes against women.

Dr. Cornelius Roelofse from South Africa shared the fact that South Africa has the unfortunate distinction of being called the rape capital of the world. To make sure that cases have been finalized, his study analyzed randomly selected data files for 2009–2011 in the Limpopo Province, Thulamela Municipality of South Africa, an extremely rural area. The cases analyzed were adjudicated by the courts, however, there was a relationship between rape and HIV that left victims in need of further support.

Reporting on a campus-community partnership between the University of Louisiana-Monroe and the surrounding community, Dr. Robert Hanser from the USA discussed how grant funding led to their coordinated domestic violence program. This program provides public awareness, prevention, and intervention services throughout Northeast Louisiana.

Finally, a broad-based examination of human trafficking as a national and international concern was the focus of Drs. Barfield-Cottledge and Kuanliang's presentation. Their paper provided information about human trafficking, transportation, and border concerns in the United States and other parts of the world. Although attempts have been made to address these issues, human traffickers continue to victimize vulnerable women, men, and children.

## Panel Session 3: Enhancing Best Practices in Policing and Political Relationships (Chair: Agnes Nemeth, Hungary)

The goal of this session was to describe cooperative practices among law enforcement, political entities, and academics. Representatives from five very different countries that span three continents shared best practices collaborative models that have been used by police in conjunction with other community organizations.

Expounding upon issues discussed in their forthcoming book, *Collaborative Policing: Police, Academics, Professionals, and Communities Working Together for Education, Training, and Program Implementation*, Max Edelbacher, Austria, presented a paper exploring various ways that academics and criminal justice practitioners collaborate to offer both formal and experiential learning courses for students in higher education for Dr. Peter Kratcoski, USA, and himself. Particular attention was on how academics and justice practitioners assure that the goals outlined in their paper are achieved. Following a similar theme, Drs. Huff-Corzine and Corzine, USA, explained how the Orlando and Orange County, Florida, law enforcement agencies cooperated with the Orlando and Orange County mayors, the County's Public Safety Officer's Office, and the University of Central Florida's Department of Sociology faculty and graduate students to seek answers to high rates of homicide during the mid-2000s.

The next two presentations examined the importance of the public's perception of the police in their neighborhoods. Dr. Mike Perkins, Vietnam, discussed the need for police in the UK to maintain their legitimacy as defenders of the British public. Using structural equation modeling, he developed several models measuring neighborhood perceptions of the police. Based on his findings, police engagement, interactions with the public, and dealing with issues the public is concerned with significantly affect the public's perceptions of police, however, there is variation within neighborhoods. New strategies to improve public confidence and community safety are expected.

In his paper on community policing and vigilantism, Dr. Bruno Meini from Italy argues that when governments cannot provide satisfactory public safety, especially in disadvantaged neighborhoods, vigilantism is likely to develop. This is not viewed as a positive outcome because vigilantism (1) usurps state power; (2) state authorities must move rapidly to counteract vigilante violence and to prosecute offenders; and (3) the state must protect the right to life against any abuse by vigilantes. Dr. Meini suggests that community courts can be used to deal with community crime problems to more effectively respond to public safety issues.

In his paper, Dr. Srisombat Chokprajakchat, Thailand, examined problems and obstacles caused by politicians' and other outside influential figures' interference in the police promotions and transfers. Although some of the practices were viewed as fair, some aspects of the promotion and transfer process on which he reported were clearly less than fair.

This session promoted the concept of police, political, and academic cooperation. Each paper made suggestions for how to develop and improve these interactions and thereby enhance public safety.

## Theme for July 29: Violence Prevention; Community Initiatives for Crime Reduction; Addressing/Assisting Special Populations and Crime Victims; and Women in the Criminal Justice System

## Keynote Address: Preventing Extreme Violence: The Case of Mass Shootings (Dr. Frederic Lemieux, USA)

The Keynote Address for the second full day of IPES was given by Dr. Frederic Lemieux, USA. His presentation, which focused on mass shootings, made four primary points: (1) since language is the key to culture, the number and type of phrases used is revealing about attitudes toward mass shootings; (2) the effects of having bans on guns or certain types of guns needs to be studied in more depth; (3) more research needs to be done to explore the clustering of mass shootings; and (4) future research needs to focus on mass shootings cross-nationally. Among other suggestions by conference attendees that need further study were examination of similarities and differences between public, e.g., gang shootings, and private, e.g., family annihilations; and the need to cross-check media sources with official data, e.g., state or government statistics.

## Panel Session 4: Building Resilient Communities: Engaging the Community for Violence and Crime Prevention/Global and Local Partnerships (Chair: Juan Salgado, Mexico)

This session explored a variety of techniques aimed at engaging the public and enhancing the resilience, or collective efficacy, of communities. In addition, various techniques for the education of police were introduced.

Dr. Johan van Graan from South Africa asserted that there are ways to make a successful transition from military to community oversight. His case study of a South African Neighborhood Watch program illustrates the benefits of empowering communities to take ownership of their community's safety and concludes with recommendations to use neighborhood watch programs for proactive community policing ventures.

Odd Malme from Norway gave an update on the police reforms in Serbia. The goal of the police reforms being put in place is to initiate democratic policing. The primary need is for increased police training.

Deputy Director Melvin Yong from Singapore suggested in his presentation that Delta Football can positively affect the lives of boys who participate. To get the boys to participate, they use social media and other innovative tactics. Like neighborhood watch programs, Delta Football can also function as a community safety program. Negative effects of social media were discussed in the paper by Dr. George Richards from the USA. It is his assertion that bullying among school age children has increased with the advent of cyberbullying. The need for law enforcement and schools to work together to reduce cyberbullying is suggested. Of course, there is also a need to involve parents in the reduction of bullying as well.

Dr. Branko Lobnikar explored policing in multicultural communities in Slovenia, his home country. With a more democratic state, community policing started being used; a method that has more issues and problems where the percentage of minorities, especially Roma, are larger. Police must receive special training to respond to people from cultures or subcultures different from their own; a realization that could benefit most police worldwide. Briefly stated, responses must be tailor-made for the ethnic group with which a police officer is working.

Professor Rick Sarre, Australia, introduced issues related to policing the cross-border region of Australia. This area spans three jurisdictions, is primarily comprised of Aboriginal peoples, and is very sparsely populated. This presentation reports on a 12-month evaluation of how well combining these jurisdictions has worked to accomplish the goal of greater community safety. Overall, there are needs for (1) more agencies to come on board; and (2) improved communication among those agencies that do participate.

Finally, police officers must frequently interact with citizens who speak a language different than their own. As an example of how to educate police about handling interpreted interviews, Sedat Mülayim, Lecturer, from Australia offered a new training video that was particularly produced to assist police affect better control over suspect-witness interaction in interpreted interviews. The video, which is the first of a series produced solely for police training purposes, covers common areas of concern when conducting these interviews and ways to minimize effects on the quality of evidence.

## Lunch Speaker: Gary Burns, South Australia

## Police/Media Cooperation: Communicating with the Community

Our lunch speaker, Gary Burns, explained that some of the main problems he faces are organized crime, cybercrime, and alcohol-fueled violence – some that leads to sex crimes. To combat these crimes, the police in South Australia where he works use social media to communicate and connect with the community; a rather new, but highly successful method that can include the community in bringing an offender to justice. With the improved police/media cooperation, they have not only improved their communication with the community, but also have been able to increase their successful responses to the types of crimes noted above.

The afternoon sessions were devoted to special populations. The first dealt with women's experience in the criminal justice system; the second explored issues related to K-12 schools; and the third reported on crime victims.

## Panel Session 5: Gender Issues in Criminal Justice (Chair: Lee Rankin, USA)

Linda Mayberry from the United States started the discussion of gender issues in the criminal justice system by identifying practices that would improve programs for women working in prisons, jails, and so on. As she points out, women are all too frequently excluded, harassed, disadvantaged economically, and discriminated against. Programs are needed that integrate women into all stages of the criminal justice system – planning, task forces, training programs, and so on. In the *INL Guide to Gender in the Criminal Justice System*, which is available at www.state.gov/documents/organization/222034.pdf, the authors explain that their goal is to advance the priority of gender equality within the criminal justice system. It splits the discussion into five parts: (1) discusses how integrating gender will advance broader Department of State policies; (2) addresses integrating gender at the planning stage; (3) outlines two approaches to adding women to the project implementation stage; (4) explains measurement and evaluation processes; and (5) explores program partnerships and coordination. If followed, women employed in the U.S. criminal justice system would experience greater equality and a safer environment at work.

Christiaan Bezuidenhout reported on women's lack of employment as police officers in South Africa. The police are comprised of only 25% women in spite of women making up 54% of the population. According to the most recent United Nations figures for 2011 (United Nations Statistics Division, 2012), 44% of women vs. 61% of men 15 years and older are engaged in economic activity. When employed, women comprise 63.2% of part-time workers; however, women are more likely than men to be unemployed. The unemployment rate for women is 27.2%, whereas for men it is 22.3%. Thus, the reason for women's low level of employment in policing is not due to the lack of women seeking employment or their lack of workforce participation. Bezuidenhout argues that there are all sorts of reasons that women are not police officers including a number of myths about women:

- women are not strong enough to do the work;
- women are not career motivated;
- policing is not a feminine thing to do;
- women cannot run in heels.

The first three myths are easy to dismiss and the fourth simply means that women's uniforms should include flats or walking shoes. As Bezuidenhout points out in his conclusion, there is no reason that women cannot work in policing. It is a matter of making a cultural change, which is not an easy task.

Compared to South Africa, the U.S. exhibits even fewer women employed in policing. The police are comprised of only 15% women in spite of women making up 50.8% of the population. According to the most recent U.S. Bureau of Labor Statistics (BLS) for 2013 (U.S. Bureau of Labor Statistics, 2014), 57.2% of women vs. 69.7% of men 16 years and older are employed. When employed, 26% of women worked part-time, which is likely related to their slightly lower rate of unemployment. The unemployment rate for women is 7.1%, whereas for men it is 7.6%. Thus, the reason for women's low level of employment in policing is not due to the lack of women seeking employment or their lack of workforce participation. Thus, as Jim Albrecht from the U.S. explained, there is a need to mainstream women in policing to make it a more appealing type of employment for women. Among the changes needed are:

- equality in promotions;
- providing facilities for women;
- making the workplace free of discrimination.

In conclusion, Albrecht asserted that "Women are often peacekeepers in the home. Thus, women can keep the peace in their community too."

According to Erica Umbricht and Laurent Engler, there are also impediments to retaining women in policing in Switzerland even if they originally choose policing as a career. Currently, women make up 25% of the police force despite advertising that encourages women to apply. They have also considered having more special events for women. They want to increase the percent of women in administrative positions; however, current policies make this nearly impossible. Specifically, an officer must be on the street for a required period of time before s/he can be considered for a promotion. The problem is that if an officer is on leave for a while, they must start counting the years toward being considered for a promotion all over again. Of course, this has a negative effect on women of child-bearing age because each time they have a child and need a short leave, they must start counting their time to consideration for a promotion at zero. Thus, very few women in policing advance to administrative positions in Switzerland.

The next presentation moved from women workers in policing to preliminary results of a study being undertaken to examine police response to domestic violence at the international level. Dr. Diana Peterson reported for the larger U.S. research team including Julie Schroeder, Olga Osby, Safiya Omari, and Warren Yoder that the study is under way. Results will be reported at a later date.

## Roundtable: Intersection of Police and Schools in Conflicted Areas of Serbia and Bosnia-Herzegovina

The goal of the Dayton Agreement was to enact reform measures among the police in Bosnia-Herzegovina. It was unsuccessful due to police corruption. New reform is now under way.

## Panel Session 6: Combatting Violence in the Schools (Chairs: Larry French and Michael Palmiotto)

Following directly from the Roundtable discussion, Larry French from the USA noted challenges that exist in assessing critical needs of schools and police in Bosnia-Herzegovina. Many of the school children in the Balkans are victims of wars in the region and still suffer the aftereffects. French recommends more training for teachers and police, who work with these traumatized children so their symptoms can be addressed.

Kyung-Shick Choi from the USA applied routine activities theory to school bullying in an effort to understand the everyday risk of victimization in U.S. schools. Choi recommends having school resource officers in K-12 schools, exploring the "hotspots" where much of the bullying occurs, having structured school rules in place, and keeping a focus on cyberbullying.

By way of commentary, we should be aware that school is one of the safest places that children can be (National Crime Prevention Council, 2015).

The final presentation in this session was given by Agnes Nemeth for Hungary. Nemeth outlined a number of programs that police officers may use in Hungarian schools. Among the recommendations was one based off of the DARE program that has been used in U.S. schools. DARE did not work well in the U.S. and may have even increased drug use in some school populations.

## Panel Session 7: Assisting Special Population and Crime Victims (Chair: Karine Bates, Canada)

This session covered a broad range of persons in need of special assistance, as well as crime victims, in general. Tiffiney Barfield-Cottledge and Attapol Kuanliang from the USA opened the session with a discussion of the link between Alzheimer's disease and missing persons. People afflicted with Alzheimer's are faced with having extreme forgetfulness, which during the latter stages can lead to fear of people and situations that were normal parts of their pre- and early stage-Alzheimer's life. Police need to be aware that as a result of Alzheimer's disease, the person may be confused and anxious, which can easily lead to aggression toward the officer. Thus, when searching for an Alzheimer's patient, police need to be careful about how they approach the person. One new technique that officers may find helpful is an app that tells officers how to respond to an Alzheimer's patient along with a notice of their home address.

Max Edelbacher from Austria switched his presentation from one focusing on the elderly to the relationship of organized crime and the informal economy. He explained recent changes in the Mafia, as well as in financial issues related to organized crime. Edelbacher advised that all of us are affected by organized crime and that there must be a political will, an awareness, and an increase in the political transparency before much can be done to reduce or eradicate crimes of this type.

Lanying Huang from Taiwan and Liqun Cao from Canada discussed the policing of non-citizens in Taiwan. Taiwan found itself in need of people to work so it brought in immigrants, who were looking for employment. In fact, it brought in many immigrants. In addition to the worker immigrants, there are 490,000 marriage immigrants. Of course, many more of the marriage immigrants are women rather than men. To police the immigrants, the Taiwanese police have developed two strategies:

1. Assess the risk that the type of immigrant represents and use the type of surveillance that works best for that category of immigrant; and

2. Increase the use of networked policing. This type of policing often improves the relationship between the police and immigrant populations because police responses are tailored to the specific immigrant group.

Susumu Nagai from Japan completed a basic study of the psychology and assistance given to survivors of homicide cold cases. Homicide survivors need police officers to show empathy when they are being questioned or dealt with in any way by anyone in the criminal justice system. The second wave of victimization, that endured at the hands of the criminal justice system (Orth, 2002), including the police, never goes away! Police need to LISTEN to these homicide survivors, these victims. They need to feel comforted and be treated carefully. Nagai's recommendations mirror those for homicide survivors diagnosed with PTSD (Doerner & Lab, 2015; Freedy, Resnick, Kilpatrick, Dansky, & Tidwell, 1994; Miller, 2009; Vessier-Batchen & Douglas, 2006).

The final paper in this session was presented by Zora Sukabdi from Indonesia. The focus of her work is on healing bombing victims. These survivors have symptoms that are much like those of homicide survivors. They need someone to listen and respond with empathy. Police need to treat them with compassion so their fear and reactions to that fear stay in control. Sukabdi, who works directly with bombing victims, shares her strategies with police in an effort to help them better understand how these victims may respond to behavior by the police.

## Theme of the Day: Promoting Best Practices for Police Effectiveness, Safety, and Professionalism Closing Ceremony and Sightseeing Tour

## Panel Session 8: Promoting Officer Health, Safety, Retention, and Effectiveness (Chair: Juan Salgado, Mexico)

Kerry Kuehl is a U.S. physician, who, among other things, does physical exams on police officers. The leading cause of death among police officers is cardiovascular disease followed by cancer. Police tend to have unhealthy lifestyles. Night shift work has the same effect as smoking a pack of cigarettes each day. Like night shift nurses, who have two times more cancer than day shift nurses, night shift police are also in greater danger of developing cancer as well. Police also have more than the average numbers of heart attacks, high suicide rates, sleep deprivation reported as 40%, and the shift workers develop obesity due to the sedentary requirement of their jobs. Only about 3% listen to their physician so the quality of life police report falls in 85th place on job satisfaction and they spend an average of $9,000 each year on medication. The SHIELD, Safety & Health Improvement: Enhancing Law Enforcement Departments, is a study concerned with saving lives, improving officers' quality of life, and saving money. Once the SHIELD program was established, enough money was saved from officers no longer needing the same amount of sick time to allow more hires. Clearly, after hearing this presentation the rest of us wanted the SHIELD program at our places of employment too.

The second presentation is also very important to law enforcement. Lee Rankin from the U.S. reported on a one-year evaluation of an on-officer body camera system. The researchers were looking for any impact the camera system may have on citizen complaints, use of force incidents, and prosecutions. The evaluation started with 25 volunteer and 25 assigned officers on the street. There were two six-month evaluations; the first six months officers were required to activate the system each time they had contact with a citizen. During the second six months, they were to activate the camera system at their discretion. At the end of the first six months, there were 40% fewer complaints and a 75% decrease in the use of force. During the second six months, there was a 42% decrease in activation with discretion. Other findings include:

- 80% of the officers gave more accurate accounts for use in court;
- 70% thought the camera system made them act more professional, but just over half wanted to continue using the cameras;
- volunteers were more likely to activate when given discretion;
- the police were more effective in their interactions with citizens.

In conclusion, although many police officers are resistant to change, once they see something work, they are more likely to put the new equipment to good use.

Turning to training issues, Linda Mayberry from the U.S. described IPET, the International Police Education and Training Program, which is supported by the U.S. Department of State, Bureau of International Narcotics and Law Enforcement Affairs. Mayberry's primary job is to bring various groups together to help police departments implement changes where they want to see change occur. The critical issue is the proper selection of participants. IPET has been implemented in Armenia, Morocco, Haiti, Tunisia, Egypt, Iraq, Nepal, and Nigeria; places where they want to see increased sustainable reform. Mayberry's job is to choose the countries after assessing their readiness to start the year-long program.

Daniel P. Leclaire from the U.S. described the Applied Sociology Program at Boston University, where police officers can take classes on police professionalism online. Due to their flexible schedule the program grew from 50 to over 500 in two years. The online program does not allow the instructor to see the students or vice versa. On the positive side, online courses make money. Still, they are more costly to run, in part, because he recommends a TA for each 15 students. I encourage the department to evaluate the outcomes, e.g., grades, for face-to-face vs. online classes to see what sort of effect the online courses have in comparison to face-to-face courses.

Blake Randol from the U.S. discussed communication effectiveness, who shares information and why at the University of Wisconsin-Milwaukee. He finds the same sort of lack of sharing in some departments and agencies. Thus, case evaluation cannot be properly conducted. He encourages people to work together rather than in isolation.

The final paper in this session was presented by Gerald Dapaar Gyamfi from Ghana. His focus was on risk management and external factors related to retention and commitment to the organization. Retention was influenced by the officer's tenure in their organization and was significantly and positively related to commitment to that organization. Women were more committed to their organizations and scored higher than men even though they had a higher attrition rate, mostly due to pregnancy, and men dominated the workplace.

## Official Reporter's Summary and Closing Ceremony

A farewell address, vote of thanks, presentation of gifts and certificates rounded out the official symposium events.

## References


Adki, S. (2014). *Strategies in prevention of crime against women in India – with special reference to combined state of AP and Telanagana.* Paper presented at the 25th Annual Meeting of the International Police Executive Symposium, Sofia, Bulgaria, July, 2014.

Albrecht, J. (2014). *Gender mainstreaming, rule of law and criminal justice administration: Training and policy recommendations.* Paper presented at the 25th Annual Meeting of the International Police Executive Symposium, Sofia, Bulgaria, July, 2014.

Barfield-Cottledge, T., & Kuanliang, A. (2014a). *Human trafficking: A global examination.* Paper presented at the 25th Annual Meeting of the International Police Executive Symposium, Sofia, Bulgaria, July, 2014.

Barfield-Cottledge, T., & Kuanliang, A. (2014b). *The relationship between Alzheimer's and missing persons: An examination.* Paper presented at the 25th Annual Meeting of the International Police Executive Symposium, Sofia, Bulgaria, July, 2014.

Bates, K. (2014). *Community initiatives to facilitate access to justice in India.* Paper presented at the 25th Annual Meeting of the International Police Executive Symposium, Sofia, Bulgaria, July, 2014.

Bezuidenhout, C. (2014). *Women in criminal justice: Reality or myth?* Paper presented at the 25th Annual Meeting of the International Police Executive Symposium, Sofia, Bulgaria, July, 2014.

Burns, G. (2014). *Police/media cooperation: Communicating with the community.* Speech given at the 25th Annual Meeting of the International Police Executive Symposium, Sofia, Bulgaria, July, 2014.

Choi, K-S. (2014). *Criminal opportunity structures and crime: Do routine activities in everyday life influence the risk of bullying victimization at school?* Paper presented at the 25th Annual Meeting of the International Police Executive Symposium, Sofia, Bulgaria, July, 2014.

Chokprajakchat, S. (2014). *Political interference in the promotions and appointments of the Royal Thai Police.* Paper presented at the 25th Annual Meeting of the International Police Executive Symposium, Sofia, Bulgaria, July, 2014.

Doerner, W. G., & Lab, S. P. (2015). *Victimology* (7th ed.). Waltham, MA: Elsevier.

Edelbacher, M., & Kratcoski, P. (2014a). *Police practitioner – academic collaboration in training and education in criminal justice.* Paper presented at the 25th Annual Meeting of the International Police Executive Symposium, Sofia, Bulgaria, July, 2014.

Edelbacher, M., & Kratcoski, P. (2014b). *The relationship of organized crime and the informal economy.* Paper presented at the 25th Annual Meeting of the International Police Executive Symposium, Sofia, Bulgaria, July, 2014.

Freedy, J. R., Resnick, H. S., Kilpatrick, D. G., Dansky, B. S., & Tidwell, R. P. (1994). The psychological adjustment of recent crime victims in the criminal justice system. *Journal of Interpersonal Violence, 9*, 450–468.

French, L. (2014). *Challenges in assessing critical needs of schools and police.* Paper presented at the 25th Annual Meeting of the International Police Executive Symposium, Sofia, Bulgaria, July, 2014.

Govender, D. (2014). *Community-based participatory approach to prevent residential burglaries and house robberies.* Paper presented at the 25th Annual Meeting of the International Police Executive Symposium, Sofia, Bulgaria, July, 2014.

Gyamfi, G. D. (2014). *External retention factors in relation to organizational commitment: Empirical evidence from Ghana Police Service.* Paper presented at the 25th Annual Meeting of the International Police Executive Symposium, Sofia, Bulgaria, July, 2014.

Hanser, R. (2014). *Coordinated community response to domestic violence.* Paper presented at the 25th Annual Meeting of the International Police Executive Symposium, Sofia, Bulgaria, July, 2014.

Huang, L., & Cao, L. (2014). *Policing non-citizens in Taiwan.* Paper presented at the 25th Annual Meeting of the International Police Executive Symposium, Sofia, Bulgaria, July, 2014.

Huff-Corzine, L., & Corzine, J. (2014). *Crossing the great divide: The development and effectiveness of working relationships between law enforcement personnel and academic researchers.* Paper presented at the 25th Annual Meeting of the International Police Executive Symposium, Sofia, Bulgaria, July, 2014.

Koutsenok, I. (2014). *Treatment of Drug Offenders – What Works and How to Make it Work.* Keynote Address presented at the 25th Annual Meeting of the International Police Executive Symposium, Sofia, Bulgaria, July, 2014.

Kratcoski, P. C., & M. Edelbacher (Eds.). (2015). *Collaborative Policing: Police, Academics, Professionals, and Communities Working Together for Education, Training and Program Implementation.* Boca Raton, FL: CRC Press.

Kuehl, K. (2014). *The SHIELD (Safety & Health Improvement: Enhancing Law Enforcement Departments) study: Feasibility and findings.* Paper presented at the 25th Annual Meeting of the International Police Executive Symposium, Sofia, Bulgaria, July, 2014.

Leclaire, D. P. (2014). *New technologies for the advancement of higher education for police professionalism of criminal justice employees.* Paper presented at the 25th Annual Meeting of the International Police Executive Symposium, Sofia, Bulgaria, July, 2014.

Lemieux, F. (2014). *Preventing extreme violence: The case of mass shootings.* Keynote Speech presented at the 25th Annual Meeting of the International Police Executive Symposium, Sofia, Bulgaria, July, 2014.

Lobnikar, B. (2014). *Policing multicultural communities in Slovenia.* Paper presented at the 25th Annual Meeting of the International Police Executive Symposium, Sofia, Bulgaria, July, 2014.

Malme, O. (2014). *Police reform in Serbia – status 2014.* Paper presented at the 25th Annual Meeting of the International Police Executive Symposium, Sofia, Bulgaria, July, 2014.

Mayberry, L. (2014a). *Guide to gender in the criminal justice system.* Paper presented at the 25th Annual Meeting of the International Police Executive Symposium, Sofia, Bulgaria, July, 2014.

Mayberry, L. (2014b). *A new approach to international policing: International police education and training.* Paper presented at the 25th Annual Meeting of the International Police Executive Symposium, Sofia, Bulgaria, July, 2014.

Meini, B. (2014). *Community policing and vigilantism: Two alternative strategies for fighting neighborhood crime.* Paper presented at the 25th Annual Meeting of the International Police Executive Symposium, Sofia, Bulgaria, July, 2014.

Miller, L. (2009). Family survivors of homicide: I. Symptoms, syndromes, and reaction patterns. *The American Journal of Family Therapy, 37*, 67–79.

Mulayim, S. (2014). *Quality management strategies for police officers in interpreted-interviews – a training video.* Paper presented at the 25th Annual Meeting of the International Police Executive Symposium, Sofia, Bulgaria, July, 2014.

Mulayim, S., & Lai, M. (2014). *Communication with ethnic communities in community policing – views of ethnic community members.* Paper presented at the 25th Annual Meeting of the International Police Executive Symposium, Sofia, Bulgaria, July, 2014.

Nagai, S. (2014a). *Telephone fraud in Japan.* Paper presented at the 25th Annual Meeting of the International Police Executive Symposium, Sofia, Bulgaria, July, 2014.

Nagai, S. (2014b). *A basic study on psychology and assistance to survivors in cold cases of homicide.* Paper presented at the 25th Annual Meeting of the International Police Executive Symposium, Sofia, Bulgaria, July, 2014.

National Crime Prevention Council. (2015). *School safety.* Retrieved February 22, 2015, from www.ncpc.org/topics/by-audience/parents/school-safety/.

Nemeth, A. (2014). *Police officers in schools – Hungarian practice.* Paper presented at the 25th Annual Meeting of the International Police Executive Symposium, Sofia, Bulgaria, July, 2014.

Orth, U. (2002). Secondary victimization of crime victims by criminal proceedings. *Social Justice Research, 15,* 313–325.

Perkins, M. (2014). *Public confidence modeling: A locally based approach to police performance management.* Paper presented at the 25th Annual Meeting of the International Police Executive Symposium, Sofia, Bulgaria, July, 2014.

Peterson, D., Schroeder, J., Osby, O., Omari, S., & Yoder, W. (2014). *Preliminary results of pilot study: International police response to domestic violence.* Paper presented at the 25th Annual Meeting of the International Police Executive Symposium, Sofia, Bulgaria, July, 2014.

Randol, B. (2014). *Sources of communication performance in the investigative units of local law enforcement: Who shares information and why?* Paper presented at the 25th Annual Meeting of the International Police Executive Symposium, Sofia, Bulgaria, July, 2014.

Rankin, L. (2014). *On-officer body camera system: End of program evaluation and recommendations.* Paper presented at the 25th Annual Meeting of the International Police Executive Symposium, Sofia, Bulgaria, July, 2014.

Richards, G. (2014). *Cyberbullying, creating partnerships for prevention.* Paper presented at the 25th Annual Meeting of the International Police Executive Symposium, Sofia, Bulgaria, July, 2014.

Roelofse, C. (2014). *Victim support and adjudication of sexual offences in the Thulamela Sexual Offenses Court in the Venda Region, Limpopo Province of South Africa.* Paper presented at the 25th Annual Meeting of the International Police Executive Symposium, Sofia, Bulgaria, July, 2014.

Salgado, J. (2014). *Rights-based approaches to criminality and violence prevention.* Paper presented at the 25th Annual Meeting of the International Police Executive Symposium, Sofia, Bulgaria, July, 2014.

Sarre, R. (2014). *Policing the cross border region: Can this unique strategy embrace crime prevention and build community resilience?* Paper presented at the 25th Annual Meeting of the International Police Executive Symposium, Sofia, Bulgaria, July, 2014.

Sukabdi, Z. (2014). *Healing bombing victims.* Paper presented at the 25th Annual Meeting of the International Police Executive Symposium, Sofia, Bulgaria, July, 2014.

Umbricht, E., & Engler, L. (2014). *Impediments to retaining women in policing.* Paper presented at the 25th Annual Meeting of the International Police Executive Symposium, Sofia, Bulgaria, July, 2014.

United Nations Statistics Division. (2012). Retrieved February 22, 2015, from http://unstats.un.org/unsd/demographic/products/indwm/.

United States Department of State. (n.d.) *INL guide to gender in the criminal justice system.* Retrieved February 21, 2015, from www.state.gov/documents/organization/222034.pdf.

U.S. Bureau of Labor Statistics. (2014). *Women in the labor force: A databook.* Retrieved February 21, 2015, from www.bls.gov/opub/reports/cps/women-in-the-labor-force-a-databook-2014.pdf.

Van Graan, J. (2014). *Multi-sector cooperation in preventing crime: The case of South African neighborhood watch as an effective crime prevention model.* Paper presented at the 25th Annual Meeting of the International Police Executive Symposium, Sofia, Bulgaria, July, 2014.

Versteegh, P., & Hesseling, R. (2014). *The B3W matrix: Managing a more effective way to tackle residential burglary.* Paper presented at the 25th Annual Meeting of the International Police Executive Symposium, Sofia, Bulgaria, July, 2014.

Vessier-Batchen, M., & Douglas, D. (2006). Coping and grief in survivors of homicide and suicide decedents. *Journal of Forensic Nursing, 2*(1), 25–32.

Yong, M. (2014). *Delta League – changing lives through football.* Paper presented at the 25th Annual Meeting of the International Police Executive Symposium, Sofia, Bulgaria, July, 2014.

# Global Strategies for Crime and Violence Prevention

# I

# Coordinated Community Response to Domestic Violence and Sexual Assault on the College Campus

# 1

ROBERT HANSER

## Contents



## Abstract

The Coordinated Community Response Team (CCRT) has been hailed as a premier system of response to domestic violence issues in past literature. The CCRT, as a partnership between multiple agencies within the community, is highlighted, with the CCRT in Northeast Louisiana and the University of Louisiana at Monroe (ULM)'s involvement in this initiative being showcased. Amidst the university's work on campus and in the community to address domestic violence, new legislation and legal requirements for investigating, processing, and reporting acts of victimization on campus have transformed the role of the university's CCRT, making its mission all the more important, both internal and external to the campus. The result is a genuine partnership between practitioners and researchers, on and off campus, who work together to provide public awareness, prevention, first-responder, and intervention services in a comprehensive manner throughout Northeast Louisiana.

**This project was supported by Grant No. 2009-WA-AX-0024 awarded by the Office on Violence Against Women, U.S. Department of Justice. The opinions, findings, conclusions, and recommendations expressed in this publication/program/exhibition**

**are those of the author(s) and do not necessarily reflect the views of the Department of Justice, Office on Violence Against Women.**

Coordinated Community Response Teams (CCRTs) have developed as a primary action mechanism for crimes of domestic violence throughout various areas of the United States. These teams include a number of agencies and partners who, working collaboratively, seek to enhance and optimize services for survivors of domestic violence. At the same time, these collaborative initiatives also seek to hold domestic violence offenders accountable for the crimes that they commit. This chapter provides a discussion of how these partnerships have developed on college campuses as funded initiatives and showcases the Violence Prevention and Intervention Program (VPIP) of the University of Louisiana at Monroe, which serves as an example of a well-run and operated CCRT on campus, and a partner to the larger community-wide CCRT led by the region's primary advocacy organization, The Wellspring, Inc.

In addition, this chapter discusses legislation in the United States that has significantly impacted college campuses in relation to domestic violence, dating violence, sexual assault, and stalking. Included in this discussion is the emergence of civil remedies and forms of related liability through the Title IX federal statutes, enforced by the Office on Civil Rights (OCR), as related to gender discrimination and sexual harassment in institutions of higher education. Likewise, recent legislation titled the Campus Sexual Violence Elimination Act of 2013, also referred to as the Campus SaVE Act, is presented. This act serves as an update to outdated sexual assault policy requirements for institutions of higher education and, at the same time, this act also provides a broader range of obligations related to prevention, training, and reporting of incidents of domestic violence, dating violence, sexual assault, and stalking. Further, the campus SaVE Act also enhances existing victims' rights provisions and the requirements of universities to make those rights known through a good faith dissemination of this knowledge.

The impact of this legislation on the VPIP as a CCRT is important to understand. As these legal changes have occurred throughout the nation, there has been a rise in prominence of the VPIP, both on campus and off campus, within the region of Northeast Louisiana. Indeed, due to much of this legislation, the scope and authority of those individuals involved in these efforts has increased, both in terms of workload and in terms of jurisdictional reach. Further still, as a result of this legislation, efforts to prevent these behaviors has resulted in an expansion in responses and activities under civil law and has also resulted in an enhanced partnership with criminal justice agencies throughout the community.

## Literature Review

Notions of establishing a coordinated community response to domestic violence emerged during the late 1990s and early 2000s as the Duluth model of response to domestic abuse increasingly became the most widely regarded model for addressing domestic violence in communities. The Duluth model originated in Duluth, Minnesota, and had its roots in the shelter movement of the 1970s as a means of protecting women who survived incidents of domestic violence. Eventually, it became clear that the mission of eradicating domestic violence would require collaborative efforts among many parties, not just the police. Rather, emergency rooms and medical centers would need to be involved, social workers were needed, school systems with children from abusive homes would need to be involved, employers for these women and/or their abusive partners might need to be involved, and many others would need to be included to ensure that survivors were given a realistic opportunity to escape their abusive environments.

Eventually, demands for accountability from domestic abusers became an area of focused attention, as well. With this came the development of batterers' intervention programs, which were designed to provide psycho-educational classes to perpetrators of domestic violence. Education for these offenders would revolve around their acceptance of the harm that they did to their loved ones and also to their need to change their views and attitudes towards women. With this effort came the support of courthouses, probation offices, and, of course, the police. It is important to consider that, with the addition of programs aimed at holding domestic abusers accountable, a two-pronged approach to addressing domestic violence developed (one prong aiding victims, the other prong holding offenders accountable). Also important to note is the fact that along both prongs, the use of a comprehensive response was implemented, one that included multiple parties and stakeholders throughout the community.

The very first Coordinated Community Response Team (CCRT) was developed in Duluth, Minnesota, during the early 1980s (Gender Violence Institute, 2013). This CCRT model worked with partner agencies to develop more effective responses to domestic violence. These teams bring together advocacy programs, law enforcement, corrections, human services, and victim services agencies to coordinate response using an integrated infrastructure of case processing. These teams examine policies and procedures, training initiatives, assessment processes, evaluations, and community awareness campaigns among their collaborators. The goal is to maximize saturation of services and to ensure that an overlap of prevention, response, and intervention approaches exists within a given jurisdiction. Further, the use of CCRTs has been adopted as a best practice for intervening in community-wide crimes of domestic violence (Domestic Abuse Intervention Program, 2013; Office on Violence Against Women, 2007). Lastly, this model of intervention has been replicated in other countries throughout Europe as well as the countries of Australia and New Zealand (Domestic Abuse Intervention Program, 2013; Gender Violence Institute, 2013).

In keeping with the idea of a community-wide response to domestic violence, the work of Salazar, Emshoff, Baker, and Crowley (2007) points toward the need to create an infrastructure that supports a systemic-level and ultimately societal change in awareness, prevention, and intervention. Salazar et al. (2007) examined and compared two CCRTs to see if they were effective in applying increased sanctions for male domestic violence offenders (i.e., arrests, convictions, sentencing, and service delivery of batterer intervention programs). As one might expect, in one program, improvements were seen in the number of offenders sentenced to probation and mandated to attend a batterer's intervention program. Oddly enough, there was no change in these outcomes for the second program. From this research, it is clear that it is important to examine the processes involved (not just the outcomes) with CCRTs and their impact on the criminal justice system's response to domestic violence.

Though a bit dated, one study is unique and worth inclusion because the researchers examined recidivism rates of offenders in the jurisdiction of a CCRT (Shepard, Falk,

& Elliott, 2001). These researchers found that when compared to a prior baseline period, offenders had significantly lower rates of recidivism during a three-year period. Further, two variables were found to be particularly related to these reductions in recidivism: (1) whether the offender was mandated by the court to attend a batterer's intervention program and, (2) if the offender completed the program. From this early research, it can be seen that offender accountability and engagement in intervention programming can be integral to reducing further recidivism in communities. Thus, it is important that CCRTs include, whenever possible, programs that work with the offender, as well as the victim.

Klevens, Baker, Shelley, and Ingram (2008) evaluated 10 CCRTs and found that, when matched with similar communities that had no CCRT, there was no impact on the rates of domestic violence. While this may be surprising, the issue as to whether CCRTs have good outcome evaluations is not the point to this current article. What is important is that Klevens et al. (2008) also noted that there was considerable variability between CCRTs in both the array of services provided as well as the quality of those services. Their conclusion was that different levels of impact upon domestic violence issues existed from one CCRT to another and that it was more a point of interest to examine these differences for clues in optimizing responses to crimes of domestic violence in the future.

In response to this point, the work of Cox, Finkelstein, Perez, and Rosenbach (2010) examined CCRTs in 14 states using a mixed model of evaluation (both quantitative and qualitative research approaches were used). Their research identified how federal funding initiatives had resulted in improvements in internal CCRT capacity and also demonstrated how external supports with collaborators was effective in reducing domestic violence in the surrounding community. From this research, it was found that CCRTs that included advisory boards and/or leaders who had routine contact and rapport tended to fare better, internally and externally, in providing services, both for victims and in offender accountability programs (i.e., batterer intervention programs). This observation is important because this one single feature was found to be associated with effective responses to both prongs of addressing domestic violence and because this also turned out to produce partnerships that consisted of more intrinsically motivated agency partners rather than those who were motivated extrinsically by money and other material rewards. In other words, the "buy-in" among leaders of agencies who sat on the advisory board was more sincere and this, presumably, also resulted in more vigorous efforts among personnel in each of these partner agencies.

Lastly and even more specific to this current chapter, Holtfreter and Boyd (2008) examined the effectiveness of CCRTs that operated on college campuses. These researchers did not evaluate the effectiveness of such programs but instead, interviewed service providers affiliated with a campus-based CCRT. From these interviews, it was found that these service providers indicated that there was a need for increased training on issues related to domestic violence, dating violence, sexual assault, and stalking. Likewise, service providers highlighted a need for more resources with which they could perform their tasks and functions. It is with this note in mind that a shift in focus will now be given to the efforts of the Office on Violence Against Women (OVW) to fund and support such programs on college campuses, resulting in the eventual funding and development of our current program of interest, the Violence Intervention and Prevention Program (VPIP) of the University of Louisiana at Monroe.

## Office on Violence against Women Minimum Standards

In 2007, the Office on Violence Against Women (OVW) developed minimum standards for CCRTs addressing violence against women on college campuses, noting that funded campuses would be required to "create a coordinated community response to violence against women on campuses" (p. 3) and that "multi-disciplinary response should involve the entire campus as well as the larger community in which the campus is located" (p. 3). In addition, funded programs require campuses to do the following:

> Develop partnerships with at least one local nonprofit, nongovernmental victim services organization within the community which the institution is located and one or more of the following criminal justice or civil legal agencies: external law enforcement, prosecution, civil legal assistance providers, systems-based victim services units, or judiciary and court personnel. An applicant who is partnering with campus law enforcement or campus security must still partner with a criminal justice or civil legal agency. (p. 3)

These requirements are important to this current chapter because it is this program of funding and these requirements upon which the Violence Prevention and Intervention Program (VPIP) were established. While the concept for campus CCRTs is similar to those in the community, they consist of a number of partners that are unique from those off campus and that are exclusive to college campuses. For instance, some of the partners might include the following:

1. Students, especially victims;
2. Campus-based victim services providers and violence prevention programs;
3. Campus law enforcement or department of public safety;
4. Faculty and staff;
5. Student groups, including those representing diverse or underserved student populations;
6. Athletic departments;
7. Sororities and fraternities;
8. Student health centers;
9. Counseling centers;
10. Campus housing authorities and residence hall assistants;
11. Campus disciplinary boards and/or judicial boards.

Each of the above partners is likely to be critical to a coordinated response on a college campus but would not be likely to be found in most CCRTs based in jurisdictions that are separate from the college campus.

In conducting such collaborative partnerships, OVW notes that first and foremost, campuses should work in tandem with experts on addressing issues related to domestic violence, dating violence, sexual assault, and stalking. From these experts, an advisory committee or task force should be developed which will be tasked with reviewing protocols, policies, and procedures of the different offices, particularly in relation to violence against women. Further, it is expected that such collaborators will work together on a consistent basis, holding scheduled meetings and developing formal policies and protocols for responding to campus-based acts of domestic violence, dating violence, sexual assault, and stalking. The key function of these meetings should be to develop and maximize responses to these crimes and to improve service delivery for survivors of these crimes.

In addition, the most effective form of campus CCRT will be one that also networks and partners with off-campus agencies and service providers. As such, it is expected that campus programs will create written policies that reinforce the partnerships between offices on campus as well as partner agencies off campus (i.e., the district attorney, area police, community-based domestic violence services center, probation departments, the batterer intervention program, and so forth). In addition, routine meetings should be set regularly that bring these partners, on and off campus, together. This is precisely what has occurred with the VPIP at the University of Louisiana at Monroe.

## Violence Prevention and Intervention Program

The Violence Prevention and Intervention Program (VPIP) of the University of Louisiana at Monroe serves as a Coordinated Community Response Team (CCRT) that networks and partners with a multitude of offices on campus as well as a variety of agencies throughout the community. This organization is a hybrid form of CCRT that incorporates partners from two communities – the university campus community and the broader regional community. Specifically, the VPIP is designed to provide awareness education to students, faculty, and staff on campus regarding the prevalence and dynamics of these types of crimes and also provides training for bystanders and potential victims of these forms of victimization.

In establishing and fulfilling this mission, numerous agreements and Memoranda of Understanding were generated between the offices on campus, as well as various external agencies throughout the community. Some of these agencies were the Ouachita Parish Sheriff's Office, Monroe Police Department, West Monroe Police Department, and the 4th Judicial District Attorney's Office, as well as the Family Justice Center. The partnerships developed by these and other organizations are not simple "paper" partnerships; they are living partnerships that reflect interconnections between these offices and agencies and ULM, in general, and the VPIP, in particular. Indeed, this is reflected by the fact that every semester, persons from at least one of these agencies (and usually each agency) agree to come to campus to speak on issues related to domestic violence, dating violence, sexual assault, and/or stalking. Likewise, the Co-Directors are active with these agencies in the community and serve in various capacities, including membership on the Stopping Abusive Family Environments (SAFE) Task Force, the Louisiana Coalition Against Domestic Violence (LCADV), and the Northeast Louisiana Law Enforcement Training Advisory Board (NLLETAB). Further, the directors also are active in training law enforcement throughout the region and network with these agencies on other social service projects, as well. This creates a formal and informal relationship with these agencies and their administrators which facilitates integration between the outside community and the campus community. It is in this manner that the VPIP operates to successfully bring together both worlds so as to optimize ULM's response to domestic violence, dating violence, sexual assault, and stalking on campus.

## Non-Profit Service Providers

While there are many non-profit agencies throughout Louisiana, including a diverse array of Non-governmental Organizations (NGOs), the chapter will showcase one organization as being of particular importance. This organization is the Wellspring Alliance, Inc., which serves as the primary organization to lead the community in addressing domestic violence in the region. Even more specifically, this organization maintains and operates a large-scale facility that is designed to be a one-stop location whereby survivors of domestic violence can receive an array of services (safety provision, legal assistance, medical assistance, childcare assistance, and so forth) simultaneously. This facility is known as the Family Justice Center (FJC) of Northeast Louisiana.

The Family Justice Center also serves as an information and service center for those who seek assistance with domestic violence, sexual assault, or stalking. The primary function of the Family Justice Center is to make services more accessible to victims of domestic violence by integrating the services of social workers, clergy, counselors, medical staff, legal advocates, prosecutors, and law enforcement, as well as community volunteers. It is also the location where over a dozen agencies and collaborators meet, on a quarterly basis, as the CCRT for Northeast Louisiana, to strategize and monitor progress in response and intervention programs.

The Family Justice Center model has been identified as a best practice in the field of domestic violence intervention and prevention services by numerous local, state, and national organizations. The Family Justice Center has, as part of its leadership and governance, a steering committee that consists of multiple members from around the community. Among the various administrators of the facility, there are representatives of Monroe Police Department, West Monroe Police Department, Ouachita Parish Sheriff's Office, Children's Protection Services, the Monroe City and Ouachita Parish school systems, a judge from the Fourth Judicial District, and assistant district attorneys from the District Attorney's Office, as well as a university representative from ULM.

This steering committee helps to facilitate the exchange of information between these agencies and also serves to coordinate community responses to domestic violence. The coordinated and collaborative approach used by this governing body has received commendations from various grant funding agencies. Further still, the Department of Criminal Justice has, on numerous occasions, been involved with community-based surveys that have provided data analysis regarding community perceptions on domestic violence. Likewise, the ULM Violence Prevention and Intervention Program, whereby Monroe and West Monroe Police Departments, the Ouachita Parish Sheriff's Office, the Family Justice Center, the ULM Police Department, and other campus organizations, have come together under Memoranda of Understanding, to educate faculty, staff, and students in regard to domestic abuse, date rape, and stalking on the ULM Campus. This is a specific example of how non-profit service providers and agencies have come together to fight crime; in this case, domestic crime.

Lastly, the Family Justice Center has consistently published its Ouachita Parish Domestic Violence Community Response Manual, which provides guidance to community members and agencies throughout the Northeast Louisiana region. This manual is written by experts in domestic violence response who are employed in various capacities throughout the community. Among these experts, area university faculty have been contributors to this manual. This is yet another clear and specific example of how collaborative partnerships between non-profit agencies, community members, and other government entities can and do exist in the region, providing enhanced information exchange and community awareness regarding criminal activity (in this case, domestically violent criminal activity).

## The Emergence of Title IX

Simply put, Title IX is a set of federal laws that prohibit discrimination on the basis of sex in schools that receive federal funding. This also includes the athletic programs for such schools. More specifically, Title IX states the following:

> No person in the United States shall, on the basis of sex, be excluded from participation in, be denied the benefits of, or be subjected to discrimination under any education program or activity receiving Federal financial assistance. (United States Department of Labor, 2016, p. 1)

With the above in mind, Title IX covers state and local school systems, including institutions of higher education, if they receive federal funds for educational programming. Among these agencies are approximately 16,000 local school districts and over 3,200 colleges and universities. All schools, programs, and activities that receive federal education funds are required to operate in a nondiscriminatory manner. These programs and activities include, among others: admissions, recruitment, financial aid, academic programs, student treatment and services, counseling and guidance, discipline, classroom assignment, grading, vocational education, recreation, physical education, athletics, housing, and employment.

Further, this statute also affords protection to individuals who exercise their rights under Title IX and/or who reports Title IX violations. When complaints are filed, the Office for Civil Rights (OCR) is tasked with enforcing Title IX protections. The primary means of enforcing compliance is through the investigation and resolution of complaints filed by people alleging sex discrimination. However, because so many institutions fall within the jurisdiction of the OCR, not all of the policies and practices of institutions receiving federal funds can be investigated. Thus, OCR provides guidance and assistance to schools, universities, and other agencies to assist with voluntary compliance with this law.

Initially, the OCR investigated issues related to gender inequality and discrimination that was, more or less, associated with working conditions or access to education. Some examples would include the following:

1. Disproportionate funding of athletic programs and scholarships for female students.

2. Inequitable pay for female faculty who hold positions similar as male faculty.
3. Discrimination against female students who are pregnant.

It is clear that these issues, while discriminatory, were not initially problems that would warrant potential intervention from criminal justice agencies. This remained the case until April 4, 2011, when the Assistant Secretary for Civil Rights published the landmark and historical "Dear Colleague Letter," a 19-page document sent to a multitude of educational institutions throughout the United States and publicly disseminated for all to see. This document produced sweeping change in regards to the application of Title IX requirements for educational institutions.

## The Dear Colleague Letter

At the outset, the U.S. Department of Education determined that the Dear Colleague Letter would serve as a significant guidance document under the Office of Management and Budget's Final Bulletin for Agency Good Guidance Practices. In this letter, the Assistant Secretary for Civil Rights made clear that Title IX and other similar statutes prohibited discrimination on the basis of sex in educational programs and activities. However, this document, in one day, broadened out significantly the scope of behaviors that Title IX would, henceforth, preside over with the following statement:

> Sexual harassment of students, which includes acts of sexual violence, is a form of sex discrimination prohibited by Title IX. In order to assist recipients, which include school districts, colleges, and universities in meeting these obligations, this letter explains that the requirements of Title IX pertaining to sexual harassment also covers sexual violence, and lays out the specific Title IX requirements applicable to sexual violence. (Office for Civil Rights, 2011, p. 1)

It is, perhaps, difficult to understand how comprehensive and thorough this one document was in regard to gender-based claims within institutions of higher education.

To give a better picture as to the substantive change that this letter has generated, consider that, since this time, there has been a proliferation of Title IX investigators and Title IX administrators – persons who are specially trained and hired for the sole purpose of processing Title IX complaints – among thousands of colleges and universities throughout the United States. Indeed, the Association of Title IX Administrators (ATIXA) has emerged as a leading advocate for gender equity in higher education and has provided conferences, training workshops, and certification to thousands of individuals at Title IX investigators and as Title IX coordinators in dozens of major cities throughout the United States. This organization has developed standards and guidelines related to liability issues, the need for awareness programs, prevention programs, judicial processing, and intervention programs that are available to campuses around the nation.

Much of these developments are necessary in order to demonstrate that agencies are responding to the concerns articulated in the Dear Colleague Letter which, among other things, pointed toward research on sexual assault on campuses as being epidemic and troubling (Ali, 2011). Indeed, research by the National Institute of Justice found that approximately 1 in 5 women are victims of completed or attempted sexual assault while in college and also made note that, in 2009, as part of the mandatory reporting requirements, colleges and universities reported approximately 3,300 forcible sex offenses (Ali, 2011).

## Title IX Processes after the Dear Colleague Letter

What has emerged is a complete change in organizational culture across hundreds of campuses around the nation. Campuses now require faculty and students to attend mandatory trainings on awareness of Title IX issues and compliance procedures. Further, many campuses have seen, as a result of this awareness, a spike in reported incidents (Association of Title IX Administrators, 2014). This implies that students and faculty are more aware, more likely to recognize gender-based victimization, and are more willing to report this victimization, as time continues. In response to this rise in reporting, universities across the United States find it necessary to send staff and/or faculty to training with organizations such as ATIXA to gain certification and expertise as official investigators of Title IX complaints or as Title IX coordinators who act on behalf of the university to process these complaints in a thorough, fundamentally fair, and legally defensible manner.

Given the overlap that was generated between Title IX expansion due to the Dear Colleague Letter and CCRT requirements set by the OVW, some staff and faculty at universities found that they would ultimately end up fulfilling multiple roles in sexual assault prevention efforts on campuses. For instance, one of the Directors of the VPIP is also a certified Title IX investigator and a certified Title IX coordinator. He has acted as the Lead Investigator of Title IX issues for nearly three years and at the Assistant Title IX Coordinator for nearly a year at ULM. This is while also providing awareness training to students and faculty on issues related to dating violence, sexual assault, and stalking, and also providing bystander training to students on campus.

## Scope of Title IX as Administrative Law

The Title IX investigative process is one that is civil in nature, being governed by administrative law set by the university itself and subject to the standards of most all liability standards common to other avenues to civil litigation. This means that investigations, judicial panel proceedings, coordination of cases, and other procedures all operate under a burden of proof known as a preponderance of the evidence. It is not uncommon for institutions to place the following statement at the end of reports that are generated: "The standard of proof required is a preponderance of evidence, i.e., the evidence demonstrates that it is more likely than not that the conduct occurred. This standard is often referred to as '50% plus a feather'." (Sokolow, 2014, p. 1)

This is, of course, a much lower burden of proof than is required in criminal courts (being based on proof beyond a reasonable doubt, sometimes equated to a 95% likelihood), and this, therefore, provides universities some advantage when compared to official police and courtroom agencies that must meet a much more stringent level of proof. Further, the jurisdiction of universities is much greater than one might imagine. Indeed, whether on or off campus, if a Title IX violation occurs that involves a university student, faculty member, or staff person of the university, it falls within the jurisdiction and purview of the university. In other words, if a student is at her home off campus and she suffers damages under Title IX from another student, faculty, or staff, that case can (and often will) be investigated by that university, with administrative sanctions being imposed. These even include events that happen in other countries, such as when students and/or faculty engage in study abroad programs or when international students return home from the United States. Thus, the scope of Title IX governance and oversight has been broadened significantly, both in terms of how it has been defined and in terms of who falls under its jurisdiction, regardless of distance or borders that may be involved.

## The Campus SaVE Act of 2013

The Campus Sexual Violence Elimination Act, called the Campus SaVE Act, is a very new legislative development and considered historical because it has revamped the means by which colleges/universities are required to address sexual misconduct on their campuses. Prior to this, the Clery Act of 1990 governed the processes by which campuses reported incident-based data to the federal government. The Clery Act, named after a tragically slain student, Ms. Jeanne Clery, amended federal financial aid laws so that colleges and universities receiving federal funds would be required to disclose campus crime statistics and security information.

As a means of updating the Clery Act and addressing some gaps and oversights associated with this act, the Campus SaVE Act revises the mandatory reporting process to be more closely aligned with current Title IX developments and to also encourage more vigorous awareness campaigns and prevention training than was provided in the past. This act requires that universities disclose incidents of domestic violence, dating violence, sexual assault, and stalking in their annually reported crime statistics, and that they report them as the appropriate categories, without modification. In addition, both students and employees who report victimization will be provided written notice of their rights (Clery Center, 2014) to the following:

1. Change academic class schedules, living arrangements, transportation, and/or working situations to avoid a hostile environment.
2. Obtain and have enforced restraining orders from criminal courts and/or a no-contact directive under university administrative law.
3. Be given full disclosure and information related to the university's disciplinary process as well as the range of sanctions that can be imposed.
4. Receive information and assistance from counseling, health, victim advocacy, legal assistance that is available on campus and in the community-at-large (Clery Center, 2014).

In addition, the SaVE Act provides clarification on standards for university disciplinary procedures related to incidents of domestic violence, dating violence, sexual assault, and stalking. This clarification aids in reinforcing actions under Title IX but goes beyond the traditional scope of Title IX, which is related to gender equity and sexual assault, and makes clear that requirements to investigate and address infractions will include acts of domestic violence, dating violence, and stalking. These are acts that are sometimes addressed through less direct means at some universities. The SaVE Act puts a stop to this and ensures that all of these actions are included within the scope of university disciplinary policy and procedure (Clery Center, 2014). Specifically, the SaVE Act ensures the following:

1. That proceedings include a prompt and impartial investigation and resolution that is conducted by staff who receive annual training on domestic violence, sexual assault, and stalking.
2. Both parties will be allowed to have other persons present during the institutional disciplinary proceeding and/or other related meetings.
3. Each party will receive a formal written outcome of the disciplinary proceeding that will be given at the same time (Clery Center, 2014).

It should be pointed out that campuses that already have active and well-constructed Title IX work groups likely already follow the above procedures. However, their work tends to be tightly focused on issues specific to Title IX allegations (Association of Title IX Administrators, 2014). While this is true, some universities have utilized their Title IX investigators in Equal Employment Opportunity (EEO) complaints, as well, because the processes of investigation, fact finding, and resolution are very similar (they are both grounded in civil law with administrative remedies usually provided, when applicable).

As with EEO workflow, it is very likely that individuals who will be tasked with providing investigations and overseeing additional complaints under the Campus SaVE Act will be these same individuals. While this does, of course, add to the volume of their workload, this is probably the most prudent approach and the most financially sound approach, as these individuals are already appropriately trained to handle such incidents, needing only a minimal degree of additional training, if any at all. However, universities should be careful to not simply "dump" additional duties on these individuals if they wish to consider themselves insulated from liability. It will be necessary to discern how they have added to and modified their current system to accommodate these additional requirements. Thus, some additional resources will be required of universities due to the SaVE Act.

Lastly and perhaps even more important, is the fact that the SaVE Act requires universities to provide awareness and prevention programming for students and employees that address issues of domestic violence, dating violence, sexual assault, and stalking. This is a substantial addition to prior legislative mandate under the Clery Act and under Title IX. On the other hand, universities, such as ULM, that have been awarded campus grants, in the past, to prevent domestic violence, dating violence, sexual assault, and stalking from the OVW, will already have this type of programming in place. Such is the case with ULM and its VPIP. Indeed, it is the sole purview of the VPIP to provide this type of prevention and awareness programming. Regardless of grant funding, the SaVE Act requires that universities will provide these education programs (Clery Center, 2014), which shall include the following:

1. Primary awareness campaigns and prevention programs for all incoming students as well as new employees at the institution.
2. Bystander intervention training that gives safe, effective, and clear directions on how observers of potential incidents can assist and/or intervene without causing undue harm to themselves or others in the vicinity.
3. Continual awareness and prevention programming that occurs, ideally, on a routine schedule, throughout the academic year (Clery Center, 2014).

As was noted earlier regarding the broadening out of incidents requiring more vigorous and specific investigation and disciplinary processing, the requirements for awareness and prevention programming will also generate substantially more work for university staff. There will, of course, be some faculty and staff who are ideal candidates for providing such training, but this will often be doled out as a collateral duty to individuals who likely already have numerous obligations and commitments. It will be important for universities to make certain that resources exist and are provided so as to ensure that they can demonstrate good faith compliance and, even more importantly, so that students, staff, and faculty, can be afforded the awareness necessary to remain safe and free from victimization in the learning environment.

## How Recent Legal Developments Have Impacted the CCRT at ULM

Changes in Title IX processes as a result of the Dear Colleague Letter as well as new standards promulgated by the Campus SaVE Act, have placed the Violence Prevention and Intervention Program into a more active and visible role within the university structure. In addition, the efforts of this initiative have extended to the surrounding community as members of law enforcement come onto campus to provide trainings and other forms of collaboration. Further, members of the VPIP are active on committees in the region and throughout the state of Louisiana, such as with the SAFE Task Force of Northeast Louisiana, the Louisiana Coalition Against Domestic Violence (LCADV), and the Louisiana Foundation Against Sexual Assault (LaFASA), which are both statewide advocacy and oversight bodies in the state of Louisiana. These activities throughout the community and throughout the state have allowed VPIP personnel to make outside agencies and advocacy organizations aware of the issues that confront campuses in Louisiana and in the United States. This has resulted in a series of trainings being offered during the LCADV and LaFASA annual conferences on topics that are pertinent to campuses. At the same time, individuals from the university who network with these organizations have been able to bring back to the campus what they have learned, externally, to further improve on-campus response to domestic violence, dating violence, sexual assault, and stalking. The back-and-forth flow of intellectual capital has improved and enhanced the overall response throughout the region.

Indeed, even the emphasis on the two-pronged approach to crimes of domestic violence has been accentuated with these internal and external partnerships. For instance, one of the directors of the VPIP, who is also an appointed Title IX coordinator and investigator for ULM, is also the lead facilitator for the Batterer's Intervention Program (BIP) in the region, working in partnership with several judicial districts throughout Northeast Louisiana. The university, when appropriate, has provided assistance with this initiative in the form of faculty time and commitment, graduate student involvement, as well as evaluative research projects. The result is a program that works closely in alignment with area police authorities, probation and parole authorities, various district courthouses, as well as other BIPs throughout the state. On some occasions, offenders in the BIP are also students at ULM and/or assaulted individuals who were, themselves, university students. This, again, demonstrates the degree of overlap that exists between the campus community and the regional community-at-large along each prong of response.

Current grant reporting requirements through OVW require that organizations such as the VPIP and the Family Justice Center provide information on collaboration with area BIPs. Indeed, the lead facilitator of the BIP provides semi-annual data to these organizations to facilitate full reporting of activities. This again shows how all of these types of programming overlap in response, making further sense of the collaborative relationships between programs to aid victims and hold offenders accountable. The introduction of the Campus SaVE act will simply further cement this connection as, in some respects, the argument can be made that a true expert on domestic violence victimization is also someone who understands the mindset and behavior of those who perpetrate such crimes. Having effective CCRTs in response to incidents of domestic violence, dating violence, sexual assault, and stalking, simply ensures that experts working to prevent such crimes leave no stone unturned and also ensure that this social ill is addressed from a multiplicity of perspectives and approaches, thereby further enhancing our ability to keep people safe on campus as well as the broader community.

## References

Ali, R. (2011). *Dear colleague letter.* Washington, DC: United States Department of Education.

Association of Title IX Administrators (2014). *Certification events.* Malvern, PA: ATIXA. Retrieved from: https://atixa.org/.

Clery Center (2014). *The Campus Sexual Violence Elimination (SaVE) Act.* Wayne, PA: Clery Center for Security on Campus. Retrieved from http://clerycenter.org/campus-sexual-violence-elimination-save-act.

Cox, P. J., Finkelstein, D. M., Perez, V. E., Rosenbach, M. L. (2010). Changes in capacity among local coordinated community response coalitions (CCRs) supported by the DELTA Program. *Journal of Family Social Work, 13*(4), 375–392.

Domestic Abuse Intervention Program (2013). *What is the Duluth model? Why it works.* Duluth, MN: Domestic Abuse Intervention Program. Retrieved from www.theduluthmodel.org/about/index.html.

Gender Violence Institute (2013). *Coordinated community response* (CCR). Clearwater, MN: Gender Violence Institute. Retrieved from www.genderviolenceinstitute.org/contactus.html.

Holtfreter, K., & Boyd, J. (2008). A coordinated community response to intimate partner violence on the college campus. *Victims & Offenders: An International Journal of Evidence-based Research, Policy, and Practice, 1*(2), 141–157.

Klevens, J., Baker, C. K., Shelley, G. A., & Ingram, E. M. (2008). Exploring the links between components of coordinated community responses and their impact on contact with intimate partner-violence services. *Violence Against Women, 14*(3), 346–358.

Office for Civil Rights (2011). *Dear colleague letter.* Washington, DC: United States Department of Education. Retrieved July 24, 2017, from: www2.ed.gov/about/offices/list/ocr/letters/colleague-201104.html.

Office on Violence Against Women (2007). *Minimum standards for creating a coordinated community response to violence against women on campus.* Washington, DC: United States Department of Justice.

Salazar, L. F., Emshoff, J. G., Baker, C. K., & Crowley, T. (2007). Examining the behavior of a system: An outcome evaluation of a coordinated community response to domestic violence. *Journal of Family Violence, 22*(7), 631–641.

Shepard, M. F., Falk, D. R., & Elliott, B. A. (2001). Enhancing coordinated community responses to reduce recidivism in cases of domestic violence. *Loyola Law Review, 47*(1), 359–371.

Sokolow, B. (2014). *The Title IX coordinator and the preponderance of evidence.* Washington, DC: The NCHERM Group, LLC. Retrieved from www.ncherm.org/wordpress/wp-content/uploads/2013/03/TNG-TOW-01-20-2014.pdf.

United States Department of Labor (2016). *Title IX, Education amendments of 1972.* Washington, DC: United States Department of Labor. Retrieved from www.dol.gov/oasam/regs/statutes/titleix.htm.

# Different Communities, Different Approaches
## Avoiding a 'One Size Fits All' Approach to Neighbourhood Policing Strategies*

2

MIKE PERKINS

## Contents



### Abstract

This chapter presents the results of a survey evaluating the views of 1322 residents of York, UK around their perceptions and attitudes towards crime, their local area, and the police with the aim of understanding the main factors affecting public confidence within the city.

The study uses Structural Equation Modelling to develop several models which are evaluated to examine whether differences in public confidence in the police exist across disparate local communities with varying degrees of neighbourhood perceptions.

The results indicate that even in a relatively small city such as York, the factors which most affect an individual's views of the police can vary wildly depending on an individual's perceptions regarding their local area. The results suggest that policing strategies aimed at improving public confidence must be altered depending on the views residents hold regarding their local communities.

## Introduction

Public confidence is a concept that underpins the entire system of policing in the United Kingdom. If the public lose confidence in the police, their ability to maintain public order will be diminished, which could have potentially disastrous consequences on a national scale. As the police of England and Wales depend on the authority that they can command, rather than the force that they can deploy as a final resort (Hough, 2003), it is therefore essential for public order that the police do everything in their power to maintain their image as the legitimate defenders of the British public.

Because of this, a full understanding of how public confidence can be improved is extremely important to forces, as it will help ensure that any potential erosions in confidence due to falling police numbers and reduced visibility are offset by the introduction of new strategies and operations aimed at increasing public confidence. This study takes the view that the accurate measurement and understanding of the drivers behind this ephemeral concept are extremely important, if improvements in public confidence levels are to be achieved.

Whilst a large number of factors have been previously evidenced as having an effect on public confidence, studies examining the simultaneous effects of these factors on public confidence are limited. Whilst all of these studies have examined public confidence using a similar methodology as the present study, several of these studies are based on data collected from countries outside of the UK (Dukes, Portillo, & Miles, 2009; Hinds & Murphy, 2007). According to Kautt (2011), the empirical research on public confidence in the UK is limited. Therefore, more research is required in the UK to establish both the key drivers of public confidence in smaller urban environments, and a more holistic understanding of these issues, as transferring public confidence policy and practice to the UK from other countries is risky, given the differences in national contexts (Kautt, 2011).

The present research aims to remedy this, by examining the factors that affect public confidence in a smaller urban environment, and showing how these factors can differ dramatically at a neighbourhood level. It is well recognised that perceptions of the police can differ quite significantly by local area and that both the social and structural characteristics (geodemographics) of a neighbourhood can affect these perceptions (Ashby, 2005; Dunham & Alpert, 1988; Jackson, Bradford, Stanko, & Hohl, 2013; Jacob, 1971; Reisig & Giacomazzi, 1998; Reisig & Parks, 2000). Due to this well-established link, we do not test whether these neighbourhood differences influence public confidence or perceptions of the police in general. Instead, we assess whether the perceptions residents hold regarding their local area affects an overall proposed model of public confidence. Doing this allows us to examine where changes might be required to policing operations aimed at influencing the factors in certain types of areas in the city in question. This will allow us to answer the research question 'Does the framework of public confidence in York differ on a neighbourhood basis?'

By testing the homogeneity of a model of public confidence in York, we can see whether residents in different types of wards may react differently to certain styles of policing or neighbourhood changes. According to Williamson, Ashby, and Webber (2006): 'The failure to take neighbourhood context into consideration in recent decades in criminological research has resulted in findings at a level of generality that may have limited relevance to practitioners and the residents in particular neighbourhoods' (p. 207). In addressing this issue, we allow the North Yorkshire Police (NYP) the potential to adapt their policing styles based upon the specific characteristics of each local area. In doing so, 'officers will be freed from a "one-size-fits-all" model of policing' (Hawdon, 2008, p. 198) and police managers can design effective, and therefore more cost-effective initiatives to improve public confidence in York.

The remainder of this chapter is structured as follows. A brief background of the area of analysis is given. This is followed by an introduction to the methodology setting out the study, as well as the factors that are to be explored. The overall model of public confidence in York developed from the data is shown, followed by a detailed exploration of how this model is affected at the neighbourhood level due to the perceptions residents hold about their local area. Implications for the police force in question are also discussed.

The unitary authority of York is the major population centre of North Yorkshire with a population of 198,000 residents from a North Yorkshire total of 796,000 (Office for National Statistics, 2011). In terms of comparison, this makes York the 86th largest local authority in England (Office for National Statistics, 2012). Despite its relatively small size, the city is ranked as the fourth best performing economy of 64 UK cities, and scores highly for overall levels of employment, education, and health (City of York Council, 2013). Covered by its own Safer Neighbourhood Command policing district, the urban area of York provides a contrast to the rural remainder of the county and this has clear implications for policing activities in the county. Because of the potential differences in both the policing strategies and the priorities of residents in these two different areas, a study examining the drivers of public confidence in North Yorkshire as a whole would provide results that would likely not prove useful to either area. In order to maximise the potential of the research, the focus of this study was therefore chosen to be the city of York.

## Methodology Overview

As we wished to examine the effects of a number of different factors on public confidence, and at the same time, examine the interactions between these factors, we decided to use Structural Equation Modelling (SEM) in order to analyse the underlying factors affecting Public Confidence in the police of York. Structural Equation Modelling is 'a technique to specify, estimate, and evaluate models of linear relationships among a set of observed variables in terms of a generally smaller number of unobserved variables' (Shah & Goldstein, 2006, p. 149). SEM is a form of multi-linear regression modelling, which allows for the simultaneous examination of relationships between multiple factors, whilst also accounting for error in the measurement instrument. It also allows for an assessment of the directional relationships between hypothetical constructs that cannot be measured directly, by examining the relationships between all measured items that act as indicators of the underlying constructs.

This research uses SEM to explore the impact of a number of different factors on the public confidence situation in York, and develop a model aimed at explaining public confidence in the city. This model seeks to explore public confidence in York in a holistic manner by examining how each of the factors interact with each other to affect public confidence. The factors that will be used to explore public confidence in the study are listed below:

1. Public CONfidence (PCON): The primary dependent variable of investigation in the study.
2. Police DEALing with local concerns (PDEAL): Whether York residents believe the police are dealing with the issues that matter in York.
3. Police and the COMmunity (PCOM): Whether York residents believe the police are engaging with their community.
4. Police INTeractions with the public (PINT): The perceived quality of interactions between the police and the public in York.
5. Fear Of Crime (FOC): York residents' worry about specific crimes occurring to them.
6. Local Area Problems (LAP): The perceptions that York residents hold about the problems that exist in their local area.
7. Local Area Cohesion (LAC): The perceptions that York residents hold regarding the social cohesiveness of their local area.
8. Local Area SAFEty (LASAFE): How safe York residents perceive their local area to be.

These factors emerged from an in-depth survey, which was distributed via various methods to different groups of York residents over a two-month period. This survey was designed to draw out the participants' attitudes towards the police and their local area, and also collected detailed demographic information.

Calls for survey participants were disseminated using a variety of methods. As well as links to the electronic survey being emailed directly to participants through the use of a public safety mailing list, links to the survey were made available online on a number of different websites including those of the University of York, the NYP, The City of York Council, Safer York Partnership (the local public safety body). The survey was widely publicised in the local area, with extensive online, radio, and newspaper coverage.

## Results

### Preliminary Data Analysis

Including survey responses entered manually after the completion of a paper based survey, 1518 surveys were started on the SurveyMonkey data collection platform. Following the removal of 196 respondents for non-completion or and non-qualification, 1322 valid, fully completed survey responses were retained for analysis; a completion rate of 90%.[1]

As this survey was publicised widely throughout the city of York it is difficult to calculate an accurate response rate for the entire survey. However, this was possible for one survey sub-sample of 6364 emails sent as a mail-shot via a Safer York Partnership mailing list. By examining the number of people who opened this email (1717), and the number of valid responses obtained through this channel (681) we can see that the follow-through rate was 39.6% which is in line with the average email response rate of 36.3% found by Sheehan (2001).

### Survey

The attitudes held by residents of York in relation to the police and public confidence broadly matched the positive views previously discovered in explorations in the wider North Yorkshire area carried out by NYP and through previous British Crime Surveys. Because the overall goal of this study is to understand the factors relating to public confidence in the police of York, before a detailed analysis of the underlying factors is undertaken, some key variables in the study are analysed in order to gain an insight into the overall views and perceptions held by York residents. The following figures are taken from the un-weighted data.[2]

- 71.6% of respondents have confidence in the police in York (19.5% strongly agree, 52.1% tend to agree that 'Taking everything into account, I have confidence in the police in York').
- 86.6% of respondents are very or fairly satisfied with their local area as a place to live.
- 73.4% feel that York as a whole is a safe place to live.
- The most commonly reported concern in residents' local area was 'rubbish or litter lying around' with 18.9% of respondents reporting some level of concern with this issue.
- 17% of respondents had been victims of crime in the last 12 months.
- 80% of respondents who had been in contact with the police in York over the last 12 months rated their experiences as either positive or very positive.

### Factor Analysis

In order to prepare the data for analysis with Structural Equation Modelling (SEM), Exploratory Factor Analysis (EFA) and Confirmatory Factor Analysis (CFA) were used to explore the relationships between the variables in the study, assign these variables to appropriate factors, and then test the relationships between these factors.

Following EFA, a nine-component solution was revealed, showing that the majority of the items loaded onto their theorised factors, thus supporting the conceptualisations of the factors chosen for examination in the study. During CFA, these nice components were reduced to an eight-factor measurement model. This model was confirmed as valid by passing tests for convergent, discriminant, and nomological validity, and compared with competing models as per suggestions by Hair, Black, and Babin (2010).

## The New Framework of Public Confidence in York

### Factor Development

In order to aid discussion, the factors in this study are split into three factor groupings (based upon their underlying characteristics) and examined with reference to these groupings. These groupings are shown in Table 2.1.

The first factor grouping consists of the perceptions that the police are dealing with the issues that matter to residents in York (PDEAL), the perceptions of police engagement with the local community (PCOM), and the perceptions of interactions with representatives of the police (PINT). There is a body of evidence suggesting that these factors not only have a direct effect on public confidence, but that they can be directly affected by police activities (Hohl, Bradford, & Stanko, 2010; Wünsch & Hohl, 2009). This grouping is therefore named 'Police Influenced Factors' (PIFs), as it is made up of those factors that the police could potentially influence through some form of direct intervention or strategy.

The second factor grouping contains those factors that are more representative of respondents' perceptions of their local area, which would not be easily altered by the actions of the police. These factors include the perceptions of local area safety (LASAFE), the perceptions of local area problems (LAP) and the perceptions of local area cohesion (LAC). Whilst evidence exists that these factors have an effect of some form on public confidence, there is no evidence suggesting that these factors can be directly influenced by the police (Cao, Frank, & Cullen, 1996). Whilst some form of indirect effect by the police may be possible, and indeed desirable, these factors represent deeply seated views of respondents that may be difficult to alter, especially over the short term. This factor grouping is therefore named 'Local Perspective Factors' (LPFs).

The final factor grouping consists of the remaining factor that falls in-between the previous two groups: the fear of crime (FOC). The FOC factor falls between the two previously described factor groupings due to the possible, indirect effect that the police may have on changing an individual's fear of or worry about specific crimes occurring. Whilst someone's worry about crime could be described as an internal social perspective, it is important to

**Table 2.1 Factor Groupings**

| Police Influenced Factors (PIFs) | Local Perspective Factors (LPFs) |
|---|---|
| PDEAL: Police dealing with local concerns | LAP: Local area problems |
| PCOM: Police and the community | LASAFE: Local area safety |
| PINT: Police interactions with the public | LAC: Local area cohesion |
| **Intermediary Factor (IF)** | FOC: Fear of crime |

note that the FOC factor assesses the worry about specific crimes occurring, rather than a general fear of, or worry about crime, which is assessed through the LASAFE factor. As there is strong evidence in the literature which suggests that the fear of crime can be affected by the perceptions of a local area (Brunton-Smith, 2011; Jackson & Bradford, 2009; Jackson, Bradford, Hohl, & Farrall, 2009; Jackson & Sunshine, 2007; Skogan, 1986) this factor could be indirectly affected through any changes in the LPF grouping. For example, if the police or other local bodies (such as the City of York Council or Safer York Partnership) are successful in reducing the visible signals of community disorder, it is conceivable that the perceptions held by residents in the area could improve to reflect these changes. However, any such reductions will take time to 'seep into the public consciousness' (Stanko & Bradford, 2009, p. 327), and affect FOC, therefore any changes in this factor would be very difficult to quantify. As this factor falls partly into both of the previously described factor groupings, it is called the Intermediary Factor (IF).

## The Structural Model

The model was developed based upon three key theoretical links between the different factor groupings discussed above, as well as the relationship between the Police Influenced Factors (PIFs) and public confidence (PCON). Previous studies have established all of the links proposed in the model shown below. By combining evidence from previous studies, along with the careful use of specification searches, trial-and-error, and re-examinations of the original data, a structural model of public confidence in York was developed. This model is shown in Figure 2.1 along with the bootstrapped, standardised path estimates calculated by the IBM SPSS AMOS analysis software for the model.[3]

The results of the structural model give a holistic view of public confidence in York. As well as showing the direct effects of PCOM, PDEAL, and PINT on PCON, the model shows how the factors that failed to show a direct impact on public confidence in initial analysis actually affect the overall framework of public confidence in York through a multi-step process summarised as follows:

1. The model shows how the drivers of confidence are rooted in an individual's perceptions of their local area; i.e. the Local Perspective Factors. Specifically,

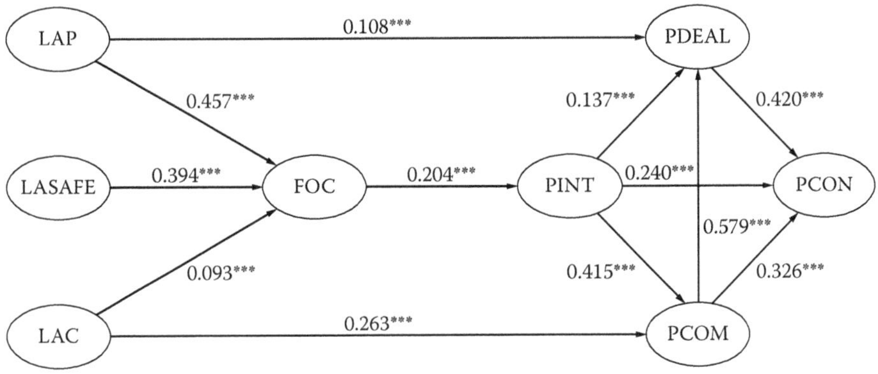


**Figure 2.1** Revised Structural Model of Public Confidence in York.

their perceptions of local area safety (LASAFE), local area/social cohesion (LAC), and local area problems/disorder (LAP).
2. These local area perceptions all influence the specific worries and fears about crime in a local area (FOC).
3. As well as directly influencing FOC, these local area perceptions influence the general perceptions an individual has about the police. This is shown through the effects LAP has on the public perceptions of how well the police are dealing with local concerns (PDEAL), and the effects LAC has on the perceptions of the police relationship with their community (PCOM).
4. In conjunction with the FOC factor, all of the LPFs exert an influence on the perceptions of the quality of public-police interactions (PINT).
5. These perceptions of public-police interactions affect the more general perceptions an individual holds about the police; in terms of whether they think the police are dealing effectively with local concerns and engaging with their community.
6. Finally, these general perceptions of the police (in addition to the perceptions of police-public interactions) directly affect public confidence as shown in the simple structural model. This suggests that strategies aimed at improving public confidence should focus on improving these factors, all of which can potentially be modified through specific operations or behavioural changes.

Goodness of fit indices revealed that all measures were within a range that would suggest a good fit of the data to the model.[4]

We now use the locational data gathered in the survey to assess whether this framework of public confidence is consistent throughout York, or if certain local and neighbourhood characteristics affect the relationships shown in the revised structural model.

## Testing the Homogeneity of the New Framework of Public Confidence in York

### Preamble

The structural model presented above provides a new perspective on public confidence in York through the development of a novel framework showing the multifaceted, interacting effects of a number of factors on public confidence. In this analysis, we use the locational data collected in the study to test whether the structural model is homogenous throughout York, or whether there are differences present from one area of the city to another. This is performed by examining whether the perceptions someone has about their area has a moderating effect[5] on the relationships specified in the structural model.

Doing this allows us to uncover any existing subtleties in the data set that may affect the general implications for policing operations in York if public confidence is a key concern. We test whether any recommendations and implications suggested by the model can be applied with confidence by the NYP throughout the whole of York, or whether a certain degree of caution must be taken in the development of any new operations aimed at maintaining or improving public confidence throughout different areas of the city.

The purpose of this testing is primarily aimed at assessing whether potential differences could exist in York, and therefore whether police managers need to be aware of the general applicability of initiatives or operations that they may wish to implement in order to influence the factors discussed in the revised structural model. This analysis does not claim to offer specific advice as to where exactly in York differences to policing operations on a ward-by-ward basis may be necessary. Instead, it uses the general concepts of highly perceived areas of the city, versus poorly perceived areas, to offer guidance that policing managers and front-line officers could use to assist in making their own judgements about where in York changes may be required based upon their unique local knowledge. To this end, we offer a contribution to practice as well as theory; however, given the vast array of locational, socio-economic, and demographic differences that may be present from one York ward to another, we do not seek to offer detailed explanations of why such differences may occur, simply whether differences do, or do not exist.

## Framework Testing Development

Respondents to the survey were required to enter their full residential postcode in order to complete the survey and qualify for the prize draw. It was recognised that some respondents might not have felt entirely comfortable with this; however, both reassurances and incentives were offered to encourage respondents to answer accurately. This postcode information was used in this particular analysis to assign each survey response to one of the 22 electoral wards within York, which allowed us to perform comparisons of the data on a ward-by-ward basis. For the purpose of this analysis, wards were used as a proxy for the term 'neighbourhood' that had been used throughout the survey.

Examinations of neighbourhood differences and their impact on perceptions of the police typically focus either on resident perceptions of their local area (Schafer, Huebner, & Bynum, 2003), or use quantitative variables linked to deprivation such as mean income, crime rates, etc. (Williamson et al., 2006). As residents' perceptions of their local areas were obtained in the survey, this type of information was used to classify the wards in York depending on the general perceptions held by the residents of the wards. Categorising neighbourhoods in this manner means that we gain a more accurate representation of the neighbourhood characteristics, social cohesiveness, and problems that are actually perceived by residents.

In order to rank and categorise these neighbourhoods in terms of the perceptions of residents living in them, we used the scores obtained in the survey with respect to the Local Perspective Factors (LPFs) of LAP, LASAFE, and LAC. Individual scores for these three variables were summed together to form a new case variable of 'Total Local Area Perceptions' (TLAP), with higher scores on this variable indicating generally poorer perceptions of the local area. An average score per ward for this variable was then created by summing the total scores of each resident then dividing this by the number of survey responses obtained per ward.

As it is only possible to compare two groups together in multigroup SEM (Hair et al., 2010), in order to see where differences in the revised structural model may lie, we compiled the responses of a number of similarly ranked wards together in order to assess group differences between wards which residents perceived positively, versus wards which residents perceived negatively. The survey responses for the top five scoring wards in York (in terms of their low total scores for the TLAP variable) were combined to create one group named 'Highly Perceived Wards' (HPWs) (n = 120) and the responses for the bottom five scoring wards were combined to create the second group of 'Poorly Perceived Wards' (PPWs) (n = 373). Five wards were combined in each instance to give a minimum number of 100 cases per group and reduce any problems with the scores for one ward overly affecting the results of the analysis, whilst still maintaining adequate differences in the scores between the groups to allow any differences to be tested.

## Framework Testing Results

To test the hypothesis that differences in the path estimates will occur between the two groups, we must test for the equivalence of paths when the revised structural model is run simultaneously for both groups, then test for significant differences between these path estimates (Byrne, 1994).

This is achieved by obtaining the critical ratios of differences table produced by AMOS, and using the 'Stats Tools' software package (Gaskin, 2012) to compare the path estimates and calculate p-values to determine the significance of the differences between the estimates. Testing for differences in path estimates this way allows us to evaluate the strength and direction of any changes in the path estimates found between the models (Arbuckle, 2011).[6]

The results of this analysis are shown in Table 2.2.

## Framework Testing Discussion

The results table shows an estimation of the unstandardised regression weights for each path in the revised structural model for the two groups in question, as well as the p-values for each of these estimates. The Critical Ratio (CR) value (*z*-scores) for the comparison of each path is shown in the far right column. The paths where significant differences

**Table 2.2 Public Confidence Framework Testing: Structural Model**

| Relationship | | | Highly Perceived Wards | | Poorly Perceived Wards | | |
|---|---|---|---|---|---|---|---|
| | | | Estimate | p | Estimate | p | Critical Ratio |
| LAP | → | FOC | 0.348 | 0.000 | 0.281 | 0.000 | –0.672 |
| LASAFE | → | FOC | 3.298 | 0.006 | 0.514 | 0.000 | –2.3** |
| LAC | → | FOC | 0.076 | 0.476 | 0.093 | 0.010 | 0.148 |
| FOC | → | PINT | 0.358 | 0.007 | 0.387 | 0.000 | 0.183 |
| LAC | → | PCOM | 0.471 | 0.000 | 0.195 | 0.000 | –2.275** |
| PINT | → | PCOM | 0.247 | 0.000 | 0.340 | 0.000 | 0.999 |
| LAP | → | PDEAL | 0.283 | 0.000 | 0.105 | 0.000 | –1.957* |
| PINT | → | PDEAL | 0.101 | 0.255 | 0.038 | 0.471 | –0.608 |
| PCOM | → | PDEAL | 0.679 | 0.000 | 0.484 | 0.000 | –1.293 |
| PCOM | → | PCON | 0.148 | 0.139 | 0.424 | 0.000 | 2.161** |
| PINT | → | PCON | 0.304 | 0.000 | 0.244 | 0.000 | –0.655 |
| PDEAL | → | PCON | 0.516 | 0.000 | 0.468 | 0.000 | –0.396 |

*Notes:* *** p-value < 0.01; ** p-value < 0.05; * p-value < 0.10.

were found are highlighted in the table. A positive $z$-score shows that the path estimate is larger in the Poorly Perceived Wards, and a negative score shows that the path is stronger in the Highly Perceived Wards. We immediately see that there are four paths in the model that are significantly different across the two groups, therefore suggesting that the structural model developed is not completely homogenous throughout York.

An initial comparison of the overall levels of public confidence between the two groups in these areas shows that in both groups, generally positive perceptions of the police exist,[7] suggesting it is not the perceptions of the police that are causing these differences in the paths within the model, but the perceptions of the local area. We now briefly explore the differences found within the model with reference to the two groups.

### Highly Perceived Wards

We first examine the three paths that are stronger in the HPWs. These are the relationships between LASAFE and FOC, LAP and PDEAL, and LAC and PCOM. The negative CR value for these links suggests that any changes in the independent variable in the HPWs will result in a greater change in the dependent variable in comparison to the PPWs.

The stronger path estimate in the HPWs between LASAFE and FOC, suggests that in the HPWs, where the perceptions of safety are higher than in PPWs,[8] residents are more aware of the subtle changes in their area that affect their fear of crime. As residents' perceptions of safety in the HPWS are almost at 100%, it is unsurprising that small changes in this level will result in extremely large changes in associated fear of crime. Whilst perceptions of local area safety are by no means low in the PPWs at 79%, even this small difference has a noticeable effect on the FOC factor.

The link between neighbourhood geodemographic characteristics and the fear of crime is well recognised (Ashby, 2005; Brunton-Smith & Sturgis, 2011; Skogan, 1986; Williamson et al., 2006), with residents in areas where high levels of social capital exist typically exhibiting lower levels of fear of crime. This analysis adds a further dimension to this view by showing that in these types of areas (represented by HPWs[9]), not only do residents exhibit lower levels of worry about crime,[10] but also that perceptions of local area safety are more important drivers of the fear of crime for these residents than individuals resident in PPWs.

In the HPW, the strengthened links between LAP and PDEAL, and LAC and PCOM, suggest that the 'expressive' model of policing (Jackson and Bradford, 2009; Jackson and Sunshine, 2007), where the public hold the police more accountable for maintaining the values and morals that appear to underpin community life, is shown to be stronger than in PPWs. In the HPWs, as signs of local area problems increase, and perceptions of social cohesion decrease, this will have a stronger effect on the perceptions held by residents of HPWs that the police are failing in their role as moral guardians or the 'social glue' of the community. The weaker, but still significant relationships between these factors in the PPWs suggests that this expressive model of policing holds true throughout York, although the difference in the estimates could suggest that residents in PPWs may not be as responsive to changes in their neighbourhood than residents in HPWs.

If residents are accustomed to seeing signs of social or community disorder in their local area (i.e. if they live in PPWs), then small increases or decreases in these signs will not affect the perceptions they hold regarding the effectiveness of the police in dealing with these problems or engaging with the community. This may be due to a perception that they feel the police are already failing in their duty to deal with disorder, as shown in the data by the lower perceptions of police effectiveness experienced by the residents in PPWs;[11] however, the generally high confidence in the police shown by residents in these areas counters this argument somewhat.

However, if residents are not used to these signs of disorder (i.e., if they live in HPWs), then any perceived increases in disorder will result in larger associated decreases in their perceptions that the police are dealing effectively with problems and engaging with the community. This demonstrates once more, how residents of HPWs may be more attuned to the signs of social and community disorder than residents of PPWs.

### *Poorly Perceived Wards*

The only path shown to have a greater effect within PPWs was that between PCOM and PCON. This shows that in areas where residents have poor perceptions of their local area, the strength of the relationship between the perceptions of police-community interactions and public confidence is significantly stronger than the same link in HPWs.

This indicates that residents of PPWs feel that the police do not understand the problems affecting the local area and are therefore failing to successfully engage with the community.[12] Therefore, if they perceive the police to be improving in this area, this will have a relatively large change on overall confidence perceived by residents of PPWs. This suggests that small additional efforts by the police to engage with the local community could have large beneficial effects in these types of wards or neighbourhoods.

The reverse of this also appears to be true. Residents of HPWs (with high levels of perceived safety and cohesion, coupled with low levels of signs of disorder) have better perceptions of police-community engagement than residents of PPWs. They may therefore feel that additional police interaction within the community is not required, due to the (assumed) absence of these signs of community and social disorder. This could be indicative of a feeling that relationships between the police and the community within HPWs are already acceptable, and that additional police operation looking at improving police-community relations in these sort of areas would be unwarranted due to the relatively smaller increases in public confidence that could be obtained from any policing efforts.

### *Caveats*

We offer a few notes of caution with regards the interpretation of these results. As the critical ratios are calculated using unstandardised regression weights, they are subject to the large factor loading effects of the one path between each factor and its composite items that is fixed to a regression weight of one. This has the potential to potentially skew the calculations of the other factor loadings, especially in those factors where there are only a small number of items per factor. This issue, along with the 99% levels of perceived safety in the HPWs group[13] serves to explain the very large regression weight of 3.298 between LASAFE and FOC in this model. Finally, the differences present in the sample sizes of the two groups means that, due to the increased statistical power, the estimates for the PPWs group may be more accurate than in the HPWs group. Therefore, the exact magnitude of the differences in the paths between the models may not be entirely dependable. With these caveats in mind, we draw the following conclusions.

## Conclusion

Even within a small, relatively homogenous city such as York, this analysis has shown that there are differences in the overall framework of public confidence depending on the perceptions people hold about their local areas. In order to account for this, policing operations must be altered depending on the specific neighbourhood context. Whilst this may already occur to some degree, this study provides a base of evidence to support any future changes.

We propose that both police managers and front-line officers consider the views of local residents as to what needs to be changed in their areas, as well as the evidence offered here, when making decisions as how best to serve the local areas in which they operate. Whilst local neighbourhood policing teams may already have some idea as to the style of policing strategies that will work best in the areas they are serving, this analysis serves to highlight the importance of adapting policing operations depending on the type of area they are serving to make the most efficient use of limited resources.

Exactly why these differences occur remains unknown and underexplored in the literature (Brown & Benedict, 2002; Hawdon, 2008). We offer a contribution to knowledge by showing how individual perceptions of a local area seem to affect certain relationships in the new framework of public confidence in York. In addition, we show how the NYP operating in York can adapt their policing styles, depending on the geodemographic characteristics of the areas they are operating in, thus addressing the literature gap identified by Hawdon (2008), who states:

> By understanding which policing style generates positive resident views of police in various types of neighborhoods, officers will be freed from a 'one-size-fits-all' model of policing. Instead, they can tailor their policing to the neighborhoods they patrol. Community policing, currently considered the best style of policing, is expensive. However, it may not be necessary to implement community policing in certain neighborhoods where less expensive styles may be equally effective. (p. 198)

Because it is generally acknowledged that the police are less effective in controlling issues of crime if they do not have the confidence of the public in terms of assisting police with their duties (Fitzgerald, 2010), it would seem clear that an opportunity to improve public confidence through relatively minor changes in police operations or behaviour should be welcomed by the police. However, given the sceptical nature of police culture, coupled with the inherent resistance to change shown by officers (Jackson et al., 2013; Wisniewski & Dickson, 2001; Wood, Fleming, & Marks, 2008), it is understood that compliance to any such changes may be low, unless mangers and decision makers can convince front-line officers that this would be beneficial to them.

The police should not see improving public confidence as a box-ticking exercise, begrudgingly carried out simply to comply with targets or the requirements of police performance management systems. Instead, the importance of public confidence needs to be embedded in policing culture if the police wish to retain the public perceptions of them as the legitimate guardians of modern society and secure their ability to maintain order in the UK.

## Acknowledgements

The author is grateful for the support of the North Yorkshire Police who provided funding for this study.

## Notes

* This chapter was previously presented at the International Police Executive Symposium 2014, and was subsequently included in a special issue of *Police Practice and Research* (Volume 17, Issue 2, 2016).

1 The likely cause of this high response rate was a survey incentive of two £50 Amazon vouchers available in a prize draw to all fully completed survey responses.

2 In order to ensure that the results of the analysis were representative of the population of York, weighting variables were created for age, gender, ethnicity, and ward location using the most recently available figures. A total weighting value was created by multiplying these individual weights together, which had the effect of altering significance levels by altering the sample size. In order to counter this, a relative total weight was created by dividing the total weight by its mean. This technique retained the distribution patterns of the weighted sample, but maintained the original sample size. This relative total weight was applied to the data set before further analysis was carried out.

3 *** shows the path estimate is significant at the $p \geq 0.001$ level.

4 CMIN: 2492.53, DF: 641, CMIN/DF: 3.89, PNFI: 0.854, p-value Sig.: 0.00, CFI: 0.952. NFI: 0.936, RMSEA: 0.047.

5 A moderating effect occurs when a third variable (in this case, perceptions of local area) changes the relationship between two related factors in an SEM model (Baron & Kenny, 1986).

6 Because we are only interested in the equivalence of regression weights between latent factors, we do not test for either factorial equivalence (Jöreskog, 1971) or latent mean structure equivalence (Byrne & Stewart, 2006).

7 62% of HPWs residents had high levels of overall confidence compared to 64% of PPWs (mean item values for all 'strongly/agree' responses in the PCON factor).

8 99% of HPWs residents agreed that they felt safe in their local area compared to 79% of PPWs residents (mean item values for all 'strongly/agree' responses in the LASAFE factor).

9 87% of HPWs residents agreed that their local area exhibited cohesive qualities compared to 46% of PPWs residents (mean item values for all 'strongly/agree' responses in the LAC factor).

10 66% of PPWs residents agreed they were not concerned about specific crimes occurring in their area, compared to 90% of HPWs residents (mean item values for all 'strongly/agree' responses in the FOC factor).

11 43% of PPWs residents agreed that the police were effective in dealing with the problems in York, compared to 54% of HPWs residents (mean item values for all 'strongly/agree' responses in the PDEAL factor).

12 42% of PPWs residents agreed that the police were interacting with their communities, compared to 54% of HPWs residents (mean item values for all 'strongly/agree' responses in the PCOM factor).

13 99% of HPWs residents agreed that they felt safe in their local area compared to 79% of PPWs residents (mean item values for all 'strongly/agree' responses in the LASAFE factor).

## References

Arbuckle, J. L. (2011). *IBM SPSS Amos 20 user's guide.* New York: IBM.

Ashby, D. I. (2005). Policing neighbourhoods: Exploring the geographies of crime, policing and performance assessment *Policing & Society, 15*(4), 413–447.

Baron, R. M., & Kenny, D. A. (1986). The moderator-mediator variable distinction in social psychological research: Conceptual, strategic, and statistical considerations. *Journal of Personality and Social Psychology, 51*(6), 1173–1182.

Brown, B., & Benedict, W. R. (2002). Perceptions of the police: Past findings, methodological issues, conceptual issues and policy implications. *Policing: An International Journal of Police Strategies & Management, 25*(3), 543–580.

Brunton-Smith, I. (2011). Untangling the relationship between fear of crime and perceptions of disorder evidence from a longitudinal study of young people in England and Wales. *British Journal of Criminology, 51*(6), 885–899.

Brunton-Smith, I., & Sturgis, P. (2011). Do neighborhoods generate fear of crime? An empirical test using the British crime survey. *Criminology, 49*(2), 331–369.

Byrne, B. M. (1994). Burnout: Testing for the validity, replication, and invariance of causal structure across elementary, intermediate, and secondary teachers. *American Educational Research Journal, 31*(3), 645–673.

Byrne, B. M., & Stewart, S. M. (2006). Teacher's corner: The MACS approach to testing for multigroup invariance of a second-order structure: A walk through the process. *Structural Equation Modeling, 13*(2), 287–321.

Cao, L., Frank, J., & Cullen, F. T. (1996). Race, community context and confidence in the police. *American Journal of Police, 15*(1), 3–22.

City of York Council. (2013). *York at a glance.* York: City of York Council.

Dukes, R., Portillo, E., & Miles, M. (2009). Models of satisfaction with police service. *Policing: An International Journal of Police Strategies & Management, 32*(2), 297–318.

Dunham, R. G., & Alpert, G. P. (1988). Neighborhood differences in attitudes toward policing: Evidence for a mixed-strategy model of policing in a multi-ethnic setting. *Journal of Criminal Law and Criminology, 79*, 504–523.

Fitzgerald, M. (2010). A confidence trick? *Policing: A Journal of Policy and Practice, 4*(3), 298–301.

Gaskin, J. (2012). Stats tools package (GroupDifference). http://statwiki.kolobkreations.com.

Hair, J. F., Black, W. C., & Babin, B. J. (2010). *Multivariate data analysis: A global perspective.* Upper Saddle River, NJ: Pearson Education.

Hawdon, J. (2008). Legitimacy, trust, social capital, and policing styles: A theoretical statement. *Police Quarterly, 11*(2), 182–201.

Hinds, L., & Murphy, K. (2007). Public satisfaction with police: Using procedural justice to improve police legitimacy. *Australian & New Zealand Journal of Criminology, 40*(1), 27–42.

Hohl, K., Bradford, B., & Stanko, E. A. (2010). Influencing trust and confidence in the London Metropolitan Police: Results from an experiment testing the effect of leaflet drops on public opinion. *British Journal of Criminology, 50*(3), 491–513.

Hough, M. (2003). Modernization and public opinion: Some criminal justice paradoxes. *Contemporary Politics, 9*(2), 143–155.

Jackson, J., & Bradford, B. (2009). Crime, policing and social order: On the expressive nature of public confidence in policing. *The British Journal of Sociology, 60*(3), 493–521.

Jackson, J., Bradford, B., Hohl, K., & Farrall, S. (2009). Does the fear of crime erode public confidence in policing? *Policing, 3*(1), 100–111.

Jackson, J., Bradford, B., Stanko, B., & Hohl, K. (2013). *Just authority? Trust in the police in England and Wales.* Oxon: Routledge.

Jackson, J., & Sunshine, J. (2007). Public confidence in policing: A neo-Durkheimian perspective. *British Journal of Criminology, 47*, 214–233.

Jacob, H. (1971). Black and white perceptions of justice in the city. *Law & Society Review, 6*(1), 69–89.

Jöreskog, K. G. (1971). Simultaneous factor analysis in several populations. *Psychometrika, 36*(4), 409–426.

Kautt, P. (2011). Public confidence in the British police: Negotiating the signals from Anglo-American research. *International Criminal Justice Review, 21*(4), 353–382.

Office for National Statistics. (2011). *Census result shows increase in population of Yorkshire and the Humber*. Retrieved May 2013, from www.ons.gov.uk/ons/rel/mro/news-release/census-result-shows-increase-in-population-of-yorkshire-and-the-humber/censusyorkandhumbernr0712.html.

Office for National Statistics. (2012). *Population estimates for England and Wales, Mid 2011*. Newport, Wales: Office for National Statistics.

Reisig, M. D., & Giacomazzi, A. L. (1998). Citizen perceptions of community policing: Are attitudes toward police important? *Policing: An International Journal of Police Strategies & Management, 21*(3), 547–561.

Reisig, M. D., & Parks, R. B. (2000). Experience, quality of life, and neighborhood context: A hierarchical analysis of satisfaction with police. *Justice Quarterly, 17*(3), 607–630.

Schafer, J. A., Huebner, B. M., & Bynum, T. S. (2003). Citizen perceptions of police services: Race, neighborhood context, and community policing. *Police Quarterly, 6*(4), 440–468.

Shah, R., & Goldstein, S. M. (2006). Use of structural equation modeling in operations management research: Looking back and forward. *Journal of Operations Management, 24*(2), 148–169.

Sheehan, K. B. (2001). E-mail survey response rates: A review. *Journal of Computer-Mediated Communication, 6*(2).

Skogan, W. (1986). Fear of crime and neighborhood change. *Crime and Justice, 8*, 203–229.

Stanko, E. A., & Bradford, B. (2009). Beyond measuring 'how good a job' police are doing: The MPS model of confidence in policing. *Policing, 3*(4), 322–330.

Williamson, T., Ashby, D. I., & Webber, R. (2006). Classifying neighbourhoods for reassurance policing. *Policing & Society, 16*(02), 189–218.

Wisniewski, M., & Dickson, A. (2001). Measuring performance in Dumfries and Galloway constabulary with the Balanced Scorecard. *The Journal of the Operational Research Society, 52*(10), 1057–1066.

Wood, J., Fleming, J., & Marks, M. (2008). Building the capacity of police change agents: The nexus policing project. *Policing & Society, 18*(1), 72–87.

Wünsch, D., & Hohl, K. (2009). Evidencing a 'good practice model' of police communication: The impact of local policing newsletters on public confidence. *Policing, 3*(4), 331–339.

# Community-Based Participatory Approach to Prevent Residential Burglaries and House Robberies

# 3

DORAVAL GOVENDER

## Contents



### Abstract

Based on the principles of community-based participatory research (CBPR), this chapter provides insight on the vital role that can be played by the community in preventing residential burglaries and house robberies. The aim of this chapter is to obtain knowledge on how unlawful entry is gained to commit residential burglaries and house robberies and to encourage homeowners on the designing and evaluation of security measures. Accordingly, this chapter considers a sample of homeowners and stakeholders in the Garsfontein, Pretoria East neighbourhood, in Gauteng, South Africa for informal interviews and observation of their residential security measures. Findings indicate that the residential security measures are not effectively and efficiently designed, neither are they being regularly evaluated to manage security risks. A public meeting was held with the community to inform them of the findings and encourage homeowners to design and evaluate their residential security measures with the object of preventing residential burglaries and house robberies.

## Introduction

In South Africa, particularly in the last decade, people's efforts to protect themselves against crime have become much more visible. People have come to realise that the police on their own cannot control crime as effectively as they believed and hoped. Compared to other crimes, burglaries and house robberies are on the increase. 'Residential burglaries and house robberies is a daily occurrence in communities' (Olutola, 2011; see also Burger 2006, p. 107; Zinn, 2010, p. 27). 'Residential burglaries and house robberies differ with regards to modus operandi' (Snyman, 2003, p. 539). 'Residential burglaries' in South Africa refers to categories where property is stolen. In these crimes there is no threat of violence between a perpetrator and the victim. In most cases, the victim will be unaware that the crime has occurred until they notice their property missing (Crime Statistics South Africa, 2013). On the other hand 'house robbery' is the term formulated by the South African Police Service (SAPS) to describe a robbery where the perpetrators overpower, detain, and rob the occupants inside their residence (Zinn, 2010). If one compares the South African meaning of residential burglary to the United States of America, a household burglary is defined as burglaries in which a household member was a victim of a violent crime. Burglary is classified as a property crime except when someone is violently attacked or threatened while at home during the burglary. The National Crime Victimisation survey categorises such attacks as a personal (rape/sexual assault, robbery, and aggravated and simple assault) rather than a property crime (household burglary, theft, and motor vehicle theft) (Catalano, 2010).

This chapter considered a sample of homeowners and stakeholders in the Garsfontein, Pretoria East neighbourhood for informal interviews and observation of their residential security measures, because Garsfontein is one of the many affluent residential areas in South Africa which reports a high number of residential burglaries and house robberies to the local police. Demographically speaking, Garsfontein's cosmopolitan population is representative of the national population of South Africa and to a limited extent the African continent (Walker & Serrano, 2006). Garsfontein residents reported 866 and 936 cases of residential burglaries in the 2012 and 2013 years respectively (Crime Statistics South Africa, 2013). Garsfontein residents reported 40 and 57 cases of house robberies in the 2012 and 2013 years respectively. In both these crimes unlawful entry was gained into the victims' premises. If one considers residential burglaries and house robberies for the period 2012–2013 there was an increase in Garsfontein (Africa Check, 2013; Crime Statistics South Africa, 2013).

Research alone does not indicate conclusively whether security measures actually reduce burglaries and house robberies, as with strategies dealing with other crimes. Against this background this research seeks to provide evidence that a community-based participatory approach does help in the prevention of burglaries and house robberies. This chapter explores the issues of community assets, needs, and participation and empowerment in the prevention of residential burglaries and house robberies. This collaboration between UNISA, the Community Policy Forum, and other stakeholders aimed at addressing residential burglaries and house robberies invited community members interested in being part of the collaboration, to step forward and agree to participate in the public meeting to include homeowners.

Drawing from the principles of community-based participatory research; the author approached this partnership using a collaborative, equitable process where all stakeholders such as the community, police, and the private security companies identified mutual benefits (Israel et al., 2003). The partnership allowed the community-university partnership to discuss the issues of importance with all the stakeholders.

## Criminological Theories and Models

Administrative criminologists and rational choice theorists view crime as being driven by opportunity. According to the rational choice theory a residential burglary/house robbery involves a series of sequential decision-making judgements by the burglar/house robber. The initial decision to burgle or rob a home may be motivated by personal needs, whilst the selection of a suitable house is taken after proper reconnaissance work is done on the said house, based on experiential knowledge and environmental cues associated with 'good targets'. Once a decision is made on a target, it becomes relatively fixed and can influence criminal behaviour, thereby becoming self-reinforcing (Cornish & Clark, 1986). Introduced by Cohen and Felson (1979) the routine activity theory encourages a triangular understanding of crime causation where the three factors leading to a criminal act taking place are as follows: a motivated offender, a potential victim/target, and the absence of a capable guardian (Police). If these three factors exist simultaneously a crime event is likely to occur (Patterson & Pollock, 2011).

Over the past two decades, security measures have become more established in residential areas (Yen, 2008). Robert Peel's dream of a truly preventative police force as being 'substantially accomplished' through private security rather than through the state police thus holds true. This is evident in the fact that private security, while still retaining 'traditional' private security tasks, engages in more and more law enforcement duties (Shearing & Stenning, 1982). Homeowners have responded with increased security measures. These vary from the installation of electronic devices for electronic surveillance such as closed circuit surveillance cameras, alarm systems, panic buttons, electronic gates, and intercom systems, to physical modifications such as burglar bars, security gates, fences, and walls around properties. The extent and nature of the changes depend, among other things, on the location of people's homes, their financial abilities, the measure of security perceived to be necessary, and the perceptions about the risk of victimisation. However, for many urban South Africans the implementation of these measures is not enough. They want to live in a more secure neighbourhood. This has led to an increase in the number of security villages and enclosed neighbourhoods. Security villages include different types of developments with different uses, ranging from smaller townhouse complexes to larger office parks and luxury estates. These areas are purpose-built by private developers for whom security is the foremost requirement in spite of the importance of other lifestyle considerations. Another type of gated community is the enclosed neighbourhood. These neighbourhoods are characterised by road closures, with fences or walls around entire neighbourhoods in some cases. Security companies are contracted to control access to these gated communities. Application to the municipalities for the right to restrict access is essential, and residents can apply to enclose their neighbourhoods on security grounds alone (Landman & Liebermann, 2005).

Security service providers in South Africa are currently utilising a Security Risk Management Framework to manage security risks. This framework is located primarily in the routine activity theory, which views the need for basic day to day protection against criminal elements. The primary aim of the framework is to manage security risks confronting assets, whose risks are largely of a criminal nature. The framework focuses on identifying, measuring, and analysing crime risks (Abrie, 2008; Fay, 2006; Rogers, 2008).

## Role of Community Policing

In response to the rising levels of residential burglaries and house robberies, many communities started their own street committees, operating under the Community Policing Forums (CPFs) or sector policing. Concerned citizens got together, elected street committees, and then developed their own neighbourhood watch patrols. When they became better organised, some of these structures hired private security companies to conduct these street patrols (Minnaar, 2009). Different types of street policing initiatives and activities began to grow within communities, resulting in the pluralisation of street policing. The pluralisation of street policing has since grown with limited co-ordination and legal control by the South African Police Service (SAPS). There are considerable demands on, and expectations of policing in South Africa. Most demands come from the tax payers and of those who allocate funds for policing. These investors are concerned with their return on investment in policing. The most frequent question asked, is 'are we getting a return on our investment' (Edwards, 2011, p. 142). The operational strategy of police management in the 21st century is to meet the public's needs efficiently, in part by involving the public to identify their policing needs, and in part by targeting policing resources to the most important issues identified by the public (Edwards, 2011).

> Community policing, which is widely held to be the most promising fundamental change in policing, is costly in resources to address the express wants of the public, even if not solely in monetary terms. The demands of the public for police attendance have already stretched the resources of most police services to such an extent, that many are unable to cope adequately with the work. (Edwards, 2011, p. 142)

## The Requirements of Community Policing

Community policing comes at a high price, as its fundamental principle is to develop improved communication and a relationship of trust between the police and the public, which means that a police officer must build a professional rapport with individuals and groups within the community. Community policing brings with it attitudinal change within policing towards addressing the needs and concerns of the public. Community policing requires officers to be available to the community consistently and over a sufficient period of time. They should become known to individuals within the community and the officers should be committed to building long-term relationships with the community, providing a source of information to the community about crime and also providing information to other police officers about the community (Edwards, 2011). According to Burger (2007, p. 102), 'the role of community policing and more specifically sector policing, is more focussed on the monitoring of public complaints than on solving community problems'.

## Public Expectation of the Police

The first and major expectation that the public has of its police is that the police should always be available. This expectation is certainly addressed in South Africa, as the police do indeed provide 24-hour service, seven days a week, all year round. Police are called as means of a dispute resolution. When a dispute arises, members of the public need it to be resolved and if this cannot be done by negotiation between the parties present or involved, some impartial arbitrator is required, whose decisions can be enforced. It is then that the police become involved (Edwards, 2011).

## Core Policing Functions of the 21st Century

Three core policing functions were identified for the 21st century, by Les Johnston in Patterson and Pollock (2011, p. 33).

- Crime-oriented policing (Reactive) – this is the core business of the police and involves responding to emergency calls from the public.
- Community policing (Proactive) – this remains a core function of the police role, but is increasingly conducted by the police alongside the community, special constables, city ambassadors, private security personnel, government departments, and members of the community.
- Order maintenance (Reactive) – this is an increasingly peripheral police function. The police remain involved in order maintenance but mainly as a final port of call.

These three core policing functions are central to policing in South Africa. However, private security companies conduct street policing together with citizens as an initiative arising from CPF structures.

## Post-Modern Policing

Since 1 April 1913, after the establishment of the SAPS, the police were the main institution responsible for reducing crime in South Africa. By the mid-1950s, police numbers had begun to fall, crime rates began to rise, legitimacy of the police among the public began to slide, and the police were moving from being a proactive to a reactive crime fighting force (Edwards, 2011). By the introduction of the CPFs the responsibilities of citizens led to a shift in focus from crime and offenders to crime prevention and community safety (looking at the causes of crime and finding solutions to community problems). This restructuring of response to crime involved a post-modern pluralistic policing approach where the police's previous monopoly of control of policing services fragmented and was increasingly undertaken by a multitude of policing providers from the statutory, voluntary, and commercial sectors (Patterson & Pollock, 2011). In South Africa we have pluralised policing to a large extent. Some of the forms of pluralised policing includes private bicycle patrols, private security foot and vehicle street patrols, business watch, neighbourhood watch, sector policing, street committees, car guards, policing by the SAPS, the Metro Police, Traffic Police, Special Investigation Units (SIUs) and other government departments.

Community policing in South Africa was originally intended as an alternative policing model to assist the police to prevent crimes in communities, and soon became subsumed into other forms of policing. In essence, community policing faded into the background whilst sector policing was pushed forward by the SAPS, ostensibly in support of community policing (Minnaar, 2009).

## Community-Based Participatory Approach

The community-based participatory approach goes beyond consultation and involvement, and so espouses working collaboratively with community partners who share common goals and interests (Hashagen, 2002). Community-based participatory research constitutes a worldview, and therefore an approach for conducting research (Israel, Eng, Schulz, & Parker, 2005). Researchers are of the view that crime should be studied in a social context, so as to improve community participation, ensure the sharing of experiences and concerns of people, and encourage 'a shared ownership of the crime problem' (Spinks, Turner, McClure, & Nixon, 2004, p. 180). It is because of this growing concern that Community Policing Forums (CPFs) were legislatively established in South Africa, so that there is constant communication between the police and the communities regarding crime issues (South Africa, 1996). Since community engagement is central to this study, it was decided to use the community-based participatory research approach to empower affected communities and to build knowledge for further research. This was based on a transactional relationship, which operated within the existing structure of the CPF, where the communities collaborated with other stakeholders, because each has something that the other perceives as useful.

## Security Measures

Security measures integrate people, procedures, and equipment for the protection of people and property on premises against theft, sabotage, or other malicious human acts. The design of an effective and efficient framework for managing risks require a methodical practical approach in which the designer weighs the objective against available resources, and then evaluates the proposed design to determine how well it meets the objective. Without this kind of careful assessment, the homeowner might waste valuable resources on unnecessary protection or, worse yet, fail to provide adequate protection at critical points of the premises. Knowledge of the modus operandi of burglars and house robbers operating in the neighbourhood would be vital in the designing and evaluation of security measures. It is therefore important that all security information be collected about recent residential burglaries and house robberies in the neighbourhood, so that the actions of the burglars and robbers may be examined. This will help to design the most appropriate security measures with deterrent value. For example, it will be unwise to protect a residence in a low risk area, with the same level of protection as a residence in a high risk area.

## Methodology

The aim of this chapter is to obtain knowledge on how unlawful entry is gained to commit residential burglaries and house robberies and to assist homeowners on the designing and evaluation of security measures. The author uses the case study design to describe the partnership between the researcher and the community in the prevention of residential burglaries and house robberies. The intervention methodology of participatory action research (PAR) was used to facilitate a process of social enquiry into the problem of residential burglaries and house robberies in the Garsfontein area, by creating a context for active community participation (Hope & Timmel, 2003). The context for the initiative and the methodological framework for the empirical study is outlined. It discusses the partnership, along with pertinent issues relevant to the problem of residential burglaries and house robberies in Garsfontein, Pretoria East. The researcher finally shares the findings of the empirical study and discusses the importance of designing and evaluating security measures to prevent residential burglaries and house robberies.

Ethical clearance was obtained from the University of South Africa to conduct this study within the broader framework of the author's community engagement project. Informed consent was obtained from the SAPS, the CPF, and other participants. The study employed a case study design because the case study design is more than a method of collecting data. It also provides the elements in designing a case study, with the understanding that the case study design is a continuous process throughout the study (Miles & Huberman, 1994). A case study involves empirical investigation of a phenomenon within its real life context, using specific methods and procedures to collect and analyse the data (Yin, 2009).

The case study approach enabled the researcher to personally observe the locations of entry, to interview various role-players, and to study the particulars of every case. In the field research the individual case was defined as a residential burglary/house robbery event that occurred in the case study area of Garsfontein. Another reason for the choice is that the interviewees for the qualitative study could be easily accessed by the author. The strategy of enquiry was to explore in depth the design and evaluation of the security measures. Data sources for this study included literature relevant to security measures, responses from the participants, and the observation field notes. An interview guide with two questions was designed and developed, aimed at the target group, namely 10 homeowners from the case study area. An observation guide was also developed based on vulnerabilities, threats, and security risk control measures. The questions for the interviews and the observation were developed on the basis of relevant literature (e.g. books written by security professionals, academics, and other experts) and with the assistance of the police, security service providers, and the community members belonging to the CPF.

A pilot study was undertaken prior to the data collection phase in order to refine the contents of the interview questions and to determine the best practices and procedures to be followed during interviewing sessions, as well as to evaluate the appropriateness of the research design.

The study was structured around the following research objectives:

1. To identify people from the community who have been victims of residential burglaries and/or house robberies.
2. To determine how entry was gained into the premises.
3. To encourage homeowners to design and evaluate security measures to prevent residential burglaries and house robberies.

The year 2013 represented the period of data collection and analysis, as it was the year in which the fieldwork was undertaken and data collected. Data collection took place over a period of six months. The following two questions were put to the participants:

1. Have you been a victim of a residential burglary or house robbery?
2. If you were a victim, can you explain how entry was gained into your premises?

The study was conducted in partnership with the CPF of a burglary-prone neighbourhood of Garsfontein. One street was identified in the Garsfontein neighbourhood by the author, which the author will hereinafter refer to as street X. Street X was selected randomly using probability sampling and the simple random sampling technique. All the streets in this suburb were put into a hat and the specific street was selected for study. The 10 individual cases also served as units of analysis. Ten houses and their owners were randomly selected on Street X in Garsfontein, Pretoria East, using the systematic random sampling technique, by choosing every third house on the street, one from the left and another from the right. Those who responded comprised of three females and seven males with an average age of 40–70 years old. Most of the respondents were employed, and had a maximum of 12 years of formal education or more.

Participants for the interviews were briefed on the purpose and significance of the study prior to the interviews. Consent was obtained from the participants. Confidentiality and anonymity of the participants were discussed. The participants supported the study by voluntarily taking part. The participants were asked to be frank and detailed in their responses and were requested to respond in the language of their choice. It was hoped that the responses would contribute to the development of knowledge. They had the option to withdraw from the interview at any time, if they so wished. Informal and in-depth individual interviews and observation were used as research methods of acquiring information for this study. Data was collected using interview questions and observation. In-depth interviews were conducted by making individual appointments with the house owners one by one at their homes at their convenience. These one-to-one interviews were conducted on Tuesday and Wednesday evenings about 17:00. Informal interviews were conducted with the local police, CPF members, and security service providers using the accidental sampling method. This was done at the CPF meetings as the author came across them individually. Observation of the security measures was conducted at the 10 houses of the respondents to determine the existing security measures and to identify vulnerabilities and risks that may provide unlawful entry for a burglar or robber. Observation was conducted by the author on the outer layer protection (perimeter fencing, perimeter access gate, security lighting, Closed Circuit Television (CCTV) installation) and the inner layer protection (windows, doors, burglar bars, alarms).

The author's experience was used as a primary source and literature was used as a secondary source in this study. The interviews were conducted in English in the respondents' own homes.

The observation results and the participants' responses were coded during data transcription and documented in a field journal. Categories of responses were created through open coding, developing categories, and evolving into thematic coding. Observations were also documented by the author during the study. They were used where appropriate in the study. The validity of the data was achieved through triangulation of the sources.

Data was obtained from a sample group of 10 homeowners from one particular street and from other stakeholders who were purposively interviewed and by observing the security measures of the 10 homes of the respondents. The researcher took into consideration the number of residents on the street when the sample group of 10 homeowners were selected.

The interpretive approach to data collection and analysis, as described by the data analysis spiral (Creswell, 2009), provided analytical guidelines for reviewing the responses. The author read through the recorded interview notes and the observation field notes to obtain a total picture of the data. This involved repeated readings of the responses and transcripts to develop familiarity with the content and delineate emergent themes. This resulted in aggregating similar responses and inserting these under appropriately formulated themes. The further analysis of the aggregated responses under the themes led to a refinement of the themes and/or moving some responses to more appropriate themes. Each theme was interpreted in relation to the context in which the study was conducted. The emergent themes were interpreted from which main findings were made by the researcher.

## Results

Once the findings were known, an announcement was made for a public meeting with the residents of the specific sector where the findings were made known as follows:

Many of the homeowners and partners were of the view that residential burglaries/robberies mainly take place when the victims are away from their homes, sometimes during the night or in the early hours of the morning when the victims are asleep in their homes. The burglars and robbers target homes where they can easily force the window or door open, and where there is no alarm system. Tuesday and Wednesdays seem to be the main days during which they target the victim's homes. These residential burglaries take place between 10:00 and 12:00 during the day, during the night from 22:00 to 24:00, and during the early hours of the morning from 02:00 until 04:00.

The researcher found that many homes had more security measures than were needed to address the threats prevalent in the neighbourhood, whilst others had too few security measures. However, the security measures were not sufficient to stop the burglar/house robber from gaining entry, since none of the security measures at the 10 homes was designed with the object of preventing residential burglaries/house robberies. Burglars/robbers usually look for design features that fit their description of a 'good target'. These may include design features of the house that could allow easy access to and escape from the house, for example, concealed entrances, and easily removable windows (Van Zyl, Wilson, & Pretorious, 2003), Some homeowners mentioned that in some cases of burglary, unlawful entry was gained by damaging the old welding of the 'Devil Fork' perimeter fencing gate and lifting the gate off the rail. This also led to the gate motor being damaged and the wirings pulled out of the gate motor box. Some burglars also gained unlawful entry by climbing over the perimeter fencing to gain access into the premises. This happens at homes where the perimeter fencing is not fitted with electrified barbed wire or where no alarm systems are installed.

Observation by the author indicated the presence of basic perimeter fencing at all 10 houses, some of them having old, rusted barbed wire. The perimeter fencing including the fence gates and alarms are also cheaply maintained by street vendors, who obtain access to the gate locking codes/frequencies during repairs. The dogs also become used to them when they conduct maintenance work on the fences, the gates, windows, and doors of the houses. Sufficient lighting was available from the street. The house of one of the homeowners that was not installed with an alarm system preferred not have an alarm system as they feared confrontation with the robbers in the event of the alarm going off.

Many of the gates did not have upper clamps to prevent the gates from being lifted off the rail. None of the 10 houses were fitted with CCTV cameras, which could have helped in recording the robbers' actions for identification by the police on a 24-hour basis (Abrie, 2008; Minnaar, 2012).

Most of the homeowners and stakeholders found that once the adversary was inside the premises (yard), unlawful entry was gained into the homes by damaging the inside pedestrian gates and neatly removing the putty of the lounge or kitchen window panes. The burglar bars are bent and the window is left wide open for easy exit, in the event of being confronted by the owner/occupier. Dining room doors and burglar bars are also damaged to gain entry. The sliding door at the front entrance of a house is sometimes forced open to gain entry into the house. The kitchen door is also forced open and the burglar bar gate damaged to gain entry into the house.

The most common housebreaking implements which were allegedly used to obtain unlawful entry into houses and found at the burglary/robbery crime scenes in Garsfontein included crowbars and screwdrivers. Zinn (2008) in his interviews with incarcerated burglars/robbers found that an axe, a hammer, a crowbar, a wrench, a shovel, and an iron pipe were identified as common housebreaking implements used to gain entry into homes.

## Discussion

Based on the principles of community-based participatory research, this chapter provides insight on the vital role that can be played by the community in preventing residential burglaries and house robberies, which was presented to the community to encourage homeowners.

## Design of Security Measures

The first step in the process is to design security measures to specifically prevent residential burglaries and house robberies, 'Understanding the modus operandi of residential burglaries and house robberies is necessary in order to sufficiently protect vital parts of the home or to avoid overprotection of nonessential areas' (Garcia, 2001, xvii; Garcia, 2008, p. 15; Institute of Nuclear Materials Management (INMM), 2004). 'A tour of the neighbourhood and the house in question as well as interviews with the occupants of the house is necessary' (Garcia, 2008, p. 3). According to Zinn (2010, p. 29),

> valuable information on crime trends, criminal networks including modus operandi can be obtained by studying the criminal profiles of known burglars/robbers by conducting case docket analysis of convicted burglars/robbers or by personally interviewing them. This will provide an understanding of the needed security measures for the house as well as an appreciation for the activities and safety constraints. A thorough characterisation of the house and the criminal activities of street gangs and other elements within the neighbourhood is an absolute necessity.

Characterisation of the neighbourhood and interviews with police, CPF members, and the neighbours are crucial (Minnaar, 2012). The police and their partners will be able to help with some of the information needed by the homeowners in a specific sector.

'Targets may include a specific home, or assets, information and people occupying specific homes. A thorough review of the house and its assets, information and people occupying it should be conducted' (Garcia, 2008, p. 4).

> A burglar/robber would tend to search for a suitable house in the area he knows best. If the burglar has specific knowledge of a particular house and its occupants, or has gained inside information through reconnaissance work, that house will be more vulnerable than other potential targets of which he has no knowledge. (Brown & Altman, 1981, p. 58)

In identifying the risk and defining the threat, specific information should be considered. 'The threats need to be defined by answering the following three questions about the adversary, such as what class of adversary should be considered, what is the range of the adversary's tactics, and what are the adversaries' capabilities?' (Garcia, 2008, p. 4).

'For any given house there may be several risks, such as a criminal outsider, a disgruntled maid, gardener or tenant, competitors or a combination of the above' (Garcia, 2008, p. 4). The security measures must be designed to protect the home against all these risks. 'Choosing the most likely risk, designing the security measures to overcome this risk and then testing to verify the system performance against the other risks will facilitate the process of preventing the threat from occurring' (Garcia, 2008, p. 4). Zinn interviewed 30 convicted, incarcerated perpetrators of house robberies and discovered that the methods used to gain unlawful entry to commit house burglaries/robberies included: climbing over the wall or fence; crawling through under the fence; forcing or breaking open door or window; forcing burglar bars apart; cutting or breaking a small section of a window and using the handle to open the window, simultaneously breaking the inner burglar bars; using a key to open the door and shifting tiles on the roof and making holes to get into the ceiling (Zinn, 2008).

Given the information obtained in the characterisation of the premises, target identification, and risk identification, the designer will be able to define the threat to the homeowner. 'The objectives of protection should be to deter, detect, delay and respond to the residential burglar or house robber' (Garcia, 2008, p. 4). No owner can protect everything all the time. This would be unrealistic, impossible, and unnecessary. We need to recognise those homes which already have outer layer protection (perimeter fencing, perimeter access gate, security lighting, CCTV, alarms, etc.) and inner layer protection (windows, doors, burglar bars, alarms, etc.). There is no need to double these efforts. Once the vulnerable points have been identified those crucial elements in the assets should then be determined in order to design appropriate security measures (Muller, 2002).

It could be stated that on average most residences provide relatively easy access to burglars as a result of inadequate security measures (Van Zyl et al., 2003). In designing security measures to detect, delay, and respond to the burglar/house robber, the designer must understand the characterisation of the house, activities, and the assets being kept at the house, identified risks, and the defined threat. The goal of the security measures should be to reduce crime, increase detection, and prevent losses. The envisaged security measures should be able to accomplish their goal by fulfilling their objectives through deterrence, detection, delay, and response or a combination of some or all of the objectives (Garcia, 2006).

Security measures may be designed to include strategies encompassing 'Crime Prevention through Environmental Designing' (CPTED), street committees, neighbourhood watch, sharing of information, and electronic networking with other service providers and organisations. Many of these have served as best practices in the law enforcement environment. The challenge is for owners to make themselves aware of current and innovative design and communication strategies. This knowledge should be coupled with the latest information on issues of changes in cultural values, crime, technology, market conditions, and political conditions (Opolot, 1999).

When designing new security measures, it is advisable to determine how best to combine the outer and inner layers of protection system elements such as fences, barriers, sensors, procedures, communication devices, and security personnel into security measures that can achieve the protection objectives. 'The resulting security measures should meet its objectives within operational, safety, legal and economic constraints' (Garcia, 2008, p. 5).

## Evaluation of the Security Measures

Soon after a residential burglary/house robbery occurs at a residence, there is a tendency of homeowners to improve security by generally upgrading existing burglar bars at the windows, security gates at the front and back doors, installing of security lights, acquiring a dog, and to foster friendly relations with the neighbours (Van Zyl et al., 2003). Evaluation should be continuously carried out on the security measures. It has to begin with a review and thorough understanding of the protection objectives that the security measures must meet. The security measures should be quantitatively and qualitatively monitored and evaluated for vulnerabilities on a continuous basis. Sophisticated analysis and evaluation techniques can be used to estimate the minimum performance levels achieved by security measures. These techniques include qualitative and quantitative analysis of the security measures. Systems that are designed to protect high-value critical assets generally require a quantitative analysis. Systems protecting lower value assets may be analysed using less rigorous qualitative techniques. Qualitative analysis is more suitable for lower consequence loss assets and so will be better able to withstand loss or damage of that asset. In qualitative analysis the analyst has to define the threats and targets and evaluate system performance, but these should be tailored to meet the budget and time constraints for the analysis (Garcia, 2008; Minnaar, 2012).

### Recommendations

It is recommended that homeowners take ownership for the designing and re-designing of security measures to prevent residential burglaries and house robberies. They should engage with security practitioners for guidance on how to design and evaluate their security measures to specifically protect their homes against specific threats such as residential burglaries and house robberies.

## Conclusion

This chapter illustrates that the community-based participatory approach in safety and security is a dynamic and evolutionary process. Community policing is a philosophy that promotes and supports strategies to address the causes and reduce the fear of crime and social disorder through problem-solving tactics and police community partnerships. Street crimes have not changed much over the years, as people have always fought each other, stolen each other's property, abused alcohol and drugs, and generally engaged in various forms of anti-social behaviour and non-compliance. Security measures can be effective against street crimes which occur in the vicinity of the streets and public places being policed. These can be loosely referred to as 'street crimes' and include such offences as robbery, burglary, theft of and from vehicles, drugs and alcohol, prostitution, other miscellaneous thefts and assaults arising from public order incidents and non-compliance. Many owners are not aware of vulnerability analysis or risk assessments; therefore they do not consider the design and evaluation of the security measures.

## References

Abrie, S. (2008). *Security risk management*. Study guide for PSMN03X. Pretoria: UNISA Press.

Africa Check (2013). *FACTSHEET South Africa: Official crime statistics for 2012/13*. Retrieved February 25, 2014, from https://africacheck.org/factsheets/factsheet-south-africas-official-crime-statistics-for-201213/.

Brown, B. B., & Altman, I. (1981). Territoriality and residential crime: A conceptual framework. In P. J. Brantingham & P. L. Brantingham (Eds.), *Environmental criminology* (pp. 55–76). Beverly Hills, CA: Sage Publications, Inc.

Burger, F. J. (2006). Crime combatting in perspective: A strategic approach to policing and the prevention of crime. *Acta Criminologica, 19*(2), 105–118.

Burger, J. (2007). *Strategic perspectives on crime and policing in South Africa.* Pretoria. Van Schaik Publishers.

Catalano, S. (2010). *Victimization during household burglary. National Crime Victimization Survey.* Bureau of Justice Statistics. Washington, D.C.: U.S. Department of Justice.

Cohen, L. E., & Felson, M. (1979). Social change and crime rate trends: A routine activity approach. *American Sociological Review, 44*(4), 588–608.

Cornish, D. B., & Clarke, R. V. (1986). Situational prevention, displacement of crime and rational choice theory. In K. Heal & G. Laycock (Eds.), *Situational crime prevention: From theory into practice* (pp. 1–16). London: Her Majesty's Stationery Office.

Creswell, J. W. (2009). *Research design: Qualitative, quantitative and mixed methods approach* (3rd ed.). Thousand Oaks, CA: Sage Publications, Inc.

Crime Statistics South Africa (2013). info@crimestatssa.com. Retrieved February 27, 2014, from www.crimestatssa.com/national.php.

Edwards, C. (2011). *Changing policing theories for 21st century societies* (3rd ed.). Sydney: The Federation Press.

Fay, J. J. (2006). *Contemporary security management.* Oxford: Elsevier/Butterworth Heinemann.

Garcia, M. L. (2001). *The design and evaluation of physical protection systems.* Boston: Butterworth Heinemann.

Garcia, M. L. (2006). *Vulnerability assessment of physical protection systems.* Boston: Butterworth Heinemann.

Garcia, M. L. (2008). *The design and evaluation of physical protection systems* (2nd ed.). Boston: Butterworth/Heinemann.

Hashagen, S. (2002). *Models of community engagement. Scottish Community Development Centre.* Retrieved February 28, 2012, from www.dundeecity.gov.uk/dundeecity/uploaded_publications/publication_283.pdf.

Hope, A., & Timmel, S. (2003). *Training for transformation: Book 1.* London: Intermediate Technology Development Group Press.

INMM. (2004). *Global best practices for physical protection.* Retrieved July 2, 2014, from www.inmm.org/Physical Protection.htm.

Israel, B. A., Eng, E., Schulz, A. J., & Parker, E. A. (2005). *Methods in community based participatory research for health.* San Francisco: Jossey-Bass.

Israel, B. A., Schulz, A. J., Parker, E. A., Becker, A. B., Allen, A. J., & Guzman, J. R. (2003). Critical issues in developing and following participatory research principles. In M. Minkler & N. Wallerstein (Eds.), *Community based participatory research for health* (pp. 53–76). San Francisco: Jossey-Bass.

Landman, K., & Liebermann, S. (2005). *Planning against crime: Preventing crime with people not barriers.* Retrieved December 13, 2015, from www.issafrica.org/uploads/LANDMAN.PDFSA.

Miles, M. B., & Huberman, A. M. (1994). *Qualitative data analysis: An expanded sourcebook* (2nd ed.). Thousand Oaks, CA: Sage Publications, Inc.

Minnaar, A. (2009). Community policing in a high crime transitional state: The case of South Africa since democratisation in 1994. In D. Wisler & I. D. Onwudiwe (Eds.), *Community policing: International patterns and comparative perspectives* (pp. 19–53). Boca Raton, FL: CRC.

Minnaar, A. (2012). Private security companies, neighbourhood watches and the use of CCTV surveillance in residential neighbourhoods: The case of Pretoria-East. *Acta Criminologica, 1*, 103–116.

Muller, M. L. (2002). *Gathering competitive information. Nuts and bolts business series/competitive intelligence series: A practical guide for leaders: Guide 3.* Randburg: Knores.

Olutola, A. A. (2011). *Crime prevention and the criminal justice systems of Nigeria and South*

*Africa: A comparative perspective.* D.Tech thesis. Pretoria: Tshwane University of Technology, Tshwane.
Opolot, J. S. E. (1999). *An introduction to private security: A comparative introduction to an international phenomenon.* New York: Austin & Winfield.
Patterson, C., & Pollock, E. (2011). *Policing and criminology: Policing matters.* Devon: Learning Matters Ltd.
Rogers, C. (2008). A security risk management approach to the measurement of crime in a private security context. *Acta Criminologica, 3,* 155–166.
Shearing, C. D., & P. C. Stenning (1982). 'Snowflakes or good pinches? – Private security's contribution to modern policing. In R. Donelan (Ed.), *The maintenance of order in society* (pp. 96–105). Ottawa: Canadian Police College.
Snyman, C. R. (2003). *Criminal law* (4th ed.). Durban: Butterworths.
South Africa. (1996). *The constitution of the Republic of South Africa.* Act No. 108 of 1996. Pretoria: Government Printer.
Spinks, A., Turner, C., McClure, R., & Nixon, J. (2004). Community based prevention programs targeting all injuries for children. *Injury Prevention, 10,* 180–185.
Van Zyl, G. S., Wilson, G. D. H., & Pretorious, R. (2003). Residential burglary in South Africa: Why individual households adopt reactive strategies. *Acta Criminologica, 16*(3), 107–123.
Walker, J. P., & Serrano, A. M. (2006). Formulating a cosmopolitan approach to immigration and social policy: Lessons from American (North and South) indigenous and immigration groups. *Current Issues in Comparative Education, 9*(1), 1–9.
Yen, J. (2008). A history of community psychology in South Africa. In C. van Ommen & D. Painter (Eds.), *Interiors: A history of psychology in South Africa* (pp. 385–412). Pretoria: *Unisa* Press.
Yin, R. K. (2009). *Case study research: Design and methods* (4th ed.). Thousand Oaks, CA: Sage Publications, Inc.
Zinn, R. (2008). The modus operandi of house robbers in the Gauteng Province. *Acta Criminologica, 21*(2), 56–69.
Zinn, R. (2010). Inside information: Sourcing crime intelligence from incarcerated house robbers. *SA Crime Quarterly, 32,* 27–35.

# Crossing the Great Divide
## The Development and Effectiveness of Working Relationships between Law Enforcement Personnel and Academic Researchers

# 4

LIN HUFF-CORZINE AND JAY CORZINE

### Contents

## Abstract

After a sharp spike in violent crime between 2004 and 2006, the Public Safety Director for Orange County, Florida, requested an in depth analysis of possible causes for the increase with suggestions to address the problem, especially among juveniles. Recommendations included increased informal contact between law enforcement and teens and more after school programs, among others. The current Orange County Sheriff incorporated three of the suggestions into his five initiatives when he ran for and won election to the office. This chapter outlines the development of a continued association between our Department of Sociology Crime Lab and the Orange County Sheriff's Office. It also identifies factors that are necessary for continuing this type of mutually beneficial relationship among local government agencies, law enforcement, and academe.

The barriers impeding academic researchers and police from forming mutually beneficial collaborations are not as impenetrable as once believed. The value of research in effectively implementing newer approaches to policing, including problem oriented policing (POP), hot spots policing, intelligence led policing, and predictive policing is acknowledged (Santos, 2014). The "pulling levers" strategy developed by David Kennedy and others at Harvard and associated with the original Ceasefire Program in Boston has been replicated with varying levels of success in several cities in the United States (U.S.). We are personally aware of several academic colleagues in U.S. cities, who have developed collaborative research projects with local law enforcement agencies, e.g., the Blocks in Chicago. And, the same type of progress has been made in other nations (Guillaume, Sidebottom, & Tilley, 2012; Marks, 2009).

Yet, the time for unbridled optimism about the future of police-academic collaborations is not the rule. There are still differences that separate the two groups. Although some of the reasons for what we term "the great divide" are based on the personalities of individuals in both law enforcement and academia, most of the obstacles are lodged in the structures and cultures of their respective organizations. Both law enforcement organizations and universities in the U.S. are hierarchical and bureaucratic and typically with more rigid levels and degrees of vertical formal control in police agencies. A recent effort to use trained undergraduate students from our university to assist in cold case homicide investigations with a local sheriff's office, for example, was approved at the departmental level within one week and no further approval at higher levels of the university was required. After the successful navigation of several levels of bureaucracy at the sheriff's office, however, the proposal was eventually rejected by the County Sheriff approximately six months later.

On the other hand, sometimes academic researchers work at their own pace. Especially when responding to changes in crime patterns, the police want and need analyses that can inform deployment patterns and prioritize goals in a short period of time. Because academics have teaching and service assignments in addition to research, many, if not most, academics conduct research at a slower pace. The lack of a consensus timetable may create tensions for both parties. Notably, problems resulting from the different timetables followed by academics and practitioners have been noted for many types of community organizations, including non-governmental organizations (Nyden and Wiewel, 1992).

The occupational culture of police officers is often less than hospitable to outsiders. Authors have long noted a belief among the police that only they can know anything useful about policing. Moskos (2008) and others have commented on a deep concern, especially among patrol officers, to avoid "trouble," and outsiders whose intentions are suspect can be viewed as dangerous. This is also true for academics. When Corzine, one of the authors, was on the faculty at the University of Nebraska (UNL), he developed a trusting relationship with the Assistant Chief of Police in Lincoln, Nebraska. The Assistant Chief would periodically call because a faculty member at UNL had requested data, and he wanted to know if they could be trusted. Specific animosity directed at academics has likely eased with the increasing number of law enforcement agencies requiring a bachelor's degree for incoming officers and the growing influx of retired law enforcement personnel into the ranks of academic researchers, at least in the U.S., but suspicions have not disappeared. A more common issue is that some police believe that academic researchers simply have nothing useful to offer. They are not evil, simply superfluous.

On the other side of the divide, there have always been academics in the U.S. who dislike the police for various reasons. They are basically irrelevant to the purposes of this chapter, however, because while they may be vocal critics of the police, they are unlikely to seek collaborative relationships with them.

The primary purpose of this chapter is to describe the development of a collaborative relationship between researchers based in the Department of Sociology at University of Central Florida (UCF) and regional law enforcement agencies in the Orange County Metropolitan Area, notably the Orange County Sheriff's Office and the Orlando Police Department. By most reasonable criterion, the collaboration has been a success. The original research led to policy changes by both agencies, the dropping of proposed ordinances by the Orlando City Council and the Orange County Commission, collaboration on additional projects, ready access to criminal justice data for academic researchers, and the hiring of sociology graduate students by the Orlando Police Department (OPD). Before describing the development of the relationship, we will briefly highlight selected, relevant characteristics of Orange County, Florida.

## Orange County, Florida

Orange County, Florida, had a recorded population of 1,145,956 in the 2010 census. It is a "majority-minority" county with a 46% non-Hispanic white population in 2010 and nearly 25% of the population who speak a language other than English at home. With a household median income of $41,311 and a family poverty rate of 8.8%, its economic standing is in the middle range for Florida counties. Although 19% of the population in

2010 was born outside the U.S., the largest group is Puerto Ricans who are citizens of the U.S. by birth.

The largest segment of the local economy is tourism with over 50 million visitors to Orange County annually. Its tourism industry is best known for Disney's Magic Kingdom, but the county is also the home of Universal Studios Florida, SeaWorld Orlando, and dozens of other theme parks, or "attractions," as they are called locally. As will be discussed later, the centrality of tourism to the region's economy was an important factor in the early stage of the collaboration between local law enforcement agencies and UCF sociologists.

Orange County reflects the dominant pattern of decentralized law enforcement in the U.S., with 11 municipal agencies, a university police department, and a sheriff's office. The two largest law enforcement agencies in Orange County are the Sheriff's Office with over 2400 sworn and civilian employees and the Orlando Police Department with over 800 employees. The Orlando Police Chief is appointed by the city's mayor and is a non-partisan position. The Orange County Sheriff is elected by voters with candidates typically running as Democrat or Republican, the two major political parties in the U.S. In contrast to the multiple police agencies in the county, there is a single jail that is used by all law enforcement agencies for processing arrestees. It holds inmates who are awaiting trial or serving sentences.

Politically, Orange County has more registered Democratic than Republican voters but neither party dominates local politics. At the beginning of the collaboration described below, Buddy Dyer, the Orlando mayor, was a Democrat; Rich Crotty and Kevin Beary, the Orange county mayor and sheriff respectively, were Republicans. Buddy Dyer remains the Orlando mayor currently, while Rich Crotty has been replaced by Teresa Jacobs, a Republican, and the current Orange County Sheriff is Jerry Demings, a Democrat. Demings was previously both Orlando Police Chief and the Director of Public Safety for Orange County, a position that has since been eliminated because of budget problems.

## The Development of the Relationship

Because there was a large increase in violent crimes between 2004 and 2006, in mid-August 2006, Buddy Dyer, Mayor of Orlando, Florida, the largest city in Orange County, decided to launch a special taskforce charged with finding new, successful ways to combat serious violent crime using police, volunteers, and community resources. The taskforce, entitled "The Mayor's Safe Orlando Task Force," was to be comprised of 15–20 members led by Stanley Stone, Vice President of Human Resources and Diversity at Valencia Community College, which is located in Orlando (Orlando Sentinel, 2006).

Shortly thereafter, the first open meeting of the Mayor's Safe Orlando Task Force met at City Hall. Members of the Task Force, representing a broad spectrum of the business, education, religious, law enforcement, and service communities (see Appendix 4.1), were given their charge by the Mayor. He started by stating that "Keeping Orlando safe is the top priority of my administration," and gave the Task Force 120 days to complete its work (Dyer, 2006, p. 1). The benefits of using the task force model, which he does regularly, the Mayor explained, were twofold:

1. Community leaders were given a forum to identify and resolve crime-related concerns, and
2. It provides a place where important information can be solicited and gathered from the general public.

To emphasize the significance of the work to be completed by the Task Force, Jeffrey Goltz, an OPD Captain and a UCF PhD, shared the following data on the 37 murders that had occurred in the City of Orlando between January 1 and August 11, 2006:

> Twenty-four victims were African-American (65%), nine were white (24%), and four were Hispanic (11%). Eleven of the victims were in their teens to mid-20s (30%). Twenty-five suspects or arrestees are African-American (76%), five are white (15%), three are Hispanic (9%), and twenty-two are teenagers to mid-20s in age (67%). Although the suspect ages range from young to old, the statistics indicate that the majority of the suspects are teens or young adults, and many of the homicides involved the use of a firearm (81%) and drug activity or robbery were the motives in many cases. (Goltz, 2006, p. 1)

Captain Goltz continued his discussion of Orlando murders by focusing on sociological perspectives, pointing out the importance of attending to potential juvenile offenders and the suggestion that Hirschi's Social Control Theory would be a good place to start looking for ways to reduce crime, in general, and murder, specifically (Goltz, 2006, pp. 1–2). Briefly stated, Hirschi's theory asserts that people, including juveniles, will commit crime and other deviant acts unless there are sufficient social controls in place to inhibit such behavior. Specifically, Hirschi argues that as long as an individual's (1) *attachment*, the bond with others based on respect, love, or affection; (2) *commitment*, the bond that focuses on ambition and aspirations to reach and maintain one's social capital; (3) *involvement* in conventional activities; and (4) *belief* in the need to obey conventional rules and laws are strong, juveniles are not likely to commit crime, including homicide (Einstadter and Henry, 2006, p. 193).

## The Mayor's Safe Orlando Task Force

With Dr. Stanley H. Stone as Chair of the Safe Orlando Task Force, the agenda and meeting times were set. Sociologists, Dr. Lin Huff-Corzine and Dr. Jay Corzine, attended these meetings regularly and, with time, became known as Task Force Consultants. The 120 days passed and the Task Force asked for more time. By March 1, 2007, however, it offered 33 Recommendations; according to Dr. Stone, 24 of the 33 Recommendations had been implemented along the way (see Appendix 4.2). The Task Force had been split into three small sub-committees, Law Enforcement, Prevention, and Re-Integration. Each sub-committee submitted a report listing short-term, intermediate, and long-term goals aimed to reduce crime, especially violent offenses, in Orlando.

As consultants, Jay Corzine and Lin Huff-Corzine were approached by Mayor Dyer's office and asked to become a part of the prevention strategy that he was initiating.

Following acceptance, we traveled to each and every Orlando neighborhood with the Mayor and members of the OPD and other city agencies to discuss issues related to violence in their neighborhoods and anything else on attendees' minds. This traveling show, entitled Mayor Buddy Dyer's Public Safety Information Series, featured the Mayor, who talked to citizens about Orlando's public safety efforts and encouraged attendees to help reduce and prevent crime. Attendance was normally sparse and often citizens were more interested in the timing of trash pick-up or people driving too fast on their streets, but the Mayor maintained a positive attitude; answering questions and taking information, and then returning to the issues of violent crime and the part they could play in helping keep the streets safe.

## Violent Crime in Orange County

At about the same time that we were making the rounds of Orlando neighborhoods, we were approached by Jerry Demings, Orange County Public Safety Officer, who had served on the Task Force, to undertake a broader, research-based study for the County. With the approval of his supervisor, Orange County Mayor Rich Crotty and funded by the Sheriff's Office, Mr. Demings secured our services to examine crime in Orange County from 2004 through 2006.

By May 1, 2007, all paperwork, including Institutional Review Board approval, was complete and our study began. We were charged with examining data from the Orange County Sheriff's Office, the County jail, the Orlando Police Department, and the Office of Juvenile Justice and then providing Mr. Demings with a series of reports containing recommendations based on the findings. Based on the Mayor's Safe Orlando Task Force statistics, we were asked to examine violent crime, especially (1) homicide and robbery that had skyrocketed in Orlando between 2004 through 2006; (2) juvenile offenders, with a focus on the potential advantage of setting a curfew for teens; and (3) the effect of gang activity on crime in the County.

To gain cooperation from the various offices, Mr. Demings brought representatives from all of the organizations together with our team of three faculty and five students. Normally, U.S. law enforcement agencies are quite hesitant to share data among themselves, let alone with academics. Thus, when Mr. Demings explained that he wanted all of the agencies to provide us with their data so that we could combine the information from each into one dataset, we were not surprised to hear people tell him that it just could not be done. In fact, one person explained that "We've been trying to do that for two years, and we just cannot make it happen." Mr. Demings simply replied that he expected them to let our team give it a try and that if any office did not comply, they would have to answer to him. Needless to say, everyone cooperated and once the data were secured from all of the agencies, it took less than two weeks to combine the information and prepare a dataset ready for analysis.

## Orange County Violent Crime Statistics

We started our investigation by exploring the general violent crime picture for Orange County, including Orlando. We found that between 2004 and 2006, violent crime in Orange County, Florida, did, in fact, experience a spike, which was primarily fueled by two offenses, homicide and robbery. Specifically, between 2004 and 2006, the homicide rate increased 87% and the robbery rate increased 67%, whereas aggravated assault increased 10.2% and rape decreased 4.4% (Corzine et al., 2007b).

Table 4.1 shows the number of homicide, robbery, sexual assault, and aggravated assault victims. Especially shocking was the jump in homicide victims from 56 in 2004 to 120 in 2006, and the rise in robbery victims by nearly 1000 from 2948 in 2004 to 3933 in 2006.

To give the statistics a context to better understand them, we turn briefly to a description of Orange County. According to the 2000 Census, the median age of Orange County residents was 33.3 years, while 68.6% were White and 18.2% Black. Just over half of the population, 50.5%, were women and the remainder, 49.5%, were men (U.S. Census Bureau, 2000). By 2010, the median age had increased to 33.7 years, the percent White decreased to 63.7% and the Black population increased to 20.8%. The percent of women increased just a bit to 50.8% of the total, and men decreased a bit to 49.2% of the total population (U.S. Census Bureau, 2010).

In comparison to the average population demographics for Orange County, victims were most likely to be 25–34 years old (see Table 4.2). Although large percentages of victims were listed as either having unknown or missing data for race, the percentages of White victims equaled or were greater than the percentages for Blacks. Still, because of their relative percentages in the population, Black victims were overrepresented, while White victims were underrepresented in each of the three years studied.

Finally, women were underrepresented and men overrepresented among Orange County victims between 2004 and 2006 (Corzine et al., 2007b).

In comparison to the average population demographics for Orange County, suspects, like victims, were most likely 25–34 years old (see Table 4.3).

The percentages of White suspects were consistently lower than the percentages for Black suspects. Thus, for each of the three years studied, Blacks showed greater percentage overrepresentation among suspects than was indicated among victims, and White suspects were underrepresented in larger percentages than was the case among White victims. Finally, and not surprisingly, women were consistently underrepresented and men overrepresented among Orange County suspects between 2004 and 2006 (Corzine et al., 2007b).

**Table 4.1 Violent Crimes in Orange County, Florida, 2004–2006**

| Year | Murder | Robbery | Sexual Assault | Aggravated Assault | Total |
|---|---|---|---|---|---|
| 2004 | 56 | 2795 | 805 | 2948 | 6604 |
| 2005 | 64 | 3836 | 944 | 3468 | 8312 |
| 2006 | 120 | 4876 | 1033 | 3933 | 9962 |
| **Total** | **240** | **11507** | **2762** | **10349** | **24878** |

**Table 4.2 Violent Crime Victims' Age, Race, and Gender, Orange County, Florida, 2004–2006**

| Characteristic | Year | | |
|---|---|---|---|
| | 2004 | 2005 | 2006 |
| **Age** | | | |
| Under 18 | 996 (16.7%) | 1136 (14.9%) | 1426 (15.6%) |
| 18–24 | 1514 (25.3%) | 1863 (24.4%) | 2492 (27.2%) |
| 25–44 | 2512 (42.0%) | 3380 (44.2%) | 3752 (41.0%) |
| 45 and Over | 958 (16.0%) | 1262 (16.5%) | 1489 (16.3%) |
| **Race** | | | |
| White | 2089 (34.9%) | 2127 (27.8%) | 2635 (28.8%) |
| Black | 1738 (29.1%) | 2127 (27.8%) | 2545 (27.8%) |
| Other | 37 (0.6%) | 53 (0.7%) | 75 (0.8%) |
| Unknown/Missing | 2116 (35.4%) | 3334 (43.6%) | 3908 (42.7%) |
| **Gender** | | | |
| Men | 3452 (57.7%) | 4502 (58.9%) | 5708 (62.3%) |
| Women | 2519 (42.1%) | 3127 (40.9%) | 3438 (37.5%) |
| Unknown/Missing | 9 (0.2%) | 12 (0.2%) | 13 (0.1%) |
| **Total** | **5980 (100%)** | **7641 (100%)** | **9159 (100%)** |

**Table 4.3 Violent Crime Suspects' Age, Race, and Gender, Orange County, Florida, 2004–2006**

| Characteristic | Year | | |
|---|---|---|---|
| | 2004 | 2005 | 2006 |
| **Age** | | | |
| Under 18 | 590 (16.8%) | 923 (16.9%) | 1174 (21.4%) |
| 18–24 | 1132 (32.3%) | 1963 (35.9%) | 2039 (37.2%) |
| 25–44 | 1429 (40.8%) | 2085 (38.1%) | 1853 (33.9%) |
| 45 and Over | 353 (10.1%) | 499 (9.2%) | 409 (7.5%) |
| **Race** | | | |
| White | 1456 (41.6%) | 1960 (35.8%) | 1868 (34.1%) |
| Black | 2013 (57.4%) | 3442 (82.9%) | 3537 (64.6%) |
| Other | 14 (0.4%) | 28 (0.5%) | 24 (0.4%) |
| Unknown/Missing | 16 (0.5%) | 40 (0.7%) | 46 (0.8%) |
| **Gender** | | | |
| Men | 2845 (81.2%) | 4603 (84.2%) | 4716 (86.1%) |
| Women | 642 (18.3%) | 853 (15.6%) | 722 (13.2%) |
| Unknown/Missing | 17 (0.5%) | 14 (0.3%) | 37 (0.7%) |
| **Total** | 3504 (100%) | 5470 (100%) | 5475 (100%) |

## Homicide in Orlando

To separate the findings for the County as a whole from the City of Orlando, we were asked to examine homicides within the city limits so that comparisons and more effective law enforcement decisions could be made. Homicides in Orlando revealed that there were 17 victims in 2004, 22 in 2005, and 49 in 2006. Thus, the significant increases noted for the County also held for the City.

## Orlando Homicide Victim and Suspect Characteristics

As can be seen by comparing the results examining the characteristics of homicide victims and suspects in Orlando (Tables 4.4 and 4.5), the ages of victims are spread across the age categories to a greater extent than are suspect ages. Over the three-year period, for example, there are six victims but only one suspect who was 61 years old or older.

In addition, greater percentages of Blacks are involved as both victims and suspects, and men are much more likely to kill and be killed. In each case, these patterns are consistent with the findings for Orange County, as well as for homicide in the U.S.

## Weapons, Motives, and Dispositions: Orlando Homicides

Compared to the patterns of weapon choice to commit a homicide in the U.S., the statistics for Orlando appear to fit the norm (see Table 4.6). Most of the homicides were committed with firearms; 76.5% in 2004, 61.9% in 2005, and 73.5% in 2006. Following as a distant second choice, Orlando homicide offenders used knives/cutting instruments.

When exploring the motive, it appears that robbery was the major reason for committing a homicide in Orlando, at least in 2006. The statistics for motive during 2004 and

**Table 4.4 Homicide Suspects' Age, Race, and Gender, Orlando, Florida, 2004–2006**

| Characteristic | Counts and Percentages by Year | | |
|---|---|---|---|
| | 2004 | 2005 | 2006 |
| **Age** | | | |
| 0–20 | 4 (25.0%) | 2 (18.2%) | 18 (39.1%) |
| 21–30 | 10 (62.5%) | 5 (45.5%) | 18 (39.2%) |
| 31–40 | 1 (6.3%) | 1 (9.1%) | 4 (8.7%) |
| 41–50 | 1 (6.3%) | 1 (9.1%) | 3 (6.5%) |
| 51–60 | 0 | 2 (18.2%) | 2 (4.3%) |
| 61–70 | 0 | 0 | 1 (2.2%) |
| 71 and Over | 0 | 0 | 0 |
| **Total** | **16** | **11** | **46** |
| **Race** | | | |
| White | 3 (18.8%) | 3 (23.1%) | 5 (10.4%) |
| Black | 13 (81.3%) | 10 (76.9%) | 38 (79.2%) |
| Hispanic | 0 | 0 | 5 (10.4%) |
| **Total** | **16** | **13** | **48** |
| **Gender** | | | |
| Men | 16 (100%) | 13 (100%) | 45 (95.7%) |
| Women | 0 | 0 | 2 (4.3%) |
| **Total** | **16** | **13** | **47** |

**Table 4.5 Homicide Victims' Age, Race, and Gender, Orlando, Florida, 2004–2006**

| Characteristic | Counts and Percentages by Year | | |
|---|---|---|---|
| | 2004 | 2005 | 2006 |
| **Age** | | | |
| 0–20 | 5 (29.4%) | 2 (9.5%) | 9 (18.8%) |
| 21–30 | 5 (29.4%) | 7 (33.3%) | 16 (33.3%) |
| 31–40 | 3 (17.6%) | 5 (23.8%) | 8 (16.7%) |
| 41–50 | 2 (11.8%) | 3 (14.3%) | 7 (14.6%) |
| 51–60 | 0 | 2 (9.5%) | 6 (12.5%) |
| 61–70 | 1 (5.9%) | 2 (9.5%) | 1 (2.1%) |
| 71 and Over | 1 (5.9%) | 0 | 1 (2.1%) |
| **Total** | **17** | **21** | **46** |
| **Race** | | | |
| White | 6 (35.3%) | 5 (22.7%) | 14 (28.6%) |
| Black | 11 (64.7%) | 17 (77.3%) | 30 (61.7%) |
| Hispanic | 0 | 0 | 5 (10.2%) |
| **Total** | **17** | **22** | **49** |
| **Gender** | | | |
| Men | 13 (76.5%) | 18 (81.8%) | 41 (83.7%) |
| Women | 4 (23.5%) | 4 (18.2%) | 8 (16.3%) |
| **Total** | **17** | **22** | **49** |

**Table 4.6 Homicide Weapon, Motive, and Disposition, Orlando, Florida, 2004–2006**

| Characteristic | Counts and Percentages by Year | | |
|---|---|---|---|
| | 2004 | 2005 | 2006 |
| **Weapon** | | | |
| Firearm | 13 (76.5%) | 13 (61.9%) | 36 (73.5%) |
| Knife/Cutting Instrument | 2 (11.8%) | 3 (14.3%) | 6 (12.2%) |
| Personal/Unarmed | 1 (5.9%) | 2 (9.5%) | 3 (6.1%) |
| Vehicle | 1 (5.9%) | 0 | 3 (6.1%) |
| Blunt Object | 0 | 3 (14.3%) | 1 (2.0%) |
| **Total** | **17** | **21** | **49** |
| **Motive** | | | |
| Robbery | 5 (29.4%) | 4 (19.0%) | 22 (48.9%) |
| Drug-Related | 0 | 0 | 3 (6.7%) |
| Sexual Assault | 0 | 0 | 0 |
| Domestic | 5 (29.4%) | 3 (14.3%) | 4 (8.9%) |
| Argument | 0 | 0 | 13 (28.9%) |
| Retaliation | 0 | 1 (4.8%) | 1 (2.2%) |
| Child Abuse | 0 | 0 | 1 (2.2%) |
| Murder/Suicide | 1 (5.9%) | 0 | 0 |
| Other | 6 (35.3%) | 13 (61.9%) | 1 (2.2%) |
| **Total** | **17** | **21** | **45** |
| **Disposition** | | | |
| Cleared by Arrest | 10 (58.8%) | 9 (40.9%) | 31 (63.3%) |
| Justified | 2 (11.8%) | 0 | 0 |
| Cleared by Exception | 1 (5.9%) | 0 | 2 (4.1%) |
| Not Cleared | 4 (23.5%) | 13 (59.1%) | 16 (32.7%) |
| **Total** | **17** | **22** | **49** |

2005 should be viewed with caution because of the large percentages reported as Other Motive.

Clearances by arrest or exception for homicides during 2004 through 2006 (Table 4.6) ranged from a low of 40.9% in 2005 to 64.7% in 2004 and 67.4% in 2006. Nationally, 62.6% of all homicides were cleared by arrest or exception in 2004; 62.1% in 2005; and 60.7% in 2006 (Federal Bureau of Investigation [FBI], 2004, 2005, and 2006). Thus, Orlando increased its clearance rates, but room for further improvement remains.

## Orange County Gang Activity

To gain insight about how gang activity may be related to violent crime in Orange County, we obtained data about the total number of people who had been booked into the Orange County jail for a gang-related violent crime by either the Orange County Sheriff's Office or the Orlando Police Department (Table 4.7).

Then, from that total we separated out those who were identified as gang members.

Among those, who were booked for a violent crime between January 1, 2004, and December 31, 2006, a total of 51 different gangs were identified. And, similar to the rising count of violent crimes, the number of gang members booked for violent crime rose from 22 in 2004 to 43 in 2005, and 75 in 2006. Latin Kings members were the most likely to be booked with 16 bookings during 2006. Following at a distant second were the Netãs with 10 members booked during 2006.

## Demographics for Gang Members Booked for Violent Crimes

Findings shown in Table 4.7 (above) provide the age, race, and gender of persons booked for violent crimes during 2004 through 2006, who were identified as gang members. Compared to the previous year, the average age ranges from 26.4 to 28.5 years, which is not a major difference; however, in 2006 the lower end of the age range dropped by 5 years and the upper limit was 10 years younger than it was in 2005. This downward trend means that younger gang members were becoming involved in violent crime.

The race of gang members is surprisingly consistent. The percentages of Black gang members booked for violent crime ranges from 36.4% to 39.5%, while the percentages

**Table 4.7 Age, Race, and Gender of Gang Members Booked for Violent Crimes, Orlando and Orange County, Florida, 2004–2006**

| Counts and Percentages of Gang-Related Booking Demographics | | | | | | |
|---|---|---|---|---|---|---|
| Year | Age Range and Average | Race | | Gender | | Total Individuals |
| | | Black | White | Women | Men | |
| 2004 | 21–40 (28.5) | 8 (36.4%) | 14 (63.6%) | 0 (0%) | 22 (100%) | 22 (100%) |
| 2005 | 20–52 (26.9) | 17 (39.5%) | 26 (60.5%) | 2 (4.7%) | 41 (95.3%) | 43 (100%) |
| 2006 | 15–42 (26.4) | 28 (37.3%) | 47 (62.7%) | 2 (2.7%) | 73 (97.3%) | 75 (100%) |

for Whites ranges from 60.5% to 63.6%. Thus, for each year "Whites outnumber Blacks, although the surnames of the inmates and their gang affiliations indicate that a high proportion of White gang members are Hispanics" by ethnicity (Corzine et al., 2007b, p. 5). As we would predict, given past research on gang activity (e.g., Miller, 2001), over 95% of the gang members in Orange County, who are booked for violent offenses, are men.

## Violent Crimes for which Gang Members Are Booked

During the three years studied, gang members were more often booked for homicide and robbery than for aggravated or sexual assault. Thus, most violent crimes in Orange County are not officially gang-related (see Table 4.8).

However, the statistics in Table 4.8 indicate that gang members were not responsible for a significant amount of violent crime in Orange County. The largest percentage of violent crime that gangs were booked for was for homicide in 2005, but even that was held to just over 6% (6.2%) of the total. Thus, our work indicates that the community needs to look elsewhere for the majority of the homicide and robbery offenders.

## A Curfew: Are You Kidding?

The comparison of adult and juvenile robbery suspects (see Table 4.9) shows that there was a consistent increase in juvenile suspects from 2004 through 2006. However, caution must be used when reading too much into statistics such as these. Of the robbery suspects ages 60.1% were unknown in 2004, 56.5% in 2005, and 61.3% in 2006 (Huff-Corzine et al., 2007).

Results in Table 4.9 indicate that 8% or fewer of the homicides are committed by juveniles. Compared to adults, juveniles were suspected of killing 41 fewer of the 50 total homicide victims in 2004; 43 fewer of the 50 homicides in 2005; and 69 fewer of the 76 homicide victims in 2006. Of course, the victims killed by juveniles are just as important to the community and their families as those killed by adults. The issue here is that juveniles as a whole do not need the finger pointed at their age group. They do not commit the majority of the homicides; instead, juveniles consistently commit less than 10% of the Orlando and Orange County homicides.

**Table 4.8 Total Bookings of Gang Members for Violent Crimes, Orange County, Florida, 2004–2006**

| Counts of Gang-Related Bookings and Percentages of Specific Crime During the Year in Question | | | | | |
|---|---|---|---|---|---|
| Year | Murder | Robbery | Sexual Assault | Aggravated Assault | Total Individuals |
| 2004 | 6 (4%) | 40 (2%) | 0 | 46 (0.5%) | 22 (0.3%) |
| 2005 | 14 (6.2%) | 74 (4%) | 2 (0.5%) | 86 (1%) | 43 (0.6%) |
| 2006 | 12 (4.5%) | 85 (4.2%) | 2 (0.5%) | 89 (1%) | 75 (1.1%) |

**Table 4.9 Counts and Percentages of Juvenile and Adult Suspects in Homicide, Robbery, Sexual Assault, and Aggravated Assault in Orlando and Orange County, Florida, 2004–2006**

| Offense | Counts and Percentages by Year | | |
|---|---|---|---|
| | 2004 | 2005 | 2006 |
| *Homicide* | | | |
| Adult Suspect | 45 (90%) | 45 (90%) | 76 (87.4%) |
| **Juvenile Suspect** | **4 (8%)** | **2 (4%)** | **7 (8%)** |
| Age Unknown | 1 (2%) | 3 (6%) | 4 (4.6%) |
| **Total** | **50** | **50** | **87** |
| *Robbery* | | | |
| Adult Suspect | 538 (33.8%) | 923 (35.9%) | 994 (30.1%) |
| **Juvenile Suspect** | **97 (6.1%)** | **194 (7.6%)** | **286 (8.7%)** |
| Age Unknown | 956 (60.1%) | 1452 (56.5%) | 2026 (61.3%) |
| **Total** | **1591** | **2569** | **3306** |
| *Sexual Assault* | | | |
| Adult Suspect | 357 (59.4%) | 557 (65.8%) | 589 (62.7%) |
| **Juvenile Suspect** | **102 (17%)** | **116 (13.7%)** | **103 (11%)** |
| Age Unknown | 142 (23.6%) | 173 (20.4%) | 248 (26.4%) |
| **Total** | **601** | **846** | **940** |
| *Aggravated Assault* | | | |
| Adult Suspect | 1274 (58.5%) | 1884 (72.2%) | 1509 (54.4%) |
| **Juvenile Suspect** | **206 (9.5%)** | **238 (9.1%)** | **262 (9.4%)** |
| Age Unknown | 696 (32%) | 487 (18.7%) | 1002 (36.1%) |
| **Total** | **2176** | **2609** | **2773** |

Juvenile suspects show the highest percentages for sexual assault, though none greater than 17%. Even aggravated assault is committed by juveniles less than 10% of the time. In brief, violent crime is committed approximately nine times more often by adults than by juveniles (Huff-Corzine et al., 2007).

## Juvenile and Adult Victim Characteristics

Victims of violent crime in Orlando and Orange County, similar to juveniles and adults involved in violence as suspects, are much more likely to be adults than juveniles (see Table 4.10). The one violent crime that juveniles experience at percentages similar to adults is sexual assault (Huff-Corzine et al., 2007).

In 2004, 50.6% of the sexual assault victims were juveniles, a statistic that increased to 53.4% in 2005, but decreased to 47.6% in 2006. Since the total number of sexual assaults increased each year, the count jumped by nearly 100 cases between 2004 and 2005, and then dropped by 3 cases in 2006.

## Juvenile Suspects Involved in Robbery by Time of Day

Our analysis of the four types of violent crime; homicides, robbery, sexual assault, and aggravated assault, illustrate that robbery is the only one that shows an increase. Between

**Table 4.10 Counts and Percentages of Juvenile and Adult Victims in Homicide, Robbery, Sexual Assault, and Aggravated Assault in Orlando and Orange County, Florida, 2004–2006**

| Offense | Counts and Percentages by Year | | |
|---|---|---|---|
| | 2004 | 2005 | 2006 |
| *Homicide* | | | |
| Adult Victims | 47 (85.5%) | 53 (88.3%) | 109 (93.2%) |
| **Juvenile Victims Suspect** | **7 (12.7%)** | **5 (8.3%)** | **7 (6%)** |
| Age Unknown | 1 (1.8%) | 2 (3.3%) | 1 (0.9%) |
| **Total** | **55** | **60** | **117** |
| *Robbery* | | | |
| Adult Victims | 1542 (76.4%) | 2153 (80.2%) | 2849 (82.8%) |
| **Juvenile Victims** | **1221 (6%)** | **159 (5.9%)** | **222 (6.5%)** |
| Age Unknown | 355 (17.6%) | 371 (13.8%) | 369 (10.7%) |
| **Total** | **2018** | **2683** | **3440** |
| *Sexual Assault* | | | |
| Adult Victims | 325 (46.4%) | 381 (45.1%) | 484 (51.4%) |
| **Juvenile Victims** | **354 (50.6%)** | **451 (53.4%)** | **448 (47.6%)** |
| Age Unknown | 21 (3%) | 12 (1.4%) | 10 (1.1%) |
| **Total** | **601** | **846** | **940** |
| *Aggravated Assault* | | | |
| Adult Victims | 1900 (86.7%) | 2353 (89.5%) | 2361 (84.5%) |
| **Juvenile Victims** | **231 (10.5%)** | **213 (8.1%)** | **338 (12.1%)** |
| Age Unknown | 61 (2.8%) | 62 (2.4%) | 96 (3.4%) |
| **Total** | **2192** | **2628** | **2795** |

2004 and 2006, the number of juvenile robbery suspects grew from 97 to 286. Still, the number of cases for which the age was unknown makes it questionable to rely on these counts. Maybe more young robbers were caught causing the count to rise without any more actual robberies being committed by juveniles.

Nevertheless, it was suggested that the increase in violent crime between 2004 and 2006 resulted from an increase in serious juvenile crime. The final table provides data to assist leaders decide whether a curfew for juveniles would help reduce the robberies in Orlando and Orange County (Huff-Corzine et al., 2007). Our recommendation was that it would not reduce crime, and with that finding the Orange County Commission and the Orlando City Council stopped their efforts to pass a juvenile curfew.

Specifically, as shown in Table 4.11, juveniles tend to commit more violent crimes between 4 p.m. and 10 p.m. than during any other six-hour time period studied.

**Table 4.11 Counts and Percentages of Juvenile Suspects Involved in Robbery in Orlando and Orange County, Florida, by Six-Hour Time Periods, 2004–2006**

| Year | 10:01 a.m.–4:00 p.m. | 4:01 p.m.–10:00 p.m. | 10:00 p.m.–4:00 a.m. | 4:01 a.m.–10:00 a.m. | Total |
|---|---|---|---|---|---|
| 2004 | 26 (26.8%) | 39 (40.2%) | 24 (24.7%) | 16 (8.2%) | 97 |
| 2005 | 41 (21.1%) | 85 (43.8%) | 52 (26.8%) | 92 (32.2%) | 194 |
| 2006 | 58 (20.3%) | 117 (40.9%) | 92 (32.2%) | 19 (6.6%) | 286 |

Logically, a curfew for juveniles soon after school until 10 p.m. does not make sense. This is the time when after school activities, e.g., sports, scouts, etc. are scheduled, and a curfew would hurt the majority in a vain attempt to control the few trouble makers. Thus, our recommendation was to rule out the idea of a curfew unless it was imposed for a more reasonable time, e.g., 9 p.m. to 4 a.m., which would include part of the time with the highest count of robberies by juveniles (Huff-Corzine et al. 2007).

## Summary

In summary, please note the reasons the community leaders became active in trying to understand and prevent violent crime included:

1. They have a real moral interest in neighborhood safety. Doing their jobs well is a high priority.
2. We live with Mickey and Minnie Mouse, Donald Duck, Pluto, the Chipmunks, and a whole host of Princesses that we must protect because tourism is our bread and butter. Unless we keep the various theme parks safe, we hurt our economy.

Knowing this, it is understandable that not only did law enforcement and academics team up to search for an answer to the rising violent crime rate in Orlando and Orange County, but it was spearheaded by politicians, the Orlando Mayor being the first to react. Notice too, however, that the Task Force examined Orange County as a whole, and although the Orange County Public Safety Officer, Jerry Demings, was on the Task Force for Orlando, when it came time to visit neighborhoods, the wording there too was Orlando Public Safety Information sessions.

Once the Task Force had nearly completed its work, the Orange County Public Safety Officer could see that Orlando statistics were buried in the larger numbers for Orange County, that actually envelopes Orlando and several other communities. Thus, Mr. Demings asked that we complete a study that separated the statistics so that the areas where violence were most prevalent could be better identified and focused on by the appropriate law enforcement agency – OPD or the Orange County Sheriff's Office (OCSO).

The final presentation we made about our findings and recommendations based on those results was to the Orange County Commissioners, another level of political organization (Corzine et al., 2007a). Formulated around the community's social institutions and guided by sociological theory we offered the following policy recommendations, which are presented in no particular order:

1. Assign more law enforcement officers to serve in community-oriented, targeted, proactive capacities.
2. Overhaul the Juvenile Justice System to bring the consequences in line with the offenses and adopt measures to get firearms out of the hands of juveniles.
3. A curfew is not recommended for reasons noted above, as well as because enforcement is problematic and it has not proven effective in other cities.

4. Schools need to expand the numbers and types of activities after school and on weekends, e.g., music, dance, art, sports, and add or re-establish vocational training.
5. Encourage families in need to seek support from schools and churches and increase the availability of family life courses.
6. Churches should organize activities after school and on weekends, like schools, and they need to work closely with law enforcement and other community groups.
7. Economy – plan work assignments for low income teens, perhaps on community renewal.

We completed the presentation by saying that "Youth Programs are Crime Prevention Programs." The results were well received. In fact, the Public Safety Officer ran for and won his bid for Orange County Sheriff using several of our policy recommendations as his platform. And, the community has kept him in office for a second term. The Mayor too, continues to be very popular and won his more recent bid for another term for which his TV commercials could have come directly out of our findings. Basically, in one he is shown working with elementary school children in after school tutoring programs and in another he is reading to a group of preschoolers.

What this study indicates is that, in some communities, having a top down approach, but one that includes community members, and keeps citizens informed has a greater chance of success than either trying to start a grass roots change movement or having new programs put into place by leaders without community input. In our example, political leaders, law enforcement for the city and the county, academics, and people from all walks of life united to produce change, and it worked.

The development of the research collaboration described above has been maintained with additional projects completed in subsequent years. Along with a doctoral student in the Department of Sociology, the authors completed a study of non-lethal assaults on law enforcement officers for the OPD. For the same agency, a mapping study of the overlap between gang members' home addresses and "hot spots" for burglary and automobile theft was completed. The authors and other Sociology faculty have also been involved as consultants and research partners, sometimes including a Memorandum of Understanding, with other Central Florida law enforcement agencies as well, specifically the Seminole and Brevard County Sheriffs' Offices. Thus, Central Florida area law enforcement and academics have established working relationships to study and respond to and help prevent crime in our own cities and neighborhoods.

## Appendix 4.1: Safe Orlando Task Force Members

### Chair

Dr. Stanley H. Stone
Valencia Community College

**Members**

Ms. Margaret Anglin
Business Owner

Reverend Willie Barnes
Macedonia Missionary Baptist Church

Ms. Ann Brown Payne
Minority & Women's Business Alliance

Mr. Greg Clendenin
Business Owner

Mr. Jerry Demings
Director of Public Safety

Orange County Government
Mr. David Glicken

Lawyer
Father Miguel Gonzalez

Orlando Diocese
Ms. Brandy Hand

Lawyer
Director, Association of Junior Leagues International

Reverend Charles Jackson
Hurst Chapel A.M.E. Church

Reverend Randall James
The First Orlando Foundation

Mr. Douglas A. Kelly
Corporate Counsel

Marriott Law Department
Ms. Sarah Kelly

Business Owner
Mr. Kelly S. Klatt, CPP

Director of Safety & Security
Loews Hotels at Universal

Dr. Percy Luney
Lawyer

Mr. Myron Marshal
Business Owner

Dr. Lance McCarthy
Metropolitan Orlando Urban League

Ms. Beverlye Neal
Florida State Conference NAACP

Mr. Ramon Ojeda
Hispanic Chamber of Commerce

Mr. James Orr
Asst. Director, Amateur Scouting
at Detroit Tigers Orlando location

The Honorable Belvin Perry, Jr.
Orange County Judge

Mr. Bob Pickerill
Business Owner

Mr. Ronald O. Rogers
Business Owner

Mr. Randy Tuten
Orlando Public Safety

Ms. Annetta Wilson
Media Training Business Owner

Ms. Martha Wright
Jones High School

Mr. Dean Luis Zayas
Ana G. Mendez University System

## Appendix 4.2: Mayor's Safe Orlando Task Force Recommendations

### Law Enforcement Sub-Committee

#### *Short-Term Recommendations (up to 1 Year)*

1. Form Patrol Tactical (TAC) Squads
2. Establish Serious Habitual Offender Comprehensive Action Program (SHO-CAP) Assistance
3. "Citizens United for Safe Neighborhoods" Initiative

#### *Intermediate Recommendations (1–3 Years)*

1. Gun Bounty Program
2. Recruitment and Incentives for Employment with Police
3. Re-establish Community Policing (COP) Initiatives
4. Re-district Patrol Divisions to redistribute "first responder" workload for increased proactive activities – to include COP activities

### *Long-Term Recommendations (up to 5 Years)*

1. Downtown/Central Patrol Initiatives
2. Increase Staffing for Drug Enforcement
3. Consider Impact Fees for Police Services (especially in areas with rapid growth)

## Prevention Subcommittee

### *Short-Term Recommendations and Top Priorities*

1. Implement a community-wide mass media marketing campaign
2. Encourage business and community partnerships to address crime prevention and barriers of economic poverty
3. Insure the availability of adult-supervised after school activities for all elementary, middle, and high school students
4. Increase focus on the impact of faith-based organizations and job partnerships
5. Implement successful in-school suspension programs
6. Establish educational scholarship programs for high-risk students

### *Intermediate Recommendations (1–3 Years)*

1. Establish more incentive-based youth and adult literacy programs
2. Support families of school-aged children
3. Provide more effective life management skills classes for at-risk youth in schools and in the community
4. Expand the Orlando Police Department Super Kids and Gang Resistance Education and Training (GREAT) programs
5. Insure that all Orange County Public School children in middle and high schools receive education about domestic violence in dating relationships
6. Re-establish the Orlando Police Department's Gang Prevention program

### *Long-Term Recommendations (3–5 Years)*

1. Establish Teen Advisory Boards in Communities
2. Utilize the Teen Court and other existing diversion programs
3. Expand the Orlando Police Department's community-oriented policing efforts
4. Establish a Crime Prevention Council and Coordinator

## Re-Integration Subcommittee

### *Short-Term Recommendations (up to 1 Year)*

1. Create a Re-Entry Council
2. Open a HELP Center (Helping Ex-offenders Live Productively)
3. Advocate for a Governor's Ex-Offender Task Force

### *Intermediate Recommendations (1–3 Years)*

1. Re-Entry Council and Faith-Based Organizations work together to secure funding to develop transitional housing and related services
2. Re-Entry Council identifies and recommends funding sources to enhance existing local re-entry programs

### *Long-Term Recommendations (3–5 Years)*

1. Re-Entry Council to secure funding and begin operation of mobile mini-HELP Centers
2. Re-Entry Council to secure funding for expansion of services including possible additional HELP Centers

## References

Corzine, J., Huff-Corzine, L., Mustaine, E., Polczynski, C., Bachmann, M., Grantham, M., & Libby, N. (2007a). *Street gangs and violent crime in Orange County, 2004–2006: An analysis of trends in gang-related crime.* Report prepared for the Orange County Attorney's Office.

Corzine, J., Huff-Corzine, L., Mustaine, E., Libby, N., Polczynski, C., Grantham, M., Bachmann, M., & Eson, J. (2007b, October 7). *Violent crime in Orange County.* Presentation to Orange County Commissioners, Orlando, Florida.

Dyer, Mayor B. (2006). Letter to Mayor's Safe Orlando Task Force members.

Einstadter, W. J., & Henry, S. (2006). *Criminological theory: An analysis of its underlying assumptions* (2nd ed.). Lanham, MD: Rowman & Littlefield.

Federal Bureau of Investigation. (2004). Uniform Crime Report. *Crime in the United States, 2004.* "Offenses Cleared." U.S. Department of Justice.

Federal Bureau of Investigation. (2005). Uniform Crime Report. *Crime in the United States, 2005.* "Clearances." U.S. Department of Justice.

Federal Bureau of Investigation. (2006). Uniform Crime Report. *Crime in the United States, 2006.* "Clearances." U.S. Department of Justice.

Goltz, Captain J. W. (2006). Introduction to the Mayor's Safe Orlando Task Force members.

Guillaume, P., Sidebottom, A., & Tilley, N. (2012). On police and university collaborations: A problem-oriented case study. *Police Practice and Research, 13,* 389–401.

Huff-Corzine, L., Mustaine, E., Corzine, J., Grantham, M., Libby, N., Bachmann, M., & Polczynski, C. (2007). *Violent juvenile crime in Orange County: Is there a need for a curfew?* Report prepared for the Orange County Attorney's Office.

Marks, M. (2009). Dancing with the devil: Participatory action research with police in South Africa. *South African Crime Quarterly, 30,* 27–34.

Miller, J. (2001). *One of the guys: Girls, gangs, and gender.* New York: Oxford University Press.

Moskos, P. (2008). *Cop in the hood: My year policing Baltimore's eastern district.* Princeton, NJ: Princeton University Press.

Nyden, P., & and Wiewel, W. (1992). Collaborative research: Harnessing the tensions between the researcher and practitioner. *The American Sociologist, 23,* 43–55.

Orlando Sentinel. (2006). Mayor to form task force to find ways to curb crime. *Orlando Sentinel.* Retrieved from http://articles.orlandosentinel.com.

Santos, R. B. (2014). The effectiveness of crime analysis for crime reduction: Cure or diagnosis? *Journal of Contemporary Criminal Justice, 30,* 147–168.

U.S. Census Bureau. (2000). American FactFinder. Profile of General Demographic Characteristics: 2000 Census Summary File 1 (SF-1) 100-Percent Data for Orange County, Florida.

U.S. Census Bureau. (2010). American FactFinder. Profile of General Population and Housing Characteristics: 2010 for Orange County, Florida.

# The B3W Matrix
## Managing a More Effective Way to Tackle Residential Burglary

# 5

PETER VERSTEEGH AND
RENÉ HESSELING

## Contents

## Abstract

By instituting a combination of Intelligence-Led Policing, Problem-Oriented Policing and Community Policing – The Best of Three Worlds – The Hague Police Service wants to enhance the effectiveness of the approach to crime and insecurity. The authors studied how residential burglaries are dealt with in the 31 police teams of The Hague Police Service with respect to this combined strategy. On the basis of a B3W-scale and a three-dimensional B3W-matrix the quality of the approach is evaluated and visualised. An important question is whether the way of implementing the B3W approach is associated with the development in the number of residential burglaries in the 31 teams. Finally, some possibilities to strengthen the current approach to residential burglaries on the basis of the research results are discussed.

## Introduction

A review of recent scientific publications from the Netherlands and other countries has provided the police in the Netherlands with three safety strategies which, after thorough study, have proven to be effective: Problem-Oriented Policing, Community-Oriented Policing and Intelligence-Led Policing (Versteegh et al., 2013). It was concluded that the success of Problem-Oriented Policing (POP) according to the SARA model (Scanning, Analysis, Response and Assessment) is primarily due to the joint approach of the relevant safety partners to the most crucial safety problems. An appropriate combination of preventive and repressive measures is implemented for each safety problem. Such a problem-oriented approach is based on an in-depth problem analysis in which the role played by the offenders, victims and environmental factors in creating the problem is examined (Newburn, 2008). The effectiveness of Community-Oriented Policing (COP) can especially be ascribed to the great involvement of citizens in safety management, whereby information about the most pressing local problems and the wishes and expectations of neighbourhood residents partly determines local priorities (Home Office, 2007; Skogan, 2006). The positive contribution to safety of Intelligence-Led Policing (ILP) can mainly be attributed to the coordinated efforts of the police based on analysed information and knowledge (intelligence), result-led management by the police force management team (accountability) and enhancement of learning ability (Jones, 2008; Ratcliffe, 2009). Furthermore, several authors state that integration and synchronisation of COP, POP and ILP seems to be a promising strategy (e.g. Baker, 2009; Ratcliffe, 2008; Scott et al., 2008; Tilley, 2008).

Besides combining the elements from the different strategies a recurring research finding is that the approach proves to be most effective if it is focused on the main crime types (hot crimes), locations (hot areas and hot spots), times (hot times), modus operandi, offenders (hot shots and hot groups) and victims (hot and repeat victims) (Versteegh et al., 2013). So we believe that the effectiveness to tackle specific crime problems could be increased by focusing on specific – local – crime problems (e.g. a hot spot of residential burglary or a hot group) and when the success factors of the three safety strategies are implemented in their interrelationship in the organization of the police. In other words, a combined safety strategy based on The Best of Three Worlds (the B3W strategy), while not new, remains an active topic within the police and in the academic world there as the debate continues about which safety strategy works best (Weisburd and Braga, 2006). What is new is the combined implementation of the different elements of POP, ILP and COP.

Since 1 January 2013 there has been one National Police in the Netherlands with ten regional units and one national unit. One of the regional units is The Hague Police Service consisting of seven districts with 29 basic teams (at the moment of the study there were 31 teams). The Hague Police Service adopted The Best of Three Worlds strategy as a fundamental element in its safety policy. The question we pose is whether the basic teams indeed implemented the B3W strategy to tackle crime problems, more specifically with respect to residential burglaries. We have chosen residential burglaries because taking action against residential burglaries is a national and almost always a local priority of the police in the Netherlands. Therefore, we studied how residential burglaries are dealt with in the service area of The Hague Police Service, and evaluated the approach in the basic teams against the B3W strategy: is the approach using a combination of problem-oriented policing, intelligence-led policing and based on an active involvement of citizens effective?

Next, we wanted to know whether there was a connection between the B3W approach started in 2012 and the development in residential burglaries in the first nine months of 2013. Finally, we dealt with some possibilities to strengthen the current approach to residential burglaries on the basis of the research results.

## Method

In the first months of 2013, one or more practical experts from all 31 police teams (division as in 2012) filled out a largely standardised questionnaire per police team with a total of 15 questions. In line with the safety strategy of The Hague Police Service, we measured the extent to which there was focus on specific local problems with residential burglaries (e.g. a hot spot or repeat victimisation), a problem analysis based on Clarke and Eck's (2003) triangle problem analysis, and an appropriate combination of victim-focused, place- or location-focused and offender-focused measures in the approach to residential burglaries (Clarke and Eck, 2003; Wortley and Mazerolle, 2008). We also studied whether different safety (information) products – especially crime scans, problem analyses, action plans and evaluations – played a role in the internal and external management of the approach to tackle residential burglaries. In the Netherlands, the mayor and the chief public prosecutor make local agreements about the police deployment. The question was also asked about cooperation, if any, with safety partners, the directive role of the municipality and the (active) involvement of neighbourhood residents. Each municipality draws up a public safety and security plan, which serves as a basis for the mayor's management of the police. Finally, the police experts were asked about the success and failure factors. The answers were processed and analysed with the aid of SPSS and Excel.

In addition to the survey we also used geocoded residential burglary figures. Because of the reorganisation of the police in the Netherlands we used for the year 2009 the police statistics obtained from the Central Bureau of Statistics Netherlands (CBS). Since the year 2010 we had the burglary figures available from the National Law Enforcement Database (BVH). The contribution of the combined B3W approach in 2012 on the development of residential burglaries and their continuing effect in 2013, were studied by examining the number of residential burglaries for the basic teams and districts in the first nine months of 2013 and comparing it with the same period in 2012.

## The B3W Matrix

In order to determine the quality of the approach, we developed a B3W scale based on the answers to the following questions. A maximum of 10 points can be earned on the B3W scale. These are divided as follows:

## The B3W Scale (Max. 10 Points)

### Problem-Oriented Policing (1–5 Points)

1. Problem analysis (hot spot, hot group and/or hot shots)
2. Action Plan
3. Cooperation with partners (more than the municipality and Public Prosecution Service)
4. Focus and differentiation in the measures (e.g. hot spot surveillance, focused police operations at hot spots in case of mobile banditry, improvement of hinges and locks, or individual offender focused measures)
5. Evaluation of the approach (process and/or effect)

### Intelligence-Led Policing (1–3 Points)

6. Internal discussion of relevant problem analyses (police team)
7. External discussion of relevant problem analyses (local authority over the police/safety consultations)
8. External discussion of the action plan (local authority over the police/safety consultations)

### Community-Led Policing (1–2 Points)

9. Advice on prevention and increasing willingness to report
10. Active involvement of citizens in hot spots (e.g. Neighbourhood Prevention Team, use of volunteers, neighbourhood management)

On the one hand, in this way, for each police team, but also for each district or the region as a whole, the quality of the approach can be scored on a scale from 1 to 10. On the other hand, the B3W scale can be used to check per geographic area whether the quality of the combined approach is associated with the development in the number of residential burglaries.

The three parts of the B3W scale can be represented separately and visually in a three-dimensional B3W matrix. We did so in order to see what possibilities there are for improvement. This enables police teams to see which aspects of the safety strategy need improvement. The teams can also be more easily compared so they can learn from one another. The effect of the B3W matrix will be explained in more detail in the discussion of the results at the end of this chapter.

## Self-Evaluation

Our study cannot be considered as a scientific evaluation study to test whether the combination of safety strategies employed is an 'evidence based' method that works. Deeper and longer-term evaluation research is needed for this, which, for that matter, has been conducted per strategy by many others in the Netherlands and other countries (Onrust and Voorham, 2013; Versteegh et al., 2013; Weisburd and Braga, 2006). We studied the main features of the measures taken by each police basic team to prevent and combat residential burglaries and the extent to which an approach that is more in line with the combined B3W safety strategy is also associated with a reduction in residential burglaries. In that sense, this study can be considered a self-evaluation for the purpose of providing reference points to improve the combined approach.

## Findings

### B3W in Practice

Before dealing with the possible connection between the approach and the development in the number of residential burglaries at police team level, we will describe the different elements of this approach on the basis of the B3W dimensions.

### Problem-Oriented Policing (POP)

All police teams (100 per cent) have stated that taking action against residential burglaries had priority in their service area in 2012. To test whether a problem-oriented approach was used, we will go through the elements of the SARA model. In an ideal situation, all elements appear. In other words, we expect just as many crime scans (S), problem analyses (A), responses (action plans) (R) and assessments (A) as there are police teams, of which there were 31 in total in 2012. The police teams have not gone that far in practice. In each next SARA step, the share of completed crime analysis and information products is smaller. Consequently, at present, there is what can be called a 'SARA funnel': we are putting the beginning of the cycle of POP more and more in order, but this does not hold for the next steps. See Figure 5.1.

Scanning: In 2012, 90 per cent of the 31 police teams had a crime scan available, whereby 82 per cent mentioned the tackling of residential burglaries as a point for attention of the competent authority. The assessment once again shows that hot spots of residential burglaries are a widespread and recurring phenomenon: 87 per cent of the police teams state that there is one or more (structural) hot spots of residential burglaries in their own work territory. In 85 per cent, there is a hot group (criminal or nuisance-causing group of juveniles), or there are hot shots (addicted repeat offenders), who are held responsible for this.

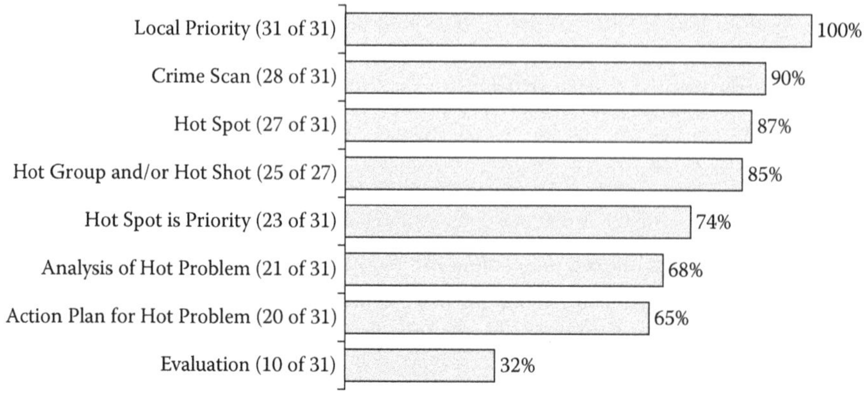


**Figure 5.1** SARA Funnel.

Analysis: An in-depth analysis is an important condition for an effective problem-oriented approach. A problem analysis has been made of two of the three (68 per cent) hot spots, as appears from the answers to the questionnaire. Based on analyses sent in, we have been left with the impression that the set-up, elaboration and quality of these analyses varies considerably in practice.

Response: Once a problem analysis has been made, an action plan almost always follows. This is also an important condition for an effective problem-oriented approach. In 65 per cent of the police teams, there is a written action plan for tackling residential burglaries.

Assessment: Assessment of the approach is not (yet) customary. In only one of the three police teams (32 per cent) was there an explicit assessment of process and effect. It is indeed clear that most police teams follow the development in the number of residential burglaries, particularly on the basis of Early Warning, an instrument used to follow the development in the number of crimes on a weekly basis in light of the medium-long term (past four weeks and as of 1 January), and to identify undesired developments in crime at an early stage. This model was taken over from the New York Police, who have been monitoring crime in this way since the 1990s.

## Intelligence-Led Policing (ILP)

In which management consultations are the main safety intelligence products discussed? We limit ourselves here to discussing the local crime scan, a problem analysis (of a hot spot or hot group) and the action plan. This choice ensues from the idea that the discussion of precisely these products expresses the focus of the action. We make a distinction between discussion within the police team (internal management) and discussion with the competent local authority (external management).

Just as in SARA, there seems to be an 'ILP funnel': in each following stage of management (strategic, tactical and operational), the share of safety and crime analysis products discussed is smaller. See Figure 5.2. In other words, the competent authority still seems to be insufficiently involved – especially in the tactical and operational stage – in managing the joint, problem-oriented approach to residential burglaries. In strategic management, the central question is which safety problem should be tackled with priority; in tactical

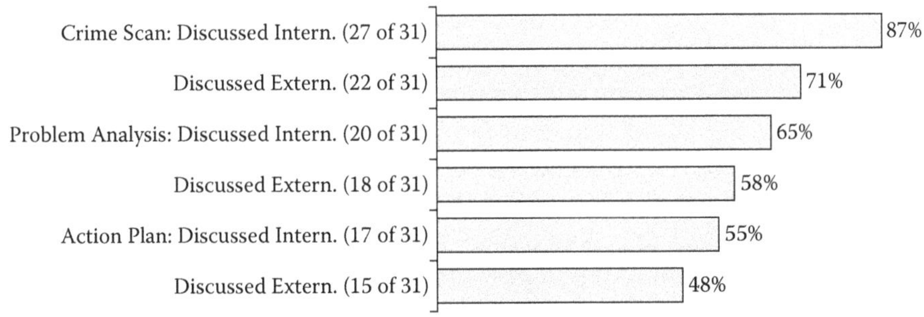


**Figure 5.2** ILP Funnel.

management, the main issue is the way in which the safety problem can be prevented and/or tackled most effectively. Operational management relates to actual implementation of the problem-oriented approach.

A vast majority of the police teams (87 per cent) have used the local crime scan in the police organisation in the strategic management or determination of the points for attention for the problem-oriented approach. A lesser number of teams (71 per cent) – but still a considerable number – have presented the crime scan to the local authority (mayor, public prosecutor and chief of police) or to the Community Safety Partners for discussion in the 34 municipalities in the area of the unit, The Hague. In about two out of three police teams (65 per cent), the problem analysis was discussed internally. It was discussed externally even less often (58 per cent). Approximately half of the police teams discussed an action plan internally (55 per cent) and externally in the consultations with the local authority or The Hague safety consultations (steering group) with the safety partners (48 per cent).

### Community-Oriented Policing (COP)

Many police teams work together with safety partners in tackling residential burglaries. The public administration division of the municipality is, for instance, involved in all cases (100 per cent) and the Public Prosecutor works together with 94 per cent of the teams. Housing corporations often (90 per cent) play a role as well in the approach. Two out of three teams (65 per cent) cooperate with the Community Safety Partners. This is remarkable if we realise that the individual-oriented approach of repeat offenders (hot-shots) is an effective instrument to reduce crime. Community Safety Partners such as the tax department (23 per cent) are still not employed often enough in tackling residential burglaries. Regarding citizen participation: the residents are represented in three out of four of the police teams (77 per cent); more specifically, neighbourhood watch teams are employed in two out of three teams (66 per cent). In about half of the police teams (45 per cent), there is occasional contact with residents in tackling residential burglaries.

## Quality of the Approach

By using the above-mentioned B3W scale, we tested the quality of the approach of each district and police team to residential burglaries in 2012 against the guiding safety strategy of the Police Unit of The Hague: problem-oriented, intelligence-led and with the involvement of citizens. The police teams in The Hague region prove to have obtained an average score of 7.3 on a scale on which a maximum of 10 points can be obtained. That is substantial, but it also shows that improvement is possible. There are in fact considerable differences between the districts. For instance, in District E – with a score of 9.0 – the B3W approach was used to a considerable extent in tackling residential burglaries. In District A, however, as can be seen, the B3W approach was used to a lesser degree in tackling residential burglaries. Within districts, for that matter, there can also be striking differences between the police teams.

## Effects of B3W: An Initial Impression

One of our questions is whether the approach is also linked with fewer residential burglaries? We realise that in the complex and dynamic practice of policing, it is extremely difficult to make statements in (scientific) terms of causality. As stated, nor was that the purpose of our research. First, we looked at the overall development of residential burglary. There was a gradual increase in the number of residential burglaries in The Hague region in the period 2005–2011, by about 35 per cent. There appears to have been a break in the trend in 2012. In that year, for the first time after a long time, the number of residential burglaries decreased slightly by 2 per cent (10,980 burglaries). This decrease continued in 2013 by 15 per cent (9358 burglaries) and in 2014 by 28 per cent (7947 burglaries) compared to 2012.

Second, we examined the effect of B3W by connecting the score of each police team on the B3W scale with the current development in the number of residential burglaries. The number of residential burglaries in the first nine months of 2013 is compared to the number of burglaries in the first nine months of 2012. Figure 5.3 clearly shows that a

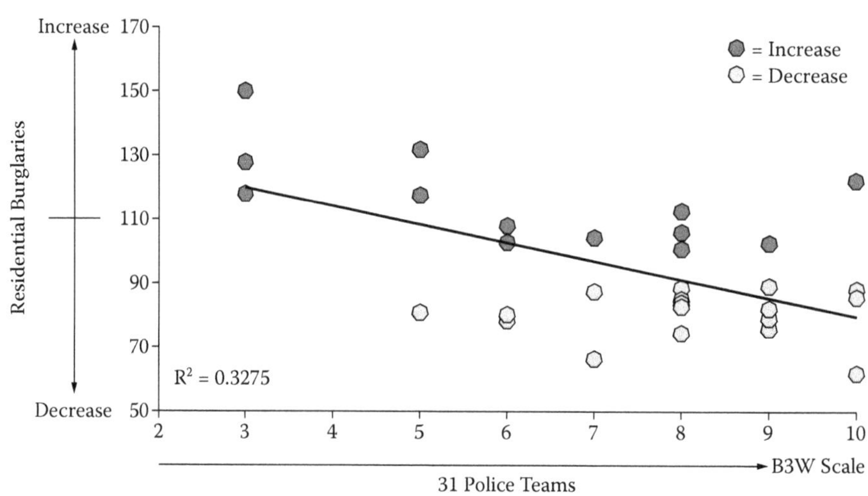


**Figure 5.3** The Hague Police Service in the B3W Matrix, January–September 2013, January–September 2012.

higher score on the B3W scale is generally linked with a greater reduction in the number of residential burglaries. In Figure 5.3, the connection between the B3W score and the development in the number of residential burglaries (Jan–Sep 2013, index: Jan–Sep 2012 = 100), per police team of The Hague Police Service is displayed.

Four police teams even prove to have obtained a 10 on this B3W scale. On paper, their approach really encompasses the 'Best of Three Worlds'. The police team with the greatest decrease in the number of residential burglaries scored an 8 on this B3W scale.

## Success Factors

A combination of the three elements mentioned is therefore indeed more often linked with positive results in reducing residential burglaries. We also asked the team experts involved with residential burglaries to indicate the success factors that played a part in this. We present these success factors in our own words and let the basic teams themselves tell what mattered according to them.

### 1. Focus and Management

This involved management and personnel in actually choosing a joint approach. A long-term focus, a contribution from Regional origin, the Criminal Intelligence Unit (CIE), the Regional Crime and the Traffic Squad was important. As was hot spot surveillance based on good information, the hot spot intervention team (HIT), the involvement of all processes, and the involvement of team members with ideas from the shop floor.

### 2. Information and Analysis

This relied on current information and intelligence position, the analysis of structural and acute hot spots (in connection with possible relocation effects), insight into hot times (capacity management) and weekly insight into nationally and locally operating offenders.

### 3. Cooperation with Partners

Partners also need a focused, active role for the municipality (especially the mayor): a Steering Group and a project group per municipality or police district; an active Public Prosecution Service; housing corporations; important roles for citizens.

### 4. Prevention and Deterrence

Specific (dynamic) control actions include: the use of ANPR (automatic number plate recognition), awareness of citizens, matrix and sidewalk signs, getting in people's good graces, flyers, deployment of the Alert Response Squad (Paraat Peloton), better hinges and locks, Police Residential Security Warranty (PKVW) and using communication channels (for example neighbourhood newspapers) of citizens, by using social media, burglary alerts, treatment of victims and reporting back.

### 5. Ability to Catch Offenders in the Act

Hot spot surveillance, willingness to report, police state of emergency (SPA), problem-oriented neighbourhood investigation, alerting citizens by providing good information, including citizens in forming a picture and monitoring, information evenings on hot spots, BITs (customized services), use of bikers, rewarding successful reporters.

### 6. Specific Tackling of Offenders

A combined individual-oriented and group-oriented (network) approach working with the burglary team in close cooperation with enforcement was vital. Knowing and being known, continued investigation for a higher clearance rate, obtaining confessions by involving parents or brothers in interrogation, using supralocal action against supralocal offenders, and regular Public Prosecutor in group action was valuable as well as early action, retaining forensic examinations of shoe tracks and tool marks, and digital investigation on the internet and ANPR.

### 7. Professionalism of Colleagues

A sense of urgency in target group policy for improving the relationship with the police and especially young Moroccans was important. Motivation, knowledge of the area, innovation orientation, an eye for prevention and other effective safety strategies are also elements that contribute to a successful approach.

## Improvement of the Approach

Finally, an even more important question may well be in what way the tackling of residential burglaries can be improved further. Which aspects of B3W need to be strengthened per basic team to achieve even better results? To answer this question, we use the B3W matrix, on which all police teams were plotted on the basis of the scores on the three 'worlds'. On the X axis, the extent of Problem-Oriented Policing (focus and differentiation) is indicated. On the Y axis, the extent of Community-Oriented Policing (active citizen participation) is plotted, and on the Z axis Intelligence-Led Policing (the extent of management). The worst scoring teams are placed at the front on the lower left side, and the very best at the back of the upper right side. See Figure 5.4.

It can be seen that most police teams where burglaries increase (dark grey) are placed low in the matrix (relatively little active involvement of citizens), a few teams are even at the very bottom at the front of the lower left side. This indicates a very moderate implementation of the B3W safety strategy. The number of residential burglaries here increased by 50 per cent, 28 per cent and 18 per cent, respectively, in the first nine months of 2013 compared to the same period in 2012.

The police teams where burglaries have decreased are clearly placed more to the right, toward the top and at the back. In the territory of these best-scoring police teams, the number of residential burglaries decreased by 38 per cent, 15 per cent and 12 per

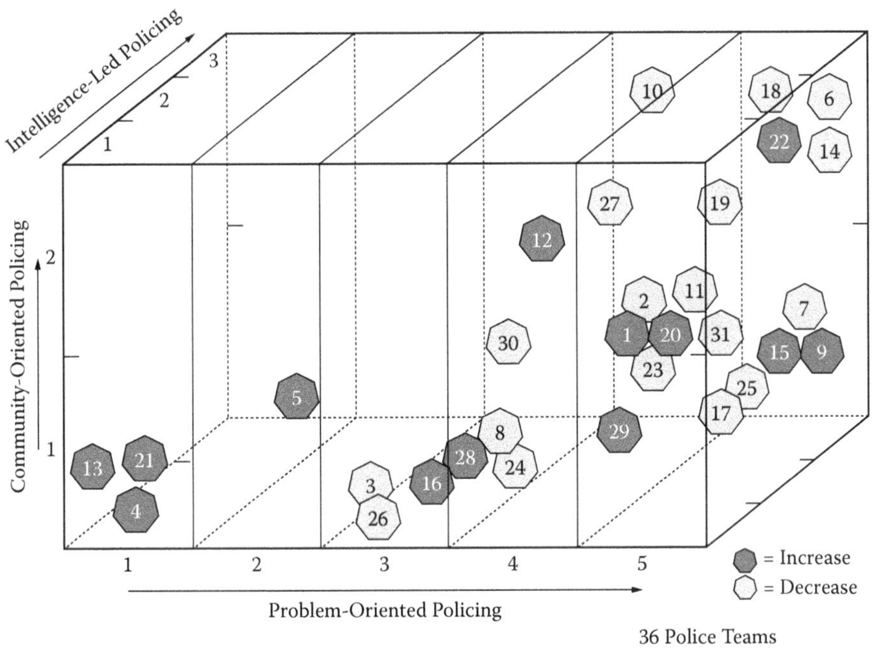


**Figure 5.4** The Hague Police Service in the B3W Matrix, January–September 2013.

cent, respectively. This indicates once again that an approach according to B3W is linked with better results.

By using the B3W matrix, the police teams where improvements are possible can see which better-performing teams they can contact to possibly learn something. Each police team can now see as well the aspect of B3W on which improvements are possible.

## Conclusions

First, the safety strategy of The Hague Police Service gives direction to an effective tackling of residential burglaries. Specifically, this concerns focus on the problem concentrations (hot spots, hot groups and hot shots) and a combination of the three elements: Problem-Oriented, Intelligence-Led and Community-Oriented Policing. The research shows – on the basis of the B3W scale – that the police teams still vary in the way in which they give shape to these three safety strategies. Second, we also see differences in the steps to be taken for optimal implementation of the three elements of the safety strategy. These differences have been called the SARA funnel and the ILP funnel. As a rule, the problem is mentioned as a priority, but it is often not worked out in problem analyses, action plans and evaluations, as well as in discussions of them with the partners in authority for an integrated and lasting approach to the problem. Third, the differences in the approach prove to be connected with the development in the number of residential burglaries in the first nine months of 2013. In the areas of the police teams that give better shape to B3W, the development in the number of residential burglaries is more favourable than the police teams that do so to a lesser degree. In short, it appears that a good application of B3W is better able to reduce the number of residential burglaries. Finally, there are, however, exceptions to this general pattern. Without optimal application of B3W, substantial decreases in the number of residential burglaries are sometimes also possible, while an optimal B3W approach (on paper) can nevertheless be linked with an increase in the number of residential burglaries. In that case, something else is presumably going on. Consequently, the world behind the results of the B3W matrix will always have to be studied in more detail as well in order to learn and improve.

Based on the research we conducted into the tackling of residential burglaries in 2012, we finally arrive at the following recommendations:

1. Each police team should try to end up in the back of the upper right corner of the B3W matrix, or bring the approach to residential burglaries more in line with the B3W safety strategy.
2. In concrete terms, this means that each police team can check which points for improvement or possibilities for Problem-Oriented and Intelligence-Led Policing and active citizen participation exist. In particular, it appears that a specific deployment of active citizens in and around hot spots of residential burglaries can certainly use an impetus in various police teams.
3. Several police teams now appear to have adopted a best practice in relation to tackling residential burglaries. These best practices could be shared more often than is now the case.
4. Discussion of such best practices with the competent authority and other safety partners could perhaps provide the possibility where necessary to give the mayor a leading role in the tactical management of the overall, problem-oriented approach to residential burglaries.
5. How can the support, involvement and professionalism of police officers be increased? How do we deal with safety management and the new alert management concept? How can shape be given in the form of peer support in order to strengthen the approach? What does that mean for 'leadership'? These initiatives could possibly be coordinated – very concretely – better than now is the case, and used in a more effective approach to residential burglaries.
6. A focused combination of SARA, ILP and COP contributes to a successful approach to residential burglaries. Giving shape to it is still customised work. Some police teams are further along in this than others. This also holds for the organisation of information. It does not seem very possible for each police team to have the necessary knowledge of analysis and approach available internally on a regular basis. It may therefore be necessary to set up a support organisation for analysis and management, project-based policing and exchanging best practices.
7. In the past years and based on the concept of Public Management, the Dutch police were primarily steered on the basis of quantitative performance indicators (e.g. counting the number of arrests made). One of the recommendations in 'The Best of Three Worlds' is to use qualitative performance indicators in

addition to the quantitative indicators. The B3W scale is a qualitative performance indicator and can also be used as such. The B3W matrix also appears to be well applicable in qualitative management. When the questionnaire is filled out per police team, the full management team should be involved.

8. In connection with repeated use of the questionnaire, it is advisable to validate the questions and data processing and computerise reports in order to facilitate comparisons.
9. Conducting the research once a year would give a view of the long-term effects of the problem-oriented approach to residential burglaries within the territory of The Hague Police Service.

## References


Baker, T. (2009). *Intelligence-led Policing: Leadership, Strategies & Tactics*, Looseleaf Law Publications, New York.

Clarke, R. V. and Eck, J. E. (2003). *Crime Analyses for Problem Solvers in 60 Small Steps*. COPS, US. (www.popcenter.org).

Home Office (2007). *Cutting Crime: A New Partnership 2008–11*, UK.

Jones, T. (2008). 'The accountability of policing', in: Newburn, T. (ed.) *Handbook of Policing*, Second Edition, Willan Publishing, Devon, UK, pp. 693–724.

Newburn, T. (ed.) (2008). *Handbook of Policing*, Second Edition, Willan Publishing, Devon, UK.

Onrust, S. and Voorham, L. (2013). Vier politiestrategieën tegen veelvoorkomende criminaliteit. Effectiviteit en werkzame mechanismen, Trimbos-instituut Utrecht.

Ratcliffe, J. (2008). *Intelligence-led Policing*, Willan Publishing, Devon, UK.

Ratcliffe, J. H. (ed.) (2009). *Strategic Thinking in Criminal Intelligence*, Second Edition, The Federation Press, Annandale, Australia.

Scott, M., Eck, J., Knutsson, J. and Goldstein, H. (2008). 'Problem-oriented policing and environmental criminology', in: Newburn, T. (ed.) *Handbook of Policing*, Second Edition, Willan Publishing, Devon, UK, pp. 221–242.

Skogan, W. G. (2006). *Police and Community in Chicago: A Tale of Three Cities*, Oxford University Press, Oxford, UK.

Tilly, N. (2008). 'Modern approaches to policing: community, problem-oriented and intelligence-led', in: Newburn, T. (ed.) *Handbook of Policing*, Second Edition, Willan Publishing, Devon, UK, pp. 373–404.

Versteegh, P., Van Der Plas, T. and Nieuwstraten, H. (2013). 'The Best of Three Worlds: more effective policing by a problem-oriented approach of hot crimes, hot spots, hot shots, and hot groups', *Police Practice and Research: An International Journal*, Volume 14, issue 1, pp. 66–81.

Weisburd, D. and Braga, A. (eds) (2006). *Police Innovation: Contrasting Perspectives*, Cambridge University Press, Cambridge, UK.

Wortley, R. and Mazerolle, L. (eds) (2008). *Environmental Criminology and Crime Analysis*, Willan Publishing, Devon, UK.

# II

# Building Resilience and Engaging Communities for Violence and Crime Prevention

# Managing Language Barriers in Policing

# 6

SEDAT MÜLAYIM AND MIRANDA LAI

## Contents



## Abstract

Since the end of the Second World War, economic migration and humanitarian resettlement in many developed countries has led to mass movements of people. Such human movements to date on a global scale have brought social, economic, and political changes to destination countries. One of the significant changes the countries have experienced is increased linguistic diversity and cultural make-up, which manifests in terms of various dynamics among citizens interacting with essential public services in their daily lives. Linguistic diversity can add to the richness of society, but it can also create challenges. One of these challenges is the effective communication in the course of public service provision including policing and crime fighting, and, increasingly, counter-terrorism and counter-extremism efforts.

Government agencies including law enforcement agencies adopt a range of communication methods. However, such methods largely appear to be top-down approaches. Certain perceived or real issues such as the feeling of being harassed or targeted by law enforcement expressed by members of some ethnic communities appear to remain the same despite decades of communication efforts. This study aims to gain insight into the preferences of ethnic communities about communication with public services in Australia, with an objective to add to the current knowledge by way of acquiring bottom-up feedback from members of a wide range of ethnic communities. A survey designed for this purpose was completed by 258 members of diverse ethnic communities with 21 language backgrounds in Melbourne, Australia. The findings are presented and their potential implications are discussed for policymakers and frontline staff. A number of research areas are identified for follow-up studies.

## Introduction

In the aftermath of the Second World War, Western developed nations witnessed a rapid change in the make-up of their communities. This was a result of economic migration and refugee and humanitarian resettlement programmes arising from wars and conflicts in Vietnam, the Middle East, parts of Africa, Asia, and South America (Fierravanti-Wells, 2015; Messina, 2007; Tanton, McCormack, & Smith, 1996). More recent events following the Arab Spring uprisings and the Syrian civil war and the emergence of extremist groups such as the Islamic State (IS) in Syria and Iraq also see the displacement of millions of people, some of whom sought refuge in safer neighbouring countries, and others in Western European countries. These mass movements of people have resulted in major social, economic, and political changes in the destination countries, many of which have traditionally been mono-lingual societies and used to a static cultural and population make-up (e.g. Australia, Germany, Sweden, and Norway).

One of the significant changes in the destination countries is an increased diversity of languages spoken in the community, which has, in turn, created different human dynamics in society and impacted on the level of integration by the new ethnic community members. Increased diversity of languages can add to the richness of a community, but it can also create challenges. One challenge is communication between newly arrived community members with various linguistic and cultural backgrounds and various public services and government agencies, including police forces and other law enforcement agencies. Members of these agencies suddenly find themselves having to deal with language barriers in questioning suspects, interviewing victims of crime, or taking statements from witnesses.

The changing demography, cultural, and linguistic make-up of our society due to people movement, leads to 'the rapidly changing social environment of policing' (Chan, 1997, p. 94). Language barriers have had an impact on proactive initiatives implemented by law enforcement in areas such as crime prevention, fighting radicalisation, and building community resilience. Imam Syed Soharwardy, founder of the Islamic Supreme Council of Canada, cited language barriers as one of the reasons that parents do not turn to authorities if they suspect their child is being radicalised (Ho, 2015). Pickering, Wright-Neville, McCulloch, and Lentini's (2007) three-year study done in Victoria, Australia, on counter-terrorism policing identifies language barriers of culturally and linguistically diverse (CALD) communities to be the most important issue identified by police. A similar study in the United States (Shah, Rahman, & Khashu, 2007) also finds that language often poses a barrier to effective policing. At the same time, Schneider (2007) reports on the Canadian experience on community crime prevention by asserting that

> the most obvious is the language barrier: poor English language skills of many residents and the lack of proficiency in predominant languages other than English among local crime prevention group leaders, CPO [Crime Prevention Office] staff and volunteers, and the police. (p. 101)

Myhill (2006) highlights the significance of community engagement for effective policing and crime prevention. He suggests that participation and engagement in various policing processes and initiatives essentially rely on communication. Communicating between the police and citizens in mono-lingual and mono-cultural societies is by no means trouble-free or straightforward, not to mention the added challenges faced by destination countries where a wide range of languages are spoken by immigrants and humanitarian settlers.

In Australia, the Federal Department of Human Services 2012–2013 annual report reveals the department used interpreters and translators of 230 languages in the provision of their services (Department of Human Services, 2013, p. 138). This indicates the sheer size of the diversity of languages and cultures within Australia, which many Western countries with large immigrant and humanitarian intake programmes are likely to be similar to. Such linguistic and cultural heterogeneity has significant implications for government on how best to achieve effective communication with citizens.

This chapter examines how policing and law enforcement agencies can communicate effectively with non-English-speaking community members in order to maintain law and order as well as protect citizens' safety and security. It explores current methods adopted in communicating with ethnic community members by policing and law enforcement agencies. Furthermore, it reports on a survey conducted in Melbourne, Australia, on community attitudes about their preferred way of communication. The aim of comparing empirical evidence with existing policy is to encourage policymakers to identify more appropriate methods and means of communication with its citizens of multicultural and multilingual backgrounds.

## Significance of Communication

A nation's proactive crime prevention strategies and fostering of community resilience relies on sound community engagement (Myhill, 2006). At the heart of community engagement is effective communication between citizens and law enforcement at all levels from local, force, regional, and national. Similarly, Lane and Henry (2004) contend that communication through community development can build community resilience and assist in crime prevention through building an 'inclusive, yet open and diverse community' (p. 206).

Under recent international political contexts, the Islamic State is seen exerting tremendous influence to radicalise people from other countries. It then attracts them to join it as foreign fighters, and increases violent extremist threats on home soil. Lone wolves seem to lead ordinary lives in domestic contexts. Increased tensions can be observed between ethnic communities and local authorities (Bowling & Philips, 2003). Among a complicated web of factors leading to home-grown radical elements and factors like marginalisation emerge as key reasons behind some local terrorist activities (NATO-OTAN, 2014; Silber & Bhatt, 2007; Zammit, n.d.). Countering marginalisation is proposed in solutions on how to counter extremism and radicalisation, especially in recent attacks and sieges on civilians on home soil perpetrated by people within the community including: the Boston bombing in April 2013, the Sydney Lindt Café siege 10 days before Christmas 2014, and the Charlie Hebdo attack in Paris in January 2015. Attention on extremism and radicalisation among home-grown communities in the West has led to numerous debates by experts, politicians, columnists, and the general public about what causes these problems and how they can be addressed. Overwhelmingly, the root causes of some of the examples cited are misguided youth, misunderstanding of religious doctrines, the lack of dialogue and information between mainstream and marginalised communities, and vulnerable community members getting the wrong message, or being brainwashed. This is then followed by debates and discussion on possible solutions to these root causes, other than the use of direct force. The solutions highlight an urgent need to get the message across, reach out to communities to embrace them, foster understanding and forge constructive dialogue (Carleton, 2014; Commonwealth of Australia, 2015; Tahiri & Grossman, 2014). They all essentially point to a recognition that there are problems with communication and there is a need for more effective communication. Governments and their agencies are in possession of a wide range of communication means and resources. Ironically as things are, extremist groups appear to use similar tools and resources, although on a lesser scale, much more effectively and more nimbly, especially in terms of online media and political and social networks (Roy, 2007). Others recognise that the narratives effectively put forward by violent extremists must be understood so that counter-narratives to combat extremism and promote integration can be developed (Carleton, 2014; Commonwealth of Australia, 2015; Sutherland, 2007).

Governments must keep pace with the needs and preferences of society when it comes to issues pertaining to homeland security. In this light, Grabosky (2009) suggests that 'law enforcement agencies should be able to anticipate what the community's security preferences are' (p. 95). Governments are unable to understand community preference if they do not have bottom-up feedback from the grassroots. In the current international security climate, to manage security needs and expectations is by no means easy, even in a mono-lingual or mono-cultural national context, not to mention the added complexities brought about by linguistic and cultural heterogeneity in countries which receive immigrants of diverse backgrounds. Such diversity is recognised as a challenge for policing in multicultural communities (Ben-Porat, 2008; Larsen, 2010; Victoria Police, 2013; Voyez, 2007). However, if properly nurtured and utilised, diversity can also become the strength of a society that is testament to the common bond of humanity.

## Communicating with Diverse Communities in Australia

Australia has a highly diverse population make-up. The 2011 Census data of Australia shows 1 in 4 people in the population were born overseas and about 1 in 5 speak a language other than English (LOTE) at home. A comparison of LOTE speakers at home over 2001, 2006, and 2011 census data shows an upward trend – 15.2%, 15.8%, and

18.2%, respectively. Settlement data across 5 years from 2008 to 2012 in terms of English proficiency (answers available in the census question: not recorded, nil, poor, good, very good) and migration stream (categories available: family, humanitarian, skilled, other) show that an average of 28% of settlers who arrived under the family stream scheme indicated their English proficiency level as either 'nil' or 'poor'. Those arriving under the humanitarian stream and said their English was either 'nil' or 'poor' was close to 75%. In addition, about 7% of some 659,245 skilled migration settlers who arrived in Australia between 2008 and 2012 under the skilled migration stream, by far the largest group among the migration streams, reported that their English proficiency level was either 'nil' or 'poor'. In summary, Australia's 186,444 new settlers (17%) across all migration streams out of a total of 1,078,920 settlers between 2008 and 2012 reported their English proficiency as 'nil' or 'poor'. As this data is self-reported, it is reasonable to assume that some of those who ticked 'good' to indicate their English proficiency and some of those who are in the 'not recorded' category (a fairly significant proportion of the skilled stream) may have English deficiencies with respect to formal written or spoken discourse. They are therefore likely to encounter difficulty in the course of various activities in their everyday interaction with public services.

Language is not a barrier for newly arrived migrants and refugees only. Australia also has more than 200 Indigenous languages (AIATSIS & FATSIL, 2005) spoken by Aboriginal and Torres Strait Islander Australians. In 2011, there were 548,370 people identified as being of Aboriginal and/or Torres Strait Islander origin who were counted in the Census, and 61,800 (11.3%) stated they spoke Australian indigenous languages at home (ABS, 2011). In addition to these statistics on spoken languages, there is also another group – deaf or hearing impaired people – who may have language barriers when interacting with public services, preventing them from fully participating in society. The number of deaf or hearing impaired people who use Auslan or sign language, vary depending on the source. The 2011 Census has 8,406 people nationwide nominating Auslan as the language they spoke at home. This figure was 5,537 in 2006, an increase of 2,869, or 51.8%. Some estimate, on the other hand, that as much as about 1% of the Australian population may need to use sign language, employing either natural sign or Auslan.

These statistics reflect a high linguistic heterogeneity, including spoken or sign languages, due to migrant, indigenous, and deaf or hearing impaired populations in contemporary Australia. What these figures tell us is that a significant section of the community will continue to have language barriers for decades to come. Therefore, from a police and broader law enforcement perspective, communication with these sections of the community will remain a challenge that merits more research for insights into what has worked and not worked in the past and new methodologies appropriate for the present and into the future.

The sorts of contacts between police and community members with low English proficiency is probably not significantly different from what the police have to deal with in other sections of the community that have no language barrier, although some areas are more common in some language groups than others. For example, the number of women prisoners with Vietnamese background in Victorian prisons is significantly higher than some other ethnic groups that have a larger population in Victoria (Le & Gilding, 2014). According to Chan (1997, p. 99), the most frequent contacts with non-English-speaking background citizens by police relate to:

- domestic violence
- property offence
- drug offences
- traffic violations
- other serious offences against the person.

However, comparing the communication methods with ethnic communities employed by New South Wales Police more than 15 years ago reported by Chan (1997) with the ones outlined by Victoria Police in 2013 (Victoria Police, 2013) reveals very little difference. The methods used by the two police forces, although more than a decade apart, broadly include:

- use of staff who are bilingual to a certain extent, e.g. with formal position titles such as multicultural liaison officers, ethnic liaison officers;
- translated information in community languages;
- recorded information in languages for hotlines;
- use of translators and interpreters in face-to-face or telephone/video-link setups, especially for legal and official matters;
- use of ethnic community leaders.

Both Chan's (1997, pp. 129–150) and Victoria Police's (2013, p. 40) reports mention the following actions undertaken by their respective forces to improve communication with ethnic communities:

1. Recruit ethnically and culturally diverse liaison police officers.
2. Recruit community liaison officers/community leaders.
3. Cultural training.
4. Set up community consultative committees.
5. Run community meetings.

The underpinning methodology for the majority of these approaches (1–3 above) is a top-down approach in the sense they predominantly facilitate a one-way channel for the person designated, be it the liaison police officer or community leader, to be the force's mouthpiece. As a matter of fact, according to Pickering et al. (2007), most Australian state and territory police agencies have dedicated multicultural advisory units that provide services to members of the Culturally and Linguistically Diverse (or CALD in short) communities, and many also have specific multicultural liaison officers. The fact that similar methods used by the two police forces have been unchanged over 15 years, despite calls for better communication with diverse communities unabating (Chan, 1995; Maguire & Wells, 2002; Pickering et al., 2007; Schneider, 2007), in the current national and international security context, points to a need for re-evaluation of police communication strategies. Myhill (2006) asserts that communication in the police-civilian partnership 'must involve two-way dialogue and good quality information and feedback' (p. 4). Kühle and Lindekilde (2010) argue that, in the context of de-radicalisation initiatives, 'the top-driven nature of the policies seems to affect legitimacy in a negative way' and recommend that 'authorities should actively seek input in the policy formulation process' (p. 129), pointing to a need for bottom-up feedback for legitimacy and effectiveness. In a similar vein, Slootman and Tillie (2006) also argue that a bottom-up approach encourages 'ownership' of initiatives by local community members. In the area of communication theory, Samovar, Porter, McDaniel, and Roy (2015) advocate the need to understand the communication party's diverse needs and how such understanding impinges on the success of the communication. They assert that 'the provision of services and products to culturally different persons entail the communication positioning of that service or product in terms that address the reality of the other culture' (Samovar et al., p. 45).

The communication strategies Chan (1997) and Victoria Police (2013) refer to have worked to a certain degree of success. Often in the absence of other options available, they may be the only methods. However, an examination of the issues that the New South Wales police received complaints about back in Chan's study and those issues expressed in Victoria Police Report show high degrees of similarities. Chan (1997) cites claims by community members, especially young people in western Sydney of harassment and the unfair targeting of ethnic groups. Victoria Police's 2013 report on police and community relations also cited identical claims by community members, especially young people in Flemington, inner-west Melbourne.

The issues raised by the police and ethnic communities at different times and in different states are strikingly similar. The only difference appears to be the ethnic community involved – it was the Vietnamese community in western Sydney in 1997, and it was some African communities in certain suburbs of Melbourne in 2013. Although community consultations and focus groups constantly feature in the toolbox of relevant decision makers' communication strategies, it is difficult to ascertain how effective such measures have been able to gauge community attitudes. It warrants further investigation on how much communication issues impact on community members' perception of being harassed or being unfairly targeted.

## A Case Study on Communication Preference

Understanding the preferences of a minority community is recognised as key to the success of policing initiatives (Grabosky, 2009). One of the few studies, albeit small and informal, was conducted by Melbourne's Metropolitan Fire and Emergency Services Board (MFB, 2008). It looked into communication with two particular Burmese ethnic communities, Chin and Karen, in Melbourne, Victoria. The same resource kit on fire awareness for these two ethnic communities was developed and disseminated, and a survey conducted to follow up on the efficacy of the information provided. It was found that there was a lack of understanding of concepts such as 'fire fighting force'. Also lacking was knowledge of using modern appliances which did not exist in these participants' home country where they came from, which is understandable given the vast difference in the levels of development between Australia and Burma. One of the most revealing outcomes of the survey was about the most preferred methods of communication. The participants were asked if they had suggestions for the MFB to improve communication. The study cites the following suggestions made by the participants:

- Conduct information sessions in Burmese, Chin, and Karen languages at churches, and at community groups and association meetings.
- Arrange for groups to visit their local fire station.
- Join with other emergency services to provide comprehensive information sessions on their role and services.
- Hold information sessions regularly to inform new arrivals as soon as possible and advertise that fire fighters are not part of the military.
- Ensure that information sessions are held in locations easily accessed by public transport as many newly arrived people from Burma may not have a driver's licence or access to a car.
- The 000 service should have access to Burmese, Chin, and Karen language interpreters.

The most significant aspect of these responses is the revelation of the participants' preferred methods of communication, pointing clearly to their preference of receiving direct communication. This contradicts the popular assumption that ethnic communities may like indirect communication methods such as using community leaders or elders (method no. 2 in the combined list by Chan (1997, pp. 129–150), and Victoria Police (2013, p. 40)). That essentially assumes ethnic communities live in a formal hierarchal structure in which information is disseminated by these leaders or elders to all members. This is clearly not the case with many ethnic communities.

In the following section, the authors report on a survey conducted in a number of ethnic communities in Melbourne, Australia. The aim of the survey is to corroborate, or otherwise, the findings reported above from the MFB study and to gain an insight into the preferences of ethnic communities about communication with government agencies. The findings of the survey can be added to the pool of existing knowledge to inform policymakers as well as frontline staff in formulating more effective strategies to communicate with ethnic communities and other communities with language barriers in various policing procedures or community building initiatives.

## Research Study

This study uses a paper-based questionnaire containing four questions to ask participants from various ethnic communities about their views on their preferred communication methods employed by public services. The participants all live in Melbourne, Australia, and are from different language backgrounds. In recognition of the different levels of literacy among the ethnic communities, the questionnaire was administered through the assistance of bilingual workers in May 2014.

The questions in the survey are:

- How long you have lived in Australia
- Your language other than English
- What is your level of English (self-assessed)

- How do you want to be communicated with by public services, e.g. social welfare, police, etc.

A total of 258 valid questionnaires were returned. Participants are from 25 different language backgrounds:

- Arabic/Assyrian/Amharic/Dinka/Nuer/Oromo/Somali (71 respondents)
- Chinese/Cantonese/Japanese/Korean (105 respondents)
- Dari/Persian (9 respondents)
- French/Greek/Italian/Spanish/Turkish (30 respondents)
- Hindi/Gujarati/Punjabi/Sinhala (19 respondents)
- Vietnamese/Chin Hakka/Nepali (24 respondents)

## Findings and Discussion

This section presents an analysis of the data collected from the participants. The length of residence in Australia was the first question asked. The authors felt it was important to capture such information from the respondents, because newcomers are reasonably expected to experience the initial linguistic and cultural challenges in a new country for their day-to-day existence, whereas those more established members of the ethnic communities, although they may have managed manoeuvring their way around the immediate community they lived in, would have accumulated more experience in dealing with various government agencies including police and other law enforcement agencies. In other words, although communication needs faced by migrants of various linguistic and cultural backgrounds in society may vary as time goes by, the challenges exist for different reasons.

The figures in Table 6.1 below show a balanced distribution of participants with 53% under 10 years in Australia, of whom 32% are newcomers between 1–5 years in Australia. The more established community members made up 47% of the respondents with over 10 years in Australia.

As discussed earlier, Australia continues to be a net migration country that receives significant numbers of new settlers through migration programmes as well as refugee and humanitarian settlement each year. A large section of these newcomers report, at or before arrival, that their English proficiency levels are either nil or poor. This study, therefore, sought to ask respondents who have all had a period of residency in Australia

**Table 6.1 How Long Have You Lived in Australia?**

| # | Answer | Response | % |
|---|---|---|---|
| 1 | 1–5 years | 83 | 32 |
| 2 | 6–10 years | 54 | 21 |
| 3 | 11–15 years | 37 | 14 |
| 4 | More than 15 years | 84 | 33 |
| | **Total** | **258** | **100** |

to respond to a similar question in assessing their own level of English. The figures in Table 6.2 show that 40% reported that they have either poor or limited English, whereas a further 29% reported they have average English skills. Just 82 participants (32%) reported their proficiency as good.

The core objective of this study was to ascertain community attitude on the preferences of communication between a diverse range of community members with language barriers and government agencies and to compare this data against the MFB study as well as current known communication methods employed by police forces and other agencies. With this in mind, the participants were specifically asked how they prefer to be communicated with by public services and were given nine options from which to choose the top three preferences. The last option 'Other' offers an opportunity for the respondents to enter text responses if they have other thoughts. The distribution of the respondents' answers is illustrated in Table 6.3 below.

Some respondents did not pick the second or the third preferences. Therefore, it must be pointed out that the corresponding totals in the last row in the table do not add up to 258. Out of the eight options provided, the highest number of respondents (n = 85, 33%) chose 'face-to-face individual meetings with officers, with the help of interpreters if needed' as their first preference, followed by 60 respondents (23%) who chose 'information brochures and flyers translated into my language' as their most favoured way of communication. The option 'Internet to access websites with translated information into my language' ranked third highest top preference for 44 respondents (17%). In relation to the second most preferred way of communication, the highest number of respondents (n = 47, 19%) chose the option 'information hotlines (spoken in my language or assisted by telephone interpreter)', followed by 44 respondents (18%) who chose the option 'Internet to access websites with translated information into my language', which also ranked third highest as the most favoured option. Forty-one respondents (16%) picked the option 'community information sessions (with interpreters in my language) in local community meeting places (e.g. community association buildings, churches, mosques, halls, community schools)', making it the third highest ranking in terms of the second preference. Moving on to the third preference of communication method, the option 'Ethnic radio or TV announcements in my language' ranked the highest, with 41 respondents (16%) choosing it. This is closely followed by the second highest number of respondents (n = 38, 15%) who chose the option 'Information hotlines (spoken in my language or assisted by telephone interpreter)' and the third preference of option 'Information brochures and flyers translated into my language' picked by 37 respondents (15%). It worth noting, though, that the third preference appears to have flatter

**Table 6.2 What Do You Think Your Level of English Is?**

| # | Answer | Response | % |
|---|---|---|---|
| 1 | Poor | 36 | 14 |
| 2 | Limited | 66 | 26 |
| 3 | Average | 74 | 29 |
| 4 | Good | 82 | 32 |
| | **Total** | **258** | **100** |

**Table 6.3 How Do You Prefer to be Communicated with?**

| | Communication Preference | First Preference | Second Preference | Third Preference | Total |
|---|---|---|---|---|---|
| 1 | Information brochures and flyers translated into my language | 60[2] | 36 | 37[3] | 133[2] |
| 2 | Face-to-face individual meetings with officers, with the help of interpreters if needed | 85[1] | 34 | 15 | 134[1] |
| 3 | Community information sessions (with interpreters in my language) in local community meeting places (e.g. community association buildings, churches, mosques, halls, community schools) | 27 | 41[3] | 33 | 101 |
| 4 | Migrant Liaison Officers or other officers who speak my language | 14 | 18 | 25 | 57 |
| 5 | Internet to access websites with translated information into my language | 44[3] | 44[2] | 23 | 111[3] |
| 6 | A leader from my community to explain to me in my language | 13 | 21 | 36 | 70 |
| 7 | Information hotlines (spoken in my language or assisted by telephone interpreter) | 1 | 47[1] | 38[2] | 86 |
| 8 | Ethnic radio or TV announcements in my language | 9 | 10 | 41[1] | 60 |
| 9 | Other | 5 | 0 | 1 | 6 |
| | **Total** | **258** | **251** | **249** | – |

*Note*: 1, 2, 3 under each preference column denote the answers which received the highest, second highest, and third highest votes.

distribution of respondent numbers in the top four, with each ranking closely followed by the next from 41, 38, 37 to 36. The last column in Table 6.3 shows the sums of each option being picked either as the first, second, or third preference, which might serve as a good indicator of the aggregate community preferences in relation to the corresponding options. The top three most preferred communication methods chosen by the respondents, therefore, are:

1. Option 2: 'face-to-face individual meetings with officers, with the help of interpreters if needed' (n = 134, i.e. 52% of the respondents);
2. Option 1: 'Information brochures and flyers translated into my language' (n = 133, i.e. 52% of the respondents);
3. Option 5: 'Internet to access websites with translated information into my language' (n = 111, i.e. 43% of the respondents).

As can be seen, the most preferred Option 2 and the second most preferred Option 1 are only one vote apart, essentially pointing to a strong inclination of respondents favouring direct interaction with public services. This is followed by Option 5 which probably reflects the increasing ease and affordability of the internet and communications technology in the community.

The survey did not seek to produce cross tabulation to ascertain if those 68% who reported their English proficiency level is not good (see Table 6.2, summation of categories 1 to 3) are the ones who chose the top three options reported above. However, with the majority of votes received by Options 1 and 2 (meaning one in two respondents in the survey favour those) and a slightly lower than 50% votes received for Option 3, it is probably safe to say that it is likely that these preferences are representative of those respondents whose English is not good. In summary, the data show us that community members, in particular those with language barriers, overwhelmingly prefer direct communication (i.e. face-to-face, information flyers, and websites), which is consistent with the responses from the Chin and Karen community members reported in the MFB Report. On the contrary, Option 4: 'Migrant Liaison Officers or other officers who speak my language' and Option 6: 'A leader from my community to explain to me in my language', which are commonly used by many government agencies, are shown to be ranked much lower by the respondents. As the authors explained earlier, this survey does not seek to measure effectiveness of these methods and the results do not mean the methods least preferred do not work or are ineffective. The findings should be viewed in the light of community attitude and preference. The reasons why Options 4 and 6 did not rank higher in the preferred methods may need to be further investigated in a more specific study. However, suffice it to say that there appears to be a growing recognition of need to look beyond the methods popularly adopted so far. Some community leaders recently admitted that the radicalised youth in some Islamic communities do not contact them (Olding, 2014) or associate with mainstream associations or groups. Another view was that community leaders and elders and some of the youth have a generational gap and do not communicate as effectively as government agencies assume they do. This probably reflects a shortcoming of this method with respect to some members of the community to which the government agencies are trying to get 'the message' across.

## Conclusion

This study aims to gain an insight into the preferences of members of ethnic communities about communication with government authorities and agencies in Australia. An objective was to add to the current knowledge in order to guide policymakers, as well as frontline staff, by way of acquiring bottom-up feedback from members of a wide range of ethnic communities.

The survey results revealed significant differences between the communication methods commonly used by government authorities and agencies and what the ethnic communities prefer. The findings in this study are in line with the views expressed by the ethnic Burmese members of the community in a previous study conducted by the Metropolitan Fire Brigade in Melbourne, Victoria. Representing a fairly comprehensive range of ethnic communities in Melbourne, the study has found that, when it comes to communication with public services, of which police and law enforcement constitute an important element, community members overwhelmingly prefer direct interaction, through face-to-face encounter or information in print or online, and with the assistance of language help, if needed, including interpreting and translating services. This finding is partly in conflict with some of the current, long established communication methods used by the government agencies. The study highlights a need to incorporate the views of the receiving end of such communication and the importance of designing bottom-up strategies for effective communication when it comes to members of the public who are not proficient in the common language of government agencies.

## Limitations of Study

There are a number of limitations in this study that need to be acknowledged. The survey was not designed to measure or compare the effectiveness of the communication methods provided in the survey options either qualitatively or quantitatively, and some of the options are no doubt being used by government agencies or organisations, including police forces. It is, rather, designed to gauge community members' preferences in the way they like to be communicated with. As a result, the ranking of the preferences must not be interpreted as one particular method being more effective or superior than the others.

The number of participants and responses from different language groups was not equal. As a result, it was not possible to undertake a cross tabulation of responses to draw links between variables or identify which particular community prefers which method more so than others. Given these limitations, caution must be exercised in generalising the findings of this study.

## References

ABS (Australian Bureau of Statistics). (2011). *Cultural diversity in Australia. Reflecting a nation: Stories from the 2011 Census.* Retrieved 8 February 2015, from www.abs.gov.au/ausstats/abs@.nsf/Lookup/2071.0main+features902012-2013.

AIATSIS (Australian Institute of Aboriginal and Torres Strait Islander Studies), & FATSIL (Federation of Aboriginal and Torres Strait Islander Languages). (2005). *National indigenous languages survey report 2005*. Canberra: Aboriginal and Torres Strait Islander Services.

Ben-Porat, G. (2008). Policing multicultural states: Lessons from the Canadian model. *Policing and Society, 18*(4), 411–425.

Bowling, B., & Philips, C. (2003). Policing ethnic minority communities. In T. Newburn (Ed.), *Handbook of policing* (pp. 528–555). Devon, UK: Willan Publishing.

Carleton, J. (2014). Expert urges two pronged approached to home grown terrorism. *Ratio National Breakfast*. Retrieved 21 June 2017, from www.abc.net.au/radionational/programs/breakfast/expert-urges-two-pronged-approach-to-home-grown-terrorism/5683148.

Chan, J. B. L. (1995). *Police accountability in a multicultural society*. Canberra: Australian Institute of Criminology.

Chan, J. B. L. (1997). *Changing police culture: Policing in a multicultural society*. Cambridge and Melbourne: Cambridge University Press.

Commonwealth of Australia. (2015). *Review of Australia's counter-terrorism machinery*. Canberra: Department of the Prime Minister and Cabinet, Australian Government.

Department of Human Services. (2013). *Annual report 2012–2013*. Canberra: Department of Human Service.

Fierravanti-Wells, C. (2015). Speech delivered at European Network of Public Service Interpreters (ENPSIT) conference: Beating Babel in Multilingual Service Settings. Retrieved 28 November 2015, from http://concettafierravantiwells.dss.gov.au/transcripts/enpsit-5-june-2015.

Grabosky, P. (2009). Community policing, east and west, north and south. *Police Practice and Research, 10*(2), 95–98.

Ho, C. (2015, 2 January). Hanson: Police service making strides in counter-radicalization efforts, but 'we need to up our game'. *Calgary Herald*. Retrieved 28 July 2017, from http://calgaryherald.com/news/crime/hanson-police-service-making-strides-in-counter-radicalization-efforts-but-we-need-to-up-our-game.

Kühle, L., & Lindekilde, L. (2010). *Radicalization among young Muslims in Aarhus*. Aarhus: Centre for Studies in Islamism and Radicalisation (CIR), Department of Political Science, Aarhus University, Denmark.

Lane, M., & Henry, K. (2004). Beyond symptoms: Crime prevention and community development. *Australian Journal of Social Issues, 39*(2), 201–213.

Larson, J. J. (2010). Community policing in culturally and linguistically diverse communities. In J. Putt (Ed.), *Community policing in Australia* (pp. 24–31). Canberra: Australian Institute of Criminology.

Le, R., & Gilding, M. (2014). Gambling and drugs: The role of gambling among Vietnamese women incarcerated for drug crimes in Australia. *Australian and New Zealand Journal of Criminology*. doi:10.1177/000486514554307.

Maguire, E. R., & Wells, W. (2002). Community policing as communication reform. In H. Giles (Ed.), *Law enforcement, communication and community* (pp. 33–66). Amsterdam and Philadelphia: John Benjamins.

Messina, A. M. (2007). *The logics and politics of post-WWII migration to Western Europe*. Cambridge: Cambridge University Press.

MFB (Metropolitan Fire and Emergency Services Board). (2008). *Resource guide: Working with communities from Burma – the Karen & Chin*. Retrieved 20 February 2015, from www.mfb.vic.gov.au/Media/docs/Working-with-Burmese-Communities-35bf0e42-585c-4410-8d79-3f18cb973f2f.pdf.

Myhill, A. (2006). *Community engagement in policing: Lessons from literature*. London: Home Office.

NATO-OTAN. (2014). *Homegrown terrorism: Causes and dimensions*. Ankara: Centre of Excellence, Defence Against Terrorism.

Olding, R. (2014). Members of Street Dawah preaching group feature heavily in Sydney's counter-terrorism raids. *Sydney Morning Herald*, 28 September. Retrieved 21 June 2017, from www.smh.com.au/national/members-of-street-dawah-preaching-group-feature-heavily-in-sydneys-counterterrorism-raids-20140927-10myuk.html#ixzz3Ebatt4tV.

Pickering, S., Wright-Neville, D., McCulloch, J., & Lentini, P. (2007). *Counter-terrorism policing and culturally diverse communities. Final report.* Melbourne: Monash University.

Roy, O. (2007). Islamic terrorist radicalization in Europe. In S. Amghar, A. Boubekeur, & M. Emerson (Eds.), *European Islam: Challenges for public policy and society* (pp. 52–61). Brussels: Centre for European Policy Studies.

Samovar, L., Porter, R., McDaniel, E., & Roy, C. (2015). *Intercultural communication: A reader* (14th ed.). Boston: Cengage Learning.

Schneider, S. (2007). *Refocusing crime prevention: Collective action and the quest for community.* Toronto, Buffalo and London: University of Toronto Press Incorporated.

Shah, S., Rahman, I., & Khashu, A. (2007). *Overcoming language barriers: Solutions for law enforcement.* New York: Vera Institute of Justice.

Silber, M. D., & Bhatt, A. (2007). *Radicalization in the West: The homegrown threat.* New York: NYPD Intelligence Division.

Slootman, M., & Tillie, J. (2006). *Processes of radicalisation. Why some Amsterdam Muslims become radicals.* Institute for Migration and Ethnic Studies, Universiteit van Amsterdam.

Sutherland, D. W. (2007, 14 March). *Threat of Islamic radicalization to the homeland. Written testimony to the United States Senate, Committee on Homeland Security and Governmental Affairs.* Retrieved 8 February 2015, from http://hsgac.senate.gov/_files/031407Sutherland.pdf.

Tahiri, H., & Grossman, M. (2014). *Community and radicalisation: An examination of perceptions, ideas, beliefs and solutions throughout Australia.* Melbourne: Victoria Police & Victoria University.

Tanton, J., McCormack, D., & Smith, J. W. (1996). *Immigration and the social contract: The implosion of Western society.* Aldershot: Avebury.

Victoria Police. (2013). *Equity is not the same: Victoria Police response to consultation and reviews on field contact policy and data collection and cross cultural training.* Melbourne: Victoria Police.

Voyez, M. (2007). Policing by consent in a diverse community. *WA Police News*, June, 26–18.

Zammit, A. (n.d.). Who becomes a jihadist in Australia? A comparative analysis. Retrieved 7 March 2015, from http://artsonline.monash.edu.au/radicalisation/files/2013/03/conference-2010-who-jihadist-australia-az.pdf.

# Community Policing and Vigilantism

## Two Alternative Strategies for Fighting Neighborhood Crime

# 7

BRUNO MEINI

### Contents



### Abstract

Community policing incorporates the logic of security by creating partnerships between the police and the public without making any distinction of rank. Since safety affects the quality of life, cooperation between the police and the public is directed to lessen the corrosive tendencies of social deviance that feed phenomena of violence. Therefore, when governments are not able to provide satisfactory public safety, especially among disadvantaged communities, what then could deter the emergence of vigilantism? The answer is positive, because vigilantism only emerges when the police do not respond adequately to popular safety and security needs; thus, citizens resort to self-help measures. Vigilantism will produce a certain number of negative implications. First, vigilantism is a system that usurps state power. Second, the state authorities need to act rapidly to counteract vigilante violent actions and to prosecute and convict perpetrators. Third, the state must strongly assert and protect the right to life against any abuse committed by the vigilantes. Finally, vigilante activities represent a serious threat to human rights and to the growth and strengthening of democratic principles at grassroots level. Community courts can represent an innovative and effective means in order to deal with community crime problems in each society. They are neighborhood-focused courts that intervene on the underlying causes of crime through a problem-solving approach in which the prosecutor partners with the police and other enforcing law actors in order to develop effective solutions to address specific public safety problems.

## Community Justice, Informal Justice, and Popular Justice

The proportion of people under the criminal justice system supervision has reached a record high in the United States of America as well as throughout the world. Consequently, there is an ongoing concerted effort to improve the efficiency of the criminal justice system. The criminal justice system is a system that is perceived as one that overprotects offenders, isolates victims, and does not take into due consideration the fears and concerns of the community. Consequently, popular pressures are mounting for reviewing the priorities of the criminal justice system, which should fundamentally expand its center of attention beyond the mere prosecution of offenders (Nicholl, 1999).

Community justice is an operating philosophy which mostly refers to all variants of crime prevention and justice activities that openly incorporate the community in their procedures and fix the enhancement of community quality of life as an objective. Community justice focuses on the actions that citizens, community organizations, and the criminal justice system can undertake to address crime and social disorder issues. It focuses on community-level outcomes, shifting the emphasis from individual incidents to systemic patterns, from individual conscience to social mores, and from personal goods to the common good. Classically, community justice is seen as a partnership between the formal criminal justice system and the community, but communities often autonomously organize strategies that directly or indirectly combat crime (Karp & Clear, 2000, p. 324).

Advocates of community justice claim that criminal justice agencies must interact with the public and learn how to listen and work with the local citizens to prevent and solve crime-related problems (Umbreit, 1994). Eduardo Barajas (1995), a program specialist for the National Institute of Corrections, identified four guiding principles and four core values of community justice. Principles of community justice comprise: the community, including individual victims and offenders, is the ultimate customer, as well as a partner, of the justice system; partnerships for action, among justice components and citizens, strive for community safety and well-being; the community is the preferred source of problem solving and citizens work to prevent victimization, provide conflict resolution, and maintain peace; and crime is confronted by addressing social disorder, criminal activities and behavior, and by holding offenders accountable for the harm they cause to victims and the community. In addition, he added that the justice system benefits the community by: striving to repair the harm caused to individual victims and communities; working to prevent crime and its negative effects; doing justice by addressing problems rather than merely processing cases; and promoting community protection through proactive, problem-solving practices focused on interventions aimed at maintaining healthy, safe, secure, and fair communities where crime cannot flourish.

In 2000, the American Probation and Parole Association (APPA) adopted a new position statement on community justice. This position statement defined community justice as "a strategic method of crime reduction and prevention, which builds or enhances partnerships within communities" (APPA, 2000). This definition summarizes the principles and core values of community justice and, specifically, places community justice in the context of community policing. In fact, the community criminal justice system reflects community policing when it directly involves the community as partners in identifying and prioritizing problems as well as in solving them (Trojanowicz & Bucqueroux, 1998).

We will now consider the concepts of formal justice, informal justice, and popular justice systems within the context of criminal justice. The formal justice system involves civil and criminal justice issues and includes formal state-based justice institutions and procedures, such as police, prosecution, courts (religious and secular), and custodial measures. The term informal justice system is used when referring to a dispute resolution mechanism falling outside the scope of the formal justice system. This term does not fit every circumstance as many terms exist to describe such systems (traditional, indigenous, customary, restorative, popular), and it is difficult to use a common term to denote the different processes, mechanisms, and norms that are currently utilized across the world (Wojkowska, 2006). Subsequently, the expression popular justice refers to "a process for making decisions and compelling compliance to a set of rules that is relatively informal in ritual and decorum, nonprofessional in language and personnel, local in scope, and limited in jurisdiction" (Merry, 1994, p. 32) (e.g., citizen patrols who oversee neighborhood safety without authorization from a police department). Theory provides two divergent orientations on popular justice. The first asserts that citizens' efforts to deal with local problems are the outcome of a growing distrust towards an intrinsically unfair and ineffective criminal justice apparatus (radical). The second upholds that existing legal control systems are correct and viable, but at the same time it expresses its concerns over declining respect for public order and state authority, rising crime rates, and insufficient resources for crime control policies (conventional) (Turk, 1987). As a final point, it is interesting to emphasize that Abel (1982) and many other scholars generally use informal justice and popular justice expressions interchangeably. Abel's reasoning presupposes that state-based justice is always formal and that popular justice is never formal but always informal. Abel's reasoning is a fallacious assumption because there is considerable informality in state-based justice systems as well. As many legal anthropologists have demonstrated, there is often significant regularization of procedures (formality) in extra-state popular justice systems. At all levels of state-based justice systems, there are unwritten customary rules which guide judges as to what they can and cannot say, write, and do. These cultural rules represent an implicit system of informal living law that controls the opinio juris of all state-based justice systems (Hund, 2008).

## Community Policing Strategy

During the 1980s, the police throughout the developed democratic world have increasingly questioned its role, operating strategies, organization, and management. This was attributable to growing doubts about the effectiveness of traditional policing strategies in safeguarding people from crime. Changes in the police emerged when the police themselves became aware of their limitations in deterring crime and inability to respond to the strong competition from the private security system whose strategies tremendously favored prevention over detection and punishment. The central issue was how the police would be able to become more effective in preventing local crime (Bayley & Shearing, 1996).

One response to the above-mentioned issue has been community policing. Its philosophy is very simple, that is to say the police and the community must work together in order to define and implement effective solutions to crime and disorder issues (Sadd & Grinc, 1994). An underlying motivation for public involvement is the belief that the police alone are neither able to create nor maintain safe communities. However, the police may be capable of supporting voluntary local efforts in order to prevent disorder and crime. In this role, the police strive to improve community schemas such as the implementation of neighborhood watches as well as youth and economic development programs (Gudell & Skogan, 2003).

Community policing is a policing strategy which constitutes a dramatic break with the past. The police strive to transform the community from being passive consumers of police protection to active co-producers of public safety (Peak & Glensor, 2012). Community policing promotes organizational strategies that support the systematic use of partnerships and problem-solving techniques to address the immediate conditions that lead to public safety issues such as crime, social disorder, and fear of crime. Community partnerships are relationships between residents and the police that address neighborhood crime-related issues. In these partnerships, organizational flexibility replaces organizational management, structured personnel, and information systems in order to be able to support collaborative agreements and to be proactive in problem solving. Problem solving is the process of engaging in the proactive and systematic examination of identified problems to develop effective responses (Cordner, 2000). Community policing has motivated police departments to become more helpful to the public through community outreach. For instance, the police work together with schools, youth services, and recreational clubs to provide educational and social supports to young people exposed to drugs, bullying, alcohol, and gangs. In addition, in the community police environment the police usually cooperate with specified groups vulnerable to problems such as local businesses, victims' groups, the elderly, storekeepers, and road users (Nicholl, 1999).

Community policing emphasizes the importance of a personalized form of control, an extension of an informal, differentiated moral system in which the police officer acts as if he or she were a member of the community. Such policing systems rely upon a decentralization of power in which the officer decides to promote order based on community needs (Wilson & Kelling, 1982). Reisig and Parks (2004) asserted that community policing strategies should include mechanisms which channel citizen input on police interventions in their neighborhood, whereas traditional police practices, which focused on suppressing crime, were initiated by authorities outside the neighborhood and have not always been consistent with community expectations. Following their aspirations, residents become an integral part of the community policing process and have the opportunity to cooperate directly with law enforcement officials to address local crime and disorder issues together. Police-community collaboration strategies will be most effective if calibrated accurately to foster and maintain a neighborhood's informal social control. Suppressive police tactics in underprivileged, crime-ridden neighborhoods may appear and be perceived as intrusive, oppressive, and inconsistent and also unfairly targeted to further estrange residents who already report high levels of disaffection with police (Reisig & Parks, 2000; Sampson & Bartusch, 1998).

The public and the police aim to reduce disorder and crime through neighborhood and order-maintenance policing strategies that are similar to those practices that are already accepted by commercial communities that utilize private policing services (Pastor, 2003). The private-sector mentality establishes the manner in which the police members view themselves, their role, and their relationships with citizens (Johnston, 1992). The process of pluralization of policing should increase public safety both in quantitative and qualitative terms. However, the pluralization of policing under the present market auspices does not provide the same level of security across society. Pluralization favors mainly affluent communities, while disadvantaged communities create favorable conditions for the emergence of vigilantism due to under-policing (Jones, van Steden, & Boutellier, 2009).

## A Significant Example of Community-Based Policing

Community-based policing in Chicago is known as CAPS (Chicago Alternative Policing Strategy). The program had its origin at the time of rising crime rates in the early 1990s and it was officially launched in 1993 in 5 of the city's 25 police districts (Skogan & Hartnett, 1997). These prototype districts were diverse in terms of their demographics, economics, crime issues, and levels of community cohesion. As such, these districts provided a valuable laboratory for testing and improving the CAPS model before being expanded citywide. The implementation of CAPS throughout the other 20 police districts began in 1994. At the heart of the plan, there was the reorganization of the city's 25 police districts into 279 police beats, equivalent to about 12 beats per area. At the median, a beat covered 48 city blocks and included about 9,000 people and 3,000 households (Skogan, 1995).

The Chicago Police Department had a new ally in the fight against crime and disorder that was the community, which was consulted and engaged on the issues of concern in relation to policing and community safety (Chicago Community Policing Evaluation Consortium, 1995). During initial phases, officers were permanently assigned to beats and trained in problem-solving techniques. Citizen committees were constituted in different neighborhoods, and police and area residents began to meet on a regular basis. Police and local citizens cooperated to identify and prioritize problems, develop targeted intervention policies, and invest community resources to address them (Scaramella, Cox, & McCamey, 2011). The following elucidation of CAPS was prepared by the Chicago Police Department and put in promotional material distributed to citizens:

> While traditional policing relied almost exclusively on police to fight crime, CAPS creates a partnership of police, residents, government agencies, and members of the community. The community shares responsibility with the police for setting crime-fighting priorities in the neighborhoods and for designing and implementing problem solving strategies. (Skogan et al., 2004, p. 88)

CAPS adopted a decentralized turf orientation model by reorganizing patrol work around small geographical areas, the city's 279 police beats, 270 of which were residential (Skogan, Steiner, DuBois, Gudell, & Fagan, 2002, pp. 4–7). As of mid-1993, police began holding neighborhood meetings in every beat in the prototype districts. These meetings were monthly and organized between small groups of residents and police officers working in the area. By the spring of 1995, they began citywide and were held in such places as church basements and park buildings all over the city. In the CAPS program, beat meetings serve as a forum for exchanging information and prioritizing and analyzing local problems. They allow police departments to develop fruitful relationships with neighborhoods' inhabitants and provide an opportunity for residents to organize their own problem-solving efforts. The meetings often feature presentations by detectives or police from special units. Representatives of city services agencies, municipal staff, school personnel, local business owners and propriety owners, and organizers from other local groups also participate (Skogan et al., 2002, p. 8). The Chicago Police Department's mission is "to protect the lives, property and rights of all people, to maintain order, and to enforce the law impartially" (Chicago Police Department, 1993, p. 13).

To better enable beat officers to work with residents and community organizations, rapid response teams were created to handle excess 911 calls. Nine or ten police officers were assigned to each police beat, and each beat had a sergeant tasked with overseeing the beat and holding quarterly meetings. Within the beats, tactical units and youth officers were expected to work more closely in support of beat officers and to exchange information with them and members of the community at beat meetings in order to identify the most appropriate solutions to neighborhood problems (Skogan et al., 2002). As a result, the Chicago Police Department decided to invest a large amount of resources to train officers and their supervisors in the skills required to track and solve problems in conjunction with the community (Skogan, 2000).

The Chicago Alternative Policing Strategy involves a significant expansion of the police mandate. Police responsibilities often include a broad range of community concerns such as social disorder, municipal service problems, and code enforcement matters previously handled by civil courts. However, dealing with crime remains at the heart of the police mission (Skogan et al., 2000). The crime theory of broken windows suggests that disorder and crime are frequently interlinked in a developmental sequence. At the community level, ignoring disorder leads to more of it just as a building with a broken window, if left unrepaired, will soon have other broken windows. One unrepaired broken window implies a decay of the neighborhood and sends a clear signal that nobody cares, not the police, not the citizens, not the community, and so breaking more windows costs nothing (Kelling & Coles, 1996). Therefore, the broken window analogy has made Chicago officials conscious of the fact that the signs of neighborhood disorder such as graffiti, abandoned vehicles and buildings, malfunctioning streetlights can all have an adverse effect on crime levels in a community. By addressing these disorder issues early on, all city agencies and the police department can prevent them from becoming serious and widespread crime problems. A procedure has been developed whereby the process is initiated through the City Service Request Form, which police officers fill out and submit to the Mayor's Office of Inquiry and Information. This request is fed into a computer that sends an electronic work order to the appropriate agency for investigation and action (Das & Verma, 2003, p. 214).

Under CAPS, the police, other government agencies, and the community work together in order to prevent crime rather than just continuing to respond harshly to an unremitting stream of apparently disconnected incidents (Goldstein, 1990). Chicago's approach is preventive and interventions are designed to be sustainable. This type of approach stands in stark contrast to zero tolerance policy in which police authorities react aggressively to crime when it occurs by punishing with an arrest of those who commit minor infractions such as loitering, public intoxication, and public disobedience. Zero tolerance policy invokes a strong police response with a minimal public involvement, whereas Chicago's CAPS strategy calls upon residents to take responsibility for their neighborhoods through partnerships and involvement with the police (Jurkanin & Hillard, 2006, p. 94).

The Chicago Police Department continues to use the CompStat model as an integral part of its community alternative policing strategy. This model is a management process within a performance management framework that synthesizes analysis of crime and disorder data, strategic problem solving, and a clear accountability structure. Ideally, CompStat facilitates accurate and timely analysis of crime and disorder data, which is utilized to identify crime patterns and issues. Based on this analysis, tailored responses are put into practice through rapid deployment of personnel and resources. An accountability structure ensures the analysis is acted upon and the responses are executed appropriately as well as assessing whether responses are effective in reducing crime and disorder (Weisburd, Mastrofski, McNally, Greenspan, & Willis, 2003). In Chicago the CompStat model is known as Deployment Operations Center, a crime-specific process which places computer-generated crime information in the hands of managers so that they can make strategic deployment decisions based on where violent crime is taking place. A 100-officer task force, known as the Targeted Response Unit, comprising specially selected and highly motivated officers, is deployed to specific locations throughout the city based on the intelligence information generated by a daily DOC analysis (Lombardo & Lough, 2007, p. 133). These efforts succeeded in reducing violent crime (murder, criminal sexual assault, robbery, and aggravated assault/battery) significantly (Chicago Police Department, 2007). This new police paradigm has come to be known as intelligence-led policing that can be described as a new dimension of community-oriented policing in that both rely on information sharing, quality analysis of data, and problem solving (Peterson, 2005). The most exhaustive definition of intelligence-led policing was given by Ratcliffe (2008) who stated that

> [i]ntelligence-led policing is a business model and managerial philosophy where data analysis and crime intelligence are pivotal to an objective, decision-making framework that facilitates crime and problem reduction, disruption and prevention through both strategic management and effective enforcement strategies that target prolific and serious offenders. (p. 6)

In addition to the monthly beat meetings, there are also District Advisory Committees (DACs) which meet regularly to advise police commanders on problems within their area. The members of the DAC are generally community leaders, school council members, ministers, business operators, and representatives of significant organizations and institutions in the district. The goal of DACs is to help police understand residents' agendas, develop district priorities, and devise solutions to community problems. However, the DACs have not resulted in being a great success because most of them have played a very limited role in planning and priority setting (Skogan, 2006, p. 70). A 2004 Northwestern University report, *CAPS at Ten*, confirmed that many members were frustrated about their unclear mandates, leadership problems and inactivity (Skogan et al., 2004). But, despite these frustrations and the fact that CAPS' effectiveness was bogged down by bureaucracy, experts say that there is reason to continue to use it in a reinvigorated version (Bowean, 2013). As a result, Mayor Rahm Emanuel and his police Superintendent Garry McCarthy pledged to revitalize the CAPS program. The central office was dismantled and resources were be shifted to each of the 25 police districts where each commander had the task to adapt the program to neighborhood needs. Specifically, each police district was allocated a sergeant and two police officers, as well as a community organizer and a youth services provider. In addition, four citywide coordinators were involved in overseeing community-oriented policing programs targeted at victim assistance, senior and youth citizens, and victims of domestic violence (Rogers, 2013). In July 2013, Chief McCarthy announced new steps in order to curb the violence. First, Twitter handles were developed and used to share information in three police districts. Second, two other social network tools were put to use to help police members solve and prevent crime. Residents can send tips via text message directly to the responding officers, and 911 callers with camera-equipped smartphones are able to alert and assist respondents by sending pictures or video of a crime. Finally, a more user-friendly website, ChicagoPolice.org, was also unveiled (D'Onofrio, 2013).

## The Phenomenology of Vigilantism

Since the 1980s, the phenomenon of vigilantism has often been studied through topics such as the rise of crime and insecurity, the involvement of local groups in political conflicts, and the possible crisis of state law enforcement agencies (Fourchard, 2008). Vigilantism consists of those acts taken by citizens who are "assuming police roles, in essence functioning as prosecutors, judges, and executioners in capturing and punishing offenders without benefit of due process or trial" (Champion, 2005, p. 263). One who takes part in vigilantism is known as a vigilante. The word is of Spanish origin and its meaning is watchman, guard, or regulator, but its Latin root is *vigil* which means awake, watchful, or observant (Kirschner, 2011).

Vigilantism is still a significant concern, especially in the African countries, as Michael L. Fleisher (2000) pointed out. In most African countries the state weaknesses have led to the chronic privatization of justice by informal security actors that further undermine the state's ability to handle these issues. Privatized justice must be regulated in order to provide effective protection of citizens and to prevent militias and vigilante groups from encroaching on state functions (Isima, 2007). A scholarly consensus does not exist as to what precisely vigilantism is, particularly as to the nature of its relationship with the state. In any case, vigilante groups question the relationship between the police and the communities they serve. A question at issue is whether such groups are tolerated or even supported by the law enforcement agencies (Omach, 2010). Another question at issue is whether these groups are forbidden and prosecuted since vigilante justice poses a challenge to authority and the legitimacy of the state (Kirsch & Grätz, 2010).

Les Johnston (1996) was the first one to establish an exhaustive criminological definition of vigilantism. He argued that vigilantism consists of six essential elements as follows: (1) planning and premeditation by those engaging in it; (2) its participants are private citizens whose engagement is voluntary; (3) it is a form of "autonomous citizenship" and, as such, constitutes a social movement; (4) it uses or threatens the use of force; (5) it arises when an established order is under threat from the transgression, the potential transgression, or the imputed transgression of institutionalized norms; (6) it aims to control crime or other social infractions by offering assurances or guarantees of security both to its participants as well as to others. It is interesting to note that Johnston rejected the idea that private security guards are vigilantes based on two grounds. First, it is a fact that numerous police forces have already discussed the prospects of establishing their own private security guards to provide police patrols. This fact implies legitimization of what private security agencies do. Second, commercial (private) security companies perform their duties within the legal spheres of the state thus providing a significant example to distinguish a profitable activity from a voluntary activity (Sharp & Wilson, 2000).

Johnston's approach is useful for distinguishing vigilantism from mere establishment violence. For instance, the actions of paramilitary punishment squads in Northern Ireland constituted vigilantism because they were directed towards infractions of institutionalized norms (such as joyriding and burglary). On the other hand, when paramilitaries assassinated innocent civilians, shot soldiers, or bombed buildings, they performed acts of political violence. These acts are inefficient to handle the internal regulation of social deviance (Silke, 1999).

Vigilante justice is an extrajudicial punishment that is motivated by the dissatisfaction with state justice. Punishment is undoubtedly a common feature of different phenomena of vigilantism but it must be distinct from mere acts of violence because it is premeditated, systematic, calculated, and often displays ritualistic and quasi-judicial characteristics (McCorry & Morrisey, 1989). Vigilante justice theoretically calibrates its sanctions to the severity of crime committed, but it practically punishes who is arbitrarily considered to be an offender without benefit of due process or trial. This type of justice represents a genuine threat to government authority because vigilantes usually break the law in their efforts to apprehend and punish alleged criminals (Silke, 2001).

Vigilante groups are informed by local (private) notions of security and justice which are popularly legitimate but not recognized by the state (Jones, 2008). They often justify their actions as a fulfillment of the wishes of vengeance of the community. The vengeance risks symbolizing the main ideological value for punishment which contradicts the fundamental traditional American value, namely the protection of the individual's due process rights in criminal proceedings (Zimring, 2003). The identification and characterization of some of the victims of vigilante groups has often been the result of a rough process of stereotyping through the use of superficially descriptive labels such as deviant, pedophile, murderer, Black, Jew, independent-minded woman, or witch. These labeled individuals may be punished verbally, physically, or even killed by vigilantes (Abrahams, 2002, pp. 33–34).

Vigilantes can be classified according to the nature of the participants and the degree of the organization characterizing their activities. These criteria generate the following fourfold typology:

1. *Private, Spontaneous Vigilantism* – Private citizens infrequently leap to the defense of the public order with all the vehemence of a traditional mob.
2. *Private, Organized Vigilantism* – Private citizens react to continuous criminal challenges by arranging timely and organized responses.
3. *Official, Spontaneous Vigilantism* – The official use of coercion belongs to the state which sometimes can violate the boundaries of tolerability. Sometimes official vigilantism appears to be the spontaneous overreaction of men on the line, rather than the result of any deliberate policy. The ultimate punishment of alleged criminals, of course, is nothing new. What is sometimes overlooked, however, is the violence that police at times direct at social outsiders and political groups.
4. *Official, Organized Vigilantism* – This makes reference to the cases where excessive coercion has been a long-term, deliberate policy of certain security and enforcement organizations. Clearly vigilantism has been, for a long time, the FBI's method of harassing, provoking, and entrapping "radical" political organizations (Sederberg, 1978).

Advocates of vigilantism underline the inability of state institutions in responding adequately to citizens' safety and security needs, and tend to insist firmly on concepts like *community*, *participation*, and *justice*. On the contrary, those who criticize vigilantism claim that it typically constitutes the wrong response to the inefficiency of the police and courts, and it is also a dangerous way to react to community concerns (Abrahams, 2002, p. 26).

## Conclusion

Community policing can represent the right strategy for assuring the protection of those socially disadvantaged groups that live in high crime neighborhoods. This strategy of policing focuses on partnerships between the police and the public without making any distinctions of rank. The police work strictly with members of communities in order to lessen the corrosive tendencies of social deviance that feed the phenomena of urban violence (MacDonald, 2002). Therefore, when institutions prove inadequate enforcement of criminal laws and the police are unable to respond to popular safety and security needs, citizens resort to self-help measures. The most controversial of these is the formation of vigilante groups (Pratten, 2008; Sekhonyane & Louw, 2002). In any community the emergence of vigilantism entails some significant consequences: first, the state has to reaffirm its authority on the population because vigilantism is a system of justice that usurps state power. Second, the state needs to act rapidly to counteract vigilante attacks and to prosecute and convict perpetrators. Lastly, the state must strongly assert and protect the right to life against any criminal act of vigilantism (Minnaar, 2002).

As mentioned previously, the weakness of the state in terms of guaranteeing order and security long since prompted a response from society. In the current context of representative democracy, a distinction may be drawn between responses which directly call into question the legitimacy of the state authority or that contribute to the crisis of society and of the state, such as fundamentalist religious groups, organized crime, and vigilante groups; and responses which aim to strengthen public trust in justice and respect human rights, such as community courts (Bidaguren & Estrella, 2002). Community courts are neighborhood-focused courts that attempt to harness the power of the justice system to address local crime problems and they can take many forms, but all focus on creative partnerships and problem-solving methods (Karafin, 2008). They have often strengthened the links to their communities by moving away from imposing centralized headquarters to smaller-scale neighborhood locations (Wolf, 2006). Basically, community courts are considered to be like problem-solving courts that apply a problem-solving approach to quality of life offenses. In particular, they are based on a collaboration among the justice participants (court staff, judge, defense, community social services, and community representatives), who work together to make justice visible in the places where crimes take place (Berman & Feinblatt, 2005). They also aim to build positive relationships, not only within the justice system but also outside with stakeholders such as residents, merchants, business leaders, churches, and schools (Thom, Mills, Meehan, & Chetty, 2013). Community courts apply a form of individualized justice that often "link offenders to individually-tailored community-based services (e.g. job training, treatment, safety planning, mental health counseling) to help reduce recidivism, thereby improving safety. In practice, community courts tend to foster the increased use of community and social services sentences" (Henry & Kralstein, 2011, p. 9).

While each community court is unique, it is possible to identify six common underlying principles that diversify the kind of problem-solving justice practiced in community courts from standard operating procedure in the justice system: enhanced information, community engagement, collaboration, individualized justice, accountability, and outcomes. First, community courts are dedicated to the idea that better staff training combined with better information (about litigants, victims, and the community context of crime) can improve the decision making of judges, attorneys, and other justice officials. The goal is to help practitioners make more nuanced decisions about individual defendants, ensuring that they receive an appropriate level of supervision and services. Second, community courts recognize that citizens, merchants, and neighborhood groups have an important role to play in helping the justice system identify, prioritize, and solve local problems. By actively engaging citizens in the process, community courts seek to improve public trust in justice. Third, community courts engage a diverse range of people, government agencies, and community organizations in collaborative efforts to improve public safety. By bringing together justice players and reaching out to potential stakeholders beyond the courthouse (e.g., social service providers, victims groups, schools), community courts can improve inter-agency communication, encourage greater trust between citizens and government, and foster new responses to local safety and security problems. Fourth, community courts seek to link defendants to individually tailored community-based sanctions (e.g., restitution, job training, drug treatment, and mental health counseling) by using validated evidence-based risk and needs assessment instruments. In doing so, community courts promote the use of alternative measures to incarceration in order to reduce recidivism, improve community safety, and enhance confidence in justice. Fifth, community courts seek to send the message that all criminal behavior, even low-level quality-of-life crime, has an impact on community safety. By insisting on regular and rigorous compliance monitoring and clear consequences for non-compliance, community courts work to improve the accountability of low-level offenders. Finally, community courts emphasize the active and ongoing collection and analysis of data, measuring outcomes and process, costs and benefits, in order to assess the effectiveness of operations and support continuous improvement. Public dissemination of community court research can represent a precious sign of public accountability, offering tangible evidence to local residents that the justice system addresses their concerns and solves public safety problems (Berman, 2010).

## References

Abel, R. L. (1982). *The politics of informal justice.* New York: Academic Press.

Abrahams, R. (2002). What's in a name? Some thoughts on the vocabulary of vigilantism and related forms of 'informal criminal justice'. In D. Feenan (Ed.), *Informal criminal justice* (pp. 25–40). Aldershot, Hants, England; Burlington, VT: Ashgate/Dartmouth.

American Probation and Parole Association (APPA). (2000). *Position statement on community justice.* Lexington, KY: APPA.

Barajas, E. Jr. (1995). *Moving toward community justice: Topics in community corrections.* Washington, DC: National Institute of Corrections.

Bayley, D. H., & Shearing, C. D. (1996). The future of policing. *Law and Society Review, 30*(3), 585–606.

Berman, G. (2010). *Principles of community justice: A guide for community planners.* New York: Center for Court Innovation.

Berman, G., & Feinblatt, J. (2005). *Good courts: The case for problem-solving justice.* New York: New Press.

Bidaguren, A. J., & Estrella, N. D. (2002). Governability and forms of popular justice in the new South Africa and Mozambique: Community courts and vigilantism. *The Journal of Legal Pluralism and Unofficial Law, 34*(47), 113–135.

Bowean, L. (2013, February 26). Chicago police look to revamp CAPS: Little data on whether program to involve community is effective at fighting crime. *Los Angeles Community Policing Forum.* Retrieved from www.lacp.org/2013-news-of-day/022613-News.htm.

Champion, D. J. (2005). Vigilantism. In *The American dictionary of criminal justice: Key terms and major court cases* (3rd ed.) (p. 263). Los Angeles, CA: Roxbury.

Chicago Community Policing Evaluation Consortium. (1995). *Community policing in Chicago, year two: An interim report.* Chicago: Illinois Criminal Justice Information Authority.

Chicago Police Department. (1993). *Together we can: A strategic plan for reinventing the Chicago Police Department.* Chicago: Chicago Police Department.

Chicago Police Department. (2007). *Making Chicago the safest big city in America, Chicago Police Department crime reduction initiatives: 2003–2007.* Chicago: Chicago Police Department.

Cordner, G. W. (2000). Community policing: Elements and effects. In G. P. Alpert & A. R. Piquero (Eds.), *Community policing: Contemporary readings* (2nd ed.) (pp. 45–62). Prospect Heights, IL: Waveland Press.

Das, D. K., & Verma, D. (2003). *Police mission: Challenges and responses.* Lanham, MD: Scarecrow Press.

D'Onofrio, J. (2013, July 8). CAPS using Twitter, smartphones to combat Chicago violence. *ABC Local.* Retrieved from http://a.abclocal.go.com/story?section=news/local&id=9165171.

Fleisher, M. L. (2000). Sungusungu: State-sponsored village vigilante groups among the Kuria of Tanzania. *Africa, 70*(2), 209–228.

Fourchard, L. (2008). A new name for an old practice: Vigilantes in south-western Nigeria. *Africa, 78*(1), 16–40.

Goldstein, H. (1990). *Problem-oriented policing.* New York: McGraw Hill.

Gudell, J. E., & Skogan, W. G. (2003). *Community mobilization for community policing.* Evanston, IL: Institute for Policy Research, Northwestern University.

Henry, K., & Kralstein, D. (2011). *Community courts: The research literature. A review of findings.* New York: Center for Court Innovation.

Hund, J. (2008). Critique of Abel on popular justice and the Alexandra treason trial. *Social and Legal Studies, 17*(4), 475–489.

Isima, J. (2007). The privatisation of violence and security sector reform in Africa: Nigeria and South Africa examined. *Journal of Peacebuilding and Development, 3*(2), 24–37.

Johnston, L. (1992). *The rebirth of private policing.* London: Routledge.

Johnston, L. (1996). What is vigilantism? *British Journal of Criminology, 36*(2), 220–236.

Jones, R. (2008). *State failure and extra-legal justice: Vigilante groups, civil militias and the rule of law in West Africa.* Geneva: UN High Commissioner for Refugees.

Jones, T., van Steden, R., & Boutellier, H. (2009). Pluralisation of policing in England & Wales and the Netherlands: Exploring similarity and difference. *Policing and Society: An International Journal of Research and Policy, 19*(3), 282–299.

Jurkanin, T. J., & Hillard, T. G. (2006). *Chicago police: An inside view – the story of Superintendent Terry G. Hillard.* Springfield, IL: Charles C Thomas.

Karafin, D. L. (2008). *Community courts across the globe: A survey of goals, performance measures and operations.* Newlands, South Africa: Criminal Justice Initiative of Open Society Foundation for South Africa.

Karp, T. R., & Clear, T. R. (2000). Community justice: A conceptual framework. In C. M. Friel (Ed.), *Boundary changes in criminal justice organizations: Criminal justice 2000* (Vol. 2, pp. 323–368). Washington, DC: U.S. Department of Justice, Office of Justice Programs, National Institute of Justice.

Kelling, G. L., & Coles, C. M. (1996). *Fixing broken windows: Restoring order and reducing crime in our communities.* New York: Simon & Schuster.

Kirsch, T. G., & Grätz, T. (Eds.) (2010). *Domesticating vigilantism in Africa.* Suffolk, UK: James Currey.

Kirschner, A. (2011). Putting out the fire with gasoline? Violence control in 'fragile' states: a study of vigilantism in Nigeria. In W. Heitmer, H-G. Haupt, A. Kirschner, & S. Malthaner (Eds.), *Control of violence: Historical and international perspectives on violence in modern societies* (pp. 563–592). New York: Springer.

Lombardo, R., & Lough, T. (2007). Community policing: Broken windows, community building, and satisfaction with the police. *The Police Journal, 80*(2), 117–140.

MacDonald, J. M. (2002). The effectiveness of community policing in reducing urban violence. *Crime & Delinquency, 48*(4), 592–618.

McCorry, J., & Morrisey, M. (1989). Community, crime and punishment in West Belfast. *The Howard Journal of Criminal Justice, 28*(4), 282–290.

Merry, S. E. (1994). Sorting out popular justice. In S. E. Merry & N. Milner (Eds.), *The possibility of popular justice: A case study of community mediation in the United States* (pp. 31–66). Ann Arbor, MI: Michigan University Press.

Minnaar, A. (2002). The 'new' vigilantism in post-April 1994 South Africa: Searching for explanations. In D. Feenan (Ed.), *Informal criminal justice* (pp. 117–134). Aldershot, Hants, England; Burlington, VT: Ashgate/Dartmouth.

Nicholl, C. G. (1999). *Community policing, community justice, and restorative justice: Exploring the links for the delivery of a balanced approach to public safety.* Washington, DC: U.S. Department of Justice, Office of Community Oriented Policing Services.

Omach, P. (2010). Political violence in Uganda: The role of vigilantes and militias. *The Journal of Social, Political and Economic Studies, 35*(4), 426–449.

Pastor, J. F. (2003). *The privatization of police in America: An analysis and case study*. Jefferson, NC: McFarland.
Peak, K. J., & Glensor, R. W. (2012). *Community policing and problem solving: Strategies and practices* (6th ed.). Upper Saddle River, NJ: Prentice Hall.
Peterson, M. (2005). *Intelligence-led policing: The new intelligence architecture*. Washington, DC: U.S. Department of Justice, Office of Justice Programs, Bureau of Justice Assistance.
Pratten, D. (2008). The politics of protection: Perspectives on vigilantism in Nigeria. *Africa, 78*(1), 1–15.
Ratcliffe, J. H. (2008). *Intelligence-led policing*. Cullompton, Devon, UK: Willan Publishing.
Reisig, M. D., & Parks, R. B. (2000). Experience, quality of life, and neighborhood context: A hierarchical analysis of satisfaction with police. *Justice Quarterly, 17*(3), 607–630.
Reisig, M. D., & Parks, R. B. (2004). Community policing and quality of life. In W. G. Skogan (Ed.), *Community policing (can it work?)* (pp. 207–227). Belmont, CA: Wadsworth.
Rogers, P. (2013, January 8). Emanuel, McCarthy aim to change CAPS: Mayor shifts resources of program to individual police districts. *NBC Chicago*. Retrieved from www.nbcchicago.com/blogs/ward-room/Emanuel-McCarthy-Aim-to-Change-CAPS-186084182.html.
Sadd, S., & Grinc, R. (1994). Innovative neighborhood-oriented policing programs: An evaluation of community policing programs in eight cities. In D. P. Rosenbaum (Ed.), *The challenge of community policing: Testing the promises* (pp. 27–52). London: Sage.
Sampson, R. J., & Bartusch, D. J. (1998). Legal cynicism and (subcultural?) tolerance of deviance: The neighborhood context of racial differences. *Law & Society Review, 32*(4), 777–804.
Scaramella, G. L., Cox, S. M., & McCamey, W. P. (2011). *Introduction to policing*. Thousand Oaks, CA: Sage.
Sederberg, P. C. (1978). The phenomenology of vigilantism in contemporary America: An interpretation. *Terrorism: An International Journal, 1*(3/4), 287–305.
Sekhonyane, M., & Louw, A. (2002). *Violent justice: Vigilantism and the state's response*. Pretoria: Institute for Security Studies.
Sharp, D., & Wilson, D. (2000). 'Household security': Private policing and vigilantism in Doncaster. *The Howard Journal of Criminal Justice, 39*(2), 113–131.
Silke, A. (1999). Ragged justice: Loyalist vigilantism in Northern Ireland. *Terrorism and Political Violence, 11*(3), 1–31.
Silke, A. (2001). Dealing with vigilantism: Issues and lessons for the police. *The Police Journal, 74*(2), 120–133.
Skogan, W. G. (1995). *Community participation and community policing*. Chicago: Center for Urban Affairs and Policy Research, Northwestern University.
Skogan, W. G. (2000). Community policing in Chicago. In G. P. Alpert & A. R. Piquero (Eds.), *Community policing: Contemporary readings* (2nd ed.) (pp. 159–174). Prospect Heights, IL: Waveland Press.
Skogan, W. G. (2006). *Police and community in Chicago: A tale of three cities*. New York: Oxford University Press.
Skogan, W. G., & Hartnett, S. M. (1997). *Community policing, Chicago style*. New York: Oxford University Press.
Skogan, W. G, Hartnett, S. M., DuBois, J., Comey, J. T., Kaiser, M., & Lovig, J. H. (2000). *Problem solving in practice: Implementing community policing in Chicago*. Washington, DC: U.S. Department of Justice, Office of Justice Programs, National Institute of Justice.
Skogan, W. G., Steiner, L., Benitez, C., Bennis, J., Borchers, S., DuBois, J., ... Rosenbaum, S. (2004). *CAPS at ten – Community policing in Chicago: An evaluation of Chicago's Alternative Policing Strategy*. Chicago: Illinois Criminal Justice Information Authority.
Skogan, W. G., Steiner, L., DuBois, J., Gudell, E., & Fagan, A. (2002). *Taking stock: Community policing in Chicago*. Chicago: Institute for Policy Research, Northwestern University.

Thom, K., Mills, A., Meehan, C., & Chetty, M. (2013). *Evaluating community justice: A review of research literature.* Auckland: Centre for Mental Health Research.
Trojanowicz, R. C., & Bucqueroux, B. (1998). *Community policing: How to get started* (2nd ed.). Cincinnati, OH: Anderson.
Turk, A. T. (1987). Popular justice and the politics of informalism. In C. D. Shearing & P. C. Stenning (Eds.), *Private policing* (pp. 131–146). Thousand Oaks, CA: Sage.
Umbreit, M. (1994). *Victim meets offender: The impact of restorative justice and mediation.* Monsey, NY: Criminal Justice Press.
Weisburd, D., Mastrofski, S. D., McNally, A. M., Greenspan, R., & Willis, J. J. (2003). Reforming to preserve: CompStat and strategic problem solving in American policing. *Criminology & Public Policy, 2*(3), 421–456.
Wilson, J. Q., & Kelling, G. L. (1982). Broken windows: The police and neighborhood safety. *The Atlantic Monthly, 249*(3): 29–38.
Wojkowska, E. (2006). *Doing justice: How informal justice systems can contribute?* Oslo: UNDP Oslo Governance Centre.
Wolf, R. V. (2006). Community justice around the world: An international overview. *Crime & Justice International, 22*(93), 4–22.
Zimring, F. E. (2003). *The contradictions of American capital punishment.* New York: Oxford University Press.

# Policing in Remote Australia
## Is it Possible to Ignore Colonial Borderlines?*

# 8

JUDY PUTT AND RICK SARRE

## Contents



**Abstract**

In 2009 a new criminal justice initiative was introduced to the central Australian desert region. It has become known as the Cross-border Justice Scheme. In short, the Scheme endeavours to police the region without paying heed to the colonial boundaries that separate the various state jurisdictions. The Scheme was designed to promote high quality trans-jurisdictional practice by all key criminal justice institutions, namely police, prosecutions, courts and corrections, but especially police. This chapter looks at the impetus of the Scheme from its political roots, the implementation of the Scheme, and the pivotal role played by police services, both in changing the environment in which the Scheme now operates and in contributing to some positive but limited changes in cross-jurisdictional policing cooperation.

## Introduction

In 1999 a 15-year-old Aboriginal girl in a rural community in Western Australia died in tragic circumstances. In November 2001, the Western Australian government, prompted by this death, announced an inquiry into allegations concerning family violence and child abuse in Aboriginal communities. In July 2002, the inquiry published its report: *Putting the Picture Together: Inquiry into Response by Government Agencies to Complaints of Family Violence and Child Abuse in Aboriginal Communities.* It became known as 'the Gordon Report' (Gordon et al. 2002). The report identified that no fewer than 13 agencies had been providing services to the girl, but that individual agencies had not been aware of the services being provided by each other. Moreover, there was a lack of clarity as to which agency was leading the process. It was a classic case of the right hand not knowing what the left hand (or any hand) was doing.

The inquiry also found that access to policing services by Indigenous people in remote areas was problematic (Gordon et al. 2002: 212, 226–228). There was a need, the report said, for more services, more police, more effective information-sharing between relevant agencies, better service coordination, and specific legislative initiatives and policy changes that would facilitate these reforms.

The Gordon Report provided the political opportunity for various agencies and groups to come together with the relevant governments and their departments to discuss the idea of a central Australian justice project. This had always been difficult, because state and territory borders, drawn across colonial maps, cut through and across tribal lands.

## The Region

In order to understand the consequences of the Gordon Report for policing in central Australia, it is useful to introduce to readers the geographic region under examination.

Spanning the three jurisdictions of Western Australia, South Australia and the Northern Territory, the central Australian 'cross-border' region is sparsely populated, with an estimated 7,000 people living in some 26 communities. The predominantly Aboriginal population in central Australia is highly mobile for family and cultural reasons (Sarre and Putt 2016).

A comparison of key census statistics for the region for 2001 and 2011 indicate that the estimated population of Indigenous persons in the region has dropped slightly (from 6,075 to 5,601 persons). Moreover, there has been a considerable decline in the estimated non-Indigenous population (3,497 to 1,327) although it is not known how much of this decrease was due to a decline in the resident (as against visiting) population. Indigenous people in the region seem to have maintained their use of local languages. Indeed, 94 per cent of residents surveyed as part of the evaluation reported that they spoke an Australian Indigenous language in 2001 and that proportion had not changed by 2011.

There have been signs of improvement in educational and employment outcomes over the relevant decade. In 2001, 15 per cent of Indigenous persons reported that they had received no formal education, and 70 per cent said they had completed Year 10. In contrast, by 2011, only 8 per cent said that they had had no formal schooling, and 79 per cent said they had completed Year 10. Labour participation rates were 35 per cent in 2001 but had climbed to 40 per cent in 2011. It appears there may have been a relative decline in the employment of non-Indigenous people and a slight improvement in employment opportunities for local Indigenous people. It could be argued that these data indicate a number of small yet positive changes in relation to addressing underlying factors that are said to affect offending (namely, poor education and unemployment).

That having been said, a scan of regional criminal justice data for the region compared with similar statistics compiled a decade ago indicate a substantial increase in offences coming to the attention of police.

## The Birth of an Idea

Although mechanisms have existed for many years to enable ad hoc inter-jurisdictional cooperation between various criminal justice agencies, including police, there was general agreement among key stakeholders that more was required to address the range of social and justice problems in the region and to allay the impediments to effective criminal justice responses created by jurisdictional borders. There needed to be a political solution (and a legislative base) that would make jurisdictional barriers in central Australia essentially porous (Fleming 2011).

In May 2002, senior officers from Western Australia (WA), the Northern Territory (NT) and South Australia (SA) met at a specifically convened Justice Roundtable in Alice Springs. During this period, representatives of the Ngaanyatjarra Pitjantjatjara Yankunytjatjara (NPY) Women's Council were expressing their concerns about the inadequate response to a range of social problems in central Australia. In the months that followed, a model of cooperation that could be implemented across the NPY lands began to emerge (Remote Service Delivery Project 2003).

There were other factors, too, that provided the impetus for reform. Police and other policy-makers wanted to reduce long-distance police patrolling and the often unduly lengthy transport of offenders that the conventional borders insisted upon. Furthermore, they wanted to address the limited capacity for crime prevention and early intervention permitted by conventional policing. Finally, they wanted to prevent the often lengthy delays in matters being dealt with by the courts following the arrest of suspects, to enable information-sharing between agencies and across jurisdictions, and to assist with victim protection (Lloyd et al. 2010; Fleming and Sarre 2011).

An Inter-Government Agreement between the three jurisdictions was signed in 2007. It was agreed by all signatories that a scheme for cooperative justice services would be implemented through the enactment of legislation. Identical laws were thus enacted in the parliaments of Western Australia, the Northern Territory and South Australia in 2008 and 2009, with amendments to national legislation enacted in 2009. These laws now allow police to be appointed as special officers in all three jurisdictions, and make it possible for persons who reside in, who are 'connected with' (or who commit offences in) the cross-border region to be arrested by any special officer, and to be dealt with by a magistrate sitting in any of the three jurisdictions.

There were also a number of inter-governmental and organizational agreements entered into. Cross-jurisdictional service level agreements (which gave effect to the legislation by describing how cooperation between services would work) were signed off between 2009 and 2011. They covered the appointment and management of police and justice officers, the installation of the required procedural arrangements including review and monitoring, and cost-sharing.

The Scheme became operational in 2009. Henceforth, there was not quite a 'borderless world' but a justice framework that allowed geographical and jurisdictional borders to be viewed as essentially porous. Induction and training sessions were held with various key stakeholder groups such as magistrates and within various justice agencies.

## The Challenges

There is no shortage of literature that highlights the challenges of policing in rural and remote Australia. The legacy of 200 years of colonial policing and bureaucratic neglect has left scars that are difficult to erase (Blagg and Anthony 2014). The literature reveals that a 'top-down' approach to policy formulation is always problematic (Cunneen 2001; Mazerolle et al. 2003; Sarre 2005; Blandford and Sarre 2009). Moreover, the mixture of Aboriginal customary law and the Australian 'common law' has been the subject of numerous inquiries, none of which has ever resolved the contradictions satisfactorily (Sarre 1997, 2000; Western Australia 2006).

A major reform agenda to attempt to overcome Indigenous disadvantage (principally at the behest of the Australian government) led to considerable turbulence in local community governance and widespread change. Integral to this national commitment was a significant investment in infrastructure and services in many remote communities, although much of this had translated into discrete programmes on the ground, often delivered by visiting service providers and a constellation of government and non-government service providers. There emerged a significant amount of research investigating the ways in which community safety was to be enhanced and evaluated, separate and apart from any reference to the Scheme (ACG 2010; Willis 2010; FaHCSIA 2011; Putt 2011, Blagg et al. 2015).

However, except for a very significant increase in police numbers and consequent policing operations in the cross-border region, there was not necessarily, at that time, a coordinated or strategic investment in justice services or in crime prevention measures. In truth, there are more crime prevention programmes and initiatives (such as youth services, night patrols and safe houses, and greater alcohol restrictions in some regions) than had formerly been the case, but this expansion did not occur as a result of the Scheme. Indeed, the main key change directly relating to crime reduction and the alleviation of social disruption was the roll-out of low aromatic (Opal) fuel, which had led to a drop in the incidence of the highly destructive practice of 'petrol sniffing' (d'Abbs and Shaw 2008). In terms of justice services, the main infrastructure facilities (regional prisons, court premises) remain largely unchanged. In sum, although there are more circuit courts, and the establishment of a Work Camp at a community in Western Australia since the introduction of the Scheme, there is very little tangible difference that one can observe in justice infrastructure at the local level, post-2009.

The introduction of the Scheme coincided with a significant jump in the numbers of police stationed in the cross-border region. There are now three police stations in the Ngaanyatjarra Lands (the Western Australian portion of the NPY lands) and a number of new or upgraded police stations in the south-western corner of the Northern Territory. Police are now rostered in SA in the Anangu Pitjantjatjara Yankunytjatjara (APY) Lands (the South Australian portion of the NPY lands) in such a way that there are usually two police officers at a police station at all times. The map of the cross-border region (Figure 8.1) shows the 16 police stations now established in the region. One consequence of the increased police presence has been a reduction in the duration of time between a call for assistance and a patrol arriving. Local police are now able to respond more quickly to adverse events and are better placed to deal with such events through their knowledge of the local context and links with local people. Indeed, greater social contact has allowed police to act more often in a proactive fashion, intervening before matters escalate.

## The Evaluation

Conducted over 12 months from 2012 to 2013, a formal evaluation set out to assess how well the Scheme was operating and how it impacted stakeholders, including justice service-providers (Putt et al. 2013).

### Method

Three key approaches were taken to accessing stakeholders' viewpoint. A total of 124 people in ten communities across the region were interviewed. Fifty local justice service

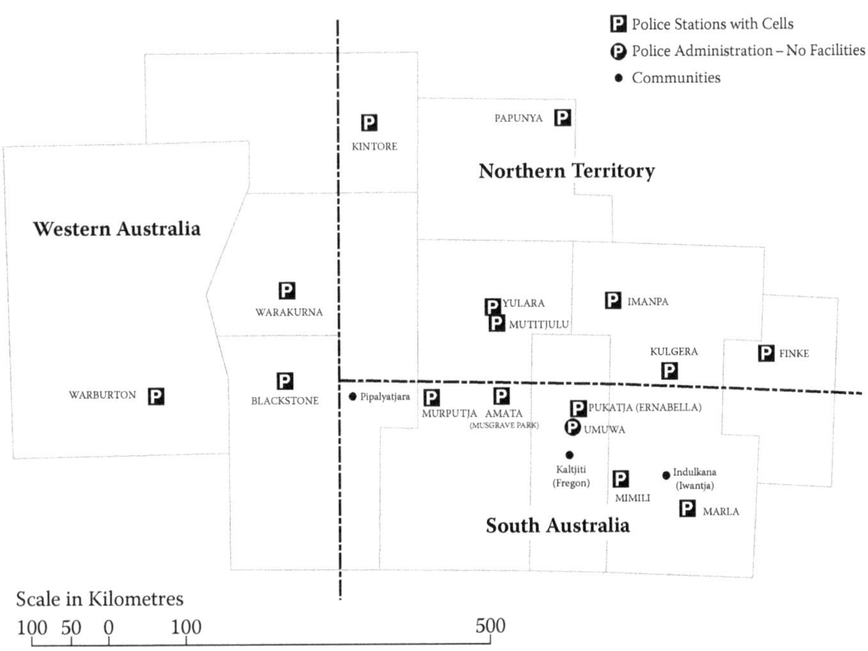


**Figure 8.1** Cross-Border Justice Scheme, Current Boundaries and Police Stations.
Source: adapted from Special Constables Manual (South Australia Police).

providers in the region participated in an online survey. More than 35 key stakeholders (typically based in a regional centre or capital city in each of the jurisdictions) participated in face-to-face or telephone interviews. With all three approaches an effort was made to include a cross-section of participants from each of the three jurisdictions.

Fieldwork was conducted in three distinct areas within the cross-border region. Each area has communities that are geographically close, and enjoy strong cultural ties. Three interview schedules were devised for community members and local justice service providers, including police and magistrates. In six communities, researchers arranged interviews with community members, police officers, clinic staff and any other service providers that may have had valuable input.

The fieldwork in several communities was timed to coincide with the visits of the Magistrates Court sessions which enabled the researchers to interview magistrates, sheriffs, prosecutors and correctional staff at around the same time. In the remaining four communities, the research concentrated exclusively on Indigenous residents of the area. The aim of the field research was to get in-depth interviews with Indigenous residents of the area to understand their perceptions and experience of the Scheme, with interviews conducted in the local language.

Of the 124 interviews conducted during the fieldwork, 84 were with local community members in the ten communities. However, very few had much to say about the Scheme itself, either because they did not know what it was or only knew of its existence because they had seen a poster about it in a local police station. In the report on the evaluation, therefore, the results from these interviews focused on the views of community members of the increase in a police presence in the region, and whether offenders cross borders to evade justice.

The input of local justice stakeholders was sought, too. The views of local police (n = 11) along with others who participated in the online survey (n = 27) were able to be captured (through fieldwork) in ten communities.

In the formal evaluation report (Putt et al. 2013), more detail is provided on the views on the Scheme of specific stakeholder groups other than police, such as magistrates and senior representatives of justice agencies.

## Responses

What follows is a summary of some of the key themes that emerged from the evaluative data specifically relating to the provision of policing services in the region and under the Scheme.

Several people interviewed identified that the quality of the delivery of policing services had improved in their region. One informant in Western Australia described her feelings about how simply having the police around in the community served to ease her stress. She said that the persons likely to start or get involved in a flare-up are much less likely to do so if the police are on hand, or if they were expected to arrive quickly. This person thought that the level of crime had decreased because of the continuous police presence and the high calibre of the relevant officers.

A long-term non-Indigenous resident commented that she thought that sometimes people would actually 'bring on' their fights when the police were in the community, in the knowledge that the police would be there to prevent them escalating too much; or to provide an excuse (for the benefit of witnesses) for someone to moderate their attack on another.

It was noted by one Indigenous interviewee that there is a strong cultural imperative in some Indigenous communities for a person who has offended to want to 'make peace' with the world. This is based on the pressing need in small-scale, kin-based societies for people not to allow disputes or conflicts to persist. In a recent and very serious case, the offender quickly handed himself in when a highly respected police officer approached him in a personal and understanding way. Reinforcements that had been brought in urgently from a nearby town were not required.

Feedback from local police generally was mixed. Some were convinced that the Scheme could be an important element in the efficient and effective delivery of justice to the region. Others said that they liked to use the Scheme's procedures, but found that they were confronted with a range of barriers that prevented them, such as the demands of paperwork. Still others believed that the Scheme was not particularly useful, and, in fact, created additional work for very little outcome.

There were mixed responses to questions about the use and impact of the Scheme. The responses ranged from those who used it extensively to those that saw it as unnecessary because so much had changed over the past ten years, primarily the big increase in local police in communities. The responses to the survey from all the local justice service providers including police indicated the overwhelming majority (96 per cent) had heard of the Scheme but one-fifth did not even know whether it had an impact on their service and nearly half (46 per cent) said it had made 'a bit' of an impact. Other survey results also highlighted that many local justice service providers did not feel they could comment on the Scheme because of their lack of knowledge and direct experience with the Scheme. For example, in response to a question about whether they would like to see changes to the Scheme, 41 per cent said yes, 20 per cent said no and 39 per cent did not know.

However, many comments by police in interviews and in the survey were positive about the Scheme. For example one police officer said it had created more work but had given them more powers, while several other officers noted it had improved communication with police across the border, improved intelligence-sharing and avoided lengthy extradition applications. Several stressed that it had not had the expected impact on their work or service, because the judiciary, the courts and Aboriginal legal services were reluctant to engage with and/or use the Scheme.

Despite evidence that the Scheme had not been widely used, several of the police interviewed described cases in which its deployment had been useful. Here are some examples:

> A guy broke into the project officer's house and stole a firearm and other stuff, and then skipped to Western Australia. South Australia police told us that they'd heard he was here. We checked it out and confirmed the rumour. So we raided him in [a community in WA] and found him with the firearm, and the offender [was] wearing the clothes he'd stolen. The South Australia police came over to [the community], interviewed and charged him.

> Picked up someone in [community A in SA] who had outstanding warrants from an offence in [regional town in WA]. We rang the [regional town] court from [community A] and he attended court in [community B in WA].

> A guy burned down a school in SA and we found him in WA. We held him in custody, and then took him to the border and the South Australia police came and picked him up. Then they charged him under SA law and he was taken to [regional town in SA].

Some cases were not as successful. Here is an example of a frustrating episode which the Scheme was not able to rescue:

> In December 2011 a bloke assaulted his wife in the NT and got locked up for it. She got the police involved. When they interviewed her they realized that he had also bashed her in another community in SA. They sent the transcript of the interview through to the South Australia police and got them to raise a complaint and make a prosecution file. [Community in SA] then forwarded the prosecution file through to [regional town in SA], who forwarded it to [regional town in NT] prosecution. They held the man on remand for the NT-based charge, but had to bail him for the SA one. They made the SA bail condition that he be present in court for the same date that the NT remand finished. The matter landed up in the SA court but the magistrate there threw the whole thing out.

The cases described above remind observers of the extent of cooperation needed between jurisdictions to prosecute successfully a cross-border case through to completion. All respondents were wary of the pitfalls:

> It's not a streamlined system. There are a lot of phone calls, calling in favours and using personal relationships. It would improve if there was more training about it, and understanding it. It's also generating work for everyone, and we're busy enough already.

In the absence of specific training many officers were loath to use the Scheme:

> Because police officers are unfamiliar with the Scheme they don't want to use it. If they do it wrong they could get into trouble with their own career, or even be sued for deprivation of liberty if they lock someone up wrongly. That is a big disincentive to using it.

An example of the need for training in the laws of different jurisdictions was given by Western Australian officers who work in South Australia:

> It's tricky – the law does change between the States – for example we do a lot of gunja [marijuana]-related stuff. In SA there are infringements for possession, and for possession of a smoking implement, whereas in WA you can't charge someone

> for possession of an implement. So you do have to know the laws in each State – at least for the areas in which we have a lot of traffic.

Better training would also provide an opportunity for police to address some of the current anomalies in the Scheme. One officer wanted to use the Scheme to involve an individual in a juvenile diversion program, but was unsure about how to manage that. This is how a colleague narrated the story:

> The Cross-border Act says that it can be used. He has got a juvenile who assaulted his wife in an NT community, then moved to a community in Western Australia. He contacted the juvenile diversion people saying that he wanted this kid to be included. They quoted the NT Juvenile Diversion Act back to him, which says that he can't be included because the person concerned has gone interstate. So the two pieces of legislation directly contradict each other. Apparently the person has to agree to it while they are in the NT – they can't move and then agree.

A number of respondents referred to the barrier of not having access to the police computer systems for the neighbouring jurisdiction:

> There is no NT computer in the [community in WA] office. You have to log in remotely using VPN, which is really, really slow. You can't print, save or anything. You have to email yourself everything, and then open it on the WA system.

A related issue is the extent to which the data systems in each jurisdiction may not be able to 'talk' to each other. The following case note gives an example of the problems that can arise:

> A man from a community close to the border got done for DUI [driving under the influence] in [regional town in NT]. Then he went to [regional town in SA] and got into trouble there and was locked up. This time the charge from [regional town in NT] was added to his other [regional town in SA] charges and they were all heard together. He lost his licence for it all. But the loss of licence didn't register on the NT system – only the SA one, because the systems don't line up. So he applied for a licence in the NT and got it.

It is not surprising that high staff turnover is seen as a significant barrier to the Scheme's success. Slow bureaucratic processes magnify this. One officer had been working at a station for almost a full year, and had still not been sworn in as a Special Constable for South Australia. That limited his role to working solely in the Northern Territory – he could not participate in multi-jurisdictional policing. As he said,

> I'll be gone from here soon, then there'll be another guy sitting here and waiting.

The very nature of the Scheme necessitates working closely with colleagues from other police services, and, in an environment with a high turnover, this can be problematic.

> At the moment it really depends on the relationship you have with the officers across the border. We used to work a lot with a particular officer. He's gone now. So we'll have to see how we go with his replacement. It really shouldn't depend so much on that relationship, because it's so important that it be used a lot.

Several respondents also said that having a single point of contact in each jurisdiction (and being aware of who that was) was useful. One respondent said that there were excellent working relationships, but that the process needed to be more formalized so that all relevant police members were aware of the correct processes and procedures and, indeed, some uniformity in the equipment worn and deployed:

> SA aren't that keen on us going down there because we wear Tasers on our belts, and the Commissioner there doesn't like them.

On the other hand, the communication channels forged by the Scheme and the consequential high degree of sharing of intelligence was cited by many police respondents as an example of the real benefit of the Scheme.

For many of those respondents who had been working in the region for a considerable period of time, the Scheme was regarded as the key impetus for the uptake and increased use of video-links, and increased awareness among local residents of the consequences of domestic violence and its criminality.

## Analysis

The evaluation unearthed a number of anticipated and unanticipated consequences of the Scheme. They are summarized in the paragraphs that follow.

The main finding from this research was that there was almost an inverse relationship between stakeholder groups' knowledge of the region versus stakeholders' knowledge of the Scheme. Local community members and service providers based in communities were unlikely to know much about the Scheme at all. The only exception to this was a number of police based in an area close to the borders who said they used it extensively. Visiting justice practitioners – such as magistrates and prosecutors who visit communities as part of circuit courts – were more familiar with the Scheme, but did not always have detailed knowledge of how it had developed nor had they used it much. Those at more senior levels in justice services, and in particular those on the Project Executive Group, were most familiar with the legislative provisions and service agreements that underpin the Scheme.

There was an expectation that many offenders would be affected by the Scheme, and that budgets would be affected thereby. However, the very low number of cases identified as 'cross-border' cases has meant that budgets have not been impacted greatly. A range of reasons were proffered for the low numbers, including delays in signing the Memoranda of Understanding, the perceived resistance and reluctance of police to change well-known practices, the poor relations between some magistrates and some police, and the lack of 'champions' at a senior police level.

It is difficult to determine whether the Scheme has operated to reduce the fear of crime in the region due to the fact that, over the period of the Scheme's implementation, there have been additional policing resources stationed in the region.

There is some suggestion that there was insufficient consultation, or consultation undertaken in a manner that befitted such a major change to justice delivery for the region, especially given that the changes would most affect the Ngaanyatjarra, Pitjantjatjara and Yankunytjatjara people and had the potential to cause significant social and family disruption to their communities (Charles 2009).

A consistent example of cross-border cooperation, referred to by several key stakeholder respondents, was the very visible police presence from all three of the police services at the sports carnivals that are convened regularly in the region.

Among key non-police stakeholders who were interviewed there was widespread support for the overall aims of the Scheme. Many such stakeholders offered very positive comments, which included the contribution of the Scheme to a justice environment that was now more flexible and effective in its responses to crime. Particularly, respondents identified the Scheme as sparking improvements to the formal and informal networks and hi-tech communications across borders.

This level of communication has had flow-on effects in the practice of justice more generally. From the point of view of collaboration and coordination across borders and between agencies, respondents reported that it is nowadays much easier to relay information from place to place in a timely fashion than it was a decade ago. Combined with the protocols in place by virtue of the Scheme, a defendant can now be dealt with, typically, at a single point and on a single occasion, thereby avoiding or reducing long-distance travel and long delays in matters being finalized.

Indeed, the heightened levels of communication and cooperation required to implement the Scheme have resulted in a diffusion of benefit across policing and other services. That having been said, the inefficiencies of geographical 'remoteness' remain, and it is almost impossible for any policy initiative to overcome, in one fell swoop, the tyrannies of distance.

The evaluation highlights that cross-border policing has been the most obvious operational beneficiary of the Scheme. There has not been the same level of, or demand for, cross-border cooperation between courts, prosecutions, community corrections, corrections and juvenile justice agencies although that is likely to grow.

The evaluation also demonstrated that there are many stakeholders who are still unsure about how the Scheme works and how it is supposed to operate. Key areas of concern raised by stakeholders relate primarily to streamlining and clarifying processes and administrative arrangements. The Scheme's proponents will now need to address these concerns. The capacity of the proponents to continue to promote the Scheme successfully will be dependent upon the commitment to it by the various sectors involved, and the resources devoted to it.

Finally, the cross-border initiative provided observers with a unique opportunity to test the idea of eliminating jurisdictional boundaries so as to deliver better justice and policing services. Developing and implementing an initiative that involved three jurisdictions and multiple agencies was no easy task. It took some years to frame and pass the legislation and to write the organizational agreements but ultimately there was enough political goodwill for it to come to fruition. Despite the low numbers of offenders being caught up in the Scheme, there are now calls for it to be extended through to other aspects in the administration of justice, such as the enforcement of fines, the operation of parole boards and appeal mechanisms.

## Conclusion

The Scheme has shown itself, through the eyes of the respondents to the evaluative study, to be a necessary but not sufficient instrument to deliver the outcomes sought by its proponents a decade ago. In the final analysis the best determinant of the success of the Scheme will be its ability to streamline justice processes and to continue to foster efficiencies. Ultimately, however, reformers should not rest until there has been a significant reduction in levels of victimization in the region. Those targets are yet to be set and measured.

## Note

* Former version previously published in PPR Sofia Special Issue.

## References

ACG (Allen Consulting Group). 2010. *Independent Review of Policing in Remote Indigenous Communities in the Northern Territory: Policing Further into Remote Communities.* Report to the Australian Government and the Northern Territory Government. Allen Consulting Group. www.allenconsult.com.au/resources/ReviewPolicingNT.pdf.

Blagg, H. and Anthony, T. 2014. '"If those old women catch you, you're going to cop it": Night patrols, Indigenous women, and place based sovereignty in Outback Australia', *African Journal of Criminology and Justice Studies*, 8(1), 103–124.

Blagg, H., Bluett-Boyd, N. and Williams, E. 2015. 'Innovative models in addressing violence against Indigenous women', *University of Western Australia State of Knowledge paper*, 1–57.

Blandford, J. and Sarre, R. 2009. 'Policing in South Australia's remote and rural communities: Preliminary observations from a novel police diversionary strategy for young Indigenous offenders', *Police Practice and Research: An International Journal*, 10(3), 187–197.

Charles, C.J. 2009. 'The national Cross-border Justice Scheme', *Indigenous Law Bulletin*, 7(12), 23–26.

Cunneen, C. 2001. *Conflict, Politics and Crime: Aboriginal Communities and the Police*, Crows Nest, New South Wales: Allen and Unwin.

d'Abbs, P. and Shaw, G. 2008. *Evaluation of the Impact of Opal Fuel. Executive Summary*, Canberra: Department of Health and Ageing.

FaHCSIA (Department of Families, Housing, Community Services and Indigenous Affairs). 2011. *Northern Territory Emergency Response Evaluation Report 2011*, Canberra: FaHCSIA. http://servicedelivery.dss.gov.au/2011/11/10/northern-territory-emergency-response-evaluation-report-2011-released/.

Fleming, J. 2011. 'Policing Indigenous people in the Ngaanyatjarra Pitjantjatjara Yankunytjatjara lands', in S. Hufnagel, C. Harfield and S. Bronitt (eds) *Cross-Border Law Enforcement: Regional Law Enforcement Co-operation – European, Australian and Asia-Pacific Perspectives.* Routledge: Oxon and New York.

Fleming, J. and Sarre, R. 2011. 'Policing the NPY lands: The cross-border justice project', *Australasian Policing: A Journal of Professional Practice and Research*, 3(1), 31–35.

Gordon, S., Hallahan, K. and Henry, D. 2002. *Putting the Picture Together: Inquiry into the Response by Government Agencies to Complaints of Family Violence and Child Abuse in Aboriginal Communities*, Department of Premier and Cabinet Western Australia, State Law Publisher, Western Australia, 31 July. www.austlii.edu.au/au/journals/AILR/2002/65.html. Reproduced in *Australian Indigenous Law Reporter* (2002), 7(4), 49.

Lloyd, J., Coates, R. and Gwilliam, C. 2010. 'The Cross-border Justice Scheme: A unique opportunity to improve justice beyond jurisdictional constraints', presentation at the *Australian and New Zealand Society of Criminology Conference*, Alice Springs, September 2010.

Mazerolle, L., Marchetti, E. and Lindsay, A. 2003. 'Policing the plight of Indigenous Australians: Past conflicts and present challenges', *Police and Society*, 7, 75–102.

Putt, J. 2011. 'Community policing in rural and remote Australia', in J. Putt (ed.) *Community Policing in Australia*, Research and Public Policy Series, Report No. 111, Canberra: Australian Institute of Criminology.

Putt, J., Shaw, G., Sarre, R. and Rowden, E. 2013. *Evaluation of the Cross-border Justice Scheme: Final Report*. Report to the Government of South Australia, Attorney-General's Department, July 2013, unpublished.

Remote Service Delivery Project. 2003. *Remote Service Delivery Project: Steering Committee, Service Delivery Model, Final Report*, Western Australia Police, unpublished.

Sarre, R. 1997. 'Is there a role for the application of customary law in addressing Aboriginal criminality in Australia?', *Critical Criminology: An International Journal*, 8(2), 91–102.

Sarre, R. 2000. 'Sentencing in customary or tribal settings: An Australian perspective', Vera Institute of Justice, New York, NY, *Federal Sentencing Reporter*, 13(2), 74–78.

Sarre, R. 2005. 'Police and the public: Some observations on policing and Indigenous Australians', *Current Issues in Criminal Justice*, 17(2), 305–313.

Sarre, R. and Putt, J. 2016. 'Policing the cross-border region', *Police Practice and Research: An International Journal*, 17(2), 126–135.

Western Australia. 2006. 'Aboriginal customary laws: The interaction of Western Australian law with Aboriginal law and culture', *Western Australia Law Reform Commission*, Project 94, Perth.

Willis, M. 2010. *Community Safety in Australian Indigenous Communities: Service Providers' Perceptions*, Research and Public Policy Series, Report No. 110, Canberra: Australian Institute of Criminology.

# Multi-Sector Co-Operation in Preventing Crime

## The Case of a South African Neighbourhood Watch as an Effective Crime Prevention Model*

9

JOHAN VAN GRAAN

## Contents



### Abstract

This case study describes the experience of effective and sustainable multi-sector co-operation in the prevention of crime between the Roodekrans Neighbourhood Watch (RNW) in Roodepoort, South Africa (SA), the South African Police Service (SAPS), private security businesses, and the local business sector. This case study is illustrated in the context of empowering communities to take ownership of community safety by facilitating a multi-sector approach. Many studies have highlighted the role of the police in driving crime prevention, however, this chapter focuses on the role and contribution of communities themselves as an effective vehicle of crime prevention drawing on multi-sector co-operation. Knowledge regarding best practices in this field of crime prevention remains a work in progress, therefore this chapter aims to contribute to the general framework for the growth of successful multi-sector community-based crime prevention initiatives.

## Introduction

The high levels of crime in South Africa (SA) continuously pose challenges for citizens and the South African Police Service (SAPS). According to Zinn (2012) the highest concentration of crime in SA that poses a risk to the general members of the public takes place in residential neighbourhoods. These crimes include residential burglaries, theft of motor vehicles and motor cycles, theft out/from motor vehicles, carjacking, business robbery and house robbery, common robbery, and general theft. As a result, there is concern in many communities regarding strategies in which crime in neighbourhoods can be prevented. One such crime prevention strategy that has been implemented by a number of communities in SA is Neighbourhood Watch.

Neighbourhood Watch in SA was first established in Johannesburg in 1985. Since the establishment of Neighbourhood Watch schemes in the United States of America (USA) and the United Kingdom (UK) there has been an expansion of such schemes around the world. The report of the 2000 British Crime Survey estimated that 27% of all households, approximately 6 million households, in England and Wales were members of a Neighbourhood Watch scheme in 2000. This amounted to over 155,000 schemes in operation (Sims, 2001). The report of The 2000 National Crime Prevention Survey 'estimates that over a quarter of the UK population and over 40% of the USA population live in areas covered by neighbourhood watch schemes' (Bennet, Holloway, & Farrington, 2006, p. 437).

It is acknowledged that there is no generic method for establishing multi-sector collaborations in community-based crime prevention initiatives. The design of such initiatives will depend on unique crime conditions, requirements, and resources of a particular community. However, this framework could be transferred to similar contexts, or adapted where necessary or even improved upon to facilitate effective multi-sector collaboration to prevent crime. The chapter makes two central points. First, it argues that the police cannot effectively control crime without public support, thus, communities play a firm role in community-based crime prevention initiatives. Second, it argues that Neighbourhood Watch projects are more effective in preventing crime in instances where such a project does not function in isolation, but actively engages in a co-operative relationship with other sectors.

## Hunter's Private, Parochial, and Public Social Orders

Hunter's (1985) private, parochial, and public spheres of social control provides the theoretical frame for this chapter. Carr's (2003) case study on 'the new parochialism' grounds the body of theory. A discussion concerning how neighbourhood organizations facilitate resident–police interactions follows whereafter the need for police–resident co-operation to effectively control crime is reviewed.

Hunter (1985, pp. 230–234) identifies three spheres of social orders – the private, the parochial, and the public – which he applies to an analysis of the nature of crime and incivility within urban communities. The private order is found in both informal and more formal primary groups where the values of sentiment, social support, and esteem are the essential resources of the social order and the basis of social control. Hunter describes that the parochial social order is based on the local interpersonal networks and interconnecting of local institutions that serve the daily and sustenance needs of the residential community – local stores (local businessmen), schools, churches (religious leaders), and voluntary associations (directors and board members) of various kinds. The institutional base of the public order is found primarily in the formal bureaucratic agencies of the state.

Given the concern with crime in urban areas attention should focus upon the public order and the institution most clearly concerned with social control in the public arena ... the police (Hunter, 1985, p. 236). However, the police are increasingly limited in their capacity to satisfy the increasing demands for their services. As a result, alternative solutions were prompted to the problem of social control by shifting the problem to other social orders, one of the results of which is what may be labelled 'the rediscovery of community'. The parochial and private social orders are often strengthened with state resources in an attempt to counteract the prevailing sense of disorder on the streets of urban neighbourhoods. The solution is not for the state to engage in direct social control, that is, to attempt to increase its efficiency in catching criminals; but rather for the state to increasingly support stronger parochial orders. This phenomenon emerges in many urban areas, for example, many local community organizations in urban neighbourhoods are often clearly concerned in their activities of social control and 'doing something' about crime (Hunter, 1985, p. 238).

## Carr's 'New Parochialism'

Carr's (2003, p. 1250) case studies of the Beltway neighbourhood in Chicago illustrate how informal social control can work in a neighbourhood that is not characterized by dense social connections but rather where community organizations and their relations with public agencies outside the neighbourhood facilitate action by citizens to control crime and disorder. Carr demonstrates that the parochial and public arenas are inseparable from each other, not independent as other scholars have argued. Carr argues that informal social control in Beltway is characterized by what he calls the 'new parochialism'. Carr explains 'new parochialism' is where diminished private and traditionally parochial forms of social control are replaced by a set of behaviours that are a combination of parochial and public controls. Instead of supervision and direct physical intervention in disputes, Beltway residents engage in behaviours that are more secure and facilitated by actors of the public sphere of control. For example, the actions of the neighbourhood problem-solving group who utilize the local politicians and city bureaucracy to close down a tavern that is notoriously known for creating crime and disorder illustrates the new parochialism. According to Carr the new parochialism is a set of practices that creates solutions at the parochial level but owes its existence and efficacy to the intervention of institutions and groups from outside the neighbourhood. Carr's study further found that residents reduced crime risks by participating in activities of local organizations that worked with police instead of directly intervening in disputes.

## Neighbourhood Organizations as Facilitators of Resident–Police Interactions: The Need to Co-Operatively Control Crime

In relation to Carr's 'new parochialism' Hawdon and Ryan (2011, p. 899) believe police and residents can co-produce public safety using strategies that range from active involvement by residents (citizen patrols, neighbourhood watches) to passive involvement by residents (residents monitor their neighbourhoods and report suspicious persons or incidents to the police). Several researchers, such as Carr (2003), have noted that residents are often reluctant to become active in crime prevention efforts because of fear of retaliation from criminals, but neighbourhood organizations can help overcome this fear by providing safe venues for residents to manage crime risk indirectly. However, evidence suggests that neighbourhood organizations can contribute to crime control and are important for stimulating resident involvement in policing efforts necessary for successful community policing (Carr, 2003; Friedman, 1994; Ohmer & Beck, 2006; Pattavina, Byrne, & Garcia, 2006). Results of Hawdon and Ryan's (2011, p. 911) study in western South Carolina revealed participation in a local anti-crime neighbourhood organization can significantly increase the probability of residents assisting police in crime-fighting efforts. Hourihan (1987, p. 129) observes participation by the public in crime prevention measures has two effects, a direct effect whereby increased patrolling or observation reduces the opportunities for crime and an indirect impact whereby a local community becomes increasingly active and integrated, and establishes the behavioural norms and social controls it considers appropriate, thereby pressuring those people who might otherwise be involved in criminal activity.

Community-based crime prevention initiatives, such as Neighbourhood Watch projects, have proven to be useful in preventing crimes such as house robbery, residential burglary, and vehicle theft. 'Police can't be everywhere 24/7, and we've seen that where Neighbourhood Watches exist and are viable in their community, we have a lower incidence of crime' (Rettig, 2010, p. 69). However, Pattavina et al. (2006, p. 226) found that residents living in high-risk neighbourhoods were more likely to become involved in community crime prevention efforts than residents living in low- to moderate-crime-risk neighbourhoods.

Neighbourhood Watch projects demonstrated even more effectiveness in preventing crime in instances where such projects do not function in isolation but actively engage in a co-operative multi-sector relationship. These projects rely on the belief that crime may be prevented if potential offenders believe that there is a high risk of being caught in particular communities. This notion is supported by Bennet et al. (2006) arguing that Neighbourhood Watch might also lead to a reduction in crime through the reduction of opportunities for crime. In addition, increased visibility by the police and communities working together serve as a proactive deterrent against crime. Blair (2005) and Bratton (2007) emphasize that now, more than ever, previous emphases on neighbourhood and problem-oriented policing achieved through partnerships must not be lost. In support of Blair and Bratton, the United Nations Office on Drugs and Crime (2013) signifies partnerships should be an integral part of effective crime prevention, given the wide-ranging nature of the causes of crime and the skills and responsibilities required addressing them. This includes partnerships working across organizations and between authorities, community organizations, non-governmental organizations, the business sector, and private citizens. Traditional crime control strategies view citizens as the passive recipients of police services, thus, citizens have historically played a limited role in the production of public order (Randol & Gaffney, 2014).

Zinn (2010) believes the most effective way of crime prevention is to improve the safety of a neighbourhood to the point that criminals avoid the entire area. Zinn further states that although SA is one of the countries with the highest crime rates in the world, several neighbourhoods in SA have achieved a low crime rate when residents employ comprehensive crime prevention strategies. However, community-based crime prevention strategies, such as Neighbourhood Watch projects carried out in a co-operative relationship, especially with the SAPS, have been introduced more successfully in SA in certain communities than others (Meyer & Van Graan, 2011). This variation in the implementation of such schemes could be attributed to factors such as quality of management and leadership, willingness of community to participate, and insufficient funding to develop infrastructure. Zinn (2010) found that in the majority of SA neighbourhoods, communities do not stand together against crime. Zinn and Kelder (2011) furthermore found in a study on the establishment of Community Safety Networks (CSNs) in SA that such networks are established on an ad hoc basis and are therefore diverse in structure and in their implementation of different crime prevention activities. Some of these networks were found to be so flawed that they fail to mobilize the community or to get them to co-operate in a joint effort in an effective campaign against crime.

Given the high levels of crime and the changing dynamics of criminal behaviour in SA, it is unlikely that community-based crime prevention initiatives, such as Neighbourhood Watch projects, can effectively prevent crime when functioning in isolation and not entering into a collaborative multi-sector partnership. In this contemporary era of community policing little emphasis needs to be placed on the significance of multi-sector community-based crime prevention initiatives, but rather on how a multi-sector approach can advance from merely being a 'talk-shop' to actively develop into an efficient and sustainable crime prevention initiative. Yilmaz (2013) expresses that neighbourhood policing supposes that policing is only most effective when it is a shared undertaking with the local community.

The significance of partnering with multi-sectors in the fight against crime is echoed by Randol and Gaffney (2014) emphasizing the increased realization that the police cannot effectively control crime without public support. Communities and citizens must play an assertive role in neighbourhood revitalization and community-based crime prevention efforts. Wood and Bradley (2009), however, caution that efforts to sustain meaningful and innovative partnerships remain profoundly challenging for police organizations.

## Methodology

This chapter describes efficient and sustainable multi-sector co-operation in preventing crime between the Roodekrans Neighbourhood Watch (RNW), the Roodepoort SAPS, private security businesses, and the local business sector. Roodekrans is a middle to upper income residential suburb situated approximately 20 miles west of Johannesburg. Roodekrans resorts under the Roodepoort police precinct within the City of Johannesburg Metropolitan Municipality. The suburb covers an area of 1.62 square miles with a population of 6,457 (South Africa, 2011). This multi-sector collaboration illustrates the benefits of entering into such an alliance and provides a general framework for the growth of successful multi-sector co-operation crime prevention initiatives.

An in-depth and comprehensive understanding of the multi-sector co-operation between the RNW, SAPS, private security businesses, and the local business sector was obtained. The case study design allowed the researcher to study the RNW in its natural setting, recognizing its intricacies and its context. In-depth interviews were conducted with the President and Chairperson of the RNW. In addition, field observations of the activities of the RNW over a prolonged period of time were conducted and official documents, such as annual reports and statistics of the RNW, were examined. The RNW is one of the largest Neighbourhood Watches in South Africa and the precinct is continuously challenged with crime which offers a unique opportunity for examining multi-sector co-operation in crime prevention.

## Brief History of Community Policing in South Africa

As stated by Schnebly (2008) a basic goal of community policing involves building a strong sense of mutual trust between the police and the community so that existing and potential crime problems can be identified and solved co-operatively. For community policing, as the adopted approach to policing in SA, to be fully appreciated it is important to provide background of the development of this approach.

Apartheid in SA impacted significantly on police–community relations. The apartheid system in SA enforced through legislation by the National Party (NP), the governing party from 1948 to 1994, was a system of racial segregation. Under apartheid, the rights, associations, and movements of the majority black inhabitants and other ethnic groups were curtailed and Afrikaner minority rule was maintained. Rauch (2000) describes the SA police as being highly militarized and hierarchical during the apartheid era. Street-level policing was conducted in a heavy-handed style, with bias against black citizens and little respect for rights or due process. Rauch further describes the job of the police under apartheid as being to enforce laws of racial segregation, to secure the minority government, and to protect the white population from crime and political disruption. The newly elected democratic government faced the mammoth task of transforming the new police service into one which would be acceptable to the majority of the population, be effective against crime, build legitimacy for the police, introduce a culture of human rights to the police, and to improve relations between the police and the black community in SA. The need for improved community–police relations was embedded in this system, and the constitutional call for community policing grew out of the extreme division that this system created between the state and the people.

During the apartheid era policing in SA was closely associated with the military and as a result SA was described as a police state. Police members received military and semi-military training and were employed in an infantry role. This resulted in an unclear distinction between the functions of the police and the military. During the apartheid era the larger SA community viewed the police as representative of an illegitimate, repressive, and unjust system. The militarized policing approach was therefore totally in contradiction with the philosophy of community policing (Van Graan, 2006). The adoption of community policing in SA after the country's birth of democracy in 1994 has brought about increasing acceptance that communities have a significant role to play in crime prevention. This increased focus on community policing in SA represented a fundamental shift in the public-private crime prevention relationship.

The first formal reference to 'community policing' as the prescribed approach for policing in democratic SA is found in the Interim Constitution of the Republic of South Africa, Act 200 of 1993 (South Africa, 1993). The newly established Government's first formal policy statement on safety and security in mid-1994 – the Minister's Draft Policy Document – placed particular emphasis on community consultation and involvement in safety and security issues. South Africa has also embedded the establishment of Community Police Forums (CPFs) in its Constitution, Act 108 of 1996 (South Africa, 1996). CPFs had been established for the purpose of mediating a relationship between the police and those they were meant to serve. This has been further supported by the SAPS Act, 68 of 1995 (South Africa, 1995) that mandates all station commissioners to establish these forums at station level. In April 1997, the Department of Safety and Security published its formal policy on community policing – the Community Policing Policy Framework and Guidelines. This policy defined community policing in terms of a collaborative, partnership-based approach to local-level problem solving. This policy marked a watershed in the development of community policing in SA and provided guidelines for the development of partnerships and local-level problem solving.

One of the five core elements of community policing in SA was defined as Partnership – the facilitation of a co-operative, consultative process of problem solving. The Department of Safety and Security's White Paper (South Africa, 1998) affirmed community policing as the appropriate methodology for enhancing policing in SA and outlined a significant role for the structures of community policing in the provision of local-level crime prevention.

With the police no longer the sole enforcers of law and order, all members of the community became active allies in the effort to enhance the safety and quality of neighbourhoods (Van Graan, 2006).

## Background and Development of the RNW

The RNW was established in February 2007 in accordance with national guidelines for community policing. The first public meeting was held in April 2007 to plan a patrolling schedule, as the primary crime prevention strategy for members to patrol the neighbourhood with their private vehicles. In April 2007, the first vehicle patrols started and have since continued uninterrupted seven days a week. Initially, the RNW was launched in Roodekrans for residents of this particular suburb only. However, residents from four other neighbouring suburbs joined the watch. Patrollers from these areas patrol across borders and also share resources. The RNW currently has 1,184 household members and 345 residents in flats representing more than 189 streets in Roodekrans and five surrounding suburbs. The RNW is the largest Neighbourhood Watch in the Roodepoort precinct and one of the largest in the country.

### Management Structure

The RNW management committee consists of 20 members. Committee members are elected annually by members at an annual general meeting. In an effort to ensure effectiveness, continuity, and the sharing of the workload deputies support the main committee members with the planning and execution of activities. Due to the rapid growth of the Neighbourhood Watch, different portfolios have evolved: Chairperson, Vice-chairperson, President, Secretary and Administration, Finance, Legal Advisor, Business and Public Relations, Membership, Crime Intelligence, Area Leaders, Support Component, Street co-ordinators, Vehicle Patrols & Equipment, Foot and Cycle patrols, Finances, Operational Room Management, and Disaster Management.

From the above it is clear that the Neighbourhood Watch operates with a sound structure and distribution of responsibilities. All portfolio heads have documented descriptions of their roles and responsibilities to ensure role clarification.

### Membership Model

The RNW follows a membership model based on an option of either joining as a patrolling member or a non-patrolling member. By benchmarking efforts with those of other effective Neighbourhood Watches, members learned that the most successful Neighbourhood Watches are those where members pay a nominal fee to belong to the watch. Paying a minimal fee imposes co-ownership and leads to members being more serious about the fight against crime. These fees are also utilized to obtain resources such as patrolling lights and street signs. Apart from the benefits of reducing crime, members are also educated of the benefits of regular interaction with their neighbours, the police, and private security businesses to facilitate a jointly co-ordinated effort to fight crime.

### Vehicle and Foot Patrols

According to the RNW Annual Report for 2013/2014 (Roodekrans Neighbourhood Watch, 2014) there were 107 vehicle patrollers patrolling the various routes, seven days a week from a total membership of 1,152 members. During the first year, 33% of all members were patrollers, however, this figure decreased to 9% in 2013/2014. Approximately 90.3% of patrollers are men and 9.7% are women. Challenges to maintain continuous citizen involvement in community policing are acknowledged by Garcia, Gu, Pattavina, and Pierce (2002, p. 3); Grinc (1994, p. 437); Hawdon and Ryan (2011, p. 899); Skogan and Hartnett (1997, p. 239); and Skogan (1994, p. 2).

The patrolling of the neighbourhood by vehicle is the key element of the RNW crime reduction strategy in a way that, as Dixon (2000) states, 'would have been unthinkable in London'. Each patroller uses his or her private vehicle, and patrol equipment (CPF signs and patrol lights) is collected from the RNW Operation Room. There are currently nine patrol routes covering five suburbs. Each patroller receives a Code of Conduct with clear guidelines, including those relevant to the safety of the patrollers. Since inception, it was decided that all patrols will be conducted in an orderly and civilized fashion in order to prevent any form of vigilantism or other forms of 'taking the law into their own hands'. Patrollers are ordinary civilians from the community, and are only the 'eyes' and 'ears' of the police, and if they approach a potential crime scene, they do not challenge a suspect. Rather, via the Operational Room, they will call the Sector Police vehicle in the area to report any potential crime risk such as a suspicious vehicle or person.

The RNW statistics indicate only 18% of crimes took place when patrols were conducted performed while 82% of crimes took place when no patrols were conducted. These statistics suggest that criminals avoid the area while patrols are being conducted as experienced by the RNW crime intelligence portfolio head in the following quote:

> When a member of the public notices anything suspicious and reports this to our radio users it enables us to act and dispatch patrollers, security companies and the police. ... the potential criminals then move out of the area resulting in a drop in criminal activity.... when we do not report suspicious activity actual crimes increase. (Roodekrans Neighbourhood Watch, 2014)

In order to address this gap, additional patrols are conducted and patrollers change their normal patterns. Special mass patrols, using more than 20 vehicles simultaneously, together with police and security businesses' involvement, are executed in crime hot spot areas when necessary. These mass patrols lead to a significant decrease in crime in periods that were previously considered to be peak times.

Additional campaigns such as foot patrols are carried out on a weekly basis. These foot patrols were launched in 2008 and take the form of community walks where groups of between two and six neighbours walk different streets in the neighbourhood. Currently, there are about 25 RNW foot patrollers. Over and above the obvious benefits of crime prevention, these walks foster relationships among neighbours, and are also used to recruit new members and identify crime risks or gaps in security that are not easily spotted when patrolling by car, for example broken fences, open entrance gates, or open garage doors.

## Street Coordinator Programme

In the interest of effective organization and to involve as many neighbours as possible, the RNW management committee decided to appoint 'street co-ordinators' from the community. A street co-ordinator is responsible for communication between neighbours of a specific street, reporting suspicious activities, welcoming new neighbours or reporting neighbours that are moving out of the area, and to sign new neighbours on as members. The RNW had 122 street co-ordinators in 102 streets as of May 2012.

## Relationship and Co-Operation Between the Police and the RNW in Preventing Crime

Marks, Shearing, and Wood (2009) are of the opinion that, in SA, the police cling to the idea of a policing monopoly and that they have been proved reluctant to explore possibilities for sharing the load of creating safety. To the contrary, the RNW is an outstanding example of an innovative police–community partnership taking shared responsibility in preventing crime to create suburban safety. Wentz and Schlimgen (2012) remark that citizen perceptions of the police are influenced by the interactions that take place between the two groups. Baker and Hyde (2011) note that police agencies in recent years have been introducing customer-focused initiatives and adopting customer service programmes, recognizing the intrinsic value police provide to the community. These authors argue that police should seek direction from its customers, the community, by stepping into their shoes to see their perspective of how policing services are delivered. Marks et al. (2009) remark that since, at least the inception of the 'community policing' movement, police organizations around the world have been on a quest to re-think both their roles and their relationships with non-state groupings.

Most information about crime comes directly from the community, and the role of the Neighbourhood Watch is to create a greater awareness of crime prevention in the community. Schnebly (2008) argues one way in which citizens can work with the police is by sharing information about neighbourhood crime through the process of crime reporting. According to Maclean (1993), of crimes known to the police, 97% of crimes are reported to the police by the public, thus, only 3% of crime is discovered by the police themselves. The role of the public in reporting crime is of the utmost importance. The importance of sharing information on crime is acknowledged by the UK Home Office (2010) stating that effective information sharing is fundamental to provide an evidence base on which partnerships can make decisions. This decision making should then help direct appropriate responses to prevent and reduce crime. Similarly, the International Centre for the Prevention of Crime (2010) agrees that crime prevention cannot be based on police or judicial assessment alone, but needs to be multidisciplinary and integrate information from a range of sources and disciplines, including other sectors. This diversity allows for a richer and more complete understanding of the causes of crime.

Initially, the RNW and sector community police forum were two separate bodies. On initiative of the police, and by means of a democratic vote by members, it was decided to merge these two forums into one body. In practice, it meant that the chairpersonship, and thus ownership of the sector crime forum, was transferred from the police to the community. This was a significant transformation in the practice of community policing. It signalled a new era for community policing with the community taking full responsibility for their own safety, with a particular focus on adopting a proactive stance on community policing, but with the necessary support provided by the police. Since then, the RNW has been operating as a sub-structure of the Roodepoort precinct CPF, with open sharing of information and reporting of crime.

Allegations about police incompetence, inefficiency, and poor service delivery have been reported regularly in the national press in many cities and towns. However, regular meetings between the RNW and the Roodepoort SAPS are held emphasizing police support and commitment to increasingly foster a co-operative relationship. Whenever police inefficiency is reported to the RNW, it is directly taken up with police management.

The sector policing concept is based on a dedicated police vehicle serving the area. They are, in most cases, able to respond within 5–10 minutes. The community patrollers will first phone the Operational Room or Sector Police if they experience a problem. The Sector Police are also involved in monthly RNW meetings to exchange ideas, review crime statistics, and to jointly plan crime prevention strategies for the next month.

## Relationship and Co-Operation Between the RNW and Private Security Businesses in Preventing Crime

It has become common to explain the proliferation of private security services as causally determined by crime rates and institutional weakness (Argueta, 2012). The private security industry in SA is an industry providing guarding, monitoring, armed reaction, escorting, investigating, and other security-related services to private individuals and companies in the country. South Africa has one of the fastest growing – in size and influence – private security industries in the world (Berg, 2007). The private security industry in South Africa currently employs more than 440,000 security officers in more than 9,000 security businesses. For each police officer in the SAPS, there are three security officers in the private sector (South Africa, 2013). These statistics put the role of private security businesses into perspective, reinforcing the relevance of engaging into a co-operative relationship with these security businesses in order to prevent crime.

From its inception, the RNW was challenged to consider co-operating with private security businesses. A process of establishing identity as well as role clarification was used to define the roles, contributions, and responsibilities of all parties. On the one hand, a Neighbourhood Watch is a community-driven organization with a distinct role. As a non-profit organization representing the needs of members as ordinary citizens of the community, the RNW philosophy is to look after the safety of residents. On the other hand, security businesses are profit-driven business entities and while they play a critical role in the overall national and local crime environment, their role is different. They provide alarm systems and react to crime as part of their armed response service to their clients. However, the RNW has built good working relations and communication with various private security businesses. At a practical level, in a neighbourhood such as Roodekrans, while only two police officers may be in the area at any given time, more than 20 security officers from different security companies will be on duty. Initially security firms would not co-operate with one another, given the fact that they treated each other as competitors. Over time, relationships were formed across company boundaries, so much so that security officers from different competitors now back one another up in collaborating at different scenes when necessary. This also enhanced the safety of the security officers themselves, given the fact that they don't operate alone anymore. Moreover, excellent relationships were formed between the security officers, the police, and community patrollers. In several cases, arrests were made when these three parties actively worked together to outperform criminals. Previously, a single party or two parties at most would inadvertently fail to apprehend criminals.

The fact that SA has one of the highest crime statistics (and stands out with the highest levels of violent crime per population ratio) in the world (Marks et al., 2009) is always put forward as the rationale why members of a Neighbourhood Watch have been encouraged to join or continue to make use of the services of private security businesses. South Africans need all mechanisms available in the fight against crime – security businesses, police, and Neighbourhood Watches. The RNW has built good working relations and communication with various private security businesses. Several joint patrols between the RNW community patrollers and private security businesses are performed. Some of these private security businesses are linked to the RNW two-way radio system to monitor and respond when necessary. As a result, improved communication and response time are facilitated that results in arrests. It is now possible for more than five security vehicles, five Neighbourhood Watch patrollers, and one or two police vehicles to arrive within minutes after an incident or risk has been reported.

## Relationship and Co-Operation Between the RNW and Local Businesses in Preventing Crime

Since the launch of the RNW, the local business community and other associations have played an integral role in the prevention of crime. These businesses and associations primarily support the RNW either through sponsorships, donations, or through providing the necessary infrastructure to successfully conduct the operational business of the Neighbourhood Watch. Prior to the inception of the RNW Operational Room local petrol stations that operate 24 hours served as the basis for the different vehicle patrol routes.

Information boards strategically erected in the suburb are sponsored by local businesses. These boards serve as an additional source of communication to residents. A local church hall has been made available for monthly membership meetings. These meetings are attended by members as well as representatives from the police, private security businesses, and local businesses. Between 70 and 120 people typically attend these meetings.

Furthermore, two local supermarkets allow the use of their parking grounds for hosting RNW open day events. Businesses also offer discount on services offered to members of the RNW. Apart from the communication channels of the Neighbourhood Watch, a local school publishes information of the RNW in its newsletter, and a number of local newspapers also continuously provide media exposure to the RNW to enhance awareness. In addition to crime prevention, the involvement of emergency medical services has also been positive to respond to vehicle accidents or serious illness or injuries in the neighbourhood. In certain cases, this high level of multi-stakeholder engagement ensured that disasters such as fires have been either effectively prevented or managed in

**Table 9.1 Successes Achieved and Challenges Experienced by the RNW**

| |
|---|
| **Successes Achieved** |
| Established 24-hour Operational Room |
| Monthly newsletter distributed to 1,082 members and networks |
| Maintaining and strengthening relationship with multi-sectors |
| Two-way radio network growth amounting to 296 radio users |
| Multi-stakeholder Crime Awareness Campaigns |
| Victim support programme |
| Executed community evacuation simulation in terms of risk management plan |
| Special crime operations with police and other role players |
| Reduction of violent crimes, e.g. armed robberies and carjacking |
| 125 patrollers collectively patrolled a number of 10,112 patrols despite decline in number of patrollers |
| Established reaction team responding to house robberies or burglaries in progress |
| Regular articles of successes achieved in various printed media |
| Regular convoy patrols with police and security businesses to create mass visibility |
| Successful marketing strategy, e.g. golf days |
| Prevention of actual crimes resulting from information provided by community, leading to arrests by police |
| Provided assistance in infrastructure development of seven Neighbourhood Watches in Gauteng, Western Cape, and KwaZulu-Natal provinces |
| Clear crime prevention strategy, sound governance structure, and distinct processes and policies |
| **Challenges Experienced** |
| Geographic nature of suburb resulted in costly radio communications network |
| Despite increase in membership majority of residents are not involved |
| Regardless of increased crime awareness many residents remain negligent |
| Utilization of technology (CCTV cameras and night vision equipment) to be optimized |
| Residents become complacent after successes have been achieved |
| Rapid growth put significant administrative pressure on committee |
| Decrease in patrolling members |

a relatively short period of time. All these efforts contributed to active business and community involvement in the campaign against crime.

Some of the successes that were achieved by the RNW during 2012/2013 (Roodekrans Neighbourhood Watch, 2013) are illustrated in Table 9.1 above. Although these successes ensured the rapid growth and sustainability of the RNW challenges were also experienced as illustrated in the table.

## Conclusion

This case study described the experience of sustainable multi-sector co-operation in the prevention of crime between the RNW, the Roodepoort SAPS, and private security businesses. Although there is no generic method for establishing multi-sector collaborations in community-based crime prevention initiatives this chapter provided a general framework for the growth of multi-sector community-based crime prevention initiatives. However, this framework does not focus on the role of the police in driving crime prevention, but it focuses on the role and contribution of communities themselves as an effective vehicle of crime prevention drawing on multi-sector co-operation.

This chapter makes two important observations. First, the police cannot effectively control crime without public support. Second, communities and citizens must play a firm role in community-based crime prevention efforts. The key finding of this study was that community-based crime prevention initiatives, such as Neighbourhood Watch projects, cannot effectively prevent crime when functioning in isolation and not entering into a collaborative partnership with other sectors, such as the police, the business sector, and private security businesses.

The author is strongly aware of and sensitive towards the fact that efforts to sustain meaningful and innovative partnerships between multi-sectors such as the police, communities, the business sector, and private security businesses remain profoundly challenging for all these sectors. This chapter has identified the following aspects as the main inhibiting factors in establishing effective and sustainable multi-sector co-operation in the prevention of crime: increasing demands on limited police resources; the reluctance of residents to become active in crime prevention efforts; Neighbourhood Watch projects that function in isolation; poor management and leadership of community crime prevention initiatives; insufficient funding to develop infrastructure of community crime prevention initiatives; community crime prevention initiatives that are established on an ad hoc basis; and many of these community crime prevention initiatives are so weak that they fail to mobilize the community in a joint effort in an effective campaign against crime.

Knowledge regarding best practices in this field of crime prevention, especially in developing countries, therefore remains a work in progress. As a result, further research is needed with regard to multi-sector co-operation in community-based crime prevention initiatives. Further research could focus on the following aspects:

- the role of multi-sector organizations to strengthen the capacity of limited police resources to enhance community crime prevention initiatives;
- the underlying causes why residents do not want to get involved in community crime prevention initiatives such as Neighbourhood Watch schemes;
- funding models to develop infrastructure of community crime prevention initiatives;
- the sustainability of community crime prevention initiatives;
- the management and leadership of community crime prevention initiatives.

## Note

* Former version previously published in PPR Sofia Special Issue.

## References

Argueta, O. (2012). Private security in Guatemala: Pathway to its proliferation. *Bulletin of Latin American Research, 31*(3), 320–335.

Baker, D., & Hyde, M. (2011). "Police have customers too". *Police Practice and Research, 12*(2), 148–162.

Bennet, T., Holloway, K., & Farrington, D. P. (2006). Does Neighbourhood Watch reduce crime? A systematic review and meta-analysis. *Journal of Experimental Criminology, 2*, 437–458.

Berg, J. (2007). *The accountability of South Africa's private security industry: Mechanisms of control and challenges to effective oversight.* Cape Town: Criminal Justice Initiative of the Open Society Foundation for South Africa.

Blair, I. (2005). *Transcript of Sir Ian Blair's speech.* Retrieved 21 September 2015, from http://news.bbc.co.uk/2/hi/uk_news/4443386.stm.

Bratton, W. (2007). The unintended consequences of September 11th. *Policing, 1*(1), 21–24.

Carr, P. J. (2003). The new parochialism: The implications of the Beltway Case for arguments concerning informal social control. *American Journal of Sociology, 108*(6), 1249–1291.

Dixon, B. (2000). *The globalization of democratic policing: Sector policing and zero tolerance in the new South Africa.* Report of a research study for the Institute of Criminology, University of Cape Town, Occasional Paper. Retrieved 12 July 2014, from www.uct.ac.za/depts/sjrp/global.htm.

Friedman, W. (1994). The community role in community policing. In D. P. Rosenbaum (Ed.), *The challenge of community policing: Testing the promises* (pp. 263–269). Thousand Oaks, CA: Sage.

Garcia, L., Gu, J., Pattavina, A., & Pierce, G. (2002). *Determinants of citizen and police involvement in community policing, final report* (pp. 3–125). Rockville, MD: National Criminal Justice Reference Service.

Grinc, R. M. (1994). "Angels in marble": Problems in stimulating community involvement in community policing. *Crime and Delinquency, 40*(3), 437–468.

Hawdon, J., & Ryan, J. (2011). Neighbourhood organizations and resident assistance to police. *Sociological Forum, 26*(4), 897–920.

Hourihan, K. (1987). Local community involvement and participation in Neighbourhood Watch: A case-study in Cork, Ireland. *Urban Studies, 24,* 128–136.

Hunter, A. (1985). Private, parochial, and public social orders: The problem of crime and incivility in urban communities. In Suttles, G. & Zald, M. (Eds.), *The challenge of social control: Citizenship and institution building in modern society* (pp. 230–242). New York: Ablex Publishing.

International Centre for the Prevention of Crime. (2010). *International report on crime prevention and community safety: Trends and perspectives* (p. 24). Montreal, Quebec, Canada: International Centre for the Prevention of Crime (ICPC).

Maclean, B. D. (1993). Let realism, local crime surveys and policing of racial minorities. *Crime, Law and Social Change, 19,* 51–86.

Marks, M., Shearing, C., & Wood, J. (2009). Who should the police be? Finding a new narrative for community policing in South Africa. *Police Practice and Research, 10*(2), 145–155.

Meyer, M., & Van Graan, J. G. (2011). Effective community policing in practice: The Roodekrans Neighbourhood Watch case study, West Rand. *Acta Criminologica: Southern African Journal of Criminology, 24*(2), 132–145.

Ohmer, M., & Beck, E. (2006). Citizen participation in neighbourhood organizations in poor communities and its relationship to neighbourhood and organizational collective efficacy. *Journal of Sociology and Social Welfare, 33,* 179–202.

Pattavina, A., Byrne, J. M., & Garcia, L. (2006). An examination of citizen involvement in crime prevention in high-risk versus low- to moderate-risk neighbourhoods. *Crime & Delinquency, 52*(2), 203–231.

Randol, B. M., & Gaffney, M. (2014). Are Block Watch volunteers different than volunteers in community-oriented policing programs? Findings from a mature COPS setting. *Police Practice and Research, 15*(3), 234–248.

Rauch, J. (2000). *Police reform and South Africa's transition.* Paper presented at the South African Institute for International Affairs conference. Johannesburg: Centre for the Study of Violence and Reconciliation.

Rettig, J. (2010). Police your community: Create a watch group. *U.S. News & World Report, 147*(11), 69–70.

Roodekrans Neighbourhood Watch. (2013). *Annual report 2012/2013.* Johannesburg: Roodekrans Neighbourhood Watch.

Roodekrans Neighbourhood Watch. (2014). *Annual report 2013/2014*. Johannesburg: Roodekrans Neighbourhood Watch.

Schnebly, S. M. (2008). The influence of community-oriented policing on crime-reporting behavior. *Justice Quarterly, 25*(2), 223–251.

Sims, L. (2001). *Neighbourhood Watch: Findings from the 2000 British Crime Survey*. London: Home Office.

Skogan, W. G. (1994). *Community participation and community policing*. Workshop on Evaluating Police Service Delivery (November 1994: Montreal). Montreal: University of Montreal & Solicitor General Canada.

Skogan, W. G., & Hartnett, S. M. (1997). *Community policing, Chicago style* (p. 239). New York: Oxford University Press.

South Africa. (1993). *The interim constitution of the Republic of South Africa, Act 200 of 1993*. Pretoria: Government Printer.

South Africa. (1995). *The South African Police Service Act 68 of 1995*. Pretoria: Government Printer.

South Africa. (1996). *The constitution of the Republic of South Africa, Act 108 of 1996*. Pretoria: Government Printer.

South Africa. (1998). *White paper on safety and security*. Pretoria: Government Printer.

South Africa. (2011). *Census 2011*. Statistics South Africa. Pretoria: Government Printer.

South Africa. (2013). *Annual report 2012/13*. Pretoria: Private Security Industry Regulatory Authority.

UK Home Office. (2010). *Information sharing for community safety. Guidance and practice advice. National support framework: delivering safer and confident communities* (p. 10). London: Home Office.

United Nations Office on Drugs and Crime. (2013). *Guidelines for the prevention of Crime ECOSOC Resolution 2002/13*. Economic and Social Council. United Nations.

Van Graan, J. G. (2006). *Obstacles impeding the transformation process in the South African Police Service* (pp. 20–21). Unpublished MTech dissertation in Policing. Pretoria: University of South Africa.

Wentz, E. A., & Schlimgen, K. A. (2012). Citizens' perceptions of police service and police response to community concerns. *Journal of Crime and Justice, 35*(1), 114–133.

Wood, J., & Bradley, D. (2009). Embedding partnership policing: What we've learned from the Nexus policing project. *Police Practice and Research, 10*(2), 133–144.

Yilmaz, S. (2013). Tailoring model in reforming police organizations towards community policing. *Journal of Organizational Change Management, 26*(5), 897–924.

Zinn, R. J. (2010). *Home invasions: Robbers disclose what you should know* (pp. 166–167). Cape Town: NB Publishers.

Zinn, R. (2012). Framework for an effective community safety network. *Acta Criminologica: Southern African Journal of Criminology, 25*(2), 50–68.

Zinn, R. J., & Kelder, N. (2011). *Basic framework for an efficient Community Safety Network* (pp. 28–29). Pretoria: Solidarity.

# III

# Assisting Special Populations, Women, and Crime Victims

# Human Trafficking

# A Global Examination of Sexual Exploitation, Corruption, and Future Implications

# 10

TIFFINEY BARFIELD-COTTLEDGE,
CYNTHIA HERNANDEZ,
JOSE CERVANTES, ATTAPOL KUANLIANG,
AND OCTAVIA S. BOLTON

## Contents



**Abstract**

Human trafficking is examined as both a domestic and international concern. While the correlation between the two is plausible, the extant literature indicates that little has been done to address these ongoing issues. This chapter provides information regarding the issue of human trafficking and transportation and border concerns in the United States as well as other parts of the World. Even though governments have attempted to address these issues, human trafficking rates have been largely unaffected by law and policies. As a result, women, boys, and girls continue to be victimized and are likewise at risk of continued victimization. While a primary goal of this work is to increase awareness regarding the nature and extent of the human trafficking, focus on global collaborative efforts, policies, and policing practices are discussed.

## Human Trafficking: A Global Examination of Perspectives, Policy, and Application

The trafficking of humans is a growing human rights concern both globally and within the United States. In the U.S. alone, all types of forced labor resulting from human trafficking has yielded a profit of approximately $32 billion. Although it is difficult to accurately quantify this growing problem due to the underground and secretive nature of trafficking networks and practices, conservative estimates suggest that over two and a half million people worldwide are in forced labor due to having been trafficked (Belser, de Cock, & Mehran, 2005; International Labour Organization [ILO], 2005). Of these estimates, children comprise 40–50% of all trafficked persons (ILO, 2005). It has been estimated that between 600,000 and 800,000 persons are trafficked across international borders annually, of which 80% are women and girls and of these approximately 43% are trafficked for commercial sexual exploitation. Women have been sold, bought, and exchanged while continually suffering from repeated physical and sexual abuse. In fact, trafficking women for prostitution is defined, for many, as a form of modern day slavery (Trafficking Victims Protection Act [TVPA], 2000).

Trafficking for the purpose of sexual exploitation, also known as sex trafficking, is a form of human trafficking that affects a large number of women and girls globally each year resulting in many silent victims who are unknown to society (Miller, Decker, Silverman, & Raj, 2007). In addition to the trafficking of women, young children are also being trafficked for profit and sexual exploitation. Specifically, child trafficking involves the recruitment, transport, and transfer of children through abduction, deception, or for exploitative purposes (Unicef, 2005). Although the research is limited, child trafficking remains a serious social concern, particularly in South and East Asia and is related to poverty, educational attainment, lack of equal opportunity and protection, and the prevalent demand for sexual acts with girls (Deb, 2009; Deb, Mukherjee, & Mathews, 2011).

## Literature Review

### International Concerns, Policy, and Prevention

The larger global perspective is similar to that of the United States, and while policies and practices are varied, human trafficking for prostitution purposes is seen as unacceptable both domestically and internationally (Macy & Graham, 2012). Research describing patterns of trafficking from and within South-Eastern Europe has assisted with efforts to effectively tackle human trafficking and associated crimes through the strategic use of the criminal justice system. Attention has primarily been placed on victims of trafficking – identifying who they are and factors that make them vulnerable. There is further need to address traffickers' behavior, law enforcement, as well as social and economic reforms (Surtees, 2008).

In Israel, trafficking women for prostitution is a serious criminal offense in which they have harsh punishments against perpetrators. In addition to laws and regulations, the Chinese also created campaigns against human trafficking and prostitution. Human trafficking in Serbia has been addressed through recent developments focused on a system of protection, assistance, and support of victims of human trafficking. This system established that victims be utilized as witnesses in criminal proceedings. And despite efforts made thus far, further improvements are needed, in terms of developing support and protection for child victims (Simeunovic-Patic & Copic, 2010). In Albania, researchers analyzed court files relating to human trafficking between 1995 and 2003. The goal was to uncover profiles and developments in trafficking network structures as well as their financial modus operandi. Findings revealed two initial profiles (an Albanian and a post-Soviet profile), which are gradually evolving into multi-ethnic and transnational profiles. In closed ethnic networks, family and clan are essential to understanding the scope of the practices operating within a relatively homogeneous culture of friendship coalitions (Leman & Janssens, 2008).

Countries in Europe also deal with human trafficking and have tried to alleviate this social problem. Motives, or push factors, associated with trafficking and why women get involved have been explained by aspirations for a better standard of living, economic difficulties, debt in their home country, and potential glorification of western countries (i.e., a pull factor). Finland, in particular, has been identified as a destination country where women have been sold into prostitution and have more opportunities to earn money compared to earning potential in their home country (Viuhko, 2010). Germaine to this is also geographic location and access of border countries which have been purported to explain transport of Russian and Estonian women to Finland. Additionally, several border security concerns involve the ease and diverse ability for transportation to Finland from Russia by ferry, train, or car. In addition to varied transportation, there are no visa requirements for Estonians to enter Finland, which only supports trafficking success.

## Port Security

Eighty percent of the entire world trade interaction occurs as the result of relationships between ports and people all over the world. One of the most significant factors related to effective policing designed to prevent and or decrease opportunities for human trafficking include border security in transit and destination countries. Since September 11, 2001, port security and regulations have increased monitoring and more countries have been identified to assist with effective implementation; however, even with these increases in security, uncertainty still remains. The importance of border security has also been heightened by the existence of recent terrorist attacks, trafficking illegal drugs, and environmental crimes such as pollution and corruption (Eski, 2011; Surtees, 2008).

In an attempt to identify varying transportation patterns associated with successful human trafficking practices, research conducted by Parmentier (2010), produced distinctions between countries of origin, countries of transit, and countries of destination of trafficked persons. Findings indicated a relationship between countries of transit and countries of destination but also brought increased attention to the likelihood that trafficked persons may spend a lengthy amount of time in a number of consecutive countries or a particular country if travel to a final destination country was abandoned. Future research honed on increased attention to port security as well as transnational insecurities is recommended. As China moved towards industrialization and urbanization in the

1980s, growth of prostitution victims also emerged (Liu, 2012). Research highlighting the relationship between economic reform policies and increased migrants into China has emerged. It is further argued that recent increases in migrant patterns impact the ease at which traffickers transport women and children into the country.

## Human Trafficking and the Law

Official criminal justice data reveal that organized crimes remain under-reported, under-detected, and, therefore, under-prosecuted (Goodey, 2008). The reality is that human trafficking is a crime that has been systematically difficult to prosecute and punish participants in this well-organized industry. Albeit limited, emerging trends among human traffickers indicate that organized systems of support exist that impede effective policing, arrest, and convictions. While the role of supporters vary, it has been learned that active traffickers operate from their home country and are the primary organizers which also impact the likelihood of them being caught (Viuhko, 2010). Also, the fact that human traffickers are supported by various intermediaries such as landlords and owners comprising an extensive network makes it difficult for police authorities to identify high level actors (Viuhko, 2010). The truth is that patterns of human trafficking are so diverse and limitations are prevalent and have been considered as paralyzing to police authorities. Even contemporary changes in the identification of traffickers as male has experienced diversity more recently. And while most traffickers are male in the Southern and Eastern parts of Europe, in other countries, such as Moldova, Romania, and Ukraine, an emergent trend has been realized in the recruitment of female traffickers. International differences are also present when examining South-Eastern Europe where human trafficking is by organized criminal groups, compared to South-East Asia where trafficking is often informal and managed through personal connections (Surtees, 2008).

## The Role of Corruption

Across the world, there are high levels of police corruption related to human trafficking and most other organized criminal activity whereby organized systems are in play. This is evidenced by the consistent patterns of trafficking of children and women within and across borders for the purpose of control and profit (Chatterjee, Chakraborty, Srivastava, & Deb, 2006; Goodey, 2003). To compound the concern, that human trafficking and related sexual exploitations of women and children remain largely ignored by police authorities only adds support to arguments suggesting the role of corruption is an extensive one. In fact, it has been found that a significant relationship exists between enforcing laws against human trafficking and the level of corruption within law enforcement. Specifically, in Latin America, Sacco Studnicka's (2010) research found that human trafficking in Brazil was largely dependent upon official corruption in 71% of the examined cases. Likewise, in China, corruption among law enforcement authorities makes it difficult to effectively measure and ban these practices (Liu & Finckenauer, 2010). These results indicate that because human trafficking is dependent on the corruption variable to combat human trafficking effectively, political corruption must be addressed at the onset of any new policy or law changes (Sacco Studnicka, 2010; Surtees, 2008).

## Social Implications

The relationship between human trafficking and prostitution is well discussed in the extant literature. Ideologies surrounding the relationship between prostitution and human trafficking maintain that certain concerns may be better examined in relation to immigration and other social and environmental conditions that lead to this behavior. Although myriad people believed that women become prostitutes because of poverty, Liu extends this definition and further explains that many women within the sex industry are not only poor but from lower-class families with limited education. Thereby establishing a generational connection similar to William Julius Wilson's *The Truly Disadvantaged* whereby the extent of poverty is exacerbated by additional factors related to limited knowledge about resources (Wilson, 1990). Some common misconceptions about the relationship between sexual abuse, prostitution, and entry into the human trafficking industry are dispelled by Liu (2012) who explains that it is not childhood experiences and sexual abuse alone that act as motivating factors, rather different situational factors. When examining data on prostitution and associated factors, support establishing these connections emerges. Specifically, in her examination, Liu (2012) reports that factors leading to the development of prostitution for women in China involved a combination of family conditions, childhood experiences, as well as education and employment histories. Relatedly, and depending on economic instability, prostitution becomes a viable option for women.

## The Victims

Victims of human trafficking have an extensive need for social services in mental and physical health. The level of damage incurred by women and children is significant. Research has shown that children who are trafficked suffer more in victimization experiences when compared to their adult counterparts. According to the Trafficking Victims Protection Act (TVPA, 2000), all minors under the age of 18 who commit a commercial sex act are considered to be victims of human trafficking whether it be fraud, force, or coercion. The vulnerability associated with being prostituted as a minor has a theorized pathway that begins with strain risk factors that act as the foundation whereby a sequence of events occurring range from running away, the consumption of drugs and alcohol, sexual denigration, and forced prostitution as a minor (Reid, 2011).

While there are social and environmental factors related to the existence and prevalence of human trafficking rates of women and children, a number of vulnerability factors used to trap these victims have been identified. A segment of the discussion on human trafficking has focused on the willing participation of women. However, the research indicates that women who willingly participate in human trafficking are often deceived about either the nature of the activity or the conditions awaiting them at their destination. These women are also misguided about the nature of activities they will be forced to engage in as well as the expected earning potential. In addition to being deceived, traffickers resort to a variety of means to ensure that women remain enslaved which includes restricting contact with family and friends and withholding legal travel documents (Viuhko, 2010). Additionally, many victims often do not trust that police and criminal justice authorities have the ability to protect them and their families from their offenders. Finally, there is concern that victims are often unaware of how to report their abuse and/or are unable to do so. It is also the case that victims are scared to report their abusers to criminal justice officials for fear of retaliation (Goodey, 2008).

### Limited Resources

To address limited resources in identifying human trafficking victims, strategies have been developed. Strategies for identifying sex trafficking victims include trafficking indicators, victim interaction strategies, immediate response strategies, and child-specific information and strategies. Several human trafficking indicators include evidence that the person is being controlled, does not have the freedom of decision making to leave, signs of physical abuse as well as indications of fear and depression (Macy and Graham, 2012). Women and children have been coined silent victims of prostitution and human trafficking largely as the result of fear, lack of knowledge about alternatives, isolation, and physical and psychological confinement, which offer some explanation as to why victims remain under the control of their traffickers (Logan, Walker, & Hunt, 2009; Viuhko, 2010). Additional fears have been reported as fear of threat and harm to family members, fear of deportation, and a general mistrust of law enforcement agents.

The growing concern regarding the general lack of knowledge and awareness of the extent to which human trafficking exists in society has been substantiated in cases where results reveal that human trafficking exists across a variety of labor sectors and is also an extremely profitable industry based in supply and demand. The nature and extent of human trafficking in the United States has been studied through the examination of data measuring levels of awareness and experiences among legal representatives. Research further highlighted a number of vulnerability factors indicating that extreme poverty is a major factor associated with being a target of human traffickers (Logan et al., 2009). And where policing is concerned, one of the main problems associated with identifying victims of human trafficking is limited resources.

## Future Implications

In attempts to address human trafficking, many countries have responded with the creation of public campaigns against human trafficking and prostitution. However, in some countries, the focus remains heavily on abolishing prostitution (Liu, 2012). And, while human trafficking appears to go hand in hand with the growth of prostitution, research demonstrating this directional correlation is lacking. Specific attention honed on protecting women's rights requires support at all levels of society and government. To assist with the long lasting traumatic effects of victimizations against women and children, research suggests the need for funding in social and therapeutic services as well as increased target hardening strategies focused on the aggressive identification of offenders and their supporters' apprehension and punishment (Herzog, 2008).

It is agreed that human trafficking for the purposes of sexual exploitation and victimization requires increased understanding and should be studied in several capacities examining the role of organized crime, mass economic migration and asylum, as well as trends in gender-based violence and inequalities (Deb et al., 2011; Goodey, 2003; Herzog, 2008). While currently garnering support, there still remains a need for public education and awareness about the dangers and impact of human trafficking on society. In 2008, Wilson and Dalton provided several suggestions for increasing awareness about the significance of human trafficking. The issue of human trafficking is a social concern that is largely misunderstood due to lack of resources and limited research. As a result, policy makers and practitioners alike have launched campaigns designed to increase awareness through training, education, and outreach programs. While successful, improving police and justice officials' law enforcement capacity, global practitioner collaboration, evidence-based program evaluations, as well as data-based decision making in legislative, legal, and regulatory changes are still needed.

One of the greatest challenges to policing human traffickers, as well as other forms of organized crime, is related to difficulty in gathering actionable intelligence. As such, it is suggested that active policing occur in communities that have been historically closed to routine policing and in areas where there is a high level of mistrust of law enforcement. To get to this, more intentional and systematic research examining perceptions of police and law enforcement is suggested (Lebov, 2010). Capturing and punishing human traffickers is at the forefront of societal concern; however, there is also a need for laws that account for protections of victimized women and children's human rights. Proposed changes in law and policy is a frontline defense for police and justice authorities. As such, there are certain definitional limitations associated with human trafficking to be addressed that will align definitional consistency, legal descriptions, and penalties for persons who traffic human beings. Parmentier (2010) suggests a comprehensive approach to addressing human trafficking that includes the development of qualitative approaches to study persons involved in trafficking organizations. Additionally, researchers have noted that human trafficking is defined in different ways depending on the country or the region; these differences need to be consistent to facilitate cooperation among law enforcement agencies. This further supports the need for definitional distinctions of human trafficking within the literature that will potentially increase the criminal justice system's ability to enforce appropriate punishments for human traffickers.

Regarding future global policy implications, it would be noteworthy to mention Gallagher and Holmes' (2008) eight essential elements of an effective response to human trafficking. These eight elements are as follows: (1) a comprehensive legal framework, in compliance with international standards; (2) a specialist law enforcement capacity to investigate human trafficking; (3) a general law enforcement capacity to respond effectively to trafficking cases; (4) strong and well-informed prosecutorial and judicial support; (5) quick and accurate identification of victims along with immediate protection and support; (6) special support to victims and witnesses; (7) systems and processes that enable effective international investigative and judicial cooperation in trafficking cases; and (8) an effective coordination among international agencies working collaboratively to reduce human trafficking.

Identifying interpersonal violence and trafficking experiences of victims remains to be an important role for existing programs focused on violence against women. While healthcare officials are often not focused on indicators associated with human trafficking, they are in unique positions to make inquiries, identify, report, and support efforts designed to combat human trafficking (Miller et al., 2007). Research suggests that the healthcare system can act to train staff on the identification of risk factors associated with possible human trafficking incidents. Developing client-responsive, culturally appropriate, and sensitive screening strategies is also needed and supported as a next step.

Additional strategies for service providers were also developed to assist in interactions with victims. Interaction strategies include building trust and rapport with potential victims, procedural issues in conducting interviews, messages that service providers should convey to potential victims, and questioning potential victims with indirect questions when he or she is alone excluding words such as coercion, trafficking, and force. According to reviewed literature, documents suggested that service providers contact the National Human Trafficking Resource Center's (NHTRC) hotline for further information on how to provide assistance to potential victims. In instances where victims may be in immediate danger, law enforcement authorities should be contacted.

Police and justice officials are also tasked with assisting with research focused on identifying more comprehensive strategies used by human traffickers beyond the scope of what is already known about offenders, to include connections to criminal networks, supporters (including corrupt partners), recruiting patterns, and transportation methodologies which act to better understand the dynamics of recruitment while also helping to formulate new responses. More honed focus should be placed on countries where there is government corruption, high infant mortality rates, large populations, and social conflict which are all known to contribute to a country's market for human trafficking (Wooditch, 2012). Having intelligence is only half the battle to defense; police authorities should also be trained and continuously briefed on changing trends, i.e., modes of transportation and identification of traffickers in order to affect reductions in the human trafficking industry.

## Conclusion

The problem of human trafficking for the purposes of sexual exploitation and victimization is a national and global concern. For some time now, it has been maintained that human traffickers need to be targeted as serious criminal offenders, which is a daunting task, given the limitations associated with difficulties identifying and prosecuting key offenders (Herzog, 2008). Human trafficking produces many related social concerns and areas of policy and practice evolution, which set the foundation for a much needed hands-on approach to impacting reductions. While it is difficult to gauge the exact extent of human trafficking, evidenced-based research has been conducted in Scotland that revealed a need for further qualitative inquiry of human trafficking survivors as well as a need for additional quantitative multi-agency data analysis (Lebov, 2010). Currently, it is more likely that low-level offenders are identified and arrested which does not significantly impact the business of human trafficking. Even with the use of harsher punishment practices, severe punishments have not weakened the human trafficking industry.

Research has its challenges and limitations and the study of human trafficking is no different. Human trafficking has several unique limitations associated with the study population of offenders and victims in that offenders are protected by those who benefit financially while victims are known as an invisible population who remain silent as a result of fear and corruption (Gozdziak & Collett, 2005; Shauer & Wheaton, 2006). And while the extant literature suggests a need for further study regarding the relationship between human trafficking and prostitution (Shauer & Wheaton, 2006), there are also links to social and environmental risk factors and their effect on propensity toward sex trafficking victimization that should be examined.

Implications of human trafficking are substantial and affect society as a whole. Research should hone the examination of situational and environmental factors and their relationship with human trafficking and persistence (Liu, 2012). It is further suggested that attention be focused on protection policies and victim identification. The larger fear is that if ignored, women and children will continue to be victims of exploitation and transported across borders as commodities. Given the relationship between human trafficking and economics, as long as services are in demand, human trafficking will exist to supply the demand. Research has been published addressing the need to better train police, to identify victims, as well as better implementation techniques to identify human trafficking activity. Moving forward the main goal should be focused on increasing awareness about the scope of the problem and developing effective strategies to fight this problem.

While some governments and legal systems perceive prostitutes as conspirators, changing perceptions identifying these women as victims in the enterprise are emerging (Herzog, 2008).

Trafficking women for prostitution (TWP) should not be portrayed as an immigration issue; and instead increased attention is needed on increasing punishment seriousness for perpetrators who victimize women and children.

## References

Belser, P., de Cock, M., & Mehran, F. (2005). *An ILO minimum estimate of forced labour in the world.* Geneva: International Labour Office.

Chatterjee, P., Chakraborty, T., Srivastava, N., & Deb, S. (2006). Short and long-term problems faced by the trafficked children: A qualitative study. *Social Science International, 22,* 167–182.

Deb, S. (2009). Child protection: Scenario in India. *International Journal of Child Health and Human Development, 2,* 339–348.

Deb, S., Mukherjee, A., & Mathews, B. (2011). Aggression in sexually abused trafficked girls and efficacy of intervention. *Journal of Interpersonal Violence, 26,* 745–768.

Eski, Y. (2011). Port of call: Towards criminology of port security. *Criminology and Criminal Justice, 11,* 415–431.

Gallagher, A., & Holmes, P. (2008). Developing an effective criminal justice response to human trafficking: Lessons from the front line. *International Criminal Justice Review, 18*(3), 318–343.

Goodey, J. (2003). Migration, crime and victimhood: Responses to sex trafficking in the EU. *Punishment & Society, 5,* 415–431.

Goodey, J. (2008). Human trafficking: Sketchy data and policy responses. *Criminology & Criminal Justice, 8*(4), 421–442.

Gozdziak, E. M., & Collett, E. A. (2005). Research on human trafficking in North America: A review of literature. *Institute for the Study of International Migration, 43*(1–2), 99–128.

Herzog, S. (2008). The lenient social and legal response to trafficking in women: An empirical analysis of public perceptions in Israel. *Journal of Contemporary Criminal Justice, 24,* 314–333.

International Labour Organization. (2005). *A global alliance against forced labour.* Geneva, Switzerland: Author. Retrieved October 10, 2013, from www.ilo.org/wcmsp5/groups/public/-ed_norm/-declaration/documents/publication/wcms_081882.pdf.

Lebov, K. (2010). Human trafficking in Scotland. *European Journal of Criminology, 7*(1), 77–93.

Leman, J., & Janssens, S. (2008). The Albanian and post-Soviet business of trafficking women for prostitution. *European Journal of Criminology, 5*(4), 433–451.

Liu, M. (2012). Chinese migrant women in the sex industry: Exploring their paths to prostitution. *Feminist Criminology, 7,* 327–349.

Liu, M., & Finckenauer, J. O. (2010). The resurgence of prostitution in China: Explanations and implications. *Journal of Contemporary Criminal Justice, 26,* 89–102.

Logan, T. K., Walker, R., & Hunt, G. (2009). Understanding human trafficking in the United States. *Trauma, Violence, & Abuse, 10*(1), 3–30.

Macy, R. J., & Graham, L. M. (2012). Identifying domestic and international sex-trafficking victims during human service provision. *Trauma, Violence, & Abuse, 12,* 59–76.

Miller, E., Decker, M. R., Silverman, J. G., & Raj, A. (2007). Migration, sexual exploitation, and women's health: A case report from a community health center. *Violence Against Women, 13*(5), 486–497.

Parmentier, S. (2010). Epilogue: Human trafficking seen from the future. *European Journal of Criminology, 7*(1), 95–100.

Reid, J. A. (2011). An exploratory model of girls' vulnerability to commercial sexual exploitation in prostitution. *Child Maltreatment, 16,* 145–157.

Sacco Studnicka, A. C. (2010). Corruption and human trafficking in Brazil: Findings from a multi-modal approach. *European Journal of Criminology, 7*(1), 29–43.

Schauer, E. J., & Wheaton, E. M. (2006). Sex trafficking into the United States: A literature review. *Criminal Justice Review, 11,* 146–169.

Sen, S. (2005). *Trafficking in women and children in India.* New Delhi, India: National Human Rights Commission.

Simeunovic-Patic, B., & Copic, S. (2010). Protection and assistance to victims of human trafficking in Serbia: Recent developments. *European Journal of Criminology, 7*(1), 45–60.

Springer, K. W., Sheridan, J., Kuo, D., & Carnes, M. (2007). Long-term physical and mental health consequences of childhood physical abuse: Results from a large population-based sample of men and women. *Child Abuse & Neglect, 31,* 517–530.

Surtees, R. (2008). Traffickers and trafficking in Southern and Eastern Europe. *European Journal of Criminology, 5*(1), 39–68.

Unicef. (2005). *Combating child trafficking.* Retrieved October 10, 2013, from www.unicef.org/publications/files/IPU_combattingchildtrafficking_GB(1).pdf.

Viuhko, M. (2010). Human trafficking for sexual exploitation and organized procuring in Finland. *European Journal of Criminology, 7*(1), 61–75.

Wilson, J., & Dalton, E. (2008). Human trafficking in the heartland: Variation in law enforcement awareness and response. *Journal of Contemporary Criminal Justice, 24*(3), 296–313.

Wilson, W. J. (1990). *The truly disadvantaged: The inner city, the underclass, and public policy.* Chicago: University of Chicago Press.

Wooditch, A. (2012). Human trafficking law and social structures. *International Journal of Offender Therapy and Comparative Criminology, 56*(5), 673–690.

# Building Community Resilience
## Strategic Role of Police with Bombing Victims*

# 11

ZORA SUKABDI

## Contents



**Abstract**

In the context where terrorism is viewed as an act of crime based on ideology, healing bombing victims using various components of society along with the support of police is critical. The approach is distinct from treatment of other crime victims. This chapter describes the strategic role of the police in transforming bombing victims into "champions" to build community resilience, based on the author's best practice. The transformation process includes five key stages namely physical rehabilitation, psychosocial rehabilitation, harmonization through group therapies and dialogues, empowerment programs, and generating change agents to deliver anti-violence messages. In the process, a collaborative work among police, professionals, experts, civil society, and other proponents is necessary in order to prevent future reciprocal acts of violence in the community.

## Introduction

Many terror attacks, such as the Bali attacks, received massive international attention due to their impact on communities (Sukabdi, 2015). In Indonesia, fatalities and wounded victims (e.g., intense pain, burns on face and body, and disability) due to terrorist bomb attack affected more than 700 people (Adi Brata in Nasrul, 2014; Satrawi, 2016). Many of the victims who survive bomb attack suffer permanent disability because of severe injuries, pain, trauma, and severe mental depression (Abas & Sukabdi, 2011). Terrorist bomb attacks not only impact first-hand victims, but also their families (Abas & Sukabdi, 2011). Widows as well as orphans suddenly emerged. Survivors and their families experience severe trauma due to terrorist bomb attack. There are those among them who also hold a sense of revenge toward the group performing terrorist bombing, and this can create new problems in society. Revenge will lead to counter-attack (time bomb), and will decrease harmony among classes or groups (Abas & Sukabdi, 2011). This chapter describes the strategic role of the police in Indonesia in transforming bombing victims into "champions" to build community resilience. It is based on the author's best practice in conducting treatment management for terrorism victims which involved Police Service officers. Moreover, as a psychologist in terrorism and radicalism, the author will describe the process of transforming bombing victims into "champions" by using psychological viewpoints.

## Terrorism as an Act of Crime Based on Ideology

Generally, the objectives of acts of terrorism can be divided into two, namely short-term objectives (e.g., attracting attention, changing political views, and maintaining the continuity of their group) and long-term objectives (e.g., establishing a state based on a certain religion, repelling invaders, and liberating the nation) (McCauley & Segal, 2009). Kruglanski and Fishman (2009) suggest that a terrorism movement is not performed without planning. Psychologically, an act of terrorism by the perpetrator is an act which occurs from a decision that has been made from careful planning. The purpose is to spread fear in a population or certain religious believer, trusting that it will achieve certain goals. In this case, violence is chosen because there is no other alternative that can be taken to achieve the goal (Kruglanski & Fishman, 2009) and to offset a force of greater authority (Crenshaw, 2009). Citations of several Islamic activists in Indonesia supporting the resistance against the Indonesian Government illustrate the issue, such as:

> There are two ways, cooperative such as in parliament, government etc., and non-cooperative such as by choosing not to cooperate and total rejection. Hence, we refuse to cooperate ... We use the non-cooperative way ... because what is true cannot be mixed with falsehood. (An Islamist militant in an interview)

> We will certainly lose if we fight using other means such as war of ideas or war of culture. (An Islamist militant in an interview)

> We do not agree on forming a party to be in parliament, they are all corrupted, even the Islamic party. We chose to fight it, not blend in it ... We do not compromise with the current system, because it is so corrupted, we fight against it ... Just give us a moment to rule the country, we assure you that Indonesia will then be excellent. (An Islamist militant in Putra & Sukabdi, 2013, p. 87)

Further, ideological terror actions can be seen as a form of reaction towards the perceived social situations, including relative deprivation (Love et al. & Post in Putra & Sukabdi, 2013; see also Gurr, 1970; Rose, 1982; Runciman, 1966; Walker & Smith, 2001). The behavior of actors of extreme terrorism (such as killing innocent people or suicide) is usually followed by moral justification to legitimize their radical approach. Moral justification usually involves a collective ideology in the name of certain community or religious people (Kruglanski & Fishman, 2009). Several moral justification used by terrorists can be in the form of fighting for independence from an oppression, fighting crime perpetrated by a certain state, serving God, etc. (Kruglanski & Fishman, 2009; Putra & Sukabdi, 2013).

The act of suicide by activists is defined as a struggle (jihad) of the highest value (Post, Sprinzak, & Denny, 2009; Putra & Sukabdi, 2013). This action is also seen as a form of sacrifice to serve God (Putra & Sukabdi, 2013), thus it is not merely an act of suicide. This is illustrated from answers of Islamic activists from the Middle East in research conducted by Post et al. (2009) as follows:

> This is not suicide. Suicide is selfish, it is weak, it is mentally disturbed. This is istishad [sacrifice for God]. (An Islamic activist, in Post et al., 2009, p. 114)

> A martyrdom operation is the highest level of jihad, and highlights the depth of our faith ... the bombers are holy fighters who carry out one of the more important articles of faith ... It is attacks when a member gives his life that earn the most respect and elevate the bombers to the highest possible level of martyrdom ... I am not a murderer. A murderer is someone with a psychological problem; armed actions have a goal even if civilians are killed, it is not because we like it or are bloodthirsty. It is a fact of life in a people's struggle the group does not do it because it wants to kill civilians, but because the jihad must go on. (An Islamic activist in Post et al., 2009, p. 114)

The perpetrators of violent extremism may have been wrong in making the decision and setting up strategies, less appropriate in choosing alternative action to obtain their goals, or miscalculate when considering several consequences from their action hence resulting in collateral damage or bombing victims. However, bombing victims are a real concern and require resolutions of all society members including legal accountability from the perpetrators.

Indonesia and various other countries view terrorism as an act of crime based on ideology (Sukabdi, 2015; see also Gunaratna & Rubin, 2011; Kruglanski, Gelfand, & Gunaratna, 2011; Rabasa, Pettyjohn, Ghez, & Boucek, 2010). In the context where terrorism is viewed as an act of crime, legal investigation (legal processing) based on valid evidence is critical. In the case of Indonesia that does not apply the Internal Security Act (ISA), law enforcement becomes the leading sector in handling terrorism and plays a major role in restoring community resilience.

## Challenges in Treating Bombing Victims

From many angles, healing bombing victims to restore community resilience is not an easy matter (Abas & Sukabdi, 2011; Wongkaren, 2012). In contrast to the handling of other crime victims, handling of bombing victims is tangent with efforts to answer why they become part of collateral damage by ideologue or by bombing actors who are highly respected (considered holy) and have a strong follower (Wongkaren, 2012). Handling of bombing victims also relates with efforts to answer questions surrounding why they become the target of crime activities of this ideology, whereas many of these bombing victims are people who diligently perform religious ritual (Wongkaren, 2012). Many bombing victims also blame the police as a representative of the government. This is due to the fact that an act of terrorism, including bombing actions, is considered by society and victims as a war between violent extremist groups and government as an authority that is considered responsible for creating injustice in economics and law (Wongkaren, 2012). Police, in this case, become the scapegoat of society, and receive no sympathy from common civilians. In many cases where police become target of terror, people form a "numb" behavior where they show no attention, have a lack of empathy, or even tend to blame police as a state institution that causes all of these actions to occur in the first place (Wongkaren, 2012).

Another issue that is no less important is the many criticisms regarding handling of bombing victims such as inappropriate treatment (e.g., lack of law that accommodates the recovery process of bombing victims) (Adi Brata in Nasrul, 2014; Satrawi, 2016) and the role of the police as protectors and guardians of the people (Wongkaren, 2012). To restore community resilience, treatment of bombing victims must be planned, structured, and directed, because the victims bring a powerful voice to build an immune system against radicalism (Wongkaren, 2012). They require assistance to receive encouragement and assistance (Wongkaren, 2012). The nation is where they live and serve; hence they require proper protection and treatment (Wongkaren, 2012).

## Strategic Role of Police in Transforming Victims into Champions

The process of assisting bombing victims by all components of society including the police as protector and guardian of the people is aimed at transforming victims into "champions." This is done in order to build high community resilience where all components of society are responsive and lend their hand in assisting crime victims. High community resilience results in society with a higher immune system hence victims do not have any implosive anger or revenge that can burst at any moment, conflict among groups, and vulnerability to provocation from any party.

At the lowest or minimum level, intervention on bombing victims tries to rehabilitate them so they are able to heal physically and to move on mentally from the tragedy.

Rehabilitation tries to restore their condition so they continue to function socially (The National Anti-Terror Agency, 2013). Furthermore, at the highest level, intervention of bombing victims tries to facilitate victims into becoming champions. As champions, not only did these bombing victims transform themselves into change agents for society, but they are also able to generate new change agents. In other words, at the level of champions, these bombing victims are actually performing "self-transcendence." Maslow's Model of Motivation (in Koltko-Rivera, 2006) explains that self-transcendence is the highest stage (sixth phase) after self-actualization as the fifth phase. To differentiate, in self-actualization, individuals explore their own potentials and contribute to others around them; whereas in self-transcendence, those individuals are able to inspire or influence other people to be able to actualize themselves or to be meaningful to their society. Both self-actualization and self-transcendence can be achieved when individuals have fulfilled their basic needs, such as psychological needs, safety needs, belonging needs, and esteem needs.

Figure 11.1 illustrates the transformation process that occurs in bombing victims based on the author's best practice in assisting them in Indonesia. During the Victim phase, which is right after the bombing occurred, bombing victims urgently require medical attention in the form of physical and psychosocial rehabilitation as they are in a state of shock and fragile condition. At this level, victims feel extremely helpless and in many cases they would rather die than live while suffering and being disabled for life. Proper treatment, namely first aid by police at the scene (e.g., referring to the nearest ER, assurance, and medical aid by police doctor), physical rehabilitation, psychotherapy, counseling, and social support from various elements of society, can make bombing victims move from the Victim phase to the Survivor phase. The police, in this case, hold an important role because they are the first to recognize and find the victims at the scene of tragedy.

During the Survivor phase, the victims have already reached emotional stability and, in many cases, are able to continue to work and function normally in society, they even create association or foundation to protect and watch over other bombing victims. They are also able to move on from the tragedy even if there are still issues lingering in themselves namely regarding who is the real actor behind the tragedy ("who?"), what is the motive ("why?"), and why they become part of the damage ("why me?"). Counseling at this time is still needed. And when bombing victims are ready, they can enter group therapy programs where they can meet with the perpetrators or bombing actors so they can get answers to their questions. This is important in helping victims move on holistically. The meeting process is not easy; hence the role of police, psychologists, and civil society (also known as non-government organizations) is extremely important in managing it. Once again, the police play a strategic role in assuring the smoothness of the process. This process will be explained in greater detail in the Harmonization/Reconciliation stage.

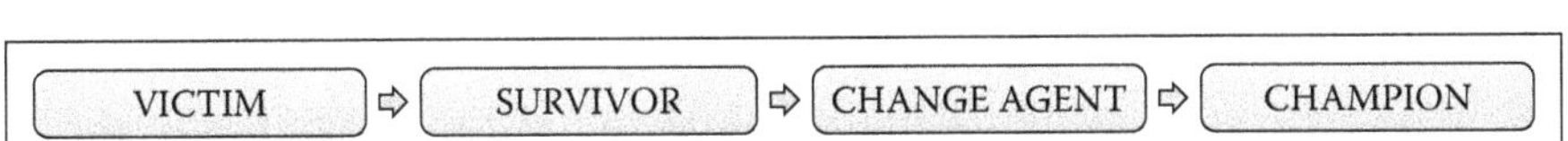


**Figure 11.1** Transformation Process of Bombing Victims.

As previously explained, in the Change Agent phase, bombing victims create a tremendous step by becoming educators or community-resource persons and by spreading the message of anti-violence to the community. At this level, assistance by police and civil society is required to ensure the safety of bombing victims in delivering their message. Moreover, the process cannot be forced. Based on the author's psychological practices, out of the more than 700 bombing victims, only around 7% are in this phase (Adiartono & Soemarno, 2010). Lastly, in the Champion phase, victims show their maximum ability by producing new change agents in various events or forums organized by their foundation or association.

There are five key stages of treatments in transforming victims into champions. Figure 11.2 explains in general treatments for bombing victims. The police hold a strategic role as protectors and guardians of the people in conjunction with civil society to restore community resilience. When bombing victims achieve their maximum, which is the level of "Champion," the community develops a "new vaccine" where the majority of people that used to be silent are becoming anti-violence due to the powerful voice of victims in raising people's alertness of the danger of radicalism and violent extremism.

## Stage I: Physical Rehabilitation

The first stage is the most critical condition which includes physical medicine and rehabilitation. During the incidence the police hold a fundamental role in helping bombing victims. The police need to quarantine the scene and provide first aid to bombing victims inflicted by immediate physical and psychological impacts of the blasts, by referring them

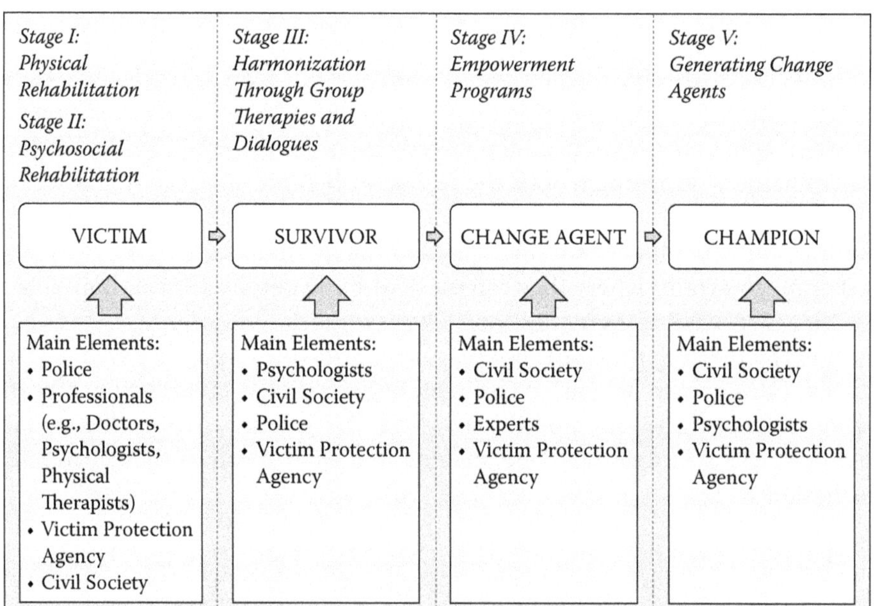


**Figure 11.2** Five Key Stages of Treatments for Bombing Victims.

to the nearest emergency unit, providing police doctors, and contacting other doctors from hospitals around the city. The damage level of bombing victims varies, from severe to minor, thus the national police need to work closely with hospitals, physical rehabilitation centers, and government entities which deal with medical-expenses support for bombing victims. Referral or recommendation from the police can expedite the first treatment of bombing victims.

Philosophically, rehabilitation is an attempt to restore to the previous condition (victim's recovery) in order to restore normal function. Amputations, skin grafts, and various other types of surgeries are included in this stage. Furthermore, treatment can be in the form of physical therapy sessions. A team of professionals such as doctors, psychologists, physical therapists, and occupational therapists is needed immensely at this stage.

Physiotherapy programs and comprehensive rehabilitation processes can take months. During this process the police and civil society need to visit bombing victims, healthcare professionals, and staff at the hospital where bombing victims are treated in order to observe and to see first-hand the healing environment experienced by bombing victims. Visits and motivation by the police create a sense of security and peace for victims, hence preventing crime or acts of revenge from the victims' families toward the perpetrators in the future.

## Stage II: Psychosocial Rehabilitation

At this stage, effective counseling or psychotherapy is applied. By definition, it is

> a process that involved a trained professional who abided by accepted ethical guidelines and has skills and competencies for working with diverse individuals who are in distress or have life problems that led them to seek help (possibly at the insistence of others) or they may be choosing to seek personal growth, but either way, these parties establish an explicit agreement (informed consent) to work together (more or less collaboratively) toward mutually agreed on or acceptable goals using theoretically-based or evidence-based procedures that, in the broadest sense have been shown to facilitate human development or effectively reduce disturbing symptoms. (Sommers-Flanagan & Sommers-Flanagan, 2012, p. 9)

This process can be in the form of conversations, dialogues, interactions, friendship, motivations, and assistance which support the mental aspect of bombing victims so they can deal with their feelings, thoughts, or behaviors.

The goal of this stage is to heal the trauma, work with adjustment problems, provide understanding, and restore the victims' psychosocial condition as much as possible to their original condition prior to the bombing disaster or tragedy. This process is very critical and difficult; hence it requires arts and collaboration from several parties including the police. Generally, counseling and psychotherapy are qualitatively the same term. Both counselors and psychotherapists engage in the same behaviors with clients, such as listening, questioning, interpreting, and explaining, yet many do so in different proportions. Psychotherapy is less directive, deeper, and longer, whereas counseling is slightly more directive and brief, more on developmentally normal but troubling issues, and focuses on practical problems (see Sommers-Flanagan & Sommers-Flanagan, 2012).

In most cases, psychological advocacy, visitation, and motivation to bombing victims from several parties including the police, public figures, state leaders, and celebrities can expedite the recovery process of victims especially the shocks that they experienced, uncertain future, trauma, depression, and extremely low self-esteem derived from lifelong disability. For cases in Indonesia, police from the anti-terrorism special forces periodically provide assistance, visitation, and various supports to bombing victims so they feel secure and motivated to live.

## Stage III: Harmonization Through Group Therapies and Dialogues

Group therapies and dialogues that bring bombing victims and their families together with the actors is an extraordinary event. This process in conducted to holistically heal the feelings of bombing victims, namely by answering questions concerning "who," "why," and "why me." Lifting the psychological burden/pressure or various questions that have been lingering within makes bombing victims feel calmer emotionally. This process is a reconciliation and peace building process. These statements by bombing victims in group therapy described their feelings:

> At that time my head was bald ... I have a wound from this part up to here ... it was embarrassing, I used to be confident when meeting people, since this incident whenever I meet new people I become less confident ... I am confused, why do they have to do this, what is their motivation, I have questions in my heart, I am confused. (A bombing victim, in Wongkaren, 2012, p. 153)

> I ... I only ask Sir, when this incident happened to me causing death to my husband, why did this happen to me, why me ... (A bombing victim, in Wongkaren, 2012. p. 153)

This stage is critical, yet important to perform. Once bombing victims have made peace with what happened to them and directly witness the legal consequences experienced by the perpetrators, then they are able to completely move on, overcome extreme hatred within themselves, and minimize vengeance so that reciprocal acts of violence can be avoided. This can increase community resilience and prevent crime in the future. Furthermore, victims are not only those hit by the bomb during an act of terror. Victims can also be families of former inmates who get a bad stigma from society. In fact, victims can also be ex-perpetrators of terror that are affected by the brainwashing process conducted by several seniors in their group. Many of the perpetrators, due to their zeal for the sake of a particular ideology and idealism, fall into acts of violent extremism thus obtaining a stigma from society as a "terrorist" which in the end causes themselves to increasingly avoid blending in with the moderate mainstream society. This drastically impacts the life of their families. They have difficulty forgetting and to move toward the betterment of themselves due to the bad stigma in society, thus this issue requires intervention. The following statements by former violent extremists in group therapy illustrate their thoughts and feelings:

> I just realized that I and my friends had the wrong target back then. (A former terror perpetrator, in Wongkaren, 2012, p. 156)

> I am confused, what was wrong with me, only enforcing Islamic shari'a, but how come I am labeled as radical, opposed by society. (A former terror perpetrator, in Wongkaren, 2012, p. 158)

Group therapy on both sides is an effort to self-heal and to raise insights on both sides. Those insights include the adverse effects of acts of terror and bombing, effects of stigma, to the effects of spiritual guidance or certain religious application that may require correction and adjustment according to the context. The insight theory was put forward by Kohler (1929), which states that learning experience can occur through "sudden comprehension" or "sudden insight" from observing and experiencing something. Significantly, insight cannot be observed by other people. Insight or enlightenment occurs personally and subjectively, and can only be felt by the individual. Even so, insight can sometimes be observed by other people. The following statement from a former violent extremist in group therapy describes this:

> The turning point for me was when I met with the victims at University of Indonesia; there I realized that Indonesia is not a war state, but a peace state. (A former terror perpetrator, in Wongkaren, 2012, p. 156)

Group therapy where there is a meeting between families of bombing victims and former terrorist inmates is rarely found in many countries. Therapy in Indonesia which is advocated by police creates a significant effect on bombing victims. They become more self-confident, assertive, have understanding of what will happen, feel relieved that they know the perpetrators, their motive, and their background, and ready to face a better future. One of a bombing victim's statements in group therapies was:

> After listening to explanation from perpetrators of terrorism, there is a reduced burden in me... (A bombing victim, in Wongkaren, 2012, p. 155)

The process at this stage involves psychologists, police, religious leaders, academics of social issue, and therapists from civil society. Involvement of the victim protection agency is something that cannot be forgotten as part of the criminal justice system. This is to ensure that the legal rights of victims are not violated (e.g., in the case of mass media presence). Pre-activities include one week of preparation that includes two major issues namely to ensure participants will attend from both sides and to establish a conducive environment for the therapy process.

Issues at this stage include safety, suspicion, awkwardness, or even tensions between the two sides at the beginning of the meeting, and information leaked to mass media.

Hence stringent security by the police (e.g., inspection of items carried by participants) is critically needed. The presence of extreme emotion (e.g., hysteria, anxiety) during this process is something that is avoided hence assessment from psychologists is required and only bombing victims with specific qualities can go through this level.

In several cases at this stage, bombing victims can display negative emotions, such as scolding the perpetrators, complaining, crying, doubting the repentance of perpetrators, or even blaming the government, even though they are still showing normal and stable emotion. The statements of bombing victims to ex-perpetrators in group therapies are as follows:

> I used to work as usual, like other people … when the bombing occurred, 80% of my body was burned, many of my bodily functions decreased, easily tired, if you can hear I'm gasping while talking as an effect from that … I also have nerve problems, it also affected my sight, you can see for yourself my current condition is like this, my arm is like this … I apply for work here and there also not accepted, I am considered physically disabled, it is difficult for me to find work. (A bombing victim, in Wongkaren, 2012, pp. 152–153)

> Frankly I am not angry with you, I am angry at the government; if there is good governance this would not have happened… (A bombing victim, in Wongkaren, 2012, p. 154)

In many other cases, bombing victims show a big heart and forgive the perpetrators but on a note that they will never repeat the act. This creates a positive effect where the perpetrators deeply regret their action and in turn want to help the victims as a form of their responsibility and even foster good relationships with the victims. In group therapy bombing victims stated to ex-violent extremists:

> Although I experience all of this, from the bottom of my heart I've sincerely let it go and forgiven. (A bombing victim, in Wongkaren, 2012, p. 154)

> I have no revenge or anything, I only hope that it is not repeated again … I really have no hatred or anything. (A bombing victim, in Wongkaren, 2012, p. 154)

> I am a mother of the victim, my child died after being hit by the bomb, at that time he was not supposed to be working, however he came because there is a meeting of mosque committee at his office, coincidently he is the head of the committee … I as the mother of the victim forgave the perpetrators … and please do not repeat this again… (A bombing victim in Wongkaren, 2012, p. 154)

Furthermore, former violent extremists stated to bombing victims in group therapy:

> Sir, if I experienced what you went through, I will also be very angry, really, it is incredible your struggle and what you experience… (A former terror perpetrator, in Wongkaren, 2012, p. 156)

> Sir, may I be allowed to visit your home? If so, I would like to apologize to your family. (A former terror perpetrator, in Wongkaren, 2012, p. 158)

This stage can also build awareness of the fatality caused by acts of violent extremism, thus increasing the immune system of society. The ultimate result of this stage is when the two sides, both victims and ex-prisoners, reach a written agreement to oppose acts of violence. Although many ex-offenders of violent extremism cases are still not involved in this activity (because they are still in prison or still out of reach from the police), it can bring insights for all parties involved. Ex-prisoners that attend as participants of dialogues and group therapies can become change agents toward their compatriots so that the life of the society is positive and progressive. In group therapy former violent extremists stated:

> Actually we the Islamic fighters only want to defend our brothers everywhere that are being oppressed ... but how come our compatriots misdirected the target... (A former terror perpetrator, in Wongkaren, 2012, p. 157)

> Sir, we are fighters, if anything in this poor country that attack you and all of us, we will rise and defend you, do not worry Sir ... we apologize for what our compatriots have done, it breaks my heart to see, your condition ... do not worry Sir. (A former terror perpetrator, in Wongkaren, 2012, p. 158)

> Sir, incredible Sir, what you experience is really difficult ... are you now able to work routinely Sir? (A former terror perpetrator, in Wongkaren, 2012, p. 156)

> I, representing the perpetrators, utter remorse and apology ... we err ... I feel sad and touched by what the victims experienced... (A former terror perpetrator, in Wongkaren, 2012, pp. 158–159)

In general, this activity is a proper learning facility for both ex-prisoners, the bombing victims and their families, practitioners in the field of violent extremism (psychologists, religious experts, experts in humanities, and academics), as well as the government to build community resilience.

## Stage IV: Empowerment Programs

Empowerment programs allow bombing victims to actualize themselves and to explore their own potential. The empowerment programs include vocational, humanitarian, educational, and social re-integration programs, even politics. Several bombing victims are getting involved in politics to change the laws and regulations concerning counter-terrorism efforts and handling of bombing victims. There are also bombing victims who become extension workers and speakers in educational and counter-narrative programs for the public. The goal is to maximize their potential, to promote the anti-violence campaign, and to endorse some changes in laws and regulations in order to prevent crime and improve community resilience. Thus, they become change agents in society. As Havelock (1970) states, a successful change agent has the characteristics of positive attitudes, adequate understanding or knowledge, and specific skills in forming a collaboration and preserving peace.

Empowerment programs need to be protected by the police as law enforcement. In addition, bombing victims also need to be accompanied by the victim protection agency. This is because in many extension programs, the victims are partnered with or collaborate with ex-perpetrators and their families, hence the agency needs to make sure that the process is productive and support the victims' development to become "champions." The lack of accompaniment of bombing victims in several counseling programs which involve collaborative work with ex-perpetrators and many parties will possibly lead to vulnerability of victims toward a subtle form of exploitation. In contrast, a productive program that is well organized can amplify the effect of the program because these bombing victims bring with them a powerful voice of the anti-violence movement or spirit in society.

Figure 11.3 describes an empowerment program model in counter-narrative to improve community resilience and to prevent crimes. In this figure, victims collaborate with ex-perpetrators to produce anti-violence messages. Organizers of the empowerment program can come from government, private sectors, or civil society. Good collaboration

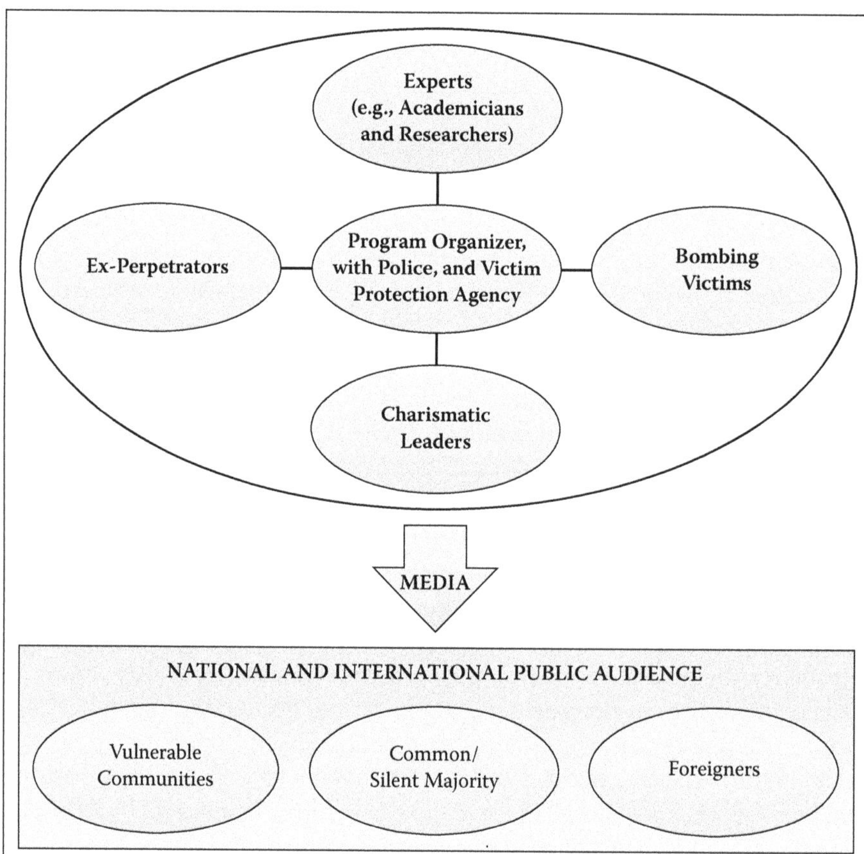


**Figure 11.3** Bombing Victims Empowerment-Program Model in Peace Campaign.

produces a quality counter-narrative program that can increase the immune system of society from acts of violence and revenge, including violence on behalf of a certain ideology or belief. In this empowerment model, the police hold a strategic position as protectors and guardians of the program. The police hold a position that is deemed critical in providing security to the parties involved in the program.

Drawing upon the "credible voices" of bombing victims and ex-perpetrators, a number of educational empowerment programs are aimed at youth in cities that are most vulnerable to violent extremism. In the programs, bombing victims as speakers draw upon first-hand narratives and explain the negative effects of violence. The audience can learn to avoid violence and provocations, and be empowered to make more positive, life-affirmative choices.

An ideal program is one that utilizes venues where students learn or where youths or communities gather, such as high schools, universities, and youth clubs. Testimonials of bombing victims, their family members, and reformed perpetrators will be "credible voices" that provide a powerful and direct testimonial about the negative impacts of violence upon society.

Periodic follow-up visits to select institutions during programs were held in order to reinforce the key message that violence is not a feasible choice and that students can make and have a better life choice by steering clear of violence. Periodic visits will over time serve to develop an ongoing relationship with school officials and students. Sustained engagement, without repetitive programming, is much more desirable, sustainable, and effective than a one-off program. At the end of the programs, the attitudes of youths or audience regarding the relative acceptability of violence will be measured. The programs are considered successful, if at the end of the program, there is a smaller percentage of the audience who still believe that violence is a legitimate expression of their grievances or to bring about change.

In vocational areas, private sectors are able to assist in providing opportunities for bombing victims to work and stay productive in society. In this case, private sectors can provide business opportunities for bombing victims that have received recommendation from professionals that have handled and observed their progress. Proper protection of the rights of bombing victims known by the police increase trust and relationship between the community and police, and also shows good governance.

## Stage V: Generating Change Agents

Treatment toward bombing victims reaches the pinnacle of success if they are able to become independent agents capable of creating new change agents or perform self-transcendence. In this case, they are able to become coaches or trainers who train prospective counselors or extension workers or speakers of anti-violence programs. In several cases, these bombing victim champions can even establish their own foundation where its management structure (e.g., founder, chairman, and caretaker) is entirely comprised of victims of terrorism, therefore they are not relying on other people who are non-bombing victims to run the operation of the foundation.

Several unique foundations, where the management structure is comprised entirely of bombing victims, are found in Indonesia. Among those foundations are ASKOBI and

Survivor Foundation. Founded in 2009, both foundations have more than 600 affiliate members (Adiartono & Soemarno, 2010; Hadisiswoyo, 2016). The organizations are open to both Indonesians and foreign nationals who have been victimized by terrorist bombing in Indonesia, or who have family members who have been victims of terrorist attacks carried out in the country. All of these foundations have already partnered successfully with police and the National Anti-Terrorism Agency as well as ex-perpetrators. In addition to public outreach activities, this foundation also provides medical and economic support to victims of terror, including programs on economic empowerment and business development for victims of violent extremism.

ASKOBI is successful in generating "change agent" students. These students continue to share with peers the message that violence is not a healthy or viable choice. ASKOBI's programs in conducting the peace campaign also reach a progressive point due to assessments of their own programs, including pre-surveys of attitude of the audience towards the acceptability of violence and extremism and follow-on surveys which measure changes in the perceptions of the audience (youths). In consultation with school officials, ASKOBI selects at least one "change agent" in each school who is identified based upon leadership potential and interest. In doing all its programs, ASKOBI performs collaborative works with the national police, clerics, or charismatic leaders, experts, researchers, other foundations, and academicians as partners or advisors.

## Conclusion

In the context where terrorism is viewed as an act of crime, legal investigation based on valid evidence is critical. In this case, law enforcement as the leading sector in handling terrorism plays a major role in restoring community resilience. Further, the approach of healing bombing victims is unique and distinct from treatment of other crime victims. The strategic role of the police is crucial in transforming bombing victims into "champions" to build community resilience. This transformation process includes five key stages: physical rehabilitation, psychosocial rehabilitation, harmonization through group therapies and dialogues, empowerment programs, and generating change agents to deliver anti-violence messages. To conduct this process, a collaborative work among police, professionals, experts, civil society, and other proponents is necessary in order to prevent future reciprocal acts of violence in the community. Finally, future papers on how the Police Service protects its officers from secondary trauma or post-traumatic stress disorder as a result of working with bombing victims or perpetrators are relevant. For this, the self-care strategies supported by the police organization for its members are important in order to build personal resilience within police officers.

## Note

* This chapter was presented in Sofia, Bulgaria, July 27–31, 2014, and originally published in the *Journal of Police Practice and Research* (PPR) special issue. It has been updated for this special edition.

## References

Abas, N., & Sukabdi, Z. A. (2011). *Move me away from terrorism.* Jakarta: Grafindo.

Adiartono, W., & Soemarno, T. (2010). *We are the bombing victims: Moving from sorrow to enlightenment.* Documentary film.

Crenshaw, M. (2009). The logic of terrorism: Terrorist behavior as a product of strategic choice. In J. Victoroff & A. W. Kruglanski (Eds.), *Psychology of terrorism: Classic and contemporary insights* (pp. 371–382). New York: Psychology Press.

Gunaratna, R., & Rubin, L. (2011). Introduction. In R. Gunaratna, J. Jerard, & L. Rubin (Eds.), *Terrorist rehabilitation and counter-radicalization: New approaches to counter-terrorism* (pp. 1–3). London: Routledge.

Gurr, T. (1970). *Why men rebel.* New Jersey: Princeton University Press.

Hadisiswoyo, S. (2016). *Bombing victims need government attention.* Jakarta.

Havelock, R. G. (1970). *A guide to innovation in education.* Ann Arbor: Center for Research on the Utilization of Scientific Knowledge, Institute for Social Research, University of Michigan.

Kohler, W. (1929). *Gestalt psychology.* New York: Liveright.

Koltko-Rivera, M. E. (2006). Rediscovering the later version of Maslow's Hierarchy of Needs: Self-transcendence and opportunities for theory, research, and unification. *Review of General Psychology, 10*(24), 302–317.

Kruglanski, A. W., & Fishman, S. (2009). The psychology of terrorism: "Syndrome" versus "tool" perspectives. In Victoroff, J. & Kruglanski, A. W. (Eds.), *Psychology of terrorism: Classic and contemporary insights* (pp. 35–53). New York: Psychology Press.

Kruglanski, A., Gelfand, M., & Gunaratna, R. (2011). Aspects of deradicalization. In R. Gunaratna, J. Jerard, & L. Rubin (Eds.), *Terrorist rehabilitation and counter-radicalization: New approaches to counter-terrorism* (pp. 135–145). London: Routledge.

McCauley, C. R., & Segal, M. E. (2009). Social psychology of terrorist groups. In Victoroff, J. & Kruglanski, A. W. (Eds.), *Psychology of terrorism: Classic and contemporary insights* (pp. 331–346). New York: Psychology Press.

Nasrul, E. (2014, June 12). Korban Teroris Tidak Diperhatikan Negara. *Republika* [Jakarta]. Retrieved June 22, 2017, from www.republika.co.id/berita/nasional/hukum/14/06/12/n726r7-korban-teroris-tidak-diperhatikan-negara.

Post, J. M., Sprinzak, E., & Denny, L. M. (2009). The terrorists in their own words: Interviews with 35 incarcerated Middle Eastern terrorists. In Victoroff, J. & Kruglanski, A. W. (Eds.), *Psychology of terrorism: Classic and contemporary insights* (pp. 109–117). New York: Psychology Press.

Putra, I. E., & Sukabdi, Z. A. (2013). Basic concepts and reasons behind the emergence of religious terror activities in Indonesia: An inside view. *Asian Journal of Social Psychology, 16*(2), 83–91. doi:10.1111/ajsp.12001.

Rabasa, A., Pettyjohn, S. L., Ghez, J. J., & Boucek, C. (2010). *Deradicalizing Islamist extremists.* Santa Monica, CA: RAND Corporation.

Rose, J. D. (1982). *Outbreaks, the sociology of collective behavior.* New York: New York Free Press.

Runciman, W. G. (1966). *Relative deprivation and social justice: A study of attitudes to social inequality in twentieth-century England.* Berkeley: University of California Press.

Satrawi, H. (2016, January 2). Menghadirkan Negara bagi Korban Terorisme. *Sindo* [Jakarta]. Retrieved June 22, 2017, from www.koran-sindo.com/news.php?r=1&n=3& date=2016-01-02.

Sommers-Flanagan, J., & Sommers-Flanagan, R. (2012). *Counseling and psychotherapy theories in context and practice: Skill, strategies, and techniques.* New Jersey: John Wiley & Sons, Inc.

Sukabdi, Z. A. (2015). A review on rehabilitation and deradicalization. *The Centre for the Study of Terrorism and Political Violence: Journal of Terrorism Research, 6*(2), 35–56.

The National Anti-Terror Agency. (2013). *National rehabilitation guidelines for terrorism perpetrators and families* (Vol. 1). Jakarta: The National Anti-Terror Agency.

Walker, I., & Smith, H. J. (2001). *Relative deprivation: Specification, development and integration.* Cambridge, UK: Cambridge University Press.

Wongkaren, Z. (2012). Group therapy and reconciliation between former terrorism offenders and terrorism victims. In S. W. Sarwono (Ed.), *Terrorism in Indonesia: Psychology perspective* (pp. 139–161). Jakarta: Alvabet.

# Women in Law Enforcement
## Reality or Myth?

# 12

CHRISTIAAN BEZUIDENHOUT

> We must oppose those knowledge and power discourses that subordinate women everywhere throughout society.
>
> – **Foucault**

## Contents



### Abstract

The world-wide perception that policing is a masculine occupation has resulted in women experiencing discrimination in this apparent masculine domain. The discrimination that policewomen experience generally stems from myths. In many cases it is accepted that the place of women is in the home, while men possess the physical power to carry out policing tasks. This contribution will look at the historical position of females in the police, the current position of female police officers in the South African Police Service (SAPS), the possible options they have to succeed, and the myths that exist regarding female police officers.

## Introduction

Since the first writings about man were analyzed it became evident that the protection of individuals and property has been the responsibility of males. In early civilizations the heads of families (usually males) regulated the behavior of their members. As societies grew and families expanded a male or a number of males were chosen to ensure the safety of the group. This means that there was always a male at the head of the family or group and it was under the leadership of either the father (*patria potestas*), the familial patriarch (*parens familiae*), or the head of the community (*parens comuniae*) that strict behavioral codes were enforced (Bezuidenhout & Theron, 2000).

Due to the fact that women were never seen as being capable of protecting themselves or their communities, they were not considered for inclusion when policing was introduced. This resulted in policing being established during the Middle Ages as an exclusively male occupation. Even when Sir Robert Peel introduced the modern policing concept in Great Britain in 1829, by means of the London Metropolitan Police Act, women were not regarded as fit to do police work. The modernization of policing in other countries, as a result of British initiatives, was also characterized by male domination (Brown & Heidensohn, 2000).

The emphasis on women not being fit for police work can be related to historical perceptions of the role of the female, data portraying females as unfit for physical protection duties, and the fact that records of the appointment of women is the vaguest amongst all historical documentation regarding policing (Roberg & Kuykendall, 1993). However, for the past 30 years, women in policing have been the subject of considerable study.

## International Historical Outline

Women who were appointed in police services in overseas countries during the late nineteenth century were referred to as "policewomen," "matrons," "prison matrons," or "police officials." The domestic tasks, which were frequently seen as their main function, included services such as doing the laundry and preparing dinners for male police officers and prisoners. It is believed that the first woman given full policing powers was Lola Baldwin from Portland, Oregon, in the United States of America (USA). She was "hired" in 1905 as a social worker and was given the responsibility to protect young girls and women. Her "crime prevention role" was seen as detached from the traditional policing role. The argument used to justify this was that females' special capacity for childcare precluded them from traditional police work. Consequently, it was argued that women could only be used for clerical work or social services involving the solving of juvenile and family problems (Grennan, 2000; Horne, 2006; Roberg & Kuykendall, 1993; Taylor, 1996). Between 1905 and 1915 various police departments in the USA followed the Portland example by appointing women.

The section female police officials were appointed to what was known as the "women's bureau" and functioned independently from the male division. These women did not wear uniforms, were not armed, and earned smaller salaries than their male colleagues despite the fact that they were often better educated and qualified than the male officials. This discrepancy between male and female police officials continued until the late 1960s. The existence of these discrepancies highlights the fact that women were not seen as true police officials from the onset (Grennan, 2000; Roberg & Kuykendall, 1993; Taylor, 1996).

During the second half of the twentieth century doctor Lois Higgins, who had been president of the International Association of Women's Policing (IAWP), attempted to improve the position of women within policing. To achieve this aim she investigated the reason why women did not form part of the male-dominated policing domain. An important reason she found for the separate establishment of the "women's bureau" was the women's belief that being separate from the men afforded them the only assurance that they could independently make progress (Champion & Rush, 1997; Dantzker, 1995; Grennan, 2000; Roberg & Kuykendall, 1993; Taylor, 1996). Factors that contributed to the women's perception that they would be hampered occupationally if they did not function independently from their male counterparts, prior to 1969 included not being permitted to undertake patrols or wear uniforms (Champion & Rush, 1997; Dantzker, 1995; Grennan, 1993; Roberg & Kuykendall, 1993; Taylor, 1996). To illustrate the position of female police officials during the beginning years of female policing Emsley (1996) states that,

> the woman police had an ambiguous position and, significantly, while they were required to have a knowledge of the duties of a constable, they were denied his key prerogative – that of arrest. If a woman police officer witnessed a breach of the law, it was her duty to enlist the help of the nearest male constable in the vicinity. (p. 35)

In this regard, Emsley (1996) points out that the perceptions and myths that existed of female police officials at the onset of female policing, as well as during the later years, have not to date been adequately explored and still exist. Brown and Heidensohn (2000) believe these myths about policewomen will never completely subside. Perceptions and socialization about a woman's weakness, procreation function, female cycle, and sexuality all preserve these myths in society and in the policing domain. They point out that both the socially constructed aspects of sexuality and the biological characteristics of a woman are the most important apparatuses that drive the myths and negativity towards women in the policing realm. They state in this regard that the

> origins of attitudes toward policewomen can be found historically in stereotypic mythology about the "good" woman, compliant and ignorant or naïve about sex other than that which is necessary for child bearing, who is protected by her father then husband and the woman who understands sex only too well and whose ways are that of all flesh leading to depravity. (Brown & Heidensohn, 2000, p. 14)

In modern times this myth still exists because the sexually active woman with different sex partners is a "tramp" or slut while the male counterpart who manages different female sex partners is still treated as the desirable stud or Don Juan.

The position of females in law enforcement has, however, improved in the USA where women represent 12–14% of all law enforcement positions (Horne, 2006; Police Employment, 2008). Although the position of female police officials was not positive in the past, the picture is not totally bleak. In countries such as Denmark, Germany, The Netherlands, Norway, and Sweden policewomen are also appointed on equal grounds and are given certain patrol duties and responsibilities. Nevertheless, while women perform as well as men in various patrol assignments and situations, they still face a significant amount of disapproval from their male colleagues (Brown & Heidensohn, 2000; Horne, 2006). Some findings show that citizens, however, have shown a greater acceptance of women in this male-dominated occupation and have greater confidence in women's ability to effectively perform difficult patrol tasks. Though they may not have the sheer physical strength of male officers, studies reveal that female officers are substantially less likely to be involved in citizen complaints about the use of excessive force than males. Male police officers are about eight times more likely to use excessive force than their female counterparts. This is especially true in Britain where the police are largely still unarmed (Morley, 2011). Female police officers tend to negotiate rather than to use physical prowess to neutralize a situation (Grennan, 2000; Horne, 2006; Roberg & Kuykendall, 1993; Taylor, 1996).

In Britain since 1976, the role of women has evolved to the extent that there are few areas of policing which do not involve the placement of female officers on the "front line" of all kinds of police work. This has been a gradual change, and it was not until 2007 that all public bodies, including individual police authorities, were required to have a Gender Equality Scheme, examining internal and external issues of gender equality. The proportion of female police officers in England, Scotland, and Wales has increased from 7% in 1977 to about 27% in 2012. This means that roughly one in four police officers are female. Morley (2011) believes that women can fulfill any function males traditionally monopolized such as traffic officers, police dog handlers, and firearms instructors. They can therefore be involved in any police activity previously dominated by male counterparts.

Police forces are becoming more diverse, more even in their gender distribution, and more aware of the need for equality of opportunity. Globally, more and more senior officers are being recruited from the female population who are often recruited for very specific managerial duties. However, there is a long way to go before police forces achieve unconditional gender equality, but things have improved in the past 30 years and continue to move towards a "genderless" representative working environment for females.

## South African State of Affairs

South Africa, which was under British rule from the late 1890s and early 1900s, was influenced by Britain with regard to female policing. Although the British started appointing policewomen on a permanent basis in London by 1915 and also supplied them with neat uniforms, South Africa responded negatively to British suggestions to follow suit. This negativity soon made way for a more positive approach due to South Africa being subjected to the same demands other countries had to face as a result of World War I.

Voluntary female police patrols were established especially in harbor cities. As these women had no powers policemen were requested to assist them at all times. Feedback from these women indicated that they could do more "good things" if they were reimbursed for their services and if official status was given to them. Some police managers realized that women could make a contribution to policing which led to the appointment of Mrs. Schelpien as a Special Patrol during January 1916. Her appointment was followed by the appointment of two further Special Patrols, namely Mrs. O'Dea and Mrs. Evans (Walsh, 1916). Despite these positive initiatives concerning female policing, it could not override the negativity and myths that existed in South Africa concerning the introduction of an official female policing component. This negativity is evident from a statement made by Gilbride (1917) in which it is claimed that,

> it is a well-established fact that the greatest ambition in a girl's life is to get married, become mistress of her own castle, as well as becoming a mother and contributing to the empty cradles, consequently even if we were to get the right class of girls to come forward and join the police, they would be with us only a year or so, when perhaps one of our Sergeants or some other likely chap would be "bagged," so that motherhood at an early stage in their career would be substituted for the Police sphere. (p. 446)

This negativity, stereotyping, and myths towards women were further reinforced by the Police Act of the time which stipulated that only men could carry out arrests. By 1919 the functioning of this "official" women's police force had deteriorated to such an extent that the City Council of Cape Town, which had been influenced by the criticism of the Minister of Justice, decided to withdraw all financial support. As a result, women policing temporarily disappeared from the scene in South Africa (Women Police, 1919; Wrottesley, 1938).

In 1944 the Centlivres and Lansdown Commissions recommended that women should be employed by the then South African Police (SAP). It was however, not until January 1, 1972, that two women were officially admitted to the SAP (First S.A. policewomen, 1971). They were Ms. Duveen Botha, then the vice-principal of a girl's secondary school, and Ms. Anna Nel, then a senior professional officer at an alcohol and drug rehabilitation sanctuary. Duveen Botha was appointed as commanding officer of the women's police with the rank of lieutenant-colonel, while Anna Nel, Botha's assistant, was appointed with the rank of major (Van Niekerk, 1988).

General Gideon Joubert, at that stage Commissioner of the SAP, announced that these two women were appointed to head women's policing and following their training at the SAP College, Pretoria, and would immediately take over the control and organization of the female component. In conjunction with this, they were also responsible for the selection of future candidates. In terms of the Police Act, they were appointed to take charge of all matters concerning women in the SAP. They were accountable to the Commissioner of the SAP (Viljoen, 1972). Joubert also confirmed that no discrimination would exist between males and females regarding salaries and other benefits. Thus, until about 40 years ago, there was no operational policewoman in the South African Police. The timeline for females in the South African Police can be summarized as follows:

- Policing in South Africa was formally established in April 1913.
- Three female "Special Patrols" were appointed in 1916–1919.
- The first official female police officers were recruited in 1972.
- The first group of women who were trained were all White.
- In July 1981 the first group of Colored females was recruited.
- In May 1982 Indian women were welcomed onto the police force.
- In July 1983 African women were welcomed onto the police force.
- The first female National Commissioner of the South African Police Service was appointed in 2012.

South Africa has undergone many changes. South Africa introduced a "welfarist" approach after apartheid was toppled in 1994. The South African Police (SAP) (as they were known before Democratization in 1994) was replaced by the South African Police Service (SAPS) (new name after 1994). Before 1994 the SAP employed a para-militaristic approach to policing, which was based on limited community involvement in policing matters. Since then the "force" has changed into a "service" with the emphasis on merged police-community partnerships. South Africa became an internationally accepted democracy in 1994 when the late President Nelson Mandela was elected as the first President of the new South Africa. This new democratic order brought about many changes in the country and also had a substantial impact on policing (Bezuidenhout, 2011; Fourie & Reynecke, 2001). The newly elected government under the leadership of the late Nelson Mandela, who was also the leader of the African National Congress (ANC), focused on the recognition of the rights of every South African citizen. He specifically declared that everyone was equal and that gender equality should become a priority in South Africa. Hence the role of women in the newly established SAPS has expanded in recent years. A growing number of opportunities were made available to women in the police service and consequently led to a progressive integration of female police officers into the police domain – an area that was significantly dominated by males before.

The first female National Commissioner of the SAPS, General Magwashi Victoria (Riah) Phiyega was appointed in 2012 (AllAfrica, 2012). However, she was suspended on October 14, 2015 pending the outcome of an inquiry into her fitness to hold office (Hunter, 2015). At the finalization of this chapter on March 10, 2016 she was still suspended as the National Commissioner of SAPS as criminal charges had been opened against her for apparently defeating the ends of justice.

Nonetheless, since her appointment in 2012 several other females have been appointed in key managerial positions and the role of female police officers has expanded in recent years. National statistics reveal that females occupy about 27% of the top management positions while males occupy about 73% of these positions (very similar to the United Kingdom). Therefore, few women hold top managerial positions and the representation of women when compared to the police population is unbalanced. One can deduce that a higher concentration of men at top management levels could result in women still facing many challenges in the male-dominated hierarchy of the SAPS. In addition, politicians in South Africa have recently announced that they want the SAPS to be 50% male and 50% female and this they want to achieve with a mass recruitment drive. Obviously the impact of these ideals will only become clear once the objective is attained and evaluated.

The government therefore introduced an en masse recruitment drive in part to address the legacy of apartheid, by promoting racial and gender representativeness in the SAPS. In so doing, they facilitated entry into the civil service by a significant number of Black African male and female police officers. The success of this drive is commendable, but open to doubt as a result of poor training, inadequate vetting of new recruits, and haphazard recruitment practices. Another drawback of mass recruitment has required a substantial investment of public funds (Bruce, 2013). The number of Black SA Police Service Act employees (operational police officers) in the service in the 2014/2015 financial year was about 76% (114,472 members out of 150,237 members) of the total operational police population, which is on par with color quotas of the current population. In addition, the SAPS also employs about 42,742 Public Service Act employees (civilians).

Currently the undivided SAPS population (top management vs. non managerial positions) looks like this:

From Table 12.1 it is still clear that women are underrepresented in the SAPS notwithstanding all the opportunities, Black empowerment initiatives by the government, and recruitment drives that have been implemented up until now.

While continuing sexist attitudes have persisted within many of the older male police communities all over the world, the public perception of the female officer has, on the whole, been more welcoming (Horne, 2006). Community members feel that female officers have brought a more "human" approach to dealing with everyday policing situations. Female police officers are also seen as being less aggressive than male officers and more likely to act with natural empathy to the public they serve. More and more interest in female policing also triggered more research endeavors about female policing. The first study focusing on the occupational achievements of female police officials was undertaken in 1973 by the Police Foundation in Washington D.C. The conclusion drawn from this study was that the job achievement of female police officials was satisfactory. This finding was of great importance as it refuted the argument that female police officials could not cope with the physically demanding nature of police work (Roberg & Kuykendall, 1993).

Up to and during the 1980s relatively little scientific data existed about the achievements of policewomen and how these women's achievements compared to that of policemen. In this regard Tracy-Stratton (1986) emphasizes that most assumptions regarding female police officials' occupational achievements were based on sexist stereotypes and myths. This view was reinforced by the tendency amongst male police officials to generalize the poor performance of a single woman to all female officials. Views such as women are only equipped to do domestic work, do not have the physical strength to execute policing tasks, and doing "men's work" should not be expected of women, were rife.

**Table 12.1 Total Operational Police Population (SA Police Service Act Employees)**

| Gender | Subtotals | % |
|---|---|---|
| Females | 39,011 | 26 |
| Males | 111,226 | 74 |
| **Total** | **150,237** | **100** |

*Source*: Annual Report: South African Police Service (2014/2015).

**Table 12.2 Achievements of Female Police Officials Compared to that of their Male Counterparts**

| Similarities Between Male and Female Police Officials | Differences Between Male and Female Police Officials |
|---|---|
| • Female police officials perform just as well as male police officials in the execution of policing tasks. Kakar (2002) could find no statistically significant differences between male and female officers' perceptions of job performance skills in administrative and supervisory tasks. A finding the current study complemented.<br>• Female police officials respond just as effectively as males to summons to defuse situations involving danger and act as competently as their male counterparts within the situation.<br>• Female police officials do patrolling as effectively as male officials.<br>• The number of arrests carried out by male and female police officials increasingly shows a similar success rate although women still arrest fewer individuals than males.<br>• The public considers female police officials to be as competent as their male counterparts. | • Female police officials are more effective during the defusing of potentially violent situations than their male counterparts.<br>• Female police officials have a less aggressive policing style than male police officials.<br>• Female police officials are reported less frequently than their male counterparts by the public for acting in an incompetent way.<br>• Female police officials handle service calls and requests (e.g., family conflict) more effectively than their male counterparts.<br>• The general public commonly sees female police officials as more pleasant and competent than their male counterparts.<br>• The community treats female police officials with more respect than their male counterparts.<br>• Contrary to male police officials, female officials experience less opposition or resistance from male offenders they arrest.<br>• Police stations are generally appraised more positively when a plaintiff had had contact with a female police official than when the contact was with a male official.<br>• Female police officials are less inclined than their male counterparts to use their firearms in dangerous situations.<br>• Female police officials are less inclined than their male counterparts to seriously injure a member of the public.<br>• Female police officials are described as emotionally more stable than their male counterparts.<br>• Female police officials are described as being more sensitive and helpful than their male colleagues with regard to the needs of members of the community. Phiyega (2012) states in this regard that "women are also found to be more empathetic and flexible, as well as stronger in interpersonal skills than their male counterparts. This enables us to read situations accurately and take information in from all sides. Women are able to bring others around to their point of view, because they genuinely understand and care about where others are coming from so those they lead people feels more understood, supported and valued."<br>• Unlike male police officials, female officials do not have the physical strength to control an offender who is big, strong, and out of control (e.g., during a rage attack).<br>• Unlike their male counterparts, female police officials are less inclined to become involved in preventative actions (e.g., to apprehend a suspicious-looking pedestrian or driver of a motor vehicle). |

Since the 1990s scientific studies concerning female police officials' occupational achievements have increasingly been undertaken and the findings compared with that of male police officials. The most important findings with regard to perceptions pertaining to similarities and differences between male and female police officials is summarized in Table 12.2 above (Aleem, 1991; Bezuidenhout, 2001 (current study 2014–2016); Cox & Fitzgerald, 1992; Flowers, 1987; Grennan, 2000; Horne, 2006; Kakar, 2002; Martin & Jurik, 1996; Roberg & Kuykendall, 1993; Shusta, Levine, Harris, & Wong, 1995; Thibault, Lynch, & McBride, 1995; Tracy-Stratton, 1986).

Although the above similarities and differences imply that women are generally successful in the executing of policing tasks this positive picture of the female police official is still not accepted by all police officials. Also many myths about female police officials still exist. To determine what perceptions male and female police officers hold towards the performance of female police officers and which myths are still sustained the author investigated the issue.

## Method

To measure the perceptions of male and female police officers pertaining to the role and ability of females on the police force I made use of an exploratory basic research approach. Cresswell's (2009) dominant-less-dominant mixed methodology strategy was followed and both quantitative and qualitative data measures were used. The dominant part of the study was the quantitative survey. Several hypotheses and sub-hypotheses were formulated for investigation in the quantitative section of the study. This chapter will, however, mainly focus on the findings of the less dominant part of the study. In this less dominant section of the research the researcher employed qualitative semi-structured interviews with male and female police officers in different units and departments of the SAPS. In the major study the quantitative findings were therefore supported by means of a qualitative technique. Also Lanier and Briggs (2014) insist that mixed methods have the potential to strengthen a study and it is applicable to any type of research. Please note that the author only selected a few findings from the quantitative section of the study to highlight the general perceptions regarding female police officers. In the survey a total of 116 items were measured. In addition, many themes had to be identified and coded in the open section (Section D) of the survey. The volume of data is too wide for a single chapter. For the purposes of this chapter only a few relevant findings will be highlighted to determine whether women in law enforcement should be deemed a reality or a myth.

## Quantitative Data Analysis Strategy

The researcher utilized the quantitative-descriptive survey research design to gather the data from the participants. A representative from the National Head Office at the SAPS assisted the researcher in contacting and distributing the questionnaires amongst 28 police stations and to Head Office in the Capital of South Africa, Pretoria (Gauteng Province).

Five hundred self-administered questionnaires using a Likert-scale format with an additional open-ended question section were distributed (about a 10% sample of police members in Pretoria). The survey consisted of four sections: Section A – Biographical information; Section B – General perception of police officers; Section C – Perception regarding female police officers; and Section D – Open ended section for own comments. Only 249 (a response rate of 49.08%) valid questionnaires were mailed back to me (see Table 12.3 below).

The data set was cleaned and statistically dissected. Descriptive measures such as means, standard deviances, and frequency tables were used to explore the data. A comparison was also drawn between the responses from the males and the females by means of the Wilcoxon signed-rank test. This non-parametric statistical test can be used when comparing two related "samples" to assess whether their population mean ranks differ (i.e., it is a paired difference test [e.g., male vs. female]). In addition, the Kruskal-Wallis one-way analysis of variance by ranks was used to analyze the data. This is a non-parametric method for comparing more than two groups that are independent, or not related (e.g., perceptions of different race groups in the sample). The one-way analysis of variance (ANOVA) was used to analyze the differences between group means (such as variation among and between groups). The General Linear Model of ANOVA was also used as different variables such as gender, age, years of service, race, and rank (see tables below) had to be considered in the measurements of the different perceptions and between groups. The Spearman's rank correlation coefficient non-parametric measure of statistical correlation between two variables was utilized to measure the internal reliability of the questionnaire. It assesses how well the relationship between two variables can be described. Statistically the questionnaire was reliable and measured what it was supposed to measure. Pearson correlations also supported internal content reliability of the Likert-scale type measuring instrument (each item was gauged). Due to word page limits I will only share a few descriptive tables to grasp the compilation of the sample better.

**Table 12.3 Sample Response Rate**

| Gender | N | % |
|---|---|---|
| Male | 137 | 55.02 |
| Female | 111 | 44.58 |
| Not indicated | 1 | 0.40 |
| **Total** | **249** | **100** |

**Table 12.4 Gender Distribution**

| Gender | N | % |
|---|---|---|
| Male | 137 | 55.02 |
| Female | 111 | 44.58 |
| **Did not indicate** | **1** | **0.40** |
| **Total** | **249** | **100** |

**Table 12.5 Age Distribution**

| Age | Males | | Females | | Total | |
|---|---|---|---|---|---|---|
| | N | % | N | % | N | % |
| 18–29 | 38 | 15.26 | 55 | 22.09 | 93 | 37.35 |
| 30–44 | 76 | 30.52 | 51 | 20.48 | 127 | 51.01 |
| 45–56 | 18 | 7.23 | 3 | 1.21 | 21 | 8.43 |
| Did Not Indicate | 6 | 2.41 | 2 | 0.80 | 8 | 3.21 |
| **Total** | **138** | **55.42** | **111** | **44.58** | **249** | **100** |

**Table 12.6 Race Distribution**

| Race | Males | | Females | | Total | |
|---|---|---|---|---|---|---|
| | N | % | N | % | N | % |
| Asian | 5 | 2.01 | 1 | 0.40 | 6 | 2.41 |
| Colored | 3 | 1.21 | 2 | 0.80 | 5 | 2.01 |
| Black | 59 | 23.70 | 30 | 12.04 | 89 | 35.74 |
| White | 70 | 28.11 | 78 | 31.33 | 148 | 59.44 |
| Did Not Indicate | 1 | 0.40 | – | – | 1 | 0.40 |
| **Total** | **138** | **55.43** | **111** | **44.57** | **249** | **100** |

**Table 12.7 Years' Service**

| Number of Years in Service | Males | | Females | | Total | |
|---|---|---|---|---|---|---|
| | N | % | N | % | N | % |
| 4–9 | 29 | 11.65 | 46 | 18.47 | 75 | 30.12 |
| 10–15 | 64 | 25.70 | 50 | 20.08 | 114 | 45.78 |
| 16–24 | 31 | 12.45 | 12 | 4.82 | 43 | 17.27 |
| 25–37 | 11 | 4.42 | 1 | 0.40 | 12 | 4.82 |
| Did Not Indicate | 3 | 1.21 | 2 | 0.80 | 5 | 2.01 |
| **Total** | **138** | **55.43** | **111** | **44.57** | **249** | **100** |

**Table 12.8 Rank**

| Rank | Males | | Females | | Total | |
|---|---|---|---|---|---|---|
| | N | % | N | % | N | % |
| Non-Commissioned | 104 | 41.77 | 76 | 30.52 | 180 | 72.29 |
| Middle Management | 26 | 10.44 | 26 | 10.44 | 52 | 20.88 |
| Top Management | 6 | 2.41 | 8 | 3.21 | 14 | 5.62 |
| | 2 | 0.80 | 1 | 0.40 | 3 | 1.21 |
| **Total** | **138** | **55.42** | **111** | **44.57** | **249** | **100** |

## Results

Several hypotheses were formulated to test different perceptions between male and female police officers regarding the role of female police officers in the police. Also different variables were tested. However for the purposes of this chapter only the main hypothesis, namely Hypothesis 1, is important to highlight. In Hypothesis 1, I postulated that female police officers would be more positive than males regarding the role of female police officers. In Table 12.9 the results from the Wilcoxon signed-rank test are presented.

In Table 12.9 it is clear that a significant difference exists between the perceptions of male and female police officers regarding all the items on The Perception of the Female Police Officer Scale. The male perceptions were mostly "neutral" while the females were noticeably more "positive."

This finding is in line with conclusions of other writers that many male police officers are generally neutral to negative toward female police officers who prefer to do operational police work (Brown & Heidensohn, 2000; Champion & Rush, 1997; Dantzker, 1995; Grennan, 1993; Horne, 2006; Roberg & Kuykendall, 1993; Taylor, 1996). Their perceptions are often based on the fact that female police officers are perceived in terms of a general prototype. They base their perceptions on different aspects such as biological differences, culture, race, education, categorization, stereotypes, experience, and own judgment. The finding supports the notion that women had been treated differently since the advent of organized policing. A neutral stance is often the safest stance as one would rather reserve a true feeling and perception. It will also be to the detriment of the male police officer who openly advocates his true perception of female colleagues, especially in South Africa where equal rights are protected by the Constitution and special recruitment and upliftment programs are in place to improve the position of females in the labor industry. This neutrality by the males in the scale section of the research was

**Table 12.9 Wilcoxon Signed-Rank Test for the Comparison of Average Scores Between the Genders by Means of the Perception of the Female Police Officer Scale**

| Gender | N | X | s | p |
|---|---|---|---|---|
| Male | 132 | 3.32 | 0.41 | |
| Female | 99 | 3.72 | 0.32 | 0.000** |

*Notes:* * = p ≤ 0.05, ≤* p ≤ 0.01.

**Table 12.10 General Linear Model of ANOVA for the Comparison of Average Scores Between Gender and Rank by Means of the Perception of the Female Police Officer Scale**

| | Male | | | Female | | |
|---|---|---|---|---|---|---|
| Rank | N | $\bar{X}$ | s | N | $\bar{X}$ | s |
| Non-Commissioned | 104 | 3,29 | | 76 | 3.74 | 0.31 |
| Commissioned | 31 | 3,39 | | 27 | 3.69 | 0.37 |

*Note:* The interaction between rank and gender was tested by means of the Perception of the Female Police Officer Scale but no significant finding (p = 0.18) was found between male and female non-commissioned and commissioned officers. However, the p value between the genders was significant (p = 0.001**).

often given a paradoxical value in the open section of the survey where comments tended to be more negative than neutral. In the qualitative section the focus was to talk about some of these negativities but also to demystify the myths about female police officers.

## Qualitative Collection and Analysis Strategies

The researcher utilized an additional method to provide supporting data gathering from face-to-face interviews by means of a semi-structured interview schedule. Ten broad questions were formulated beforehand to guide the interviews. The qualitative data provided rich information regarding the perception of male and female police officers regarding their perceptions about the role of female police officers in the police. The selected officers in this part of the study were conveniently selected in a non-probability manner. High ranking officers from both genders (five male and five female) were approached at SAPS head office to participate while the communication officers at all the stations (28 stations) were interviewed in this section. One of the broad questions in the semi-structured interview schedule was to determine whether certain myths exist regarding the performance of female police officers in the police domain.

Content analysis was used for the qualitative methodology method of data analysis. First the researcher had to understand the meaning of each participant's response to a question, and thereafter identified themes that embraced these meanings. The second step in the analysis was to assign codes to these identified main themes. This was done manually instead of using a computer software program. Having identified the different themes, the responses were classified according to these reoccurring themes. The themes became very clear as a saturation point regarding the themes was reached at an early stage after the interviews commenced. The last step in this process was to integrate the themes and responses in the text to support the findings regarding existing myths and the actual performance of female police officers (Kumar, 2005).

From these two data gathering methods the aim was to first investigate the perceptions of male and female officers regarding the role and performance of female police officers. Also the researcher aimed at addressing the myths that exist in society, in literature, and amongst certain police officers in the sample with regard to female police officers.

## Results

### Coping Strategies

Various pressure groups and activists as well as political changes have made it possible for women to enter the female domain of policing. Despite all the pressures and changes it seems as if women still occupy a small percentage of the entire police population globally (Horne, 2006). Do the myths regarding female police officers contribute to the slow progress women are making in the policing domain? Also, although the opportunity has been created for female police officers to achieve the highest ranks in the SAPS, various dangers are lurking that could affect the position of female police officers in general. In this regard research has shown that many women who are promoted to top management positions (the highest echelons) desert their fellow female workers by taking on the so-called boys' club's identity. When this happens their main objective becomes the perks the position offers them and not the plight of female workers in general. In other words, they become "one of the top boys" and often adopt a similar management style as their male counterparts (Baron & Byrne, 1997).

According to the social identity theory of Henry Tajfel (1981) women who struggle to attain a specific identity have four options to succeed. In this case, female police officers who are actively in the police can react in one of four ways to succeed or survive in the still essentially male-dominated environment. To triumph they can do the following:

### *Exit*

Exit is a strategy where the person capitulates and moves out of the situation. The female police officer who finds that she cannot attain an official police identity may opt for this strategy by resigning and either accepting another occupation more tolerant of women or assume the role of housewife.

### *Stagnant Acceptance*

Those who accept this option carry on with daily routines in a submissive way. In other words, they tolerate what is happening to them (e.g., sexual harassment or not being promoted) although intense frustration is experienced.

### *Pass*

Adopting pass as a strategy involves becoming like the dominant or controlling group (males). A female police officer who makes use of pass will try to act in a similar way to her male counterparts in order to become "one of the boys." This may, for example, involve using crude language, drinking more than the men, and acting in an aggressive way towards felons she apprehends or in her daily police duties. She basically adheres to the preconditions of the so-called sub-culture of policing. This strategy frequently fails because her gender makes her different and her behavior may threaten the male identity of her male equivalents.

### *Voice*

Voice occurs when a collective identity forms and female police officers decide to stand together utilizing the available means to achieve equality and accepting their gender. Female police officers using this strategy will develop a strong identity as POLICEwomen. In time this will result in their male counterparts accepting them as police officers and not merely as women who want to be police officers (policeWOMEN who rely on their gender to progress in a career in the criminal justice sphere). The voicing strategy can change workforce demographics and may actually speed up the attitudinal and perceptual changes (Kakar, 2002). With regard to policing, some traits make female officers different from male officers and these traits are desirable traits of contemporary law enforcement strategies such as community policing and victim support. Female police officers in the middle management echelons tend to use an interactive and participative management style where they consult with peers and fellow police officers. This is somewhat of a paradox compared to the management style of top female managers who usurp the authoritarian "boys' club" management style.

The issue of gender equality in policing and speeding up the attitudinal and perceptual changes may be addressed through a number of perspectives, but first we have to look at the myths that exist with regard to female police officers and what the perceptions of the respondents were. We also have to look at the actual perceptions of male and female police officers with regard to female officers. Policing is often still seen as a "pure form of hegemonic masculinity" and in some way this still feeds indifferent views and myths of females in the police domain (Bezuidenhout & Theron, 2000).

## Myths Pertaining to Female Police Officials

Myth One: Female police officials become sexually and romantically involved with their male colleagues (Brown & Heidensohn, 2000).

Although it cannot be denied that sexual attraction and interaction does occur among some male and female police officials and that such involvement could result in homes being broken up, it is not a phenomenon exclusive to policing. As a matter of fact, it is a phenomenon that occurs world-wide in all environments where men and women work together. Besides being farfetched to claim that all policewomen have affairs with their male colleagues, it appears that female police officials are less inclined than their male counterparts to initiate and have affairs with colleagues. Although the participants in the study indicated that certain factors could contribute to a relationship most males and females disagreed about this issue during the interviews. They did, however, highlight certain factors that could initiate sexual and emotional attraction, namely long vehicle patrol duties together, the sharing of intimate information, and relying on each other in a dangerous situation.

Myth Two: Female police officials cannot utilize physical defensive techniques because they are not strong and tough enough to do so (Emsley, 1996; Gilbride, 1917; Horne, 2006).

According to this viewpoint, females are not capable of supporting male colleagues when, for example, a fistfight occurs or a brawl in a bar has to be broken up. The use of violence is regarded as a warranted method of policing under certain circumstances. Although women are generally not as strong and fast as men, it is also undeniably so that policewomen can use firearms, tear gas, or batons as effectively as policemen. No conclusive evidence exists that female policewomen are less capable than males in resolving conflict situations. What distinguishes them from males is that they often make use of skills such as conflict resolution and negotiation techniques to handle problematic situations whereas males will use physical prowess to neutralize the situation. A recent development, especially in South Africa, is that many male and female police officers tend to become overweight which hinder both genders in functioning optimally during physical altercations or to chase a thug on foot. Although a few male respondents supported this myth the majority of the group negated it.

Myth Three: Female police officials are sick every month due to their menstrual cycle (Brown & Heidensohn, 2000).

The respondents were of the opinion that in a case where a woman is regularly ill during menstruation and she cannot successfully carry out her policing duties she should not be a police official. In reality, most female police officials do not complain of being sick during menstruation and execute their duties as competently as when they are not menstruating. Thus, despite the symptoms they may experience, they continue to do the work expected of them. This physiological characteristic is always difficult to assess as women differ significantly with regard to the effects of menstruation and the impact thereof on their daily functioning. The female respondents did highlight that their cycles could cause discomfort and also highlighted that bathroom facilities whilst on patrol are often lacking or unhygienic.

Myth Four: Female police officials expect special treatment and favors from male police officials (Emsley, 1996; Horne 2006).

The contrary is true, as most female police officials merely want to be treated as equals. Should a female police official demand preferential or special treatment on account of her gender it can be construed that she is not serious about having a career in policing. In certain situations, young good-looking female officers often bear the brunt of the unwelcome continuous attention of some male police officers who focus on her beauty and not her skills and dreams of becoming a successful POLICEwoman (as in the voice strategy to cope).

Myth Five: Female police officials are more inclined to use "deadly force" (a firearm) during confrontations because they lack the physical power to wrestle or have a fistfight (Horne, 2006).

This myth was used over a long period of time to preclude women from doing patrol work. In the earliest times a few "manly" criteria were used to select police officials such as: must be of the male gender, tall, physically burly and powerful, a hard drinker, and a good fighter (Brown, Esbensen, & Geis, 1996; Reiner, 1992; Roberg & Kuykendall, 1993). These selection criteria dissipated eventually, but influenced the thinking of the classic police thinkers for quite some time. During the 1900s up until the democratization process commenced in 1992 women were not allowed to patrol on their own. They were also not permitted to join special units such as the mounted service or the dog unit or to join the public-order-policing unit (e.g., policing of riots). The reason advanced for these restrictions was that women do not have the physical capability to do the work. In connection with these restrictions Van Heerden (1986) remarks as follows. She does the same work as a man in almost every section of the police. Only in the mounted police and task force are policewomen at present not allowed. They also do not do border duty and if patrol duty is carried out, it is always in the company of a male policeman.

The contrary is true because most female police officials are more patient than their male counterparts and would rather negotiate than use violence. The male and female respondents in the study supported this notion. Only an insignificant number of the participants thought differently. Molden (1985) claims that a well-trained female police official will be able to stand her ground if the situation demands it. If the situation warrants it, all officials whose lives are threatened, irrespective of how big or small they are, will use a firearm to protect themselves and the lives of their colleagues. Resorting to the use of deadly force is regarded as justified when police officials use it in self-defense. The South African and international news channels are currently inundated with cases of police brutality and in a significant number of cases it is male police officers who shoot to kill or use extreme brutality (e.g., the Lonmin mine incident in South Africa).

Myth Six: Female police officials are emotionally unstable and easily resort to tears.

In general women cry more than men. This is attributed to the way in which women are socialized as well as the societal view that it is normal for women to cry (Collier, 2014). From a cultural perspective police officials, and especially policemen, are expected not to cry when being confronted with upsetting scenes. They are expected to be emotionally strong, not to show any emotion, and be able to take the lead and to accept whatever happens in an accepting way. When a woman acts as a male's equal, this criterion is also applied to her. The view is based on the expectation that both male and female police officials will show the necessary professionalism and control in a situation other persons will react to with emotional outbursts. It is thus believed that the defusing of a problem will be hampered if any emotions are shown (Bradley, 1973). Half of the male respondents in the study expressed the view that women are inclined to be emotional and moody, especially during their premenstrual phase. In addition, they believed that women's emotionality has a negative effect on the execution of their policing duties. All the female respondents (100%) (in both the qualitative and quantitative sections of the research) agreed that characteristics or circumstances that are traditionally associated with women such as pregnancy, premenstrual tension, emotionality, and the rearing of children, could influence the effective execution of policing tasks. Especially pregnancy was highlighted as a factor that could have a major impact on the efficiency of female police officials. In addition to factors such as tiredness and tension experienced during pregnancy, the public's view of a pregnant policewoman may also have a negative effect on how the official executes her policing duties. Only three male respondents also believed that some female police officials use pregnancy as an excuse for not working shifts, to get transfers, or to avoid doing work that would normally be expected of them. Although some respondents indicated that having to take two months' leave before the birth of the baby is unnecessary because they could continue with most of their policing tasks, the majority claimed that this was impossible. Approximately 17% of the male respondents believe that the granting of maternity leave is a discriminatory practice because men do not enjoy such a benefit when their wives or partners have babies. They are given a few days off (usually a week), but must be back in the saddle once their days of compassionate leave are over. Women may legally stay home for months to recover and to nurture the newborn baby.

It is normal for police officials, whether male or female, to experience intense emotions when being confronted with upsetting scenes. Three of the respondents in the current study expressed the view that emotionality and depression are not determined by gender but related to the nature of police work. Thus, the psychological state of both men and women is influenced by the work that has to be done.

Although the expectations of and standards for female police officials are continuously changing and women are currently allowed more freedom to explore their femininity, women in the police service have to be careful as to how they assert themselves and what survival mechanisms could be used within the male-dominated policing domain. In this regard Tracy-Stratton (1986) points out that some male police officials "cannot accept a woman who rejects her own feminine nature to become one of the boys" (using the "pass" strategy). One of the male respondents who participated in the study indicated that female police officials could not be considered to be feminine. Despite this viewpoint it must be accepted that the environment, the type of policing tasks, as well as the unit in which the policewoman is working will determine the extent to which she will be able to express her femininity.

Legislation and policy changes have contributed to female police officials' position within the SAPS being improved to such an extent that there are many instances where women are enjoying better prospects than their male counterparts (a female chief of police in SA was appointed in 2012). The Constitution and affirmative action policies (South African Police Service, 1996) have ensured that there can no longer be discrimination against women. This means that a larger percentage of female police officials have to be appointed in the SAPS and that the woman instead of the male should be promoted when both qualify for promotion and only one position is available. This state of affairs benefits women while simultaneously causes many males to feel threatened.

A question that arises when the above is considered is whether female police officials are not artificially benefited by legal and constitutional prescription? To answer this question it is necessary to determine to what extent women are able to do work traditionally earmarked for males and whether the women's job performance is poorer than, similar to, or better than that of their male counterparts.

In this study a few derogatory comments by males were made about females in the open-ended section of the survey (quantitative section). Respondent 15 indicated that "they only want to do selected duties during the day because they are lazy." Respondent 19 stated that "women police officers are state mattresses." In other words they are sexually promiscuous and available. Respondent 87 was of the opinion the "women need to do female related duties and should not be in the police. They cannot do what a male can do as they are too weak." Respondent 156 stated that women can only do serious police work for one week in the month "as the rest of the month they go on light duty because of their female cycles." According to Martin and Jurik (1996, p. 64) an important reason for some males' non-acceptance of women in the police being as competent as men, is based on the way in which male police officials interpret their policing role. If it is interpreted in terms of traditional criteria of what "masculinity" and "femininity" involves their embedded attitudes will not easily be changed. On the whole the findings were very similar to Kakar's (2002) findings as most of the hypotheses tested insignificant. Thus, male and female police officers generally view females as competent enough to do police work or to become managers.

## Concluding Thoughts

The appointing of women to carry out official policing tasks only gained proper momentum in many countries during the 1970s. Although progress has been made female policing is an important issue on the change management agendas of many police forces globally. In South Africa many opportunities have been created albeit some artificial to allow women into the once sacred male domain. In spite of this, after more than 20 years of democracy women are still significantly underrepresented in the policing domain in South Africa. Then again this underrepresentativeness is also evident in many other countries such as the United States of America and the United Kingdom. Although women have proved themselves as capable of executing most policing tasks satisfactorily, negativity towards them within the police service has persisted. A possible reason is that various myths exist as to why women should not be seen as competent to enter an occupational field which has for centuries been considered an exclusively male domain. Despite the fact that most of these myths have been dispelled by scientific research, attitudes towards the female police official are slow to change. While research findings (the current study) show that women have certain skills and characteristics to do certain policing tasks better than their male counterparts they still struggle to be seen as equals (Horne, 2006). Even if the occupational achievements of female police officials are as good as that of their male counterparts and in some instances even better, some male police officials still cling to the traditional myths and the viewpoint that women should not be in policing. To address this problem it is essential to undertake scientific research to identify problem areas and to develop programs that will address these problems. In so doing the possibility exists to build a truly democratic police service in which gender discrimination will not feature. However, if myths continue to exist we can expect much of the same in the next 30 years. It is quite difficult to change attitudes and perceptions as they are linked to cognitive scripts which are in themselves a somewhat permanent feature in a human once they have been shaped (Bartol & Bartol, 2014). A cognitive script may be learned by direct experience or by observing others. Once learned, the cognitive script will most probably be followed and becomes an enduring way of thinking. If a young male police officer learns from his older more senior colleagues that females should not be in the police because of their gender a specific cognitive script regarding female police officers could develop. This type of thinking can have its roots in early socialization practices and taught perceptions regarding gender roles and sexuality. In this study the female participants were more positive about their role in the policing domain compared to their male counterparts. In the qualitative section of the study the majority of the respondents dispelled the myths surrounding the role of females in the police which supports the notion of females in law enforcement. Women in law enforcement are therefore a reality and not a myth.

## References


Aleem, S. (1991). *Women in Indian police.* New Delhi: Sterling.

AllAfrica. (2012, June). The appointment of the country's first female National Commissioner, Magwashi, Victoria Phiyega. *BuaNews* (Tswane). Retrieved March 3, 2016, from www.buanews.gov.za.

Annual Report: South African Police Service (2014/2015). Pretoria: Strategy, Research, Monitoring and Evaluation (Head Office). Retrieved March 7, 2016, from www.gov.za/sites/www.gov.za/files/SAPS_Annual_Report_2014-15.pdf.

Baron, R. A., & Byrne, D. (1997). *Social psychology* (8th ed.). Boston: Allyn & Bacon.

Bartol, C. R., & Bartol, A. M. (2014). *Criminal behavior: A psychosocial approach* (10th ed.). Upper Saddle River, NJ: Pearson.

Bezuidenhout, C. (2001). 'n ondersoek na die houdings van manlike en vroulike polisiebeamptes teenoor die rol van die vrouepolisiebeampte in die Suid-Afrikaanse polisiediens [An investigation into the attitudes of male and female police officers regarding the role of female police officers in the South African police service]. Unpublished doctoral dissertation, University of Pretoria.

Bezuidenhout, C. (2011). Explaining the implications of intelligence-led policing on human rights in South Africa. In J. F. Albrecht & D. K. Das (Eds.), *Effective crime reduction strategies: International perspectives.* Boca Raton, FL: CRC Press (Taylor & Francis Group).

Bezuidenhout, C., & Theron, A. (2000). Attitudes of male and female police officers towards the role of female police officers. *Acta Criminologica: South African Journal of Criminology, 13*(3), 19–31.

Bradley, A. (1973). And the constable cried when she made her first arrest. *Personality Magazine*, pp. 108–111.

Brown, J., & Heidensohn, F. (2000). *Gender and policing: Comparative perspectives.* New York: St. Martin's Press, LLC.

Brown, S. E., Esbensen, F-A., & Geis, G. (1996). *Criminology: Explaining crime and its context* (2nd ed.). Cincinnati, OH: Anderson.

Bruce, D. (2013, March). New blood: Implications of en masse recruitment for the South African Police Service. *SA Crime Quarterly, 43.*

Champion, D. J., & Rush, G. E. (1997). *Policing in the community.* Upper Saddle River, NJ: Prentice Hall.

Collier, L. (2014, February). Why we cry: New research is opening eyes to the psychology of tears. *American Psychological Association, 45*(2), 47.

Cox, S. M., & Fitzgerald, J. D. (1992). *Police in community relations: Critical issues* (2nd ed.). Dubuque, IA: Wm. C. Brown.

Creswell, J. W. (2009). *Research design: Qualitative, quantitative and mixed methods approaches.* London: Sage.

Dantzker, M. L. (1995). *Understanding today's police.* Englewood Cliffs, NJ: Prentice Hall.

Emsley, C. (1996). The origins and development of the police. In E. McLaughlin & J. Muncie (Eds.), *Controlling crime: Crime, order and social control.* London: Open University Press.

First S.A. policewomen start training next year – Gen. Joubert. (1971, November 7). *Sunday Express*, p. 3.

Flowers, R. B. (1987). *Women and criminality: The woman as victim, offender, and practitioner.* New York: Greenwood.

Fourie, M., & Reyneke, F. (2001). Introduction. In F. Reyneke & M. Fourie (Eds.), *Police management beyond 2000.* Cape Town: JUTA.

Gilbride, P. (1917, December). Policewomen: A criticism. *Nonqui*, p. 446.

Grennan, S. A. (1993). A perspective on women in policing. In R. Muraskin & T. Alleman (Eds.), *It's a crime: Women and justice* (pp. 163–176). Upper Saddle River, NJ: Prentice Hall.

Grennan, S. A. (2000). The past, the present, and the future of women in policing. In R. Muraskin (Ed.), *It's a crime: Women and justice* (2nd ed.) (pp. 383–398). Upper Saddle River, NJ: Prentice Hall.

Horne, P. (2006). Policewomen: Their first century and the new era. The police chief: The professional voice of law enforcement. *The Police Chief, 73*(9), September. Retrieved March 7, 2016, from www.policechiefmagazine.org/magazine/index.cfm?article_id=1000 &fuseaction=display.

Hunter, Q. (2015). Zuma suspends police commissioner Riah Phiyega. *Mail & Guardian: Africa's best read.* Retrieved March 7, 2016, from http://mg.co.za/article/2015-10-14-zuma-suspends-police-commissioner-riah-phiyega.

Kakar, S. (2002). Gender and police officers' perceptions of their job performance: An analysis of the relationship between gender and perceptions of job performance. *Criminal Justice Policy Review, 13*(238), 238–256.

Kumar, R. (2005). *Research methodology* (2nd ed.). London: Sage.

Lanier, M. M., & Briggs, L. S. (2014). *Research methods in criminal justice and criminology: A mixed methods approach.* New York: Oxford University Press.

Martin, S. E. & Jurik, N. C. (1996). *Doing justice, doing gender: Women in law and criminal justice occupations.* Thousand Oaks, CA: Sage.

Molden, J. (1985, June). Female police officers: Training implications. *Law and Order*, pp. 12, 62–63.

Morley, C. (2011). Public perceptions of female police officers in the UK. Retrieved July 23, 2017, from www.pitlanemagazine.com/morals-values-and-norms/public-perceptions-of-female-police-officers-in-the-uk.html/.

Phiyega, M. V. (2012, November). Remarks by the National Commissioner of the SAPS at the Annual Women's Prestige Awards, Mpumalanga, South Africa. Retrieved March 5, 2016, from www.gov.za/speeches/view.php?sid=32492.

Police Employment. (2008, May). *Women in law enforcement.* Electronic article. Retrieved March 5, 2016, from www.policeemployment.com/.

Reiner, R. (1992). *The politics of the police* (2nd ed.). New York: Harvester Wheatsheaf.

Roberg, R. R., & Kuykendall, J. (1993). *Police and society.* Belmont, CA: Wadsworth.

Shusta, R. M., Levine, D. R., Harris, P. R., & Wong, H. Z. (1995). *Multicultural law enforcement: Strategies for peacekeeping in a diverse society.* Englewood Cliffs, NJ: Prentice Hall.

South African Police Service. (1996, November). Policy document on affirmative action. Reproduced Document SAPS.

Tajfel, H. (1981). *Human groups and social categories: Studies in social psychology.* Cambridge: Cambridge University Press.

Taylor, J. (1996). International Association of Women Police. *Servamus, 89*(4), 43.

Thibault, E. A., Lynch, L. M., & McBride, R. B. (1995). *Proactive police management* (3rd ed.). Englewood Cliffs, NJ: Prentice Hall.

Tracy-Stratton, B. (1986). Integrating women into law enforcement. In J. C. Yuille (Ed.), *Police selection and training: The role of psychology.* Dordrecht: Martinus Nijhoff.

Van Heerden, T. J. (1986). *Inleiding tot die Polisiekunde* [Introduction to police science]. Pretoria: Universiteit van Suid-Afrika.

Van Niekerk, S. (1988, November 22). Pionier Duveen Botha sê op Oujaar tot siens [Pioneer Duveen Botha greets on Old Years Evening]. *Die Beeld,* p. 1.

Viljoen, M. (1972, November 26). Fyn handjies versterk arm van die gereg: Ons polisievroue [Fine hands strengthen the arm of the law: Our policewomen]. *Bylae tot Foto-Rapport,* pp. 5, 6–8.

Walsh, M. S. (1916, September). The first policewoman. *Nonqui.* The ladies supplement to the Nonqui, pp. 247–248.

Women Police. (1919, Maart 25). Ongepubliseerde skrywe van die Sekretaris voor Justitie van die Unie van Zuid-Afrika aan die Kommissaris van die South African Police [Unpublished writing of the secretary general of justice of the Union of South Africa to the commissioner of the South African Police].

Wrottesley, S. (1938, January 3). Police sift history of "special patrols." *Argus,* pp. 4–5.

# Strategies in Prevention of Crime against Women in India – with Special Reference to Telangana State

# 13

ADKI SURENDER

## Contents



### Abstract

Violence against women is a worldwide phenomenon and India is no exception. Sexual harassment and other forms of sexual violence in public spaces are an everyday occurrence for women and girls around the world – in urban and rural areas, in developed and developing countries. Some national violence studies show that up to 70 per cent of women have experienced physical or sexual violence in their lifetime from an intimate partner. This chapter reviews the growth of violence against women in India and also focus on causes for the growing problem. This study is to examine the efforts made by the Government of India, as well as the undivided State of Andhra Pradesh with special attention paid to measures taken by the newly formed Telangana State in prevention of crimes against women and, finally, suggestions are made to strengthen the actions of the governments in eradication of crime against women in India. For this purpose, the researcher mostly depended on secondary data, such as government records and reports of the police department. For first-hand information, the researcher interacted with the police personnel, NGOs and members of the women protection organizations. Further, the past experience of the researcher on this topic has also added to the analysis.

## Introduction

Violence against women is a worldwide phenomenon and India is no exception. Sexual harassment and other forms of sexual violence in public spaces are an everyday occurrence for women and girls around the world – in urban and rural areas, in developed and developing countries. According to a 2013 global review of available data, 35 per cent of women worldwide have experienced either physical and/or sexually intimate partner violence or non-partner sexual violence. However, some national violence studies show that up to 70 per cent of women have experienced physical or sexual violence in their lifetime from an intimate partner (A.P. Crime Report, 2013). Violence against women nullifies the enjoyment of human rights and fundamental freedom of women. Yet, it is perhaps the most non-recognized human rights issue. All over the world, in all life situations, women are more vulnerable than men in public and private life. According to the United Nations General Assembly resolution (1993) 'violence against women' means

> any act of gender-based violence that results in, or is likely to result in, physical, sexual or mental harm or suffering to women, including threats of such acts, coercion or arbitrary deprivation of liberty, whether occurring in public or in private life.

For discouraging increasing violence against women, the UNO declared 25th November as 'International Day for the Elimination of Violence Against Women'.

An attempt has been made in this chapter to review the growth of violence against women in India and also focus on causes for the growing problem. The important objective of the present research study is to examine the efforts made by the Government of India, as well as the undivided State of Andhra Pradesh with special attention paid to measures taken by the newly formed Telangana State[1] in prevention of crimes against women and, finally, suggestions are made to strengthen the actions of the governments in eradication of crimes against women in India. For this purpose, the researcher mostly depended on secondary data, such as government records and reports of the police department. For first-hand information, the researcher interacted with the police personnel, NGOs and members of the women protection organizations. Further, the past experience of the researcher on this topic has also added to the analysis.

## Women's Status in India

India is one of the oldest civilizations in the world with a kaleidoscopic variety and rich cultural heritage. It has achieved multifaceted socio-economic progress during the last 67 years of its independence. There are 29 states and 7 Union territories in the country and it is known as a sub-continent with a population of approximately 1.2 billion people (Census Report, 2011) which makes it the second most populated country in the world. The male population is around 624,630,000 and the female population is almost half of the total population at approximately 585,370,000 (48.37 per cent). The gender ratio is 940 per 1,000 men. Kerala, with 1,058 females per 1,000 males, is the state with the highest gender ratio and Haryana with 861 has the lowest gender ratio. It has been observed that the gender ratio was 972 females per 1,000 males in 1901 which has declined to 940 in 2011. Overall literacy rates have improved but the female literacy rate lags behind compared to the male rate. Expansion of employment opportunities has been an important objective of development planning in India. According to the Census data, the work participation rate (i.e. the proportion of employed or total workers to population) of females steadily rose from 14.22 per cent in 1971 to 25.6 per cent in 2011.

India is one of the countries that provide equal justice to women by phasing out the disparities of gender. It is a matter of pride that India is one of the first countries of the world to give women the right to vote and contest elections (Article 326 of the constitution). The principle of gender equality is also enshrined in the Indian Constitution, Fundamental Rights, Fundamental Duties and Directive Principles (Articles 14, 15 and 16 ensure equality before the law). The Constitution not only grants equality to women, but also empowers the State to adopt measures of positive discrimination in favour of women. Further, the 73rd and 74th Constitutional Amendment Act passed in 1992 provide for reservation of one-third of seats in rural and urban local bodies for women as members and as chairpersons. Many states including Telangana provide 33 per cent of reservation in education and employment sectors for women to improve their status. Despite the above activities, the crime rate against women has not decreased.

## Causes of Violence

Violence against women is a multidimensional problem encompassing economic, social and cultural issues that are varied and highly complex. Various research studies show that cultural traditions play an important role in the occurrence of violence against women. The dowry system is one of the social, as well as cultural traditions of the Indian society and became an important cause for increasing crimes against women in India. During 2009–2013 more than 8,000 cases per annum were registered under dowry death provisions in the country. It has been observed that women without family support are more vulnerable to violence than other women. In India, economic and education factors also play a vital role in violence against women. In spite of the tall talks about economic growth, women are becoming more vulnerable to discrimination and violence. Any development strategy which neglects the need for enhancing the role of women cannot lead to comprehensive socio-economic development. To increase the status of women, they must be empowered economically. Self-help groups (SHGs) were projected as the main vehicle for women's empowerment in India, but suicides among SHG members have exposed the reality of exploitative interest rates and coercive loan recovery methods by the microfinance companies (MFIs). These MFIs publicly humiliate women in order to recover their loans and therefore women are forced to opt for prostitution or take loans from moneylenders in order to repay their MFI debts. Further, in spite of increased female work participation, India has among the world's lowest level of female labour force participation – the proportion of working-age women who are either working or looking for work. Of 131 countries, India ranked 11th from the bottom in terms of women's workforce participation in 2010–2011. In addition, there is a wide gender disparity in the literacy rates in India. Despite intensive efforts for the last six decades to improve literacy levels, the achievement has not been completely satisfactory. The low female literacy rate has a significant impact on violence because it contributes to women's lack of awareness and employment opportunity (Venkat and Rukmini, 2015).

## Legal Safeguards

India has one of the most impressive sets of laws and constitutional provisions for the protection of women. To uphold the constitutional mandate, the State has enacted various legislative measures intended to ensure equal rights, to counter social discrimination, various forms of violence and atrocities and to provide support services to women. These are broadly classified into two categories:

1. Crime under the Indian Penal Code (IPC).
2. The crimes under the special and local laws (SLLs).

There are only seven types of recognized crimes against women under the Indian Penal Code (1860) and four SLLs for exclusively dealing with crimes against women. Under the IPC crimes against women include:

i. Rape (Sec. 376 IPC);
ii. Kidnapping & Abduction for specified purposes (Sec. 363–369 and 371–373 IPC);
iii. Homicides for Dowry, Dowry Deaths or their attempts (Sec. 302/ 304-B IPC);
iv. Cruelty by Husband and Relatives (Sec.498-A IPC);
v. Assault on Women with intent to outrage her modesty (Sec. 354 IPC);
vi. Insult to the modesty of Women (Sec.509 IPC);
vii. Importation of girls from Foreign Country (up to 21 years of age) Sec. 366-B IPC).

There are more than 50 special Acts in the country which are directly and indirectly related to women and crime against women. However, there are four special Acts framed by the Government of India over the years to protect the interest, status and reduction of violence against women. These gender-specific laws for which crime statistics are recorded throughout the country are:

- The Immortal Trafficking Prevention Act, 1956:
- The Dowry Prohibition (Amendment) Act, 1961;
- Indecent Representation of Women (Prohibition) Act, 1986;
- The Commission of Sati Prevention Act, 1987.

Due to many legislations and lack of uniformity in legislations regarding women protections, the enforcement agencies as well as legal prosecutors are negligent in the implementation of acts and provisions and are unsuccessful in providing safety and security to women. Capacity-building improvement has become necessary to all concerned agencies as well as NGOs to bring awareness on legislations and the need to implement the above-mentioned provisions.

## Crime against Women in India

The advancement of science and technology has brought changes in the socio-economic and political perspective that exaggerated gender discrimination in the developed and developing countries of the world including India. The above discussions highlight the fact that in the transformation of society, women are empowering themselves to achieve the status of equality on par with men, although recent government reports show that violence against women is still a growing crime in India. In New Delhi, a baseline study conducted in 2012 reveals that 92 per cent of women have experienced some form of sexual violence in public places in their lifetime, and 88 per cent of women have experienced some form of visual or verbal sexual harassment (National Crime Records Bureau (NCRB), 2013). According to the NCRB (2013) reports a crime has been recorded against women every 3 minutes and every 60 minutes two women are raped in India. Every six hours, a young married woman is found beaten to death, burned or driven to suicide. The following section discusses the types of crime and growth of crime against women in the Indian scenario.

## Types of Violence

Violence against women can broadly be divided as

i. Physical abuse, even death – like feticide, infanticide, incest, battering, rape, sati, witch hunting, genital mutilation, sexual assault at work place, forced pregnancy/sterilization, etc.
ii. Psychological abuse like mental harassment, confinement, forced marriage.
iii. Denial/deprivation of basic human amenities like health, nutrition, education, means of livelihood, etc.
iv. Commodification of women's bodies for trade/business like trafficking, prostitution, etc.

## Growth of Violence against Women

As more and more women in the country started asserting their rights, becoming educated and taking jobs, they have increasingly become targets of attacks. Crimes against women in the country as well as in the State of Telangana are on the increase. The following statistics (NCRB, 2013) speak loudly about the alarming picture of crime against women in the country and the situation in the State of Telangana is not much better.

Figure 13.1 presents the growth of crimes committed against women in India.

The figure shows that a total of 309,546 cases of crime against women (both under various sections of IPC and SLL) were reported in the country during the year 2013 as compared to 244,270 in the year 2012, thus showing an increase of 26.7 per cent during the year. These crimes have continuously increased in reporting during 2009–2013 with 203,804 cases in 2009, 213,585 cases in 2010 and 228,649 cases in 2011. The combined state of Andhra Pradesh (including Telangana State as stated earlier) which stood top with a 7.3 per cent share of the country's women population, has reported nearly 10.6 per cent of total crimes committed against women at the All India level, by reporting 32,809 cases. Uttar Pradesh State, accounting for nearly 16.7 per cent of the country's women population, has accounted for 10.5 per cent of total cases of crimes against women in the country by reporting 32,546 cases during the year 2013. The national rate of crime committed against women was 52,200 in 2013. Delhi Union Territory reported the highest rate of crime against women at 146,800 during the year 2013 as compared to the crime rate at the national level.

Table 13.1 presents the details of crimes against women during the year 2009 to the year 2013 along with percentage variation. The statistics reveal that the IPC component of crimes against women accounted for 95.6 per cent of total crimes and the other 4.4 per cent were SLL cases. The problem of gender-based violence is getting worse. It can be observed from Table 13.1 that crimes against women during the year 2013 have increased by 26.7 per cent over the year 2012 and by 51.9 per cent over the year 2009. Further, incidences like torture, molestation, kidnapping, rape, sexual assault and Dowry Act cases are continuously increasing. Especially, every day 93 women are raped in the country. There has been a gradual increase in the number of rapes reported in India – from 24,923 in 2012 to 33,707

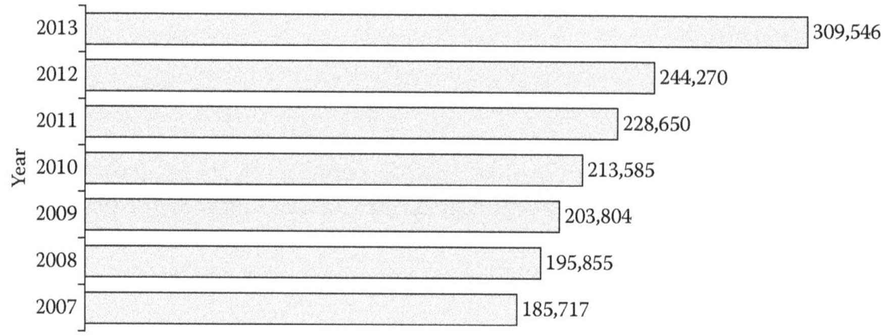


**Figure 13.1** Growth of Crimes against Women in India, 2007–2013.

Source: NCRB (2013).

**Table 13.1 Incidents of Crime against Women, 2009–2013**

| Sl. No. | Crime | Year | | | | | Percentage of Variation in 2013 over 2012 |
|---|---|---|---|---|---|---|---|
| | | 2009 | 2010 | 2011 | 2012 | 2013 | |
| 1 | Rape (Sec. 376 IPC) | 21,397 | 22,172 | 24,206 | 24,923 | 33,707 | 35.2 |
| 2 | Kidnapping (363–373) | 25,741 | 29,795 | 35,565 | 38,262 | 51,881 | 35.6 |
| 3 | Dowry (302 and 304B) | 8,383 | 8,391 | 8,618 | 8,233 | 8,083 | −1.8 |
| 4 | Torture (498A) | 89,546 | 94,041 | 99,135 | 106,527 | 118,866 | 11.6 |
| 5 | Molestation (354) | 38,711 | 40,613 | 42,968 | 45,351 | 70,739 | 56.0 |
| 6 | Sexual Harassment (509) | 11,009 | 9,961 | 8,570 | 9,173 | 12,589 | 37.2 |
| 7 | Importation of Girls (366B) | 48 | 36 | 80 | 59 | 31 | –47.7 |
| **A** | **Total IPC Crime** | **194,835** | **205,009** | **219,142** | **232,528** | **295,896** | **27.3** |
| 8 | Sati Prevention Act 1987 | 0 | 0 | 0 | 0 | 0 | 0.0 |
| 9 | Immoral Traffic (P)Act 1956 | 2,474 | 2,499 | 2,435 | 2,563 | 2,579 | 0.6 |
| 10 | Indecent Rep. Women (P) Act 1986 | 845 | 895 | 453 | 141 | 362 | 156.7 |
| 11 | Dowry Prohibition Act 1996 | 5,650 | 5,182 | 6,619 | 9,038 | 10,709 | 17.9 |
| **B** | **Total SLL Crime** | **8,969** | **8,576** | **9,508** | **11,742** | **13,650** | **16.2** |
| **GRAND TOTAL** | | **203,804** | **213,585** | **228,650** | **244,270** | **309,546** | **26.7** |

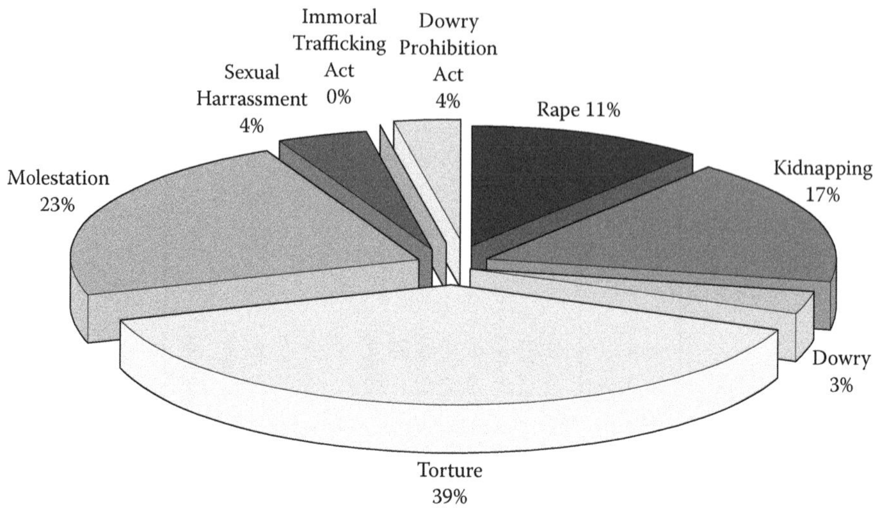


**Figure 13.2** Percentage of Crime Rate against Women, 2013.

in 2013; an increase of 35.2 per cent in the year 2013 over 2012. Figure 13.2 presents the distribution of crimes against women in India during the year 2013.

The pie chart explains that torture cases registered are highest in India (39 per cent) followed by molestations (23 per cent), kidnapping (17 per cent) and rape (11 per cent). Further, an analysis shows that every hour almost 14 torture cases, 8 molestations, 6 kidnappings and 4 rape cases were registered during 2013; overall every day 848 cases (35 cases per hour) were registered involving women, which is a serious matter from the safety and security point of Indian women. However, the number of cases registered against women has not reached 12 per cent of the total IPC cases. Table 13.2 presents the proportion of crime against women cases in India.

Many reasons can be attributed to unreported women's cases in India. Mainly, discussions with police officers and NGOs highlighted the fact that on one hand women are not willing to register their cases due to various social reasons, and on the other, the majority percentage of reported cases are not registered by the police officers, on account of the majority of cases being compromised by both parties or through counselling by the police at the time of registration of cases (MHA Crime Report, 2013). According to the social organizations (Divya, 2013), most of the sexual abuse cases, especially against minors, go unreported in the country. The number of unreported cases of child sexual abuse is much higher than reported cases. In many cases, parents are reluctant to lodge a police complaint

**Table 13.2 Proportion of Crime against Women towards Total IPC Crimes**

| Sl. No | Year | Total IPC Cases | Crime Against Women (IPC Cases) | % to Total IPC Crimes |
|---|---|---|---|---|
| 1 | 2009 | 2,121,345 | 203,804 | 9.2 |
| 2 | 2010 | 2,224,831 | 213,585 | 9.6 |
| 3 | 2011 | 2,325,575 | 219,142 | 9.4 |
| 4 | 2012 | 2,387,188 | 244,270 | 10.2 |
| 5 | 2013 | 2,647,722 | 295,896 | 11.2 |

thinking the matter would go public and it will be harmful to the victim's future. Therefore, the true picture of violence against women would be more shocking.

An important question then arises as to whether the police are approachable enough for women to access justice. The researcher noticed after discussions with the NGOs as well as victims that there was a lack of trust between the police and the public, which resulted in several incidents of violence against women going unreported (Divya, 2013). Further, as mentioned above, the police also do not show interest in registering cases and most of the cases are aimed at being settled at the initial stage of the registration; the reason is a shortage of sufficient police strength in the police stations. Another reason is due to the absence of women on the police force; the male police find it very difficult to deal with women's cases. Additionally, the investigation process is often delayed in taking the appropriate action against the violators/accused. By nature, Indian women are traditional, shy and not bold enough to talk about personal problems before policemen unreservedly (Bureau of Police Research and Development, 2013, 2014).

In addition to the above, another important fact revealed through the police records is a significant increase in the number of false cases of sexual harassment being filed. According to the women police officials, two years ago only 10 per cent of the total harassment and domestic violence cases registered turned out to be false. But now, the figure has increased nearly to 30 per cent. In view of this, the police need to undertake a more detailed enquiry and a strict investigation is required in these cases and serious action should be initiated against persons who file false cases.

## Administrative Measures of Governments

Providing safety and security is the primary responsibility of the government, either State or Central. Both the governments have made several efforts to eliminate violence against women in India. All kinds of violence against women outside and inside the domain of their homes are essentially administrative, police and legal matters. Voluntary organizations/civil society organizations have had a small role to play in this, except for mounting pressure on the official machinery to act in a non-partisan manner. Considering the above problems, apart from constitutional and from legal protections, the following measures have been taken by the government to protect women from crimes.

1. Establishment of women police stations.
2. Separate women police force.
3. Women commissions.
4. Encouraging NGOs' role.
5. 'Nirbhaya Fund'.
6. Criminal Law (Amendment) Act, 2013 (Ghosh and Rustamji, 1994).

### All Women Police Stations and Women's Protection Cells

To pay special attention to crimes against women and inspire confidence and provide free communication by the women victims, the government has come out with separate police forces with women and All Women Police Stations (AWPSs). Most of the States/ UTs including Telangana have set up AWPSs at the district level and 'women and children help desks' at the police station level. At present, there are 518 women police stations in the country. An overwhelming majority of these, 38.42 per cent, are in the State of Tamil Nadu, with 199 AWPSs. It is followed by Uttar Pradesh at 71 AWPSs, Bihar and Rajasthan with 40 AWPSs and in the undivided State of Andhra Pradesh with 26. However, there are ten States and Union Territories that still need to establish AWPSs. Apart from these AWPSs, separate women protection cells (WPCs) were established in Telangana and A.P. States under the supervision of the Crime Investigation Department (CID) intended to monitor the crimes against women and take up serious cases for investigation (Telangana State Report, 2015).

## Women Police Force

In view of increasing crimes against women and participation of women in socio-economic and political activities as discussed above, problems faced by the male police force in tackling women cases have necessitated appointing a separate women's police force in the police department (National Commission for Women Act, 1990). Further, the Criminal Procedure Code has also insisted on strict use of a female for searching another female. The present strength of the women police force in the country is 105,325 increased from 56,667 in 2009, more than 85 per cent have been added in five years and the figure rose 8 per cent compared to that in the previous year. However, women account for just 6.11 per cent of the total police force across the country. The situation is particularly bad in the Prime Minister's home state of Gujarat, which has just 3.64 per cent (2,691) women in its police force. The number is only relatively better at 4.29 per cent (7,238) in UP, which has the second largest police force in the country, and 4.33 per cent in undivided A.P. Women's organizations as well as National Women's Police Conferences demand to increase the strength of women police to 33 per cent to protect women's interests. As a result, emphasizing the need to bring policewomen to frontline duties, the Ministry of Home Affairs, Government of India has asked states to ensure that 33 per cent of their police force consists of women personnel and the Centre can play only an advisory role when it comes to states.

> It is essential that women are visible at the cutting edge level of public interface. There is a tendency to engage women police only in situations like security checks and other specialized duties relating to women, but unless they are assigned frontline duties in the police stations, there would not be an impact on the community as a whole. (National Commission for Women Act, 1990)

## Women Commissions

As a result of enhanced consciousness about the trend of increasing violence against women and girls, the government has set up the following institutional mechanisms for monitoring the violation of the rights of women:

1. National Commission for Women;
2. State Commissions for Women.

As per the recommendations of the Committee on the Status of Women in India – 1974, the Government of India established the National Commission for Women, a statutory body in January 1992, for the following functions:

- to review the constitutional and legal safeguards for women;
- to recommend remedial legislative measures;
- to facilitate redress of grievances; and
- to advise the government on all policy matters affecting women.

One can say that unless the government is particularly committed to it and ensures a primary role for women in national life, setting up commissions can only serve a limited purpose.

## NGOs' Support

In India voluntary efforts and community participation are closely linked with the eradication of many evils of society. NGOs have taken on an activist role on various gender issues and have played an effective role in promoting the causes of women at both central and state levels. There are over 6,000 NGOs in the country who receive programme funding and support from the Government of India to support women's development programmes including dealing with atrocities and crimes against women. For instance, Sarojini Rehabilitation Centre for Women, Swadhar schemes and *Ujjwala* programmes, all of which were sponsored by the Central Government.

## 'Nirbhaya Fund'

A corpus fund called 'Nirbhaya Fund' with 1,000 cores (US$164 million) was set up by the Government of India in 2013 for supporting initiatives by the Government and NGOs working towards protecting the dignity and ensuring safety of women in India. The Ministry of Home Affairs and the Ministry of Women and Child Development, along with several other concerned Ministries, worked out the details of the structure, scope and the application of this Fund (Government Order, 2014).

## The Criminal Law (Amendment) Act, 2013

The death following a brutal gang rape and assault of a 23-year-old paramedical student in India's capital Delhi on 16 December 2012 has put a spotlight on crimes against women in the country. Widespread protests and emotional outbursts spontaneously erupted across India, with women and men demanding the safety and protection of women, a change in attitudes towards women, and a change of archaic gender laws and speedy justice to bring rapists to task. Unless laws are strengthened to punish wrong-doers and justice is delivered speedily, this crime will continue unchecked. As a result, the Government of India has brought a new Act, i.e. the Criminal Law (Amendment) Act, 2013 also called the Nirbhaya women protection Act, 2013 (Nirbhaya Act, 2013).

The Criminal Law (Amendment) Act, 2013 came into force on 2 April 2013. It has amended various sections of the Indian Penal Code (1860), the Code of Criminal Procedure and the Indian Evidence Act. It has enhanced punishment for crimes like rape, sexual harassment, stalking, voyeurism, acid attacks, indecent gestures like words, and inappropriate touching. The new laws have provisions for increased sentences for rape convicts, including life-term and death sentence, besides providing for stringent punishment for offences such as acid attacks, stalking and voyeurism.

## Special Initiatives in Telangana State

Telangana was separated from Andhra Pradesh State and formed as the 29th state of India on 2 June 2014. The state has an area of 1,14,840 sq km and has a population of 35,287,000. The Telangana region was part of the Hyderabad State from 17 September 1948 to 1 November 1956, until it was merged with Andhra State to form the Andhra Pradesh State.

Without delay after the formation of the state, the Telangana government had focused on the safety and security of people especially women and adopted a zero-tolerance policy towards crimes on women (Telangana State Report, 2015). For this purpose, the State Government has constituted a Committee consisting of seven senior officers from different services under the Chairmanship of Mrs Poonam Malakondaiah, Indian Administrative Service (IAS) to suggest measures for effective implementation of

**Figure 13.3** State of Telangana in India.

Source: www.deccanchronicle.com/nation/current-affairs/270816/maps-of-new-telangana-districts-online.html.

various legislations meant for safety and security of girls and women in the Telangana State and also give suggestions on the further policy changes/steps required in this direction. The Committee made 77 recommendations on Issues relating to Safety and Security of Women and Girls in Telangana State.

The Government has announced a 33 per cent reservation for women[2] in an attempt to improve female representation in the police force and to control crimes against women. The State Police also prepared proposals to introduce a number of women police stations by recruiting more women in the police force and to set up a womens desk at all police stations with a woman receptionist on a 24/7 basis to receive complaints and take action in emergency cases. The government is also planning to appoint women counsellors at each police station in coordination with the women and child welfare department, Society for Elimination of Rural Poverty (SERP) and Social Action committees. The department also emphasizes appointing one legal advisor in each police station for the better case recording of women and First Information Report (FIR) filing.

To address crimes against women, domestic violence and dowry harassment the state government formed 340 community-managed counselling centres and 436 Mandal level social action committees in the state. As on 1 January 2015 of total of 31,991 cases were reported to these committees and counselling centres; out of these 26,052 cases are resolved.[3]

## Initiatives in Hyderabad City and Cyberabad City Police

The recent increasing crimes against women in the state capital city of Hyderabad and its surrounding areas, i.e. Cyberabad Police jurisdiction put attention on the police department and brought many reforms in the functioning of the police force in the protection of women. The following measures have been adopted by Telangana State to provide protection to women:

1. Introduced SHE taxis: the concept of SHE taxis exclusively driven by women and meant for women passengers. These taxis are provided by the government to women drivers with several security features for both the driver and passengers.
2. Hyderabad City had the police launch the ‘Hawk Eye mobile app’ for women’s safety. This app has features for women’s safety while travelling and an SOS button for accessing help in emergency situations, among others.
3. Strengthening the public transport system in the twin cities of Hyderabad and Secunderabad. All public transport buses are required to provide a wire mesh separating male and female passengers and make a separate entry for women. Special ladies’ buses were also introduced on certain routes.
4. The Government had issued certain regulations to all auto-rickshaw and taxi drivers to add GPRS systems linked to Central Police Control Room for a better controlling system and to avoid sexual harassment and kidnapping cases.
5. Another important initiative of the State Government is ‘zero tolerance for crime against women’. For this purpose, the Hyderabad city police and Cyberabad city police have formed 100 ‘SHE’ police teams to catch persons sexually harassing

**Figure 13.4** Cyberabad Police Jurisdiction Including Hyderabad City Police.
Source: cyberabadpolice.gov.in/information/PDF/Cyberabad-map.pdf.

women in public places. Each team, comprising a sub-inspector, four constables and two women constables, would carry hidden cameras to record acts of persons harassing women. They would be caught and based on the video footage, further legal action would be initiated. These teams of police personnel are deployed at 'hot spots' to observe and catch offenders red-handed with evidence. These 'SHE' systems also extended to other urban areas of the state.

## Conclusion

The conscious efforts of State and Central Governments as well as non-government organizations for the eradication of violence against women have certainly contributed to improving the situation of women to an extent. However, it is nationally accepted that the right perception of people and social transformations are necessary to deliver gender justice and free women from violence at every point in their lives. Our achievements are many, but we have miles to go in changing the mindset of people and society at large for women to stand on an equal platform with men and to free Indian women from threats of violence.

The above discussions reveal that violence against women has been increasing continuously in spite of governmental measures. It became a challenging job to all governments to actively work to combat violence against women through a variety of programs. Violence against women both inside and outside of their homes has been a crucial issue in contemporary Indian society. Women in India constitute nearly half of its population and most of them are grinding under the socio-cultural and religious structures. The conscious efforts of State and Central Governments as well as non-government organizations for eradication of violence against women by enactment of legislations, establishments of separate women's police stations, women police forces, the appointment of Women's Commissions and special funds allocated for women's safety have certainly contributed to improving the situation of women to an extent. The Telangana State government's special initiatives to improve women and girls' freedom of movement and enhance their ability to participate in education, work and in public places have been receiving appreciation from women's organizations. Although violence against women and girls, especially sexual harassment in public places, remains a largely neglected issue there still is great need to improve the situation. To improve the situation and efficiency of law enforcement agencies I would like to make the following suggestions.

## Suggestions

- The Government should enact comprehensive and uniform legislation for the efficient function and enforcement of laws to provide safety and security to women.
- Initiate strict action against police personnel found to be either displaying bias against women or neglecting their supervisory responsibilities while registering complaints of sexual offences.
- Steps may be taken by the government to improve the strength of women police forces to 33 per cent of the total strength of police forces in the country, and the number of All Women Police Stations also needs to increase. Further, for efficiently dealing with women's cases steps may be taken to ensure a sufficient number of female police officers should be appointed at all law and order police stations in the country; such steps will bring drastic changes in the attitudes of the male police.
- Sensitizing the law enforcement machinery about crimes against women, through structured training and awareness programmes, meetings and seminars, etc., for police personnel at all levels, as well as other functionaries administering the criminal justice system.
- Women's Commissions should be strengthened and fill all vacancies in the national and state level organizations to deal with women's problems efficiently and provide sufficient supporting staff and infrastructure.
- Help-line numbers should be exhibited prominently in hospitals/schools/colleges premises, and in other suitable places.

- Set up exclusive 'Crimes Against Women and Children' desks in each police station and Special Women's Police Cells in all police stations including all women's police stations as needed.
- Steps may be taken to improve socio-bio-economic conditions and a property rights act should be initiated to discourage dowry harassment cases.
- Lastly, the study suggests that teachers should be given training in the value of education, and sustained awareness campaigns on gender equality should be undertaken in all schools and colleges including gender modules to be integrated into the curriculum at every level.

## Notes

1 The Telangana State was separated from Andhra Pradesh State on 2 June 2014 and formed as the 29th State of India.
2 Statement by the Telangana State Director General of Police on 14 September 2014.
3 *Reinventing of Telangana, the first step, Socio economic outlook – 2015*, Planning Department, Government of Telangana.

## References


A.P. Crime Report (2013). *Annual Reports of State Crime Records Bureau*, CBCIDDGP Office, Hyderabad. Andhra Pradesh.

Bureau of Police Research and Development (2013). Data on Police Organizations. Ministry of Home Affairs, Government of India, New Delhi.

Bureau of Police Research and Development (2014). Data on Police Organizations. Ministry of Home Affairs, Government of India, New Delhi.

Census Report (2011). Office of the Registrar General and Census Commissioner of India, Ministry of Home Affairs, Government of India, New Delhi.

Divya, D. (2013, 21 August). A city (Hyderabad) based NGO working on children and women issues. *The Times of India*, p. 5.

Ghosh, S. K. and Rustamji, K. F. (1994). *Encyclopedia of Police in India*, Vol. II, Part A, Ashish Publishing House, New Delhi.

Government Order Ms. No. 01 (2014). Women, Children, Disabled & Senior Citizens (Schemes) Department.

Indian Penal Code (IPC) (1860). Act No. 45 of 1860. Government of India.

Indian Police Act (1861). Ministry of Home Affairs, Government of India.

MHA Crime Report (2013). National Crime Records Bureau, Ministry of Home Affairs, Government of India, New Delhi.

National Commission for Women Act (1990). Act No. 20 of 1990 of Government of India.

National Crime Records Bureau (NCRB). (2013). *Report 2013*, Ministry of Home Affairs, Government of India, New Delhi.

Telangana State Report (2015). *Reinventing Telangana, The First Step, Socio Economic Outlook 2015*. The Planning Department, Telangana State, Hyderabad.

United Nations (1993). Declaration on the Elimination of Violence Against Women, UN General Assembly resolution 48/104. UNO, New York.

Venkat, V. and Rukmini, S. (2015, 8 March). The 'second' sex. *The Hindu*, English Daily, Hyderabad. www.thehindu.com/sunday-anchor/the-second-sex/article6970203.ece.

# The Assessment of Capable Guardianship Measures Against Bullying Victimization in the School Environment

# 14

KYUNG-SHICK CHOI, SHEA CRONIN,
AND HEATHER CORREIA

## Contents



## Abstract

Policymakers, school officials, and the law enforcement community have expanded legal tools and other strategies to address bullying in recent years. This has resulted in a larger and more challenging role for law enforcement officers working in school settings. The present study seeks to understand the ways in which local law enforcement officers interpret this new role and their efforts to prevent and respond to bullying. We draw upon Routine Activities Theory as a lens to view officer perceptions of promoting guardianship and reducing target suitability of young people most at-risk for bullying victimization. Data collected from qualitative interviews of law enforcement officers working with local schools, suggest that officers see a role for law enforcement in promoting guardianship around this health and safety concern, but recognize the limitations of using arrest authority. They emphasize promoting trust and building relationship in efforts to support potential and current bullying victims.

## Introduction

Mass shootings have dominated media coverage and national discussions about crime taking place at schools since the tragic events of the shootings at Columbine, CO in 1999. Much of the public response to these terrible events has been to focus on the physical security of the school along with adding law enforcement to school grounds. At the same time, faced with perceptions and realties that school bullying has increased (School Bullying Statistics, 2013) and that it has significant consequences for victims, the national attention has also focused on bullying within schools with particular attention to bullying taking place or facilitated through social media platforms. In response, legislatures and schools have strengthened anti-bullying policies. Law enforcement agencies, both working directly within school systems or in partnership from the local community, have taken on a greater role in enforcement of new law and policy around bullying.

Recognizing the potential concerns around criminalizing school misconduct, law enforcement can be an effective component of a broader strategy to address bullying. Routine Activity Theory (RAT) (see Cohen & Felson, 1979; Felson, 1986) provides a useful lens through which to view the role of law enforcement personnel working in schools to reduce the incidence of bullying. School resources officers and other law enforcement personnel working with schools provide formal guardianship and can promote informal guardianship. Through application of community-based policing practices, officers may also be able to foster trust between students and law enforcement to facilitate open communication about bullying and other crime concerns with schools. Bullying, as a school safety and health concern, presents significant challenges that can be understood through application of RAT.

Bullying, a behavior that once was seen as normal, is currently a behavior that is shown to be a serious problem. "There is a general agreement that for a behavior to be considered bullying, it must be repetitive, and a difference of power-physical, social, or other must exist between the bully and the victim" (Jacobsen & Bauman, 2007 p. 1). Bullying takes place every day in the United States school systems and surveys suggest that about 30% of students in the United States are involved in bullying (School Bullying Statistics, 2013). The same SAFE survey also revealed that 85% of bullying cases have no intervention by a teacher or school administration (School Bullying Statistics, 2013). While some prevalence estimates suggest that bullying is a fairly common experience among young people, the forms of bullying, modalities in which it occurs, and consequences it has for victims vary considerably.

Definitions of bullying typically include both physical and non-physical forms of bullying, including bullying that takes place at least in part through social media – "cyber bullying." Although school systems are likely more responsive to physical bullying, which has more easily recognized signs, attention to non-physical forms of bullying is important because of the significant psychological and behavioral consequences attached to victimization (Jacobsen & Bauman, 2007). Research has shown that "depression, suicidal thoughts, substance abuse, and an increased predilection to crime are negative consequences associated with bullying" (Schroeder et al., 2011, p. 489). Several tragic high-profile cases have shed light on the potential harm experienced by victims of bullying, including cases where it is thought that victims had committed suicide in part due their bullying victimization (see, for example, Crawford, 2012 and Meier, 2007) – or what has been termed "bullicide" (Poland, 2011, p. 92). Even though cyber bullying and other forms of non-physical bullying may not be brought to the attention of the school systems, it is equally problematic as any other form of non-physical bullying and physical bullying. They further present unique challenges to school teachers, staff, and law enforcement personnel to intervene and respond to crimes taking place out of their direct guardianship against often highly vulnerable young people.

The purpose of this research is to examine the ways in which officers can be utilized as a source of capable guardianship and reduce the suitability of targets to prevent, intervene, and respond to bullying within schools. Implementing strategies with "model fidelity" is an important component to the success of any school-based approach to crime and victimization (Rosiak, 2009, p. 8), yet the goals and approaches of incorporating officers with schools to address the specific crime of bullying vary widely as do the characteristics and outlooks of the officers in those positions. While better connection between officers and schools may be a promising approach for dealing with bullying, previous bullying research indicates that program effectiveness varies largely due to the environments in the school systems (Black, Washington, Trent, Harner, & Pollock, 2009). A better understanding of the ways in which school-based officers can address bullying concerns might help support law enforcement and school officials to design bullying prevention programs with existing officer resources.

The study approaches the questions about law enforcement role in addressing bullying concerns though a qualitative interview methodology. Data collected through interviews with local law enforcement officers involved in schools allow us to learn how officers view their role in promoting safety within school settings and how they work with victims. The findings may be useful to improving co-guardianship between school security, teachers, and school staff (Rosiak, 2009). The following section applies the RAT perspective to the issue of bullying and outlines relevant research on bullying in schools. The chapter then describes the interview methodology before moving into findings on the ways in which officers view their roles around promoting guardianship and addressing suitable targets of bullying. The chapter concludes with a discussion of the findings in light of extant research and the potential policy implications.

## Theoretical Framework and Literature Review

Routine Activity Theory (RAT) describes three elements that are necessary to produce a crime event: motivated offenders, a suitable victim, and the absence of capable guardians (Cohen & Felson, 1979; Popp & Peguero, 2010, p. 2415). More recent restatements of RAT emphasize six components or "two triplets" around the three objects of supervision that can be used to produce positive public safety outcomes (Eck, 1994). When suitable targets are supervised by capable guardians, motivated offenders are supervised by handlers, and amenable places are supervised by managers, crime prevention is possible (Eck, 1994). Bullying as a crime phenomenon fits well within the RAT perspective because the motivation to engage in the activity is fairly prevalent within adolescent populations and the settings in which it takes place often lack capable guardianship either within schools or through various social media. At an individual level, exposure and proximity to motivated offenders in a setting that lacks capable guardianship likely increases the risk of bullying victimization, especially for those vulnerable to bullying because of personal risk factors (Hindelang, Gottfredson, & Garofalo, 1978). School resources may help promote the level of capable guardianship through a variety of methods as well as minimize the suitability of potential bullying victims and this chapter uses both components as a frame to view the roles of school resource officers. The RAT perspective also fits well with the ways in which law enforcement personnel may view their role in dealing with bullying because it is a perspective that officers trained in community policing approaches understand and apply to crime problems.

## Capable Guardianship

From the RAT perspective, the prevalence of capable guardianship is a central element in preventing crime events. In the context of bullying prevention, guardianship can take many forms, including physical security measures, formal guardianship, and informal guardianship. Although school security measures (metal detectors, closed-circuit televisions, and building designs) became a popular response to school violence in the 1990s, they prove ineffective in dealing with school crime in general (Brown, 2005) and in particular bullying problems where weapons are rare and where it takes place through a variety of methods (via social media) and locations (buses and school travel routes) outside of school. Given the limitations of physical security measures, schools have also turned to programs and other strategies to promote better informal guardianship within the schools around crime and bullying.

School administrators and law enforcement personnel promote efforts to improve the climate or environment of the school as a way of improving informal guardianship. Research by Johnson, Burke, and Gielen (2011) reported on a study where students rate statements as positive or negative regarding the issue of school violence, including bullying. The statements that students generated related to school violence, especially bullying, included "presence of school police," "school police who care about students," "school police who make sure students go to class," "school police that are aware," "teachers who care about students," teachers making sure students are safe," and "teachers not caring about students' inappropriate behavior" (p. 335). These statements were rated as either moderate or low to initiation, cessation, and severity of bullying. Statements including "teachers' disrespect towards students," "lack of supervision in certain places," "teachers not in hallway," "school police who are unnecessarily harsh," "school police not actively involved in school," "discrimination by school police," and "too much connection to teachers" were rated high in the severity of bullying (p. 335). With a balanced relationship and partnership, the teachers and school resource officers can develop a healthy relationship with students that will not impede their school environment but enhance it. The present study contributes to this research by examining the ways in which law enforcement personnel view their roles dealing with bullying concerns through developing relationships and supporting informal norms around bullying prevention.

Finally, guardianship can be produced through the formal enforcement of the school rules and regulations by school teachers, administrators, or law enforcement personnel working in partnership with schools. As bullying has been more clearly defined with criminal codes, law enforcement takes on a more significant role with the regulation of bullying behaviors in schools. Some observers contend that there is a real need to better understand the balance between the role of schools and law enforcement. As Price (2009) argues "the higher stakes for students combined with their lack of sophistication, require a more thoughtful and clear policy to set fair limits for criminal investigations in schools" (p. 550). Developing policies and procedures that can be easily followed will allow students to be able to see what will happen if they commit certain crimes while on school property. This allows all students to be treated the same as well as no questioning taking place on what the punishment is going to be. Including officers within schools has been understood to create tensions and role conflict; the present study seeks to understand how officers view their role in the enforcement of law or school policies around bullying and the general promotion of formal guardianship.

## Suitable Target

By the guardianship roles of law enforcement addressing school bullying problems, it is important to also consider the ways in which officers can better identify and work with potential victims of bullying. The perspective recognizes that victim suitability is a necessary component of many crime events and that offenders seek out victims that fit their goals whether they are instrumental or expressive. That is, suitable targets include victims that may be easy targets to successfully perpetrate a crime or ones that meet more symbolic ends (reifying power or status positions, confronting perceived threats based on racial, gender, or sexual differences). In the discussion below, it is understood that individual, social, and family characteristics place some young people at higher risk for victimization and, therefore, also make them identifiable to school and law enforcement seeking to reduce bullying victimization or intervene in ongoing situations. By applying principles connected to RAT, officers based in schools may be in a unique position to help reduce the suitability of young people with higher risk of bullying victimization.

Although some forms of teasing and harassment may be a regular occurrence within schools, research on actual bullying victimization demonstrates that it varies significantly based on individual and school characteristics. Research on individual risk for bullying is broad and findings depend on definitional issues as well as the age of participants being studied. In several instances certain psychological disorders have been implicated as not only consequences of bullying but risk factors for it. For example, Arseneault et al.'s (2006) research from a longitudinal study showed that young people with withdrawal and anxiety and depression disorders are more vulnerable to bullying. Young people also engaged in aggression at early ages and other behavioral problems at later ages are at risk for higher rates of victimization. Home life and other early life experiences have also been associated with higher bullying risk (Bowes et al., 2009). It is also recognized that there is a good deal of overlap between young people who engage in bullying and bullying victims (Baker, Lynch, Cantillon, & Walsh, 2016; Ball et al., 2008). This fact means that when officers contact bullying aggressors through law enforcement activity (i.e., investigating allegations), they are likely to be interacting with a young person who may have experienced or still be experiencing bullying. Beyond individual factors and characteristics, Hodges, Malone, and Perry (1997) demonstrate that social risk – lacking peer support and peer rejection – places young people at risk for victimization although not exclusively bullying. While studies demonstrate the victimization risk differs greatly by personal characteristics, more could be learned about the ways in which law enforcement personnel view their role in working with higher-risk populations.

## Methodology

Using a semi-structured interview methodology, this study examines the ways in which school resources officers and other school personnel conceive of their roles and activities in addressing bullying within the school. Following RAT as a conceptual framework that helps explain physical and non-physical bullying victimization within the school environment, we specifically sought to understand the ways school resources officers and staff view their role as promoting capable guardianship and building connections to students to reduce the likelihood of victimization. The following outlines the sampling techniques and interview procedures.

This study was conducted using qualitative interviews of law enforcement personnel from seven local police departments located in Eastern Massachusetts, and the study sample was generated using a snowball procedure. All participants in the study were law enforcement personnel including school resource officers, juvenile detectives, patrol officers, and dispatchers who currently or have previously worked directly with the school systems. Initially, five law enforcement personnel were asked and consented to participate in this study: two school resource officers, a juvenile detective, a patrol officer, and a retired school resource officer from local law enforcement agencies. The original five law enforcement personnel were chosen based upon their particular assignments on their police department and their daily interactions with youth in the school systems. The original participants also provided referrals to other law enforcement agencies and personnel, which were contacted for participation in the study.

The snowball sampling method yielded 18 participants who had relevant knowledge and experience in school settings and were willing to participate in this study. The final sample consisted of both male and female law enforcement personnel, mainly of patrol officers at the time of their involvement in schools, from a variety of local communities. There also existed a large variation in the years of experience, ranging from 1 year of service to over 20 years of service.

Interview questions used for this research were reviewed and approved by the Institutional Review Board (IRB) at a state university located in South Eastern Massachusetts. In order to introduce the proposed research, after approval by IRB, a letter was delivered to multiple police agencies addressed to the chief of police. The three police departments in South Eastern Massachusetts were initially chosen to participate in the study. Included with the letter was a consent document that the chief of police signed granting permission to interview the personnel of the department. Individual law enforcement officers who agreed to participate in the study were then explained the purpose of the study, the process of the study, and consented to participate in the study. The interview either took place face-to-face, by e-mail, or by phone. At the conclusion of the interviews, all responses were transcribed to facilitate analysis.

## Analysis and Findings

This study determines if having school resource officers as a form of capable guardianship in the school system will deter physical and non-physical bullying in grade schools and high schools from taking place. By interviewing a combination of 20 law enforcement officers and teachers, the data collected were then used to reveal the importance of formal guardianship in the school environment and how this task can be accomplished by implementing school resource officers. The interview measured three areas: the use of capable guardianship, extra-curricular activities, and transportation. These measurements are presented below.

### Capable Guardianship

Previous research that was conducted demonstrated the importance of formal and informal guardianship within the school environment when it came to the reduction of physical and non-physical bullying victimization in the school environment. Schools and state legislatures have crafted policies and laws designed to prevent and respond effectively to bullying within schools and enforcement of formal policies is one of the primary purposes of law enforcement officers involved in schools. Implementation likely varies considerably from local community context, school and agency characteristics, and individual officer perceptions of policies as has been seen in implementation research on police agencies. Negotiating the implementation of policies directed at the prevention of bullying was one of the first themes to emerge from the discussion of capable guardianship with the sample of law enforcement officers.

Officers tended to distinguish their enforcement roles from that of school officials. It was a commonly held view by interviewees that officers should have little role with specific school-based policy and regulations compared to their enforcing the state criminal codes. All the officers that were interviewed agreed that school policies and regulations should be handled by the school and school department unless the act is criminal. Several quotes illustrate this viewpoint:

> When it comes to school rules and regulations the behavioral problems are brought to the school staff's attention. For general school policies that are broken the students are disciplined through the school department. (Officer 2, personal communication, October 2, 2014)

> We follow the rules of the ... police department but we don't enforce the rules of the school department. If there is a discipline issues with the students (weapons, fighting, drugs, or theft) then we would assist along with school police officers assigned to the school if there is an officer assigned to that particular school. (Officer 17, personal communication, October 28, 2014)

> As the juvenile detective, if the school administration or school resource officer contact me in regards to a juvenile breaking school rules and policies then in most cases criminal complaints are being taken out by me or the [SRO]. (Officer 18, personal communication, October 29, 2014)

The distinction between behaviors regulated by school policy (i.e., "behavioral problems") and criminal behavior is not clear in policy or in practice. However, these behaviors are still regulated by both criminal code and school policy. Officers spoke about using their law enforcement role when school policy was seen as inadequate to deal with repeated situations involving the same aggressor or when the severity of a given situation warranted. One officer for example pointed to bullying responses escalating from a school warning, to school discipline, and "on the third offense" being "criminally charged and brought to the police station" (Officer 2, personal communication, October 2, 2014). Another officer discussed that he was "usually not called to investigate the bullying crime until the second offense." The distinction was further sorted out through partnership with school administrators. Even though officers viewed enforcement of formal rules around bullying as central to their role, few officers agreed that this acted as an effective deterrent to bullying. Instead officers focused on other positive aspects of the officers' involvement in schools and bullying prevention connected to the concept of capable guardianship.

One way in which officers viewed officers having an impact on bullying and other crime taking place with the school was through surveillance and prevention activities related to a general school security approach.

> The methods that the school resource officers are using are currently working. There is no way to fully prevent [bullying] from taking place within the schools but the resource officers working with the students and building a mentor relationship with the students seems to be the most effective way. (Officer 3, personal communication, October 12, 2014)

> Having a school resource officer is great for everyone involved. With the violent society that we live in and history of school violence the interaction between the school resource officer and the student is extremely positive. The school resource officer can interact with the students and build a bond with them. Students can understand what the school resource officer does and that he or she is human too. The only negative is that the school resource officer is still a sworn police officer and might have to take out criminal charges on the student that looks up to him or her as a mentor and even has a personal liking to. (Officer 3, personal communication, October 12, 2014)

> School resource officers were another form of security. I was able to receive tips from other students and faculty. These tips helped in focusing on where the trouble was initiating from. Having a school resource officer walking around the school has shown a change in students' behaviors. (Officer 1, personal communication, September 24, 2014)

> I do believe school resource officers are deterring bullying, violence, and drug activity from taking place. Having someone in uniform and the personal presence of a police officer makes a big impact on the activity that is taking place in the school. The school resource officer is only human so they are not going to be able to catch every crime. Other security measures will enhance the security at the school by giving the school resource officers extra help. (Officer 3, personal communication, October 12, 2014)

Their responses pointed to officers being in a position to collect information about school misconduct that might be serious enough to warrant law enforcement attention. Officers viewed their highly visible position and unique authority (over that of school administrators) as an asset to collecting information and intervening in developing situations.

## Target Suitability

Most young people could report instances where they felt bullied in school, but bullying victimization experiences vary considerably by a variety of risk factors according to risk surveys. Policing literature has long recognized that building connections to and developing trust between groups differentially impacted by particular crime problems is an important step to effective prevention and response. Individuals who are reluctant to report victimization experiences to capable guardians (police, school officials) for a variety of reasons (lack of trust, concerns about the response, fear of further victimization) could be at higher risk for victimization. In part, the involvement of police directly in schools stems from broader community-based policing efforts to develop relationships between young people and police agencies.

During the interviews, interviewees viewed their role through this broader community policing frame. Their comments suggested they saw it as important to have a connection with students and for students to feel comfortable speaking with officers. As one officer put it: "this interaction between the school resource officer and students is extremely positive" adding that "officers are able to interact with students and build a bond with them." Others noted that an officer working in schools can act as a "community mentor," that they can work with "kids to build trust," and that they can develop "familiarity [with] the children and their families," among other variations around the theme of developing positive relationships.

Oftentimes they highlighted that organized groups and extra-curricular activities were sources to help facilitate these relationships. One interview noted that these gave him an opportunity to work with a group of students he believed would be at higher risk for victimization:

> There was a group, Gay-Lesbian Bi-sexual-Transgender (LGBT) that I became the "sponsor" of and would go to the meetings with the students on Thursdays. Most of the students that were part of this group were occupying my school day because of who they were. This group was a way in which I could go and talk with the students at once about life in general. (Officer 1, personal communication, September 24, 2014)

Working with groups that are at higher risk for bullying victimization (as noted by the officer in interview 1), could be an effective way for school resource officers to intervene in ongoing instances of bullying. Another officer explained:

> It's important to build rapports with kids and getting to know them on a first name basis. Most kids just want someone to listen to them. Officers that allow this, make a world of difference to kids. It's important when extra-curricular activities roll around, that officers do engage these kids. This reinforces relationships so that kids know that once they leave school, everything is not over.

All police officers that were interviewed for our data believed that a police officer engagement with the student in the school environment is important but so are the extra-curricular activities, where participation in certain activities is thought to reduce victimization risk.

> I believe this can be one of the most important and rewarding parts of the school resource officer. As I stated previously, to allow the officer to interact with the students in a non-adversarial manner fosters a stronger relationship between the juveniles and the police. Our department and school resource officers do an outstanding job of participating in and creating programs for extra-curricular activities such as softball games (police vs. football players), ski trips, an open gym program instituted by one of our school resource officers as well as many more programs and events. (Officer 15, personal communication, October 23, 2014)

> The [department] has had basketball, volleyball, softball, and dodge ball games versus the middle and high school students which I have participated in. Although I was not part of it, during the summer the school resource officers would open the high school gym two nights a week for kids. I feel these events help kids to stay busy and can keep them from committing crimes out of boredom. (Officer 11, personal communication, October 23, 2014)

The officers interviewed here drew connections between their community policing role and efforts to address bullying within schools. This went beyond the idea of enforcing bullying policies or providing formal guardianship to school spaces. They discussed the centrality of developing relationships with young people so that officers could be a source to communicate potential problems around bullying.

## Discussion

School crime has received greater attention from media, policymakers, and the law enforcement community over the past several decades. Recently, this attention has refocused on the problem of bullying with recognition of the significant consequences. The involvement of law enforcement in the responses to school crime and bullying in particular has grown, yet little research has been done explicitly on the ways in which law enforcement officers working within schools see their role in bullying prevention activities and responses. We use a RAT perspective as a lens to understand the ways in which law enforcement can play a role as part of a broader set of community- and school-based responses to bullying concerns.

School resource officers can be a critical feature preventing bullying through promoting both formal and informal forms of guardianship. Fitting John Rosiak's (2009) work on school resource officers, officers in our study were consistently hesitant about using their law enforcement authority to deal with school misconduct problems. At the same time they understood that their unique authority presented a kind of "backstop" against ongoing or particularly serious forms of bullying behaviors. Although officers consistently articulated a distinction between school misconduct, how and under what circumstance they apply this distinction is not clear from our interviews. Price (2009) observes a similar phenomenon that can lead to criminalization of actions that would normally be treated as school misconduct because "police presence at school must be justified by action" (p. 549). Others (Garby, 2013) have observed concerns about implementation of zero-tolerance bullying policies. Clearly, the officers here emphasized some degree of discretion and balance even when identifying law enforcement as one potential tool for addressing behavioral problems. Although officers in this study demonstrated some reluctance to arrest, they did perceive their role in promoting formal guardianship to be through collecting information about problems, being a visible presence within schools, enforcing laws in certain situations, and making themselves available for potential victims. In facilitating this last activity, officers moved beyond their basic role in promoting guardianship to a broader view of the police role in schools.

In line with frameworks from community policing and legitimacy, officers emphasized their efforts to build bonds, connections, or otherwise promote a positive relationship with students. They recognized the importance of maintaining trust with young people generally while policing within schools but also more specifically around providing open avenues for collecting information and receiving specific reports of victimization. We see this as fitting within the RAT components of reducing target suitability by making potential aggressors aware that higher-risk groups are empowered by their connection to officers acting as mentors within schools. Officers here reported working with organized activities and student groups as one method of developing relationships. The officers recognized and framed their role as one embodying a strong service, and community orientation is encouraging given that youth mentoring, and recreational programming, can be effective (Berger, Free, & Searles, 2009). More research should be done to better understand the appropriate mechanisms for aiding officer efforts to promote trust and build relationships with students.

The present study contributes to the understanding of law enforcement's role in addressing the bullying issue though school partnerships. Although the study's aim is to understand this role through in-depth qualitative interviews, the observations made here were based on a relatively small sample of officers. Future research should expand the scope of the present study to include perspectives from school administrators, teachers, and police personnel beyond the rank of patrol officer to capture a more comprehensive view. Readers should also be cautious of generalizing the findings here to other agencies, schools systems, and legal contexts. In addition, due to practical considerations, researchers also relied on multiple interview techniques which could have led to inconsistency in the nature and quality of responses. Despite these caveats the study helps understand the ways in which officers view their difficult role in addressing school-based crime and bullying and can help to inform the policy and practice.

## Conclusion

Given the likely expansion of law enforcement involvement in the schools generally and in dealing with bullying of all kinds, this study provides some guidance to policymakers and practitioners. First, the unique position of law enforcement officers negotiating the dual and sometimes conflicting roles of law enforcement and school resource, suggest the need for policy clarification and training. Recently, for example, in the state where this study was conducted, a new law mandates all cities and towns to designate at least one school officer (Massachusetts State House, 2014), yet training is at the discretion of the chief. Interview data suggest that careful selection criteria should be used in identifying officers best suited for school-based work and that training should emphasize when and how they should intervene in school misconduct problems and in particular bullying. Relatedly, it is clear that officers working to address youth and school crime should work within established partnerships with schools, which are seen as an important technique for improving school safety outcomes (Backstrom, 2010; Fritz, 2006; Hirsch, Lewis-Palmer, Sugai, & Schnacker, 2004). This may also help ease the conflict that seems inherent in enforcing legal mandates that coexist with school misconduct policy. Finally, officers should also follow the practices emphasized within the interviews here around developing trust and bonds with students, particularly students thought to be disproportionately affected by bullying. This includes being aware of characteristics that place students at higher risk, identifying warning signs, and resources and skills to improve relationships with students. Bullying has come to be seen as a real health and safety problem within schools and law enforcement has been called upon to play a great role in prevention and intervention efforts. Understanding how agencies and officers interpret their role can help contribute to revising responses to more effectively deal with this unique school crime problem.

## Appendix 14.1: Interview Questions

Department: ___________ Male/Female Years on the Department: ___________

### Qualitative Questions

1. What are your thoughts about the incorporation of a school resource officer in a school environment? What are the positive and negative effects of having a school resource officer?
2. As a school resource officer, what actions, if any, do you take to enforce school rules and regulations that are issued by the school department?

3. When a case of physical bullying takes place in the school environment, as a school resource officer what types of actions are taken to handle such cases?
4. When a case of non-physical bullying takes place in the school environment, as a school resource officer what types of actions are taken to handle such cases?
5. When a case of cyber bullying takes place in the school environment, as a school resource officer what types of actions are taken to handle such cases?
6. When a case such as physical bullying, non-physical bullying, or cyber bullying takes place in the school environment, what are the policies and procedures of your police department in regards to handling of these cases?
7. When a case such as physical bullying, non-physical bullying, or cyber bullying takes place in the school environment, what are the policies and procedures of the school department in regards to handling of these cases?
8. As a school resource officer, how would you describe your participation with the students in the school-sponsored extra-curricular activities? What are your thoughts of school resource officers engaging in school-sponsored extra-curricular activities?
9. As a school resource officer, do you believe that you are deterring bullying from taking place in the school environment? Explain.
10. In your opinion, what methods are currently being used by the school resource officers to deter bullying from taking place that are effectively working? What, if anything, needs to be altered in regards to handling cases within the school environment involving bullying?

## References

Arseneault, L., Walsh, E., Trzesniewski, K., Newcombe, R., Caspi, A., & Moffitt, T. E. (2006). Bullying victimization uniquely contributes to adjustment problems in young children: A nationally representative cohort study. *Pediatrics, 118*(1), 130–138.

Backstrom, J. C. (2010, May). Bullying prevention is crime prevention. *The Prosecutor Feature*, 22–24.

Baker, J., Lynch, K., Cantillon, S., & Walsh, J. (2016). *Equality: From theory to action.* Dordrecht: Springer.

Ball, H. A., Arseneault, L., Taylor, A., Maughan, B., Caspi, A., & Moffitt, T. E. (2008). Genetic and environmental influences on victims, bullies and bully-victims in childhood. *Journal of Child Psychology and Psychiatry, 49*(1), 104–112.

Berger, R. J., Free Jr., M. D., & Searles, P. (2009). *Crime, justice, and society: An introduction to criminology.* London: Lynne Rienner Publishers Inc.

Black, S., Washington, E., Trent, V. T., Harner, P., & Pollock, E. (2009, January 13). Translating the Olweus Bullying Prevention Program into real-world practice. *Health Promotion Practice, 11*(5), 733–740.

Bowes, L., Arseneault, L., Maughan, B., Taylor, A., Caspi, A., & Moffitt, T. E. (2009). School, neighborhood, and family factors are associated with children's bullying involvement: A nationally representative longitudinal study. *Journal of the American Academy of Child & Adolescent Psychiatry, 48*(5), 545–553.

Brown, B. (2005). Controlling crime and delinquency in the schools: An exploratory study of student perceptions of school security measures. *Journal of School Violence, 4*(4), 105–125.

Cohen, L., & Felson, M. (1979). Social change and crime rate trends: A routine activity approach. *American Sociological Review, 52*, 170–183.

Crawford, L. (2012, October). Standing up for his son. *The Human Rights Education Center of Utah.* Retrieved November 28, 2013, from http://hrecutah.org/standing-up-for-his-son/.

Eck, J. E. (1994). *Drug markets and drug places: A case-control study of the spatial structure of illicit drug dealing.* Doctoral dissertation, University of Maryland, College Park.

Felson, M. (1986). Linking criminal choices, routine activities, informal control, and criminal outcome. In D. B. Cornish & R. V. Clarke (Eds.), *The reasoning criminal: Rational choice perspectives on offending* (pp. 119–128). New York: Springer.

Fritz, G. K. (2006). Creating a safe, caring and respectful environment at home and in school. *Brown University Child and Adolescent Behavior Letter, 22*(12), 8.

Garby, L. (2013). Direct bullying: Criminal act or mimicking what has been learned? *Education, 133*(4), 448–450.

Hindelang, M. J., Gottfredson, M. R., & Garofalo, J. (1978). *Victims of personal crime.* Cambridge, MA: Ballinger.

Hirsch, E. J., Lewis-Palmer, T., Sugai, G., & Schnacker, L. (2004). Using school bus discipline referral data in decision making: Two case studies. *Preventing School Failure, 48*(4), 4–9.

Hodges, E. V., Malone, M. J., & Perry, D. G. (1997). Individual risk and social risk as interacting determinants of victimization in the peer group. *Developmental Psychology, 33*(6), 1032.

Jacobsen, K. E., & Bauman, S. (2007). Bullying in schools: School counselors' responses to three types of bullying incidents. *Professional School Counseling, 11*(1), 1–9.

Johnson, S., Burke, J. G., & Gielen, A. C. (2011). Prioritizing the school environment in school violence prevention efforts. *Journal of School Health, 81*(6), 331–340.

Massachusetts State House. (2014). *The 190th General Court of the Commonwealth of Massachusetts.* Boston, MA. Retrieved December 2, 2015, from https://malegislature.gov/Laws/GeneralLaws/PartI/TitleXII/Chapter71/Section37P.

Meier, T. (2007, December 1). *Megan's story.* Retrieved December 2, 2013, from www.meganmeierfoundation.org/megans-story.html.

Poland, S. (2011). The phenomenon known as bullicide. *District Administration, 47*(5), 92.

Popp, A., & Peguero, A. A. (2010). Routine activities and victimization at school: The significance of gender. *Journal of Interpersonal Violence,* 2413–2436.

Price, P. (2009). When is a police officer an officer of the law? The status of police officers in schools. *Journal of Criminal Law & Criminology, 99*(2), 541–570.

Rosiak, J. (2009). Developing safe schools partnerships with law enforcement. *Forum on Public Policy Online, 2009*(1). *Oxford Round Table.* 406 West Florida Avenue, Urbana, IL 61801.

School Bullying Statistics. (2013). *Bullying statistics.* Retrieved August 14, 2015, from www.bullyingstatistics.org/content/school-bullying-statistics.html.

Schroeder, B. A., Messina, A., Schroeder, D., Good, K., Barto, S., Saylor, J., & Massiello, M. (2011). The implementation of a statewide bullying prevention program: Preliminary findings from the field and the importance of coalitions. *Health Promotion Practice, 13*(4), 489–495.

# IV

# Promoting Best Practices for Police Officer Safety, Accountability, Effectiveness, Professionalism, and Retention

# An Analysis of the Effects of On-Body Officer Camera Systems

# 15

HAROLD RANKIN

## Contents

## Abstract

This chapter focuses on the system's impact on reducing civil liability, addressing departmental complaints, enhancing criminal prosecution, and providing operational transparency of a large metropolitan police department in the Southwest. In addition, the Axon Flex body camera was evaluated for ease of use, durability, and comfort.

Fifty on-officer body camera systems were deployed throughout the department, predominately to patrol officers and divided among the four patrol divisions. Another three camera systems were assigned to the traffic division for use by motor officers.

Officers were either assigned or volunteered to assist in evaluating the on-officer body camera system. Nearly half of the evaluation officers volunteered to participate in the program. Assigned officers were chosen by their respective division commanders based on individual criteria.

## Introduction

> The nature of police work creates an environment that places individual police officers in dangerous situations where the use of force is sometimes necessary. This unique aspect of police work opens the door for higher levels of public scrutiny about how individual police officers do their jobs. (Archbold & Maguire, 2002)

This aspect of police work has not changed; however, what has changed is the increasingly litigious society the police encounter. The police operate in an environment where the allegation of misconduct has an immediate impact on the officer and the agency, which threatens to erode community trust.

Civil litigation throughout the nation has been on the rise for the past several decades. Special interest groups, social media, and the omnipresence of recording devices have helped fuel litigation against police organizations. According to Human Rights Watch (1998), civil lawsuits brought by citizens against police officers are a means of seeking accountability. Due to these lawsuits, victims and their families have been granted millions of dollars in settlements.

Technological advancements continue to improve the level of service agencies provide to their communities. Leveraging existing technology can increase efficiency, improve transparency, and may help to mitigate the allegations of misconduct.

The recent development and deployment of on-body officer camera systems appears to be a viable solution to decreasing allegations of police misconduct. Initial analysis seems to suggest that the presence of an on-body officer camera modifies suspect behavior, helps to regulate police interaction, and can be used to quickly dispel allegations of wrongdoing. In 2010 the CATO Institute's National Police Misconduct Statistics and Reporting Project (NPMSRP) tracked 925 civil lawsuits regarding police misconduct reported in the media (Packman, 2011). The NPMSRP reports that 33% of these police misconduct lawsuits resulted in a win for the victim. Of these, 74% were settled out of court and 26% resulted in a favorable judgment for the victim. The median award for all successful police misconduct litigation was $225,000 (Packman, 2011).

In 2010 the NPMSRP recorded 4,861 unique reports of police misconduct that involved 6,613 sworn law enforcement officers. The most prominent type of reported misconduct was the allegation of excessive force, which accounted for 23.8% of all reports (Packman, 2011).

The Rialto Police Department conducted a year-long study of the effects of on-body cameras. Over the course of one year, officer complaints fell by 87.5% for those officers wearing the on-body camera. During the evaluation period, Rialto officers wearing an on-body camera reduced their use-of-force by 59% (Farrar, 2013).

According to the Pew Institute, in 2011 less than 40% of adults in the United States had smartphones. However, by May 2013 the number of adults in America who own a smartphone had risen to 59%. It is estimated by the end of 2014 approximately 80% of adults will own a smartphone (Sterling, 2013). Why are these statistics important to law enforcement? Given the nature of police work, the police are often inserted into contentious situations that at times mandate the legitimate use of force. Snippets of video that depict an escalated use-of-force incident without showing what led to the event can erode public trust and spur litigation against the police for misconduct.

Allegations of police misconduct and the filing of civil lawsuits against agencies for excessive force and misuse of force can have a financial impact on governmental entities. "Most civil suits are filed based on allegations of false arrests/imprisonment, excessive use of force, negligence, improper training, constitutional violations" (Archbold & Maguire, 2002, p. 224).

Although two-thirds of all cases against departments do not result in a settlement, those that do generally result in a higher award than cases involving other departmental lawsuits (Packman, 2011).

As a new innovation in law enforcement, on-body officer camera systems have the potential to counter dramatic video that fails to provide the full story. "Body-worn, on-officer cameras also ensure that there is more than just one video recorded of a use-of-force incident" (Wyllie, 2013). It provides a view of the entire incident from the perspective of the officer. Such video may have the ability to stop the filing of claims, by providing a thorough review of the incident, which can then be adjudicated in a timely manner. According to former NYPD Commissioner Bratton, "So much of what goes on in the field is 'he-said-she-said,' and the camera offers an objective perspective" (Lovett, 2013). The value of on-body cameras has gained the support of some organizations outside the field of law enforcement. "Cameras hold real promise for making it easier to resolve complaints against police," said Peter Bibring, a senior lawyer with the A.C.L.U. of Southern California (Lovett, 2013).

In addition to dispelling an allegation of misconduct, the presence of the video might modify the behavior of the officer, as well as the behavior of the person being contacted. Rialto Chief of Police Farrar recently stated,

> When you put a camera on a police officer, they tend to behave a little better, follow the rules a little better. And if a citizen knows the officer is wearing a camera, chances are the citizen will behave a little better. (Lovett, 2013)

The Mesa Police Department experienced a reduction of overall departmental complaints as well as use-of-force complaints. The Mesa Police Department evaluated the effects of on-body cameras during a year-long study. Findings demonstrated that officers equipped with an on-body camera experienced a 40% decrease in complaints and a 75% decrease in use of force complaints (Mesa Police Department Internal Affairs, 2013).

Also many complaints against Mesa police officers were mitigated within days by the presence of the video.

> Police officials from Oakland to Greensboro, N.C., all cited the swift resolution of complaints against officers as one of the primary benefits body cameras had offered. In some cases, citizens have come to the police station to file a complaint and decided not to after they were shown the video of the incident. (Lovett, 2013)

## Resistance to New Technology

There appears to be some resistance by police officers and some political leaders to embrace the use of on-body officer camera systems. "It would be a nightmare," said Mayor Bloomberg in reaction to the order by Judge Shira A. Scheindlin, of the Federal District Court in Manhattan (Santora, 2013). Many officers have expressed that the deployment of on-body officer camera systems demonstrates a lack of trust on the part of police administration. "Officers not familiar with the technology may see it as something harmful. But the irony is, officers actually tend to benefit. Very often, the officer's version of events is the accurate version" (Lovett, 2013).

American law enforcement looks significantly different today than it did 20 years ago. Agencies that have embraced change and technology have benefited greatly from advancing the needs of the community by ensuring the ability to meet the challenges of an evolving society. Those agencies that have maintained the status quo are not only hurt by their decisions to remain the same, but are ultimately affected by the advancement of other agencies.

> Innovative police departments put less innovative police departments at a higher risk for civil litigation by improving police technology or implementing more restrictive police policies. Kappeler (2001) asserted that as police departments increase their level of technology (such as computers for record keeping or new criminal apprehension techniques), they place less innovative police departments at risk to be sued for not having specific technological advancements. (Archbold & Maguire, 2002, p. 225)

## Methodology

The on-body camera policy was implemented during two six-month periods, the first six months required mandatory activation of the on-body camera. The following six months provided on-body camera officers with discretion to activate the camera system.

To enhance the overall evaluation, the Mesa Police Department entered into an agreement with the Arizona State University School of Criminology and Criminal Justice to plan, monitor, and evaluate the deployment of the camera systems through the use of line officer surveys and field contact reports.

The evaluation of the camera system also extended to the storage, management, and retrieval of video evidence. Evidence.com was contracted as a third party vendor responsible for cloud based data storage and security.

At the onset of the study, program administrators met with the 50 Axon users to discuss expectations, answer questions, and to gain their support in providing accurate and timely feedback regarding the functionality of the camera system and their perceptions of our deployment model.

Officers were asked to complete four quarterly surveys that were intended to track their perceptions over the course of the study. The survey measured administrative burden, use of video evidence in court, citizen reactions, and officer behavior, comfort, use, and general perceptions. Officers were also asked to make recommendations to continue, expand, or eliminate the on-officer body camera system.

In addition to the Axon users, 50 non-camera system officers (comparison group) from Red Mountain, similar in age, gender, and race were identified to complete the quarterly surveys.

Both the Axon users and the comparison group were asked to complete monthly field contact cards. Axon users and comparison group officers were advised of a randomly selected day/shift per month in which they were required to complete a contact card for every contact. The contact cards contain a series of 24 questions identifying the specific call, the nature of the call, gender and demographics of the participants, suspect behavior, type of force required, victim behavior, and officer perceptions.

Officers were also asked to make recommendations to continue, expand, or eliminate the on-officer body camera system.

Upon receipt of the completed surveys and field contact cards, program administrators ensured that officer names and identification numbers were not associated with any of the completed instruments. They were then turned over to the assigned researcher for data entry and analysis.

Program administrators worked with MPD Internal Affairs to gather the following pre and post study data on the experimental and comparison groups:

- complaints regarding discourtesy;
- use of force during the evaluation period to the previous year;
- complaints regarding discourtesy and use of force between officers wearing the body cameras and those who were not.

## Stakeholders and Workgroup

An integral component of this study was to identify potential stakeholders that could be impacted by the deployment of the on-officer body camera systems. In doing so, a workgroup consisting of the records unit, evidence section, information technology unit, policy management unit, City of Mesa Prosecutor's Office, training, internal affairs, and patrol met to discuss policy implications and system integration. The objectives of the workgroup were to minimize the impact on officers and to integrate the on-officer body camera system into existing processes.

The following policies and procedures were reviewed: Public Records Requests (ADM 1734), Release of Public Information (ADM 1730), Evidence Disposition and/or Removal (ADM 1130), Evidentiary Recordings (ADM 1850), and Rule 15 Requests (ADM 440).

Based on the workgroup findings, it was determined that the greatest challenge would be integrating video evidence managed by Evidence.com, a third party data storage vendor with the existing workflow involving public records requests, redaction requirements, and Rule 15 (discovery) mandates. The workgroup submitted policy recommendations that would minimize civil liability by ensuring that video evidence could easily be identified, retrieved, and provided upon request in accordance with Arizona State law. Those recommendations were approved by the executive staff.

## Program Administration

The evaluation program has been centrally managed and administered by the Red Mountain District Coordinator and Operations Lieutenant. The Red Mountain Commander provided program oversight. A centralized administration of the evaluation program allowed administrators to work closely with the vendor, Taser International, to immediately address hardware and software needs. Furthermore, it fostered a close working relationship among stakeholders and facilitated a thorough evaluation and data collection process.

## Study Protocol

A comprehensive protocol was developed and approved, which was intended to provide Axon camera users, supervisors, and administrators with the guidance needed to successfully manage the study. The protocol was divided into two six-month segments that would provide executive staff with a comparison between two operational models.

In the first six months, camera officers were directed, "When practical, officers will make every effort to activate the on-officer body camera when responding to a call or have any contact with the public."

During the second six-month period, officers were given the latitude to "exercise discretion and activate the on-officer body camera when they deem it appropriate."

The balance of the policy remained the same throughout the entire evaluation period.

## Results

The study revealed that volunteer officers were 60.5% more likely to use the on-body camera system than their assigned counterparts. When officers were provided the discretion to activate the on-body camera system, their use rate dropped by 42% as compared to their use during the mandated activation policy timeframe. On-body camera users experienced a 40% decrease in departmental complaints and a 75% reduction in use-of-force complaints when compared to the previous 12 months.

The academic collaboration and research between Arizona State University and the Mesa Police Department to evaluate the impact of on-officer body camera systems on citizen reactions and officer behavior has produced several thousand documented contacts. On average, program officers completed 400 field contact forms per month. Although some officers expressed concern with the need to complete additional documentation, most officers were willing to assist in the study.

The initial survey produced the following results:

- Over 80% of program officers believed that the camera system would improve the quality of evidence and produce more accurate accounts of an incident.
- Over 76% of program officers believed that video evidence would help prosecute domestic violence cases when the victim was unwilling to testify.
- Less than half of program officers believed that the presence of a camera system would impact citizen reactions. Only 45% indicated that citizens would be more respectful.
- Nearly 77% of program officers believed that the camera system would cause officers to act more professionally and 81% indicated that it would make them more cautious when making decisions.
- The initial survey demonstrated some concern with the ease of use in downloading video and navigating Evidence.com.
- Very few officers believed that the camera system would increase officer safety and less than half believed their fellow officers were receptive to the presence of a camera system on scene.
- Only 23.5% of program officers expressed within the initial survey that the Mesa Police Department should adopt an on-officer body camera system.
- The results of the subsequent surveys are not yet available and the final survey results will be published by Arizona State University.

## Axon Users: Differences Between Volunteer and Assigned Users

Axon users were classified as either volunteer or assigned users. Their rate of usage was tracked throughout the study period. On average, volunteer officers produced 71 video files per month as compared to assigned officers who averaged 28 video files per month. *Officers who volunteer to wear the on-body officer camera system were 60.5% more likely to use the system than their assigned counterparts.*

## Complaints

During the evaluation period[1] (Oct–Sep) Axon users[2] were the subject of 18 departmental complaints and/or Blue Team inquiries.[3] Axon users were the subject of 30 departmental complaints/inquiries in the 12 months prior to the implementation of the evaluation program. This represents a 40% decrease in overall departmental complaints. Axon users also experienced a 75% reduction in use-of-force complaints.

### Complaints/Blue Team Analysis

#### *October 1, 2012–September 30, 2013*

**Table 15.1**

| IA Complaints/Blue Team[1] | Axon Users[2] |
|---|---|
| Evaluation Period[3] | 18 |
| Prior 12 Months | 30 |
| Percent Change | –40 |

**Table 15.2**

| Use-of-Force Complaints | Axon Users |
|---|---|
| Evaluation Period | 1 |
| Prior 12 Months | 4 |
| Percent Change | –75 |

## Redaction Requests

As previously stated, the records department receives all public records and media requests. Records supervisors are tasked with ensuring that requests are properly completed and provided to the requestor in a timely manner. At times, reports must be redacted prior to release. The majority of report redactions are completed by the records unit staff. Some complex investigations are sent to the assigned detective for redaction.

All public records requests involving on-officer video are forwarded to the officer who produced the video. Records supervisors contend that they are unable to complete the review of on-officer videos. They indicated that the process is extremely time consuming and they do not have the personnel to absorb the increased workload. On-officer video files can be several hours long, which would require them to review the video without any knowledge of the content and what might require redaction.

When an officer receives the public records video request, the officer is required to review the video in its entirety. The review consists of identifying images and information that should not be released, including National Crime Information Center/Arizona Criminal Justice Information System (NCIC/ACJIS) information, personal biographical information, juvenile faces, undercover officers, informants, nudity, and other sensitive information as determined by the staff attorney.

Any items that need to be redacted are identified by the officer by providing a description and time stamp of the selected images. The request is then forwarded to the MPD Video Services Unit (VSU) for action.

During the study period the records unit received an average of three to four public records requests per month for on-officer video. Of those requests, three requests were forwarded by officers to the VSU for action. In each of the cases, VSU had to pixilate objects from the video. The video length varied from one hour to two hours. The total time to complete these three redactions was 30.5 hours.

## Limitations and Lessons Learned

### System Integration: Evidence.com – CAD – RMS

The introduction of on-officer video presented two initial challenges when evaluating the impact on existing policy and workflow. First, unlike other evidence stored by the Mesa Police Department, on-officer video is managed by a third party vendor. This meant the existing process that manages evidence and evidence disposition would not encompass on-body video stored within Evidence.com. An unintended omission of on-officer body video caused by a disconnect in established processes could adversely impact the disposition and prosecution of criminal cases.

### Existing Process to Manage Discovery and Public Records Requests

When a case is presented for prosecution, both the prosecutor and the defense attorney review the departmental report and the evidence voucher entered into the Records Management System (RMS). The voucher itemizes the evidence in the case. Based on their review of the evidence, attorneys make discovery decisions and submit Rule 15 requests to the MPD Records Unit. The records unit processes most discovery requests and uses the evidence voucher to determine case evidence. The records unit uses the same process to fulfill public records and media requests.

Once a case is adjudicated, the evidence section looks at the evidence voucher and submits a disposition request to the case agent. The case agent and supervisor assign the appropriate case disposition and return the disposition request form to the evidence section for action.

Discovery requests, evidence disposition, public records, and media requests all rely on case information entered into RMS.

### Solution: Records Unit Access to Evidence.com

The introduction of Evidence.com as the storage solution for on-officer video represented a workflow change for the records unit, which is tasked with fulfilling records requests. As such, records supervisors were provided with access to Evidence.com and were trained in identifying and retrieving available video evidence. In doing so, every records request would require a search of Evidence.com and RMS to determine the existence of evidence under a given departmental report number.

However, the solution proved to be ineffective. It became immediately apparent that officers were not consistently adding the required departmental report number to video evidence located with Evidence.com. An initial review of video files in Evidence.com revealed that greater than 60% of all video files did not have a departmental report number or retention category. Therefore, when records supervisors looked for associated evidence, it was both difficult and time consuming to determine if video evidence existed. Within months, Axon users had produced several thousand video files, which could not be easily searched.

Additional training was provided to Axon users in hopes of achieving greater compliance with entering the required case data within Evidence.com.

## Solution: Evidence Voucher

The next attempt at developing a solution to identify discoverable evidence was to integrate RMS and Evidence.com functions. Since RMS appeared to be the avenue used by MPD to identify evidence, program administrators worked with the evidence section supervisor and members of the information technology unit to achieve system integration. The intent was to create an easy process for officers to link associated video evidence in Evidence.com with the departmental report number populated in RMS. After considerable discussion, the following solutions were developed and approved by the executive staff:

RMS Module Checkbox – Would readily identify the RMS case as having an associated on-officer video located in Evidence.com. The officer writing the report would merely check the new box located in the existing module within RMS.

CAD Benchmark – Officers were asked to verbally notify the communications dispatcher that their assigned call had an associated on-officer video, which would be stored in Evidence.com. The dispatcher would key the benchmark as an Axon call. The result of the benchmark would ensure on-body video cases were searchable in CAD.

Evidence Voucher – Officers would create a "virtual" RMS evidence voucher, which would be used by records, case agents, detectives, and the courts to link video evidence in Evidence.com to the appropriate RMS case. This step would ensure that there were no inadvertent omissions of evidence when fulfilling discovery and public records requests.

Although approved by the executive staff and incorporated into policy, this solution was met with heavy resistance by officers who felt that the additional steps were unreasonable and increased their administrative workload.

## Solution: Automated Process

Program administrators worked closely with representatives of Evidence.com to develop an automated solution that would link RMS cases with video evidence located in Evidence.com and eliminate the manual processes.

Program administrators, police information technology unit members, and representatives of Evidence.com began working on a process to achieve integration among CAD, RMS, and Evidence.com. Thus far, the process has achieved success in developing an effective algorithm that uses CAD data to identify an officer to a specific call. The algorithm then auto-populates the RMS report number for the appropriate video file located in Evidence.com.

The second phase in system integration is to automate and link RMS offense codes with Evidence.com retention categories. This will ensure that video evidence is properly retained under Arizona State law. This process is ongoing and should be implemented in the near future.

By automating the entry of the departmental report number within Evidence.com, the manual processes that were developed to link the two systems can be eliminated. This will relieve Axon users of most of their administrative time and burden associated with the program. The records unit and evidence section can now effectively handle discovery requests, public records requests, and evidence dispositions.

## Program Management

The on-officer body camera program has been managed and led by a division coordinator and an operations lieutenant. Program management of 50 on-officer body camera systems requires a considerable amount of operational commitment.

The study ended September 30, 2013, which eliminated efforts directed at processing survey and field contact cards. However, all other program functions will require administrative attention to adequately maintain a functioning on-officer camera program. These requirements include: training officers, supervisors, and administrators as they enter and leave the program; purchase, maintain, repair, and replace hardware that is worn, damaged, or lost; maintain a close working relationship with representatives of Evidence.com to ensure firmware updates and immediate resolution of software issues that arise. These duties will exponentially increase with any expansion of the on-officer body camera program.

### Program Expansion and Effective Administration

It is recommended that any consideration to expand the on-officer body camera program should be accompanied by a discussion to expand the number of personnel assigned to manage the program. Properly managed, the program is an asset to the organization; however, it can also expose the department to increased liability without effective oversight.

### Program Administration: District Coordinators

One viable option to effectively manage an expansion of the on-officer camera program would be to centralize control of the program within the Training Unit and to assign each division coordinator the responsibility of managing the aforementioned operational responsibilities for their respective divisions.

## Hardware

The camera system has exceeded expectations over the course of the evaluation period. The video quality is exceptional and the battery-life, with rare exception, will last a complete ten-hour shift. There have been some reports of battery-life degradation during extreme heat conditions, but even in those cases the degradation is negligible. Early issues involving accidental disconnections of the power cord have been fixed with new fasteners that hold the cord in place.

The biggest concern among users is the volume of the audible recording indicator (beep). Users report that the audible warning is too loud during playback and can distort key witness or suspect statements.

### Initial Purchase

The initial purchase of 50 on-officer body camera systems did not include the purchase of the hand-held tablet/player required by officers to enter the departmental report number and to set the retention category for each call while in the field. Without the hand-held tablet/player, officers could not finalize each event at the end of the call. Instead officers were required to download the entire shift's activity at the end of the work day, which would take up to six hours to complete. Officers would then have to spend the first hour of the following shift updating the previous day's events. This increased the administrative workload for the officer and reduced the amount of time in the field handling calls.

### Hand-Held Tablet/Player

The issue was remedied when Taser agreed to loan the department 30 hand-held Samsung Galaxy players for the duration of the evaluation period. The hand-held tablet/player has allowed officers to finalize the recording at the end of an event in less than two minutes. As such, it is recommended that any future purchase of an on-officer body camera system include the hand-held tablet/player.

## Policy Evaluation

Effective April 24, 2013, Axon officers were given the discretion of when to activate their on-officer body camera system. Prior to this date, the policy directed officers when practical to record every public contact.

An analysis of system usage before and after the change date revealed the following:

> Prior to April 24, 2013, Axon officers averaged 2,327 video files per month. Following the implementation of the discretionary policy, officers averaged 1,353 video files per month. *This represents a 42% decrease in system activations under the discretionary policy.*

## Recommendations

### Successful Program Implementation

The success of any new program is dependent upon the team tasked with implementing the program and the level of buy-in achieved among officers, executive staff, and the community. The camera system can be viewed as intrusive by officers and therefore officers can be skeptical about the value of the system. Until officers achieve some "wins" with the system, the implementation of the program can be a long process. As such, it is recommended that the program be implemented in stages. This allows the introduction of cameras into the field among new users, while receiving close support from the administrative team responsible for system deployment. In doing so, an agency can work with a smaller administrative team while maintaining quality assurance.

### Camera Activation Considerations

Based on the program evaluation, officers were 42% less likely to activate their camera system under a discretionary activation policy. Furthermore, there was a significant difference between officers who volunteered to participate in the program as compared to those who were assigned to the program. Assigned officers were less inclined to activate their cameras when it was their decision.

At the conclusion of the evaluation, the policy reverted back to a "near mandatory" policy, instructing officers to activate their cameras unless extenuating circumstances prevented them from doing so. Officers were also provided some latitude in activating their cameras when privacy issues were a concern. Officers were asked to document their decision regarding non-system activations.

### Data Storage and Retention

Managing evidence storage and retention are crucial to the success of any on-body camera system program. Video represents both evidence and a public record and is subject to discovery and public records laws. During the evaluation period, the 50 camera officers generated approximately 45,000 video file segments. This translates to approximately 475 GB per officer or about $750 per officer per year in storage charges. Ensuring that video segments are accurately categorized for retention and that officers properly tag their videos will allow the department to meet discovery and public records requests in the prescribed time. This can be achieved through regular administrative audits.

## Notes

1 IA Complaints/Blue Team: Blue Team inquiries and IA complaints regardless of disposition, excluding: missed training, missed court, vehicle accidents, and off-duty incidents.
2 Axon user: 50 officers assigned to wear and evaluate the Axon Flex on-body camera system.
3 Evaluation Period: October 1, 2012–September 30, 2013.

## References

Archbold, C. A., & Maguire, E. R. (2002). Studying civil suits against the police: A serendipitous finding of sample selection bias. *Police Quarterly, 5*(2), 223–249.

Farrar, W. A. (2013). *Self-awareness to being watched and socially-desirable behavior: A field experiment on the effect of body-worn cameras on police use-of-force.* Rialto, California Police Department. Washington, DC: Police Foundation.

Human Rights Watch. (1998, June 1). Shielded from justice: Police brutality and accountability in the United States. *Human Rights Watch.* Retrieved October 2, 2013, from www.columbia.edu/itc/journalism/cases/katrina/Human%20Rights%20Watch/uspohtml/uspo30.htm#P730_210368.

Lovett, I. (2013, August 21). In California, a champion for police cameras. *New York Times.* Retrieved October 3, 2013, from www.nytimes.com/2013/08/22/us/in-california-a-champion-for-police-cameras.html?pagewanted=all&_r=1&.

Mesa Police Department Internal Affairs. (2013, January 1). *2013 Summary of Mesa Police Departmental complaints.* Mesa, AZ: MPD IA.

Packman, D. (2011, April 5). *2010 NPMSRP police misconduct statistical report – draft.* The CATO Institute's National Police Misconduct Reporting Project. Retrieved October 2, 2013, from www.policemisconduct.net/2010-npmsrp-police-misconduct-statistical-report/.

Santora, M. (2013, August 13). Order that police wear cameras stirs unexpected reactions. *New York Times.* Retrieved October 1, 2013, from www.nytimes.com/2013/08/14/nyregion/order-that-police-wear-cameras-stirs-unexpected-reactions.html.

Sterling, G. (2013, June 5). Pew: 61 percent in US now have smartphones. *Marketing Land.* Retrieved October 3, 2013, from http://marketingland.com/pew-61-percent-in-us-now-have-smartphones-46966.

Wyllie, D. (2013, June 5). A tale of 2 videos: A case study in why you should have a body-worn camera. *Police One.* Retrieved October 4, 2013, from www.policeone.com/police-products/body-cameras/articles/6261737-A-tale-of-2-videos-A-case-study-in-why-you-should-have-a-body-worn-camera/.

# Information Sharing in the Investigative Units of Local Law Enforcement Agencies

## Which Units Share Information and Why?

# 16

BLAKE M. RANDOL

## Contents



### Abstract

Historically, a number of criminal justice failures in the United States and abroad have been attributed to a lack of information sharing between law enforcement agencies. To date, few studies have assessed the correlates of information sharing performance in police organizations. Using a sample of 171 criminal investigators from local law enforcement agencies, this study tests whether the correlates of information sharing identified in the policing and information sciences literature are associated with criminal investigators' reports of communication and information sharing effectiveness. Results show that several factors were associated with information sharing performance including years of investigator experience, managerial support for information sharing, and greater access to information and communication technology. Conversely, findings show that communications red tape inhibited information sharing in law enforcement agencies. Implications for research and practice are discussed.

## Introduction

The need for improved information sharing practices and collaboration in the law enforcement community has received considerable international attention in the current era of homeland security (Carter & Carter, 2009; Giblin, Schafer, & Burruss, 2009; Pelfrey, 2007, 2009). Inadequate information and intelligence sharing in a multi-agency context is a recurrent problem that has been attributed to a variety of catastrophes in the American criminal justice system. Such problems include the Federal Bureau of Investigation's (FBI) stalled investigations of terrorism suspects prior to the events of September, 11, 2001 (Brown, 2002; Garnett & Kouzmin, 2007; Kettl, 2006); the Los Angeles Police Department's (LAPD) inability to maintain order during the 1992 Los Angeles Riots (Cannon, 1997; Miller, 2001); and the New Orleans Police Department's poorly coordinated response to Hurricane Katrina (Garnett & Kouzmin, 2007; Kettl, 2006). More effective information sharing practices can potentially prevent crises in these situations.

It is important to acknowledge that information sharing is not only critical in times of crisis, but it is equally important to the day-to-day operations of the criminal justice system. Police work is inherently "information dependent" (Manning, 1992) and the police rely heavily on information sharing systems for their day-to-day operations. Numerous factors prevent information sharing in police organizations including limited incentives for detectives and command staff across jurisdictions to coordinate and exchange information (Wilson, 1984); differentiation between various organizational units such as terminology and protocols; and the distortion or blockage of information as it is transformed either vertically or horizontally (Manning, 1992). Egger (1984) refers to these problems in police organizations that impede information sharing as "linkage blindness." Linkage blindness prevents police practitioners from linking disparate facts together and connecting the dots contained in different units, thus contributing to investigative failures and poorly coordinated responses to critical incidents.

Although linkage blindness has long been recognized as a fundamental problem with the criminal justice system in the United States, prior to the era of homeland security, practitioners, policy makers, and academics gave scant attention to the issue of information and intelligence sharing in the law enforcement community. The nation's responses to the terrorism events of September 11, 2001, have stimulated a strong interest and growing body of research in the area of information sharing and the intelligence fusion process (Carter & Carter, 2009; Ratcliffe, 2002). With the publication of the 9/11 Commission Report (Kean/Hamilton, 2004) federal officials and policy makers acknowledged that problems with information sharing had prevented the early identification of suspects in terrorism cases (Pelfrey, 2009). A key finding of the report was that problems with information sharing were largely an artifact of the decentralized and jurisdictionally fragmented nature of the criminal justice system in the United States. Federal policy makers responded by creating a new cabinet level agency, the Department of Homeland Security (DHS), which centralized the administration of federal intelligence and emergency response agencies under the oversight of the Director of National Intelligence (DNI). DHS directives and other federal mandates established a new role for local law enforcement agencies in the federal national terrorism prevention system (Pelfrey, 2009), and developed a new infrastructure for the fusion of intelligence information across federal, state, local, and tribal law enforcement agencies, which Carter and Carter (2009) refer to as the fusion process.

The academic literature has addressed many dimensions of information and intelligence sharing in the law enforcement community including but not limited to: its role in day-to-day police operations (Carter & Carter, 2009; Manning, 1992; Ratcliffe, 2002); the essential role that information sharing serves in intelligence-led policing (ILP) and the intelligence fusion process (Carter & Carter, 2009; Ratcliffe, 2002); and the impediments to information sharing in a multi-agency context (Ratcliffe, 2002; Sheptycki, 2004). However, to date, a limited number of studies have directly examined the correlates of information sharing in local law enforcement agencies (Gottschalk, 2007a, 2007b; Hughes & Jackson, 2004; Sheptycki, 2004).

The purpose of this chapter is to identify and investigate the factors that either impede or facilitate information sharing between police organizations in a multi-agency context. Following the policing and information sciences literature this study models the sources of information sharing performance in the investigative units of local law enforcement agencies in the United States. More specifically, this study uses a sample of 171 criminal investigators to model the relationship that a number of factors have with information sharing practices. Explanatory factors examined in this study include the information sharing attitudes of criminal investigators, managerial support for communication, agency access to information and communications technology systems (ICT), communications red tape, and information systems red tape. This study also evaluates several control variables including organizational size, the size of the investigative unit, and the officers' years of experience in criminal investigation.

## Information Management in Policing

According to Manning (1992) police work is inherently "information dependent." Timely and accurate information is critical to the day-to-day operations and the overall success of police organizations. Police officers are confronted with an astounding amount of information on a daily basis; therefore, an important function of the police is to sort and sift through these vast amounts of information and to discern what information is valuable to the organization (Luen and Al-Hawamdeh, 2001). Police agencies use three general types of information including *primary, secondary, and tertiary* (Manning, 1992). Police principally rely on primary information which is captured in various forms including records, citizen reports, surveillance, officer experiences, and observations. Information becomes secondary once it has been processed by at least two units and it changes in its initial format and location, and subsequently becomes tertiary information once it has been processed and transferred on multiple occasions.

It is important to draw a distinction between "information" and "intelligence" because the two concepts are often confused with one another. Intelligence is generally understood as being the output or product of the analysis of items of information, which are usually collected from a number of different sources (Carter & Carter, 2009).

Presently, knowledge is collected and housed by police organizations in a variety of ways including computer-aided dispatch (CAD) systems, management information systems (MIS) (Manning, 1992), records management systems (RMS) (Chen, Zeng, Atabakhsh, Wyzga, & Schroeder, 2003), and other information and communications technology (ICT) systems (Sheptycki, 2004), such as COPLINK (Chen et al., 2003). A problem with the proliferation of CAD, MIS, and RMS systems during the digital revolution of the 1980s and 1990s was that it led to the development of fragmented and non-integrated information management systems, in which case data is often not shared or used very effectively (Hughes & Jackson, 2004).

## Information Sharing in the Era of Homeland Security

The topic of information sharing practices in the law enforcement community has received considerable attention in the current era of homeland security (Carter & Carter, 2009; Giblin et al., 2009; Pelfrey, 2007, 2009). This focus on information sharing practices occurred in a time when information and communication technologies were developing rapidly, and were widely adopted in both the United States and abroad, giving rise to the new era of "data driven" or "intelligence led policing" (Carter & Carter 2009; Ratcliffe, 2002; Sheptycki; 2004). In the United Kingdom the National Criminal Intelligence Service developed the National Intelligence Model (NIM), which achieved widely recognized success by integrating intelligence systems and facilitating multi-agency intelligence sharing practices (Ratcliffe, 2002). Observing the success of the United Kingdom's NIM, the U.S. Department of Justice (DOJ), the Office of the Director of National Intelligence (DNI), and the Secretary of the Department of Homeland Security (DHS) strongly encouraged the adoption of intelligence-driven strategies and the improvement of information sharing practices in America's law enforcement sector (Carter & Carter, 2009; McGarrell, Freilich, & Chermak, 2007; Ratcliffe, 2002).

Since 9/11, federal agencies including the DOJ and DHS have granted millions of dollars (e.g., Homeland Security Grant Program, the Urban Areas Security Initiative Grant Program) to assist state and local law enforcement agencies in the development of intelligence fusion centers (Allen, Wilson, Norman, & Knight, 2008; Carter & Carter, 2009). Fusion centers (i.e., physical plants) serve as regional hubs for the intelligence fusion process (i.e., the collection, analysis, and dissemination of criminal intelligence information) (Carter & Carter, 2009). In addition to the development of fusion centers, federal grants also assisted state, local, and tribal law enforcement agencies in developing technology infrastructure, including CAD, MIS, RMS, and ICT systems.

There is a general consensus in the extant literature that the trend of information sharing in the law enforcement community is growing (Carter, 2008; Ratcliffe, 2002). These innovations within local police organizations, particularly the growth of information systems for gathering and sharing intelligence information, have largely been fueled by the demand from state and federal entities to collect risk-related information. Ratcliffe (2002) observed that in the modern "risk society" police agencies are the primary collectors and providers of risk-related information for sources external to the policing organization. Subsequent to 9/11, local police agencies are increasingly expected to collect and share many types of information (i.e., terrorism, gangs, drug trafficking, organized crime, homicides, etc.), with state and federal agencies, and with regional fusion centers. Furthermore, local police agencies have been mandated[1] to collect and report uniform crime reports to the Federal Bureau of Investigation (FBI) for decades, and some have chosen to adopt the more comprehensive requirements of the NIBRS process.[2] After being delegated the role of being among the central gatekeepers of risk-related information many local law enforcement agencies have responded by keeping as much information as possible irrespective of its importance just in case it becomes needed. Unfortunately, local law enforcement agencies, many equipped with modern ICT systems, have become much more efficient at collecting information than they are at sharing it (Ratcliffe, 2002; Sheptycki, 2004).

## Impediments to Information Sharing

Research shows that there are a variety of complex internal and external factors that impede the flow of information across organizational hierarchies in a multi-agency context (Hughes & Jackson, 2004; Sheptycki, 2004). Using a review of the extant literature, Sheptycki (2004) identified a variety of common "organizational pathologies" with the flow of information across organizational hierarchies. Organizational pathologies that are problematic in American policing include the digital divide, duplication of investigative and crime analytic efforts, intelligence hoarding, and information silos. The digital divide is common in American law enforcement given that police organizations use a variety of different and sometimes incompatible ICT systems for storing and communicating intelligence information. Police organizations that receive technology grants[3] adopt ICT systems that are up to date and coordinated with systems that are used by federal agencies (i.e., systems used for NIBRS reporting); however, agencies with lower operating budgets are less likely to invest in ICT infrastructure[4] and are more likely to continue using dated and incompatible systems, which hampers the process of sharing information.

Several studies have highlighted the prevalent problem of information hoarding and information silos in the American law enforcement community (Kettl, 2006; Sheptycki, 2004). Research shows that the greatest challenge to effective interagency information sharing occurs when critical knowledge becomes trapped within the isolated networks contained within separate hierarchies (i.e., information silos). In which case, the information is hidden and is not shared with other units or agencies. Similar problems with interagency communications were highlighted in the 9/11 Commission's Report (Kettl, 2006). The report identified that poor communications between federal law enforcement agencies occurred for a variety of reasons including procedural restrictions on information sharing and poor communication between federal agencies including the FBI, the National Security Agency (NSA), the Central Intelligence Agency (CIA), and the Immigration and Naturalization Service (INS). Following the reports' policy recommendations, the U.S. federal government attempted to solve these problems of interagency collaboration and information sharing by establishing interagency task forces, FBI fusion centers, and by developing a new cabinet level agency, the United States Department of Homeland Security (DHS). Today, the DHS has authority over a number of intelligence and emergency management functions.

## Factors Associated with Information Sharing

Research shows that a variety of factors are associated with effective information sharing practices in the law enforcement community; which include information technologies (Chen et al., 2003; Gottschalk, 2007a, 2007b); the implementation of knowledge management strategies (Gottschalk, 2007a, 2007b; Luen & Al-Hawamdeh, 2001); technical, social, and structural factors (Hughes & Jackson, 2004); the role of leadership and organizational culture (Gottschalk, 2007a, 2007b).

Many studies have shown that developments in database technologies are improving information sharing practices in the law enforcement community (Chen et al., 2003; Gottschalk, 2007a, 2007b). The use of relational database systems can overcome the widespread problem of database fragmentation by integrating existing systems and by enabling agencies to more easily share intelligence data relating to terrorism and gang-related activity, criminal investigations for homicides, aggravated assaults, and sexual assault, and a variety of other crime related issues (Chen et al., 2003; McGarrell et al., 2007; Sheptycki, 2004). For instance, the COPLINK system which was developed by the National Institute of Justice (NIJ), the National Science Foundation (NSF), the Tucson Police Department (TPD), the Phoenix Police Department (PPD), and the University of Arizona (UA). COPLINK is a system that effectively integrates police databases and shares detailed investigative information, and therefore is increasingly being recognized as an invaluable tool in law enforcement technology (Chen et al., 2003).

Studies in organizational science have shown that public service organizations, including police departments, have more red tape than private organizations, which inhibits information sharing practices (Bozeman, 2000). Bozeman (1993) defines red tape as "rules, regulations, and procedures that remain in force and entail a compliance burden, but do not serve the legitimate purposes the rules were intended to serve" (p. 283). Pandey and Kingsley (2000) define red tape as "impressions on the part of managers that formalization (in the form of burdensome rules and regulations) is detrimental to the organization" (p. 782). Research shows that organizational red tape has an adverse impact on a variety of organizational performance measures including communication and information sharing (Bozeman & Kingsley, 1998; DeHart-Davis & Pandey, 2005; Pandey & Garnett, 2006; Scott & Pandey, 2000). The 9/11 Commission Report found that formal procedures that were developed in 1995 to control information sharing protocols between federal prosecutors and the FBI resulted in far less information being shared than was permitted under federal law. These procedures are referred to as "The Wall" (National Commission, 2004, p. 79).

A number of policing studies have shown that differentiations in organizational structures, processes, and practices are contingent upon organizational size (Langworthy, 1986; Zhao, 1996). The influence of organizational size, which is typically measured as the total number of employees, can cut both ways and has had inconsistent effects on information sharing in the public sector (Pandey & Garnett, 2006). Information sharing is often more difficult in larger and more complex organizations because they have more layers, departments, and opportunities for communication breakdowns. On the other hand, larger organizations tend to have more resources that they can dedicate to communication and information sharing including personnel, expertise, and fiscal resources. Consequently, studies have produced mixed findings concerning the relationship between organizational size, communication, and information sharing (Pandey & Garnett, 2006).

The objective of this study is to better understand how knowledge, either in the form of information or intelligence, surfaces and becomes shared between police investigators, units, or agencies to inform criminal investigations in a timely and effective manner. Employing theory from the policing and information sciences literature, this study develops and tests an exploratory model to explain information sharing performance in the investigative units of local law enforcement agencies.

## Method

The primary source of data for this study is a sample of criminal investigators that were surveyed in Washington State. The survey instrument's design and implementation procedures followed the principles set forth in Dillman, Smyth, and Christian's (2009) *Tailored Design Method.* Remark software was used to administer the internet survey over a two-month period in fall 2011 and winter 2012. Prior to sending the invitation letter a standard prenotice letter was sent to the list of criminal investigators. A week later an invitation email was sent, which included a URL to the survey, web survey instructions, and an access code. Two weeks later a thank you letter, with a reminder and instructions was sent. Four weeks later another thank you letter, with a reminder and instructions was sent. A total of 658 criminal investigators from state, county, and municipal law enforcement agencies were invited to participate in the survey and 171 officers completed the survey reflecting a survey response rate of 26%. A secondary data source that was used for this study was the United States Department of Justice's 2007 Law Enforcement Management and Administrative Statistics Survey (LEMAS). This comprehensive dataset contains information on a variety of administrative attributes of local law enforcement agencies in the United States. This study uses the LEMAS data to develop a measure of the number of information and communications technology systems that were used by the sampled law enforcement agencies.

## Dependent Variables

A single measure of *information sharing* performance was used as a dependent variable in this study. Five separate survey items were used to construct the *information sharing* scale, which are presented in Table 16.1. The survey items were Likert scale questions that ranged from 1 (strongly disagree) to 5 (strongly agree). The Cronbach's Alpha for the

**Table 16.1 Survey Items Used as Measures of Information Sharing Performance**

| Survey Items | Mean | SD | Min | Max | Factor Loadings |
|---|---|---|---|---|---|
| *Information Sharing Performance* | | | | | |
| There is good communication among various departments in your law enforcement agency | 3.53 | 1.06 | 1 | 5 | 0.72 |
| Criminal investigators handling sexual assault and homicide cases are kept informed on issues affecting their jobs | 3.58 | 0.92 | 1 | 5 | 0.61 |
| Your agency has frequent communication with other law enforcement agencies | 3.95 | 0.86 | 1 | 5 | 0.82 |
| Criminal investigators frequently share knowledge and information with investigators from other units and other law enforcement agencies | 3.93 | 0.84 | 1 | 5 | 0.77 |
| Criminal investigators in your agency are kept informed about program and policy developments outside of your agency | 3.27 | 0.96 | 1 | 5 | 0.63 |
| Cronbach's Alpha = 0.84 | | | | | |
| Eigen value = 2.56 | | | | | |
| Survey Items | | | | | Mean |
| *Information Sharing Performance* | | | | | |
| There is good communication among various departments in your law enforcement agency | | | | | 3.53 |
| Criminal investigators handling sexual assault and homicide cases are kept informed on issues affecting their jobs | | | | | 3.58 |
| Your agency has frequent communication with other law enforcement agencies | | | | | 3.95 |
| Criminal investigators frequently share knowledge and information with investigators from other units and other law enforcement agencies | | | | | 3.93 |
| Criminal investigators in your agency are kept informed about program and policy developments outside of your agency | | | | | 3.27 |
| Cronbach's Alpha = 0.84 | | | | | |
| Eigen value = 2.56 | | | | | |

*Note:* SD represents the standard deviation for each survey item. $N = 171$.

*information sharing* scale was 0.84, which is generally interpreted as a moderate to strong level of intra-scale reliability (Acock, 2008).

## Independent Variables

Several factors found in the literature to be associated with information sharing performance were evaluated in this study. Independent variables used in this study include organizational size, the size of the criminal investigation unit, the investigator's years of experience and the investigator's attitude toward information sharing, the degree of managerial support for communication, the investigator's perceptions of red tape, and the investigator's access to ICT systems.

Organizational size, the size of the criminal investigation unit, and the investigator's years of experience were used as control variables in this study. The number of full-time sworn officers employed by the respondent's law enforcement agency was used as a proxy for organizational size. There was a high bivariate correlation between organizational size and the size of the criminal investigation unit ($R > 0.7$); therefore, organizational size was recoded as an ordinal variable to reduce the threat of multicollinearity. Law enforcement agencies that employ fewer than 25 full-time sworn officers were coded as 1, agencies that employ between 25 and 49 officers were coded as 2, agencies having between 50 and 74 officers were coded as 3, agencies employing between 75 and 99 officers were coded as 4, and agencies that employed 100 or more officers were coded as 5.

The number of full-time criminal investigators (sworn or non-sworn) that work in the respondent's law enforcement agency was used as a proxy for the size of the agency's investigation unit. Given that the structure and degree of specialization within investigation units varies across agencies, respondents were asked to report the total number of criminal investigators working for their agency rather than merely the number of investigators working within their particular unit. Agencies that employed no full-time criminal investigators were coded as 1, those that have one to five investigators were coded as 2, agencies that employ six to ten investigators were coded as 3, and agencies that employ more than 10 investigators were coded as 4. Years of experience in criminal investigation was an ordinal variable on the survey instrument, in which respondents were given the following choices; less than six months of experience (coded as 1), six months to a year of experience (coded as 2), one to five years of experience (coded as 3), and more than five years of investigative experience (coded as 4).

The investigator's attitude toward information sharing was measured using a questionnaire item that asked respondents how strongly they agree or disagree to the following statement: I believe that it is critical that law enforcement agencies share information they have access to with allied law enforcement agencies. Strongly disagree responses were coded as 1, disagree was coded as 2, uncertain was coded as 3, agree was coded as 4, and strongly agree was coded as 5. To determine the investigators' attitudes concerning the degree of managerial support for communication that they receive, respondents were asked how much they agree or disagree with this statement: managers and supervisors promote communication and information sharing among different work units within your agency. Strongly disagree responses were coded as 1, disagree was coded as 2, uncertain was coded as 3, agree was coded as 4, and strongly agree was coded as 5.

Table 16.2 lists the survey items that were used to assess investigator perceptions of communications red tape and information systems red tape within their respective law enforcement agencies. These measures were adapted from prior studies of public sector communication performance (Garnett, 1997; Guy, 1992; Pandey & Garnett, 2006; Zammuto & Krakower, 1991). Two survey items were used to measure whether rules and procedures impeded communications in the police organizations that were surveyed. The first measure asked respondents whether they believed that communication in your agency is restricted in some degree by policies and procedures. The second item asked respondents if they believed that communication with other agencies is restricted by policies and procedures. Strongly disagree responses were coded as 1, disagree was coded as 2, uncertain was coded as 3, agree was coded as 4, and strongly agree was coded as 5. The communications red tape survey items were used to form a communications red tape scale. As summarized in Table 16.2, the factor loading for the two items were 0.73 and 0.71, and the Cronbach's Alpha value for the scale was 0.65 reflecting a moderate level of internal reliability.

In addition to communications red tape a measure of information systems red tape was also assessed in this study. Similar to other public sector agencies it is reasonable to expect that law enforcement agencies that have more impediments to requesting and exchanging information may have lower levels of information sharing performance. Two survey items were used to construct an information systems red tape scale. The first survey item asked respondents whether they believed that rules and procedures on preparation of information systems reports ensure that criminal investigators receive timely information. Strongly agree responses were coded as 1, agree was coded as 2, uncertain was coded as 3, disagree responses were coded as 4, and strongly disagree was coded as 5. For the second item in the scale respondents were asked whether they believed that procedural requirements for information system requests make it difficult for criminal investigators to obtain relevant information. Strongly disagree responses were coded as 1, disagree was coded as 2, uncertain was coded as 3, agree was coded as 4, and strongly agree was coded as 5. As summarized in Table 16.2 the factor loading for the two items were 0.66 and 0.53, and the Cronbach's Alpha value for the scale was 0.61.

Data from the LEMAS survey was merged with data from our survey of investigative units to develop a measure of information and communications technologies (ICT) that were used by each agency. The ICT measure is comprised of an additive index that simply measures the number of computer systems that each agency uses for the following functions: intelligence gathering, interagency information sharing, records management, criminal investigations, and crime analysis. Each of these survey items was a dichotomously coded yes or no question on the LEMAS survey. No responses were coded as 0 and yes responses were coded as 1. The Cronbach's Alpha value for this index was 0.81 reflecting a strong level of internal reliability.

**Table 16.2 Survey Items Used as Measures of Red Tape**

| Survey Items | Mean | SD | Min | Max | Factor Loadings |
|---|---|---|---|---|---|
| *Communications Red Tape* | | | | | |
| Communication in your agency is restricted in some degree by policies and procedures | 2.51 | 1.76 | 1 | 5 | 0.73 |
| Communication with other agencies is restricted by policies and procedures | 2.84 | 1.46 | 1 | 5 | 0.71 |
| Cronbach's Alpha = 0.65 | | | | | |
| Eigen value = 1.14 | | | | | |
| *Information Systems Red Tape* | | | | | |
| Rules and procedures on preparation of information systems reports ensure that criminal investigators receive timely information | 3.17 | 1.54 | 1 | 5 | 0.66 |
| Procedural requirements for information system requests make it difficult for criminal investigators to obtain relevant information | 2.34 | 1.61 | 1 | 5 | 0.53 |
| Cronbach's Alpha = 0.61 | | | | | |
| Eigen value = 1.07 | | | | | |

*Note:* SD represents the standard deviation for each survey item. $N = 171$.

## Results

### Descriptive Statistics

Table 16.3 reports the descriptive statistics for each of the dependent measures and independent measures evaluated in this study.

Results show that the mean value for the information sharing scale was 18.21 on a scale ranging from 5 to 25, which suggests that there is a fairly high level of information sharing among the police agencies in Washington State. The number of full-time sworn police officers was used as a statistical control for agency size. As previously discussed there is a high correlation between the raw number of sworn full-time officers and full-time criminal investigators, therefore, these variables were recoded into ordinal scales to reduce the threat of multicollinearity in the statistical model. Results show that within the sample there was a mean number of 3.89 officers on a scale of 5, indicating that on average the respondents represented moderate sized law enforcement agencies employing somewhere between 75 and 100 full-time sworn officers. Moreover, the mean number of criminal investigators was 2.13 on a scale of 5, thus indicting that on average respondents in the sample represented law enforcement agencies with relatively small investigative units that employed about five or fewer criminal investigators.

On average respondents had very favorable attitudes towards sharing information with allied agencies, this variable had an average value of 4.62 on a scale of 5, indicating that on average respondents had either agreed or strongly agreed with the view that it is critical that law enforcement agencies share information with allied agencies. Additionally important, the mean number of respondents that reported managerial support for communication and information sharing was 3.7 on a scale of 5, thus showing that on average respondents agreed that their supervisors supported communication and information sharing among different work units within their agency.

Interestingly, respondents held optimistic attitudes about their organizations in terms of red tape. The average value on the communications red tape scale was 5.35 on a scale of 10, and the average value on the information systems red tape scale was 5.51 on a

**Table 16.3 Descriptive Statistics for Dependent and Independent Measures**

| Variables | Mean | SD | Min | Max |
|---|---|---|---|---|
| *Dependent Variable* | | | | |
| Information sharing performance scale | 18.21 | 3.59 | 7 | 25 |
| *Independent Variables* | | | | |
| Number of full-time sworn | 3.89 | 1.22 | 1 | 5 |
| Number of investigators | 2.13 | 1.45 | 1 | 5 |
| Years of experience in investigation | 2.83 | 1.62 | 0 | 4 |
| Managerial support for communication | 3.70 | 1.09 | 1 | 5 |
| Information sharing attitude | 4.62 | 1.04 | 1 | 5 |
| Communications red tape | 5.35 | 1.94 | 2 | 10 |
| Information systems red tape | 5.51 | 1.95 | 2 | 10 |
| ICT systems | 3.21 | 1.85 | 0 | 5 |

*Note:* $N = 171$.

scale of 10. These scores indicate that many respondents perceived that red tape inhibited both communications and information requests within their respective agencies. The descriptive results also show that on average the sample of investigators had access to roughly three types of information and communication technology systems.

## Inferential Statistics

Table 16.4 reports the results of the ordinary least squares (OLS) regression model that was used to test the relationship between the hypothesized independent variables and *information sharing* practices in the investigative units of local law enforcement agencies. With the exception of two moderately sized bivariate correlations ($R = 0.58$ and $R = 0.61$), most correlation coefficients between the independent variables were low and not high enough to warrant concerns about multicollinearity in the multivariate models (Appendix Table 16.1). Also, a variance inflation factor (VIF) test was run and the highest VIF score was 2.39, which further suggests that multicollinearity in the multivariate model was not a concern. Many scholars follow the general rule of thumb that multicollinearity becomes a concern when VIF values exceed 4 (Fisher & Mason, 1981). Table 16.4 presents the standardized regression coefficients and standard errors for the OLS model. Diagnostic statistics indicate that the model fulfills the assumptions of OLS regression.[5]

The adjusted $R^2$ values reported in Table 16.4 indicate that the model explained approximately 22% of the variation in information sharing performance within the investigative units of law enforcement agencies. The F statistic for the model was statistically significant ($p < 0.001$), thereby indicating that the specified model does a better overall job of explaining variation in the information sharing practices than a baseline model with no predictors.

The results from model 1 show that more years of experience in criminal investigation, managerial support for communication, and the number of ICT systems, each had positive and statistically significant relationships with the information sharing performance within the sampled police organizations. Conversely, the findings reveal that communications systems red tape was negatively associated with information sharing performance.

**Table 16.4 Police Investigative Unit Information Sharing Performance**

| Independent Variables | Coefficients | *t*-statistics | *p*-values |
|---|---|---|---|
| Number of full-time sworn | –0.43 (0.23) | –1.84 | 0.068 |
| Number of investigators | 0.23 (0.19) | 1.21 | 0.228 |
| Years of experience in investigation | 0.44 (0.13) | 1.98 | 0.047 |
| Managerial support for communication | 1.46 (0.21) | 7.00 | 0.000 |
| Information sharing attitude | –0.01 (0.30) | –0.03 | 0.975 |
| Information systems red tape | –0.35 (0.25) | –1.38 | 0.169 |
| Communications red tape | –0.52 (0.24) | –2.11 | 0.037 |
| ICT systems | 0.50 (0.28) | 2.08 | 0.038 |
| F | 17.70*** | | |
| Adjusted $R^2$ | 0.22 | | |

*Notes*: ***$p < 0.001$, $N = 171$. Table presents results from OLS regression models. Entries are standardized coefficients and standard errors in parentheses, *t*-statistics, and *p* values. F represents the F statistic.

The findings indicate that one-unit increase in the experience level of criminal investigators was associated with a 0.43-unit increase in information sharing ($p<0.05$). Also, managerial support for communication was associated with a 1.46-unit increase in information sharing ($p<0.001$). Furthermore, the model reveals that greater agency access to ICT systems was associated with information sharing ($p<0.05$), and that one-unit increase in an agency's number of ICT systems was associated with a 0.50 unit increase in information sharing performance ($p<0.05$). On the other hand, communications systems red tape was negatively associated with information sharing ($p<0.05$), whereas a unit increase in communications red tape was associated with a –0.51-unit decrease in information sharing ($p<0.05$). Results show that several factors are associated with information sharing in local law enforcement agencies including managerial support for communication, years of investigative experience, access to technology, and communications red tape. These findings are consistent with a number of previous studies (Chen et al., 2003; Gottschalk, 2007a; Hughes & Jackson, 2004; Pandey & Garnett, 2006).

Although organizational size was not a statistically significant correlate of information sharing at the 95% level of confidence, this variable was negatively associated with information sharing at the 90% level. This finding is consistent with studies in the information sciences literature which shows that information sharing is often more difficult in larger and more complex organizations because they have more layers, departments, and opportunities for communication breakdowns (Pandey & Garnett, 2006).

An interesting finding was that communications red tape was negatively associated with information sharing. This finding indicates that criminal investigators, who found that rules and procedures inhibited their personal communications with other investigative units, also rated their respective police agencies as having poor information sharing performance. This finding is consistent with established theories of communications and the findings from prior studies (Bozeman & Kingsley, 1998; DeHart-Davis & Pandey, 2005; Pandey & Garnett, 2006; Scott & Pandey, 2000). For instance, Pandey and Garnett (2006) found that communications red tape was negatively associated with the internal communication performance in health and human service agencies.

Another important finding from this study is that managerial support for communication was a positive and significant correlate of information sharing. This result is consistent with the findings of Gottschalk's (2007a, 2007b) studies of police investigation in Norway, which found that decision leadership was associated with investigative performance. Additionally, consistent with the results of Gottschalk's studies, results from this study show that police agencies that had greater access to information and communications technologies were more likely to share information. This finding is consistent with a number of prior studies in the policing literature (Chan, 2001; Chen et al., 2003; Redmond & Baveja, 2002; Sanders & Henderson, 2012).

The study findings imply that several policy measures can be taken to improve the effectiveness of information sharing practices in law enforcement agencies. First, results show that criminal investigators with more experience reported higher levels of information sharing in their agencies. This finding suggests that law enforcement agencies that have more experienced criminal investigators in their investigative units are more likely to share information. Research suggests that law enforcement agencies experience relatively high turnover rates in their investigative units which may inhibit information sharing practices (Lynch & Tuckey, 2008). This turnover may occur for a variety of reasons including investigators requesting that they be transferred to other details due to stress or burnout, investigators being promoted, or investigator transfers to different duties for other reasons. Given this finding, law enforcement agencies can potentially improve their information sharing practices by adopting human resource policies that aimed at retaining and recruiting experienced criminal investigators. For instance, stress management programs, employee incentive programs, or promotion policies can potentially be used or altered to encourage higher retention rates.

Second, this study's findings suggest that law enforcement agencies can improve information sharing by taking measures to increase the degree of managerial support for communication and information sharing. Research shows that command staff who actively encourage criminal investigators to communicate, collaborate, and share information with investigators from other units achieve higher levels of investigative performance (Gottschalk, 2007a, 2007b). For instance, investigators who more actively communicate with their colleagues and counterparts in other organizations are more likely to find leads to their own cases and learn about new developments or innovations in their field that may improve how they conduct their own investigations.

Third, the fact that communications red tape was negatively associated with information sharing suggests that law enforcement agencies can improve their information sharing practices by taking measures to reduce procedural impediments to communication. Slightly more than 50% of investigators reported that they agreed that communication policies in their agencies restricted their communications. Rules and policies concerning communication in law enforcement agencies should be written in a manner that facilitates communication and encourages information sharing, rather than in a manner that impedes it.

Finally, results from a number of studies, including the current study, have shown that developments in IT infrastructure are associated with improved information sharing practices (Chan, 2001; Chen et al., 2003). This important finding suggests that developments in information technology are having a positive impact on the performance of police organizations. This finding supports existing federal and state programs that encourage information technology development in local law enforcement agencies, including COPLINK and information technology grants (e.g., the U.S. Department of Justice's Technology Grants); furthermore, this finding strongly suggests that these programs should be expanded.

## Study Limitations

It is important to note the limitations of this research. First, this study provides only an indirect measure of information technology, which has been shown to be an important factor in explaining information sharing practices in law enforcement agencies in several different nations (Chan, 2001; Chen et al., 2003; Gottschalk, 2007a, 2007b; Redmond & Baveja, 2002; Sanders & Henderson, 2012). Arguably model specification would be stronger if the sample of respondents had been asked whether the use of ICT systems in their agencies had improved information sharing practices. Unfortunately, this information is not available. Despite this limitation the indirect measure of ICT systems that was imported from the LEMAS survey, adds insight to this study which would not have otherwise been provided. Furthermore, the relatively low response rate among investigators that responded to the survey (26%) is another limitation that may impact the representativeness of the sample of data used for this study. Given these noted limitations it is also important to consider that criminal investigators are a difficult population to survey, and that this is merely an exploratory study and a first step toward developing a better understanding of the information sharing practices in local law enforcement agencies in the United States. Nevertheless, insights from this study can serve as a foundation for future studies of this important and understudied topic in policing.

## Conclusion

Although the academic literature has addressed many dimensions of information and intelligence sharing in the law enforcement community (Carter & Carter, 2009; Manning, 1992; Ratcliffe, 2002; Sheptycki, 2004); to date, few studies have directly examined the correlates of information sharing in law enforcement agencies (Garciano & Heaton, 2010; Gottschalk, 2007a, 2007b; Hughes & Jackson, 2004; Lippert & O'Connor, 2006; Sheptycki, 2004). This exploratory study provides a modest first step toward improving our understating of the correlates of information sharing practices in American police organizations. Further research is needed to determine the range of organizational characteristics that either facilitate or impede information sharing practices. Future research can overcome the limitations of the current study by including additional measures of occupational culture, providing more specific measures of information technology, and by including additional measures to determine more specifically the role that leadership plays in information sharing practices.

**Appendix 16.1 Bivariate Correlations Between All Variables**

| Variables | 1 | 2 | 3 | 4 | 5 | 6 | 7 | 8 | 9 |
|---|---|---|---|---|---|---|---|---|---|
| 1. Information sharing performance | 1.00 | | | | | | | | |
| 2. Number of full-time sworn | −0.21 | 1.00 | | | | | | | |
| 3. Number of investigators | −0.09 | 0.58 | 1.00 | | | | | | |
| 4. Years of experience in investigation | 0.18 | −0.10 | −0.04 | 1.00 | | | | | |
| 5. Managerial support for communication | 0.60 | −0.18 | −0.09 | 0.09 | 1.00 | | | | |
| 6. Information sharing attitude | 0.17 | −0.15 | −0.06 | 0.15 | 0.25 | 1.00 | | | |
| 7. Communications red tape | −0.21 | 0.14 | 0.09 | −0.04 | −0.03 | −0.04 | 1.00 | | |
| 8. Information systems red tape | −0.20 | 0.15 | 0.19 | −0.06 | −0.04 | −0.12 | 0.39 | 1.00 | |
| 9. ICT systems | 0.09 | −0.02 | 0.05 | 0.17 | 0.20 | 0.61 | −0.02 | −0.06 | 1.00 |

## Notes

1 Although local police departments have been mandated to report data pertaining to crime incidents it is important to note that not all police departments fully report this information.

2 The FBI's National Incident Based Response System (NIBRS) is a comprehensive incident based reporting system for crimes known to law enforcement authorities. The system collects and reports

a variety of data pertaining to crime incidents brought to the attention of law enforcement authorities including data pertaining to the nature and types of the particular offenses in the incident, characteristics of the offender(s), victim(s), information pertaining to the property stolen, damaged, or recovered, and the characteristics of suspects arrested in connection to the crime incident.

3 Examples of federal technology grant programs for local law enforcement agencies include the COPS Office Technology Imitative Grant Program (TIG) and Urban Area Security Initiative (UASI).

4 DOJ grants funded by the COPS Office including the TIG and UASI programs require grantees to match a portion of the funds for the technology developments. Therefore, more resourceful jurisdictions are better positioned to apply and receive these grants.

5 Stata was used to run the OLS regression analysis. Cameron and Trivedi's decomposition of IM-test indicates that the distribution of the dependent variable had no statistically significant problems with heteroskedasticity, skewness, or kurtosis. The Breusch-Pagan/Cook-Weisberg test further indicated no statistically significant problems with heteroskedasticity.

## References


Acock, A. C. (2008). *A gentle introduction to Stata* (2nd ed.). College Station, TX: Stata Press.

Allen, D. K., Wilson, T. D., Norman, A. W. T., & Knight, C. (2008). Information on the move: The use of mobile information systems by UK police forces. *Information Research, 13*(4).

Bozeman, B. (1993). A theory of government "red tape." *Journal of Public Administration Research and Theory, 3*(3), 273–304.

Bozeman, B. (2000). *Bureaucracy and red tape.* Upper Saddle River, NJ: Prentice Hall.

Bozeman, B., & Kingsley, G. (1998). Risk culture in public and private organizations. *Public Administration Review, 58*(2), 109–118.

Brown, D. (2002). Agency with most need didn't get anthrax data; CDC unaware of Canadian study before attacks. *Washington Post*, November 2.

Cannon, L. (1997). *Official negligence: How Rodney King and the riots changed Los Angeles and the LAPD.* New York: Random House.

Carter, D. L., & Carter, J. G. (2009). Intelligence-led policing: Conceptual and functional considerations for public policy. *Criminal Justice Policy Review, 20*(3).

Carter, J. G. (2008). The intelligence fusion process for state, local, and tribal law enforcement. *Criminal Justice and Behavior, 36*(12), 1323–1339.

Chan, J. B. L. (2001). The technological game: How information technology is transforming police practice. *Criminal Justice, 1*, 139–159.

Chen, H., Zeng, D., Atabakhsh, H., Wyzga, W., & Schroeder, J. (2003). COPLINK: Managing law enforcement data and knowledge. *Communications of the ACM, 46*(1), 28–34.

DeHart-Davis, L., & Pandey, S. K. (2005). Red tape and public employees: Does perceived rule dysfunction alienate managers? *Journal of Public Administration Research and Theory, 15*(1), 133–149.

Dillman, D. A., Smyth, J. D., & Christian, L. M. (2009). *Internet, mail and mixed-mode surveys: The tailored design method* (3rd ed.). Hoboken, NJ: Wiley.

Egger, S. A. (1984). A working definition of serial murder and the reduction of linkage blindness. *Journal of Police Science and Administration, 12*(3), 348–357.

Fisher, J. C., & Mason, R. L. (1981). The analysis of multicollinear data in criminology. *Methods in Quantitative Criminology*, 99–125.

Garciano, L., & Heaton, P. (2010). Information technology, organization, and productivity in the public sector: Evidence from police departments. *Journal of Labor Economics, 28*(1), 167–201.

Garnett, J. (1997). Administrative communication: Domains, threats, and legitimacy. In J. Garnett & A. Kouzmin (Eds.), *The handbook of administrative communication* (pp. 3–20). New York: Marcel Dekker.

Garnett, J., & Kouzmin, A. (2007). Communicating throughout Katrina: Competing and complementary conceptual lenses on crisis communication. *Public Administration Review*, December, 171–188.

Giblin, M. J., Schafer, J. A., & Burruss, G. W. (2009). Homeland security in the heartland: Risk, preparedness, and organizational capacity. *Criminal Justice Policy Review, 20*, 274.

Gottschalk, P. (2007a). Information technology in the value shop: An empirical study of police investigation performance. *International Journal of Information Technology & Decision Making, 6*(4), 751–765.

Gottschalk, P. (2007b). Maturity model for email communication in knowledge organizations: The case of police investigations. *International Journal of Law, Crime and Justice, 36*, 54–66.

Guy, M. E. (1992). Productive work environments. In M. Holzer (Ed.), *The public productivity handbook* (pp. 321–333). New York: Marcel Dekker.

Hughes, V., & Jackson, P. (2004). The influence of technical, social and structural factors on the effective use of information in a policing environment. *European Journal of Knowledge Management, 2*(1), 75–86.

Kettl, D. F. (2006). Managing boundaries in American administration: The collaboration imperative. *Public Administration Review, 66*(1), 10–19.

Langworthy, R. H. (1986). *The structure of police organizations.* New York: Praeger.

Lippert, R., & O'Connor, D. (2006). Security intelligence networks and the transformation of contract private security. *Policing and Society, 16*(1), 50–66.

Luen, T. W., & Al-Hawamdeh, S. (2001). Knowledge management in the public sector: Principles and practices in police work. *Journal of Information Science, 27*(5), 311–318.

Lynch, J. E., & Tuckey, M. (2008). The police turnover problem: Fact or fiction? *Policing: An International Journal of Police Strategies & Management, 31*(1), 6–18.

Manning, P. (1992). Information technologies and the police. In M. Tonry & N. Morris (Eds.), *Modern policing* (Vol. 15, pp. 349–398). Chicago: The University of Chicago Press.

McGarrell, E. F., Freilich, J. D., & Chermak, S. (2007). Intelligence-led policing as a framework for responding to terrorism. *Journal of Contemporary Criminal Justice, 23*(2).

Miller, A. H. (2001). The Los Angeles riots: A study in crisis paralysis. *Journal of Contingencies and Crisis Management, 9*(4), 189–199.

National Commission on Terrorist Attacks Upon the United States. (2004). *The 9/11 commission report.* New York: W.W. Norton & Company.

Pandey, S. K., & Garnett, J. L. (2006). Exploring public sector communication performance: Testing a model and drawing implications. *Public Administration Review, 66*(1), 37–51.

Pandey, S. K., & Kingsley, G. A. (2000). Examining red tape in public and private organizations: Alternative explanations from a social psychological model. *Journal of Public Administration Research and Theory, 10*(4), 779–799.

Pelfrey, W. V., Jr. (2007). Local law enforcement terrorism prevention efforts: A state level case study. *Journal of Criminal Justice, 35*, 313–321.

Pelfrey, W. V. (2009). An exploratory study of local homeland security preparedness: Findings and implications for future assessments. *Criminal Justice Policy Review, 20*, 261.

Ratcliffe, J. H. (2002). Intelligence led policing and the problems of turning rhetoric into practice. *Policing and Society, 12*(1).

Redmond, M., & Baveja, A. (2002). A data-driven software tool for enabling cooperative information sharing among police departments. *European Journal of Operational Research, 141*, 660–678.

Sanders, C. B., & Henderson, S. (2012). Police "empires" and information technologies: Uncovering material and organisational barriers to information sharing in Canadian police services. *Policing and Society: An International Journal of Research and Policy.* doi:10.1080/10439463.2012.703196.

Scott, P. G., & Pandey, S. K. (2000). The influence of red tape on bureaucratic behavior: An experimental simulation. *Journal of Policy Analysis and Management, 19*(4), 615–633.
Sheptycki, J. W. E. (2004). Organizational pathologies in police intelligence systems: Some contributions to the lexicon of intelligence-led policing. *European Journal of Criminology, 1*(3), 307–332.
Wilson, J. Q. (1984). Problems in the creation of adequate criminal justice information systems. In Information Policy and Crime Control Strategies (Ed.), *Bureau of Justice statistics* (pp. 8–11), United States Department of Justice [NCJ 93926].
Zammuto, R. F., & Krakower, J. Y. (1991). Quantitative and qualitative studies of organizational culture. *Research in Organizational Change and Development, 5*(2), 83–114.
Zhao, J. (1996). *Why police organizations change: A study of community-oriented policing.* Washington, DC: Police Executive Research Forum.

# Retention Factors in Relation to Organizational Commitment

# 17

## Empirical Evidence from the Ghana Police Service

GERALD DAPAAH GYAMFI AND JOSHUA OFORI ESSIAM

### Contents

## Abstract

Retention factors have economic implications in the organizational commitment of employees to their organization. The researchers conducted this study using 240 personnel drawn from two divisions of the Ghana Police Service (GPS) from the Greater Accra Region of Ghana and used cross-sectional research design to assess the retention factors that affect organizational commitment of the personnel. The findings revealed that organizational commitment has significant relationships with compensation, and work-life balance. It was indicated that there were no significant relationships between organizational commitment and opportunities for training and development, career opportunities, supervisor support, and job characteristic. The study observed that the female officers were more appreciative of their compensation and were more committed than their male counterparts. Long service experience was significantly related to commitment. It was recommended that more women should be encouraged to join the service.

## Introduction

Organizational commitment, according to Porter, Steers, Mowday, and Boulian (1974) is defined as "the relative strength of an individual's identification with and involvement in a particular organization" (Sholihin & Pike, 2010, p. 395). In policing, organizational commitment is a relationship that determines the extent to which the officers identify themselves with the values and mission of the service and make the effort to pursue the strategic direction of the police service. The managerial support behavior can therefore have an effect on the commitment of the officers. Behaviors such as how the police administration frames and clarifies change, supports the officers with the incentives that boost their morale, allows the officers to make inputs, and provides them with job satisfaction can affect the commitment of the officers. These behavioral factors can serve as retention strategies (Ford & Weissbein, 2003). The attitudes and behaviors are determining factors indicating the extent to which the officers are committed to the police agency.

In this study, the researchers collected data from two divisions of the Ghana Police Service, using cross-sectional research design, to ascertain the relationship between the commitment of the police officers to the service and the factors that ensure the retention of the officers. Factors considered by the researchers included opportunities made available for training and development, compensation, gender, supervisor support, and work-life balance. This study will be of benefit in ensuring improvement in the performance of police officers.

### Problem Statement

Even though research has provided that the level of organizational commitment is generally higher in the police service, as compared to the level of commitment exhibited by employees in many other public organizations such as utility services and hospitals, the level of organizational commitment in the police service decreases with the tenure of police officers (Sholihin & Pike, 2010). It has been found in the police service through an exit interview that individual officers, with the perception that they are not valued, are less committed to the service and are more inclined to leave the service based on some external pressures (Parsons, Kantt, & Coupe, 2011). Many studies on commitment to the police service have centered on some factors such as subordinate-superior relationship (Sholihin & Pike, 2010), promotion, and leadership (Rusu, 2013), while not much research has been done on the relationship between commitment and retention factors such as gender, work-life balance, and tenure of the officers (Dick, 2011). In this study, the researchers looked into these factors that affect the commitment of police personnel in Ghana.

## Literature Review

### Commitment to Organization

Organizational commitment is important to both researchers and practitioners because of its impact on organizational performance. It has influence on employees' job performance, attrition rate, and how organizations adapt to change (Hausknecht, Rodda, & Howard, 2009). Research by Su, Baird, and Blair (2009) in the Australian manufacturing industry, using a simple random sample of 500 managers, indicated that there is a positive relationship between employee organizational commitment and retention factors. The findings revealed that outcome orientations and stability – cultural factors, job satisfaction, perceived support of organization – have a direct relationship with organizational commitment. Another study by Polatci and Cindiloglu (2013) found that the size of an organization and job satisfaction are significantly related to the commitment of employees to their organizations.

The study of organizational commitment helps to clarify and bring understanding of the intensity of employee dedication and stability to continue to work with an organization. The commitment of an employee to an organization can serve as an indicator of that employee's identification with the mission, goals, and the vision of that organization (Keskes, 2014). The commitment to an organization promotes the strong desire of the employees to willingly exert great effort to act for and maintain loyal to the values of that organization. The commitment serves as a driver of an employee remaining or leaving that organization (Shaw, Delery, Jenkins, & Gupta, 1998). Organizational commitment is linked to retention of employees through knowledge sharing, improved organizational citizenship behaviors, and improved performance (Chughtai & Zafar, 2006).

### Organizational Commitment Model

Meyer and Allen (1997) wrote extensively on organizational commitment and asserted that organizational commitment has three components. These are the desire (affective commitment), the need (continuance commitment), and an obligation (normative commitment) to remain steadfast in working with that organization (Keskes, 2014). Meyer and Allen, the proponents of the affective commitment scale, opined that affective commitment involves a love and joy construct that reflects positively or negatively on the commitment of an employee. The proponents proposed a three-component model of organizational commitment based on affective, normative, and continuance factors (Keskes, 2014; Merritt, 2012). These components tend to glue employees to their organizations and have different implications to the behavior of an individual to an organization. All three components tend to relate negatively to employee turnover. Meyer, Stanley, Herscovitch, & Topolnytsky (2002) provide that affective commitment concerns an individual acceptance and the internalized values and goals of the organization that determine their strong emotional attachment to the organization. Rusu (2013) carried out a correlational analysis of the components of organizational commitment using a sample of teachers. The result indicated that the normative component of organizational commitment is about the individuals' perceived obligations to maintain employment based on morality and other principles and the norms of reciprocity. The continuance commitment is based on the assessment made by an employee on personal investment made and the perception of the cost of leaving the organization by that employee (Meyer et al., 2002). This is a type of commitment resulting from the employees' perception that there is a lack of any alternative or desirable employment opportunities available to entice the employee to leave the existing job (Vandenberghe et al., 2007).

## Job Satisfaction

Research has revealed that the retention rate of police patrol officers declines soon after recruitment due to the treatment received from their superiors (Julseth, Ruiz, & Hummer, 2011). In a study of policing, the findings also indicated that the recruits enter the police service highly motivated and committed, but soon after entering the service the motivated and committed attitudes begin to decline swiftly resulting from poor job satisfaction derived (Maanen, 1975). However, another study carried out by Ford and Weissbein (2003) revealed that there was a positive relationship between the commitment of police officers and the job satisfaction derived by the officers from their work behavior. A critical factor that determined job satisfaction was the acceptance of the officers by the external community and the operations of the police administration in providing them the strategic focus and support (Vandenberghe et al., 2007).

## Commitment to Organization

Organizational commitment is important to both researchers and practitioners because of its impact on organizational performance. It has influence on employees' job performance, attrition rate, and how organizations adapt to change (Hausknecht et al., 2009). The study of organizational commitment helps to clarify and bring understanding of the intensity of employee dedication and stability to continue to work with an organization. The commitment of an employee to an organization can serve as an indicator of that employee's identification with the mission, goals, and the vision of that organization (Keskes, 2014). The commitment to an organization expresses the strong desire of an employee to willingly exert great effort to act for and maintain loyal to the values of that organization. The commitment serves as a driver of an employee remaining or leaving that organization (Shaw et al., 1998). Organizational commitment plays an important role in the studying of an organizational behavior and it has a relationship with the attitudes and behavior of the people working in an organization.

## Career Development and Opportunities for Training and Development

Organizational leadership can inspire loyalty by appreciating the need to develop the potential of the workers and encouraging them to think critically about their personal aspirations and the development of the organizations using their abilities. This can create a psychological bond between the officers and the police service (Yasar, Emhan, & Ebere, 2014). The organizational learning climate has significant influence on the commitment of the employees to their organizations. Training and development opportunities help to equip police officers with the requisite knowledge and skills needed to enable them to make effective input into their work. This boosts their morale and increases their commitment to their services. Courtright and Mackey (2004) used the purposive sampling technique to gather data from 633 students of police training institutions on commitment of criminal justice majors to their related occupations in the Northeastern United States. The findings of the research indicate that there is a significant and positive relationship between job commitment, training, and development.

In a related research, organizational commitment was affected by the job-fit to the skills possessed by the workers, flexibility of the work, perceived balance between work and personal life, how employees feel valued as an essential asset to their organizations, and opportunities offered for advancement. The learning climate offered is also a determining factor of affective commitment (Budihardjo, 2013). The incentives provided at the police training institutions and how the instructors carry themselves or their teaching methodology and academic results have effect on the motivation, retention, and commitment of the trainees to the police service (Courtright & Mackey, 2004). The knowledge acquired from the training institutions increases the self-efficacy and boosts the organizational citizenship behavior of the officers (Chen & Kao, 2011). One study found that training had little immediate impact on the lower ranking officers but higher immediate impact on the higher ranking officers of the police agency (Quinet, Nunn, & Kincaid, 2003).

## Compensation

In compensating for the work done by police officers, the physiological, social and psychological factors should all be considered (Rees & Smith, 2008). The incentives that can influence the retention of police officers include high pay and pension payment (Parsons et al., 2011). The working conditions and how the officers learn to live with the conditions also play important roles in the commitment and retention of the officers to the police service (Rees & Smith, 2008).

## Supervisors' Support

Supervisor support plays an important role in employee commitment and retention due to the ability of the function to help achieve a high level of employee morale and motivation and stir the workers to focus on looking beyond their own self-interest to the goal of the collective group (Bakiev, 2013; Keskes, 2014). Studies into supervisors' support through the use of transformational leadership have proven that employees' organizational commitment is higher in situations where the style of leadership encourages participation in the decision-making processes (Walumba, Orwa, Wang, & Lawler, 2005). A study by Yasar et al. (2014) on the relationship between supervisor support and organizational commitment, using a survey of 21 employees from a petroleum corporation in Nigeria, found that effective leadership by supervisors inspires loyalty and enhances the desire of the workers to remain committed to the organizational goals. Research has shown that the commitment levels of police officers who express support for their supervisors and show appreciable interest have an effect on the retention of the officers (Ford & Weissbein, 2003).

## Work-Life Balance

The working climate that is influenced by culture, including the leadership style and reward system, can have an effect on the commitment and retention of officers to the police service. In a related study on commitment to teamwork, it was shown that there is a positive link between quality of working life and affective commitment (Keskes, 2014). The quality of working life is manifested in the form of the nature of trust, employee relationships, and supervisor support. It has been suggested that the relationship between quality working life and commitment is higher among the top police officers than the junior officers (Schirmeister & Limongi-França, 2012). In a study, full-time employees showed high levels of organizational commitment, and part-time employees, who also prefer to have more time to reconcile work and family life, also showed high commitment (Gonzalez Santa Cruz, Lopez-Guzman, & Sanchez Canizares, 2014). The support that is provided for police officers to have a balance between work-life and family life also determines the level of their commitment. For instance, a study in the medical field revealed that the longer amount of time the employees spent at work, the more work-family conflict they encountered (Benligiray & Sonmez, 2012).

## Job Characteristics: Organizational Commitment and Retention

Research into policing has shown that in the police service there is a direct relationship between the commitment of the officers and their retention in the service (Ford & Weissbein, 2003). In its effort to control crime and have zero-tolerance for corruption as a way of reducing social disorder, there is the need for higher autonomy and increased feedback from the community – based on strategies adapted and adopted by the police agency (Green, 2000). Police officers are highly visible to the general public, for instance those who are constantly on foot patrols, bike patrols during the day, and night patrols during the night, become committed to the police service when they experience job satisfaction (both intrinsic and extrinsic) from the police administration and through partnership with the community (Ford & Weissbein, 2003).

The work environment of the service has significant influence on the attitude and retention of the officers. It has also been revealed that organizational commitment can be used as indicators that predict absenteeism, turnover, and tardiness of police officers (Ford & Weisbein, 2003).

## Commitment and Retention: Gender Issues

Kim and Merlo (2010) carried out research on female police officers in Korea to determine the major reasons why women are committed to policing. In the study the researchers interviewed 220 female police officers. The outcome of the study revealed that the female police officers were committed to the police service because they felt they had the ability to do the work. In many countries women are underrepresented in policing and the major factors that contribute to the underrepresentation are women's attrition rate and commitment. Linden (1983) used interviews, questionnaires, and direct observation to gather data from police officers in British Columbia, Canada. The findings revealed that the major factors leading to high attrition of female police officers included the structural characteristics of the service, culture, and interpersonal relationships among the personnel.

A study in the United States by Martin (1989) indicates other factors leading to high attrition rate of female police officers include sexual harassment, pregnancy, and short maternity leave for the women of the service. Female enrollment in policing has improved in our contemporary time; however, retention rates are low due to factors relating to commitment. For instance, in a study done in Australia and New Zealand, the findings indicate that during a particular period the average recruitment rate increased upwards by 33% but the retention rate fell to 26.6% in Australia and 17.1% in New Zealand (Prenzler, Fleming, & King, 2010). Compared to many other professions, there have been some difficulties encountered in promoting and retaining female police officers (Shelley & Morabito, 2011).

## Research Objectives

The main objective of the study was to investigate the relationship between retention factors and organizational commitment in the Ghana Police Service. The specific objectives were:

- to examine the relationship between retention and commitment factors of the personnel to the police service;
- to investigate whether significant differences exist between retention factors and demographic characteristics;
- to find out the relationship between the demographic characteristics of the police personnel and commitment to the service.

## Research Hypotheses

The literature review has demonstrated that generally the commitment level of police officers to the police service/force is low and the low commitment has a significant relationship with retention of the police officers at post. The studies by Kim and Merlo (2010), Linden (1983), Martin (1989), and Shelley and Morabito (2011) indicate higher attrition rates for female police officers than men due to some retention factors in many different parts of the world. The review of literature on commitment and retention factors of police officers gives the impression that not much research has been conducted in Africa on retention factors in relation to organizational commitment of police officers to the police service or force. The lack of literature on retention factors in relation to organizational commitment in Ghana has created a gap and scarcity of empirical work conducted in Ghana (Gyamfi, 2011). Based on the above literature the following hypotheses have been proposed:

H1: Compensation has a significant relationship with organizational commitment.

H2: Opportunity for training and development predicts normative commitment.

H3: There is no significant mean difference between gender and compensation.

H4: There are significant differences between gender and organizational commitment variables.

## Methods

### Research Design

A cross-sectional survey design was used by the researchers to achieve the study objectives (Van Dyk and Coetzee, 2012). The rationale for the use of cross-sectional survey research is that research questions assist researchers in understanding the relationships among the variables at any point and time, and to investigate how the variables of organizational commitment and retention factors relate with one another, even though the design is not capable of assuming causality (Bartlett, Kotrlik, & Higgins, 2001).

### Data Collection Procedure

The researchers applied and they were granted official permission by the office of the Inspector General of Police, Ghana, to conduct the research; participation was entirely voluntary. In line with the principles that govern ethical considerations in research (Delle, 2013), the questionnaires were administered by the researchers at the police stations during the first week of January 2014. It took about one month for the data collection. The researchers gave their telephone numbers to participants for the collection of the data and any further clarification needed for the understanding of the questions. The researchers collected the data at one point in time or whenever the respondents called them for collection (Delle, 2013; Essiam, 2013, Gyamfi, 2012).

### Sample Size and Sampling Technique

Responses from the respondents remained anonymous and confidential. In all, the researchers retrieved a total of 240 questionnaires representing a 62.5% response rate through convenience sampling techniques. The convenience sampling technique was used because of the nature of the work of the police officers which usually involved movements from offices to the community and crime scenes.

### The Organizational Commitment Questionnaire

The Organizational Commitment Questionnaire (OCQ) designed by Meyer and Allen (1997) was adopted by the researchers to measure organizational commitment of the personnel of GPS. OCQ is a multi-factor instrument used for measuring employees' affective commitment (eight items, $\alpha = 0.82$), continuance commitment (seven items, $\alpha = 0.74$), and normative commitment (seven items, $\alpha = 0.83$) (Meyer & Allen, 1997). Responses were made on a 7-point Likert scale (1 – strongly disagree, 2 – disagree, 3 – slightly disagree, 4 – undecided, 5 – slightly agree, 6 – agree, and 7 – strongly agree) and the averages were estimated to yield the composite commitment scores for each respondent (Döckel, Basson, & Coetzee, 2006). The present study also obtained acceptable high internal consistency reliability: affective commitment ($\alpha = 0.87$), continuance commitment ($\alpha = 0.79$), and normative commitment ($\alpha = 0.78$). The Cronbach's Alpha for affective commitment and continuance commitment for the current study was higher than that found by Meyer and Allen (1997).

### The Retention Factor Scale

The present study adopted the Retention Factor Measurement Scale designed by Döckel (2003). The questionnaire was presented in the form of a 5-point Likert scale (1 – strongly disagree, 2 – disagree, 3 – neutral, 4 – agree and 5 – strongly agree). Van Dyk and Coetzee (2012) reported the following Cronbach's Alpha coefficients in their study as a measure of the internal consistency reliability of the instrument: compensation (thirteen items, $\alpha = 0.95$), job characteristics (four items, $\alpha = 0.67$), opportunities for training and development (six items, $\alpha = 0.88$), supervisor support (six items, $\alpha = 0.83$), career opportunities (six items, $\alpha = 0.73$), work-life balance (four items, $\alpha = 0.88$), and commitment to the organization (three items, $\alpha = 0.89$). With regards to the internal consistency reliability of the scale, the present study obtained: compensation ($\alpha = 0.90$), job characteristics ($\alpha = 0.70$), opportunities for training and development ($\alpha = 0.79$), supervisor support ($\alpha = 0.81$), career opportunities ($\alpha = 0.74$), work-life balance ($\alpha = 0.85$), and commitment to the organization ($\alpha = 0.77$).

## Results

### Demographic Characteristics of the Study Respondents

The results of the demographic characteristics of the personnel of GPS that participated in the study showed that, males 197 (69.6%) and females 73 (30.4%) participated in the study. The age ranges from less than 20 years, 2 (0.8%); 20–29 years, 93 (38.8%); 30–39 years, 111 (46.3%); 40–49 years, 27 (11.3%); and 50 and above indicated 7 (2.9%). The married participants were 162 (67.5%). Tenure of the respondents revealed that those who had served in the police service for less than 5 years were 42 (17.5%); 6–10 years were 86 (35.8%); 11–15 years were 44 (18.3%), and more than 15 years were 68 (28.3%). The demographics of the study participants broadly matched that of GPS where, for instance, the male police officers outnumber female police officers.

## Significance of Mean Differences: Gender

An independent t-test performed indicated that men and women differ significantly in their sense of indebtedness to the police service. Findings revealed that the females significantly scored higher than their male counterparts on the normative commitment (M [females] = 4.51; SD = 0.920; M [males] = 4.18, SD = 0.992]). The difference between the males and females on their normative commitment was moderate (t [238] = –2.42, p < 0.05, d = 0.34). Findings on the retention factor scale revealed that there were significant mean differences between men and women and their appreciation for their monetary and non-monetary rewards in return for their work within the GPS. That is, on Compensation, findings showed that the females were more satisfied with their rewards than the males (M [males] = 3.023, SD = 1.005; M [females] = 3.324, SD = 1.114). However, the effect size was practically small (t [238] = 2.06, p = 0.04, d = 0.28). Further findings revealed no significant mean difference between gender and the other Organizational Commitment and Retention variables.

## Mean Ratings of the Organizational Commitments and Retention Factors

Findings from Table 17.1, below, showed that the personnel of the GPS rated affective commitment (M = 5.32, SD = 1.05), indicating their emotional affiliation to the police service was high. Normative commitment was moderately high (M = 4.28, SD = 0.98). The personnel of the GPS rated continuance commitment as moderately high (M = 4.05, SD = 1.03) on the commitment variables. Among the retention factors, the personnel of the GPS rated opportunities for training and development (M = 3.95, SD = 0.56) as high, followed by career opportunities, moderately high (M = 3.55, SD = 0.31), commitment to organization, moderately high (M = 3.48, SD = 0.36), compensation, moderately high (M = 3.11, SD = 1.05), job characteristics, moderately high (M = 3.02, SD = 0.63) and supervisor support, low (M = 2.70, SD = 0.23). Work-life balance (M = 2.6, SD = 0.47) was rated the least among the retention factor variables.

## Inter-Correlation Statistics

Table 17.1 shows that all retention variables correlated positively and significantly with the overall retention factor (RF). Organizational commitment has positive and significantly

**Table 17.1 Inter-Correlation Statistics**

| Variables | Mean | Stand. Dev. | Ret. Factors | Org. Commit. |
|---|---|---|---|---|
| Normative Commitment (OC) | 4.28 | 0.98 | – | – |
| Affective Commitment (OC) | 5.32 | 1.05 | – | – |
| Continuance Commitment (OC) | 4.05 | 1.03 | – | – |
| Compensation (RF) | 3.11 | 1.05 | 0.73*** | 0.15* |
| Opport. for Train. & Dev't (RF) | 3.95 | 0.56 | 0.56*** | n/s |
| Career Opportunities (RF) | 3.55 | 0.31 | 0.15* | n/s |
| Supervisor Support (RF) | 2.70 | 0.32 | 0.20** | n/s |
| Work-Life Balance (RF) | 2.60 | 0.47 | 0.20** | –0.14* |
| Commitment to Organization (OC) | 3.48 | 0.36 | 0.28*** | –0.20* |
| Job Characteristics (OC) | 3.02 | 0.63 | 0.40*** | n/s |

*Notes:* OC, Organizational Commitment; RF, Retention Factors; *P ≤ 0.05; **PT ≤ 0.01; ***P ≤ 0.001.

lower correlations with compensation ($r = 0.15$, $p \leq 0.05$; small practical effect), while work-life balance ($r = -0.14$, $p \leq 0.05$; small practical effect) and commitment to organization ($r = -0.20$, $p \leq 0.05$; small practical effect) correlated negatively and significantly with the organizational commitment variable. Further results revealed that there were no significant relationships between organizational commitment and opportunities for training and development, career opportunities, supervisor support, and job characteristics ($p > 0.05$).

## Multiple Regression Analysis Between Organizational Commitment Variables and Retention Factor Variables

Table 17.2 presents multiple regression analysis between the organizational commitment variables and the retention factor variables. The results indicate that compensation ($\beta = 0.18$, $p \leq 0.001$), commitment to organization ($\beta = -0.18$, $p \leq 0.001$), and work-life balance ($\beta = 15$, $p < 0.05$) significantly predicted the scores in affective commitment. Further findings indicate that compensation, commitment to organization, and work-life balance also explained a small significant variance in the affective commitment ($R^2 = 0.078$, F (3,236) = 7.74, $p \leq 0.001$]. The researchers also observed that opportunities for training and development ($\beta = 0.15$, $p < 0.05$) contributed significantly and positively to the variance in the normative commitment whilst the career opportunities ($\beta = -0.17$, $p < 0.05$) variable contributed significantly and negatively to the variance in the continuance commitment.

## Significant Mean Differences Between Tenure Categories and Organizational Commitment Variables

Table 17.3 reveals ANOVA results of organizational commitment and tenure of the GPS personnel. The researchers observed significant mean differences with very small practical effect in all the variables in organizational commitment and the tenure in the service and that affective commitment (F [3,236] = 5.114, $p = 0.002$, $\eta^2 = 0.08$); normative commitment (F [3,236] = 6.619, $p = 0.000$, $M = 4.63$, $SD = 0.97$, $\eta^2 = 0.06$), and continuance commitment (F [3,236] = 2.667, $p = 0.048$, $M = 4.33$, $SD = 1.02$, $\eta^2 = 0.03$).

## Post-Hoc Tests Analyses Between Tenure Categories and Organizational Commitment Variables

Table 17.3 reveals post-hoc analyses results for organizational commitment variables with tenure categories of the personnel of the GPS. The Tukey Honestly Significant Difference (Tukey HSD) was used for normative commitment Levene's (F [3,236] = 6.62, $p = 0.766$) and affective commitment Levene's (F [3,236] = 5.118, $p = 0.934$) as assumption of homogeneity of variance were met while the Dunnette C test was used to compare tenure and continuance commitment Levene's (F [3,236] = 2.667, $p = 0.048$) as the assumption for equal variance was violated. Given the statistical significance of the omnibus ANOVA F-test, the post-hoc analyses were computed to avoid Type I error in the study findings.

Post-hoc comparison using Tukey HSD procedure to determine which of the four tenure categories means differed in relation to the normative commitment of the GPS

**Table 17.2 Multiple Regression Analysis with Retention Factors as Independent Variables and Organizational Commitment as the Dependent Variables (N = 240)**

| Variable | B | SEB | β | *t* | *p*-Value | | R | Adjusted $R^2$ | F-Value |
|---|---|---|---|---|---|---|---|---|---|
| Affective commitment (constant) | 7.24 | 0.73 | – | 9.90 | 0.000*** | | 0.299 | 0.078 | 7.72 |
| Compensation | 0.18 | 0.06 | 0.18 | 2.86 | 0.001** | | | | |
| Commitment to organization | –0.54 | 0.18 | –0.18 | –2.91 | 0.001** | | | | |
| Work or life balance | –0.24 | 0.14 | –0.15 | –1.63 | 0.007* | | | | |
| Normative commitment (Constant) | 4.71 | 0.99 | – | 4.75 | 0.000*** | | 0.184 | 0.0214 | 2.74 |
| Opportunity for training and development | 0.27 | 0.11 | 0.15 | 2.36 | 0.019* | | | | |
| Commitment to organization | –0.30 | 0.18 | –0.11 | –1.66 | n/s | | | | |
| Job characteristics | –0.03 | 0.10 | –0.02 | –0.27 | n/s | | | | |
| Continuance commitment (constant) | 7.00 | 0.89 | – | 7.90 | 0.000*** | 0.218 | | 0.0354 | 3.92 |
| Career opportunity | –0.55 | 0.20 | –0.17 | –2.74 | 0.007** | | | | |
| Commitment to organization | –0.31 | 0.18 | –0.11 | –1.68 | n/s | | | | |
| Work or life balance | 0.15 | 0.14 | –0.07 | –1.05 | n/s | | | | |

*Notes:* SE, standard error; β, beta; P probability value; t, t test; $R^2$, coefficient of determination; R, correlation coefficient; $R^2 \leq 0.12$ (small practical effect size) +++, $R^2 \leq 0.26$ (large practical effect size) *$P \leq 0.05$; **, $P \leq 0.01$; ***, $P \leq 0.001$.

**Table 17.3 Analysis of Variance – Significant Differences Between Tenure and OC Variables**

| Variables | Tenure | N | Mean | SD | F | *p*-Value | Eta-Squared |
|---|---|---|---|---|---|---|---|
| Normative Commitment (OC) | Fewer than 5 years | 42 | 4.095 | 0.981 | 6.619 | 0.000 | 0.080 |
| | 6–10 years | 86 | 4.004 | 0.948 | | | |
| | 11–15 years | 44 | 4.466 | 0.875 | | | |
| | More than 15 years | 68 | 4.630 | 0.970 | | | |
| Affective Commitment (OC) | Fewer than 5 years | 42 | 5.185 | 1.039 | 5.114 | 0.002 | 0.060 |
| | 6–10 years | 86 | 5.093 | 1.027 | | | |
| | 11–15 years | 44 | 5.275 | 0.938 | | | |
| | More than 15 years | 68 | 5.721 | 1.074 | | | |
| Continuance Commitment (OC) | Fewer than 5 years | 42 | 4.039 | 1.237 | 2.667 | 0.048 | 0.030 |
| | 6–10 years | 86 | 3.867 | 0.959 | | | |
| | 11–15 years | 44 | 4.008 | 0.881 | | | |
| | More than 15 years | 68 | 4.328 | 1.026 | | | |

*Notes:* SD, standard deviation; F, frequency; P, probability value; OC, organizational commitment; $P \leq 0.05$.

personnel. Findings indicated that police personnel who had served less than 5 years (M = 4.10, SD = 0.98) and those who had served for more than 15 years (M = 6.63, SD = 0.97) reported significant mean difference, however, the effect size was negligible. Also, small practical effect size was reported between personnel who had served for 6–10 years (M = 4.00, SD = 0.95) and 11–15 years (M = 4.47, SD = 0.87) in relation to their normative commitment toward the GPS. Conversely, the normative commitment did not differ significantly within the four categories of tenure.

Also, post-hoc test for affective commitment by tenure showed that a negligible but significant mean difference existed between the police personnel who had served less than 5 years (M = 5.19, SD = 1.04) and their senior colleagues who had served for more than 15 years (M = 5.72, SD = 1.07). However, affective commitment did not differ significantly within the tenure categories. Finally, post-hoc analyses for continuance commitment by tenure using Dunnett C test also reported a small practical effect with significant mean difference between police personnel who had served for 11–15 years (M = 4.33, SD = 1.02). Similarly, continuance commitment among the personnel of the GPS did not differ significantly among the tenure categories employed in the study.

## Discussion

The significance of retention factors in relation to organizational commitment cannot be underestimated (Döckel, 2003; Döckel et al., 2006; Van Dyk & Cotezee, 2012). The present study investigated the relationship between the retention factors as documented by Döckel (2003) and the three variables of organizational commitment by Meyer and Allen (1997) in the GPS. The present study reported that compensation, opportunity for training and development, career opportunities, supervisor support, work-life balance, commitment to organization, and job characteristics uniquely predicted the variance in the retention factor variable. The results of the findings indicate that generally the organizational commitment of the personnel to the police service was high (Parsons et al., 2011). Considering the various components of commitment, the affective component of the commitment level rated highest, followed by normative commitment and continuance commitment. This is an indication that the officers have the greatest desire to work for the service in line with the findings of Ford and Weissbein (2003).

However, the relationship between the commitment level and compensation, though positive and significant and supporting the first hypothesis, was low. Nevertheless, the effect of compensation on normative commitment was higher for the female officers than their male counterparts. The result indicates that on the retention factor scale there were significant mean differences between men and women and their appreciation for their monetary and non-monetary rewards in return for their work within the GPS. This finding rejects the third hypothesis that there will be no significant mean differences between gender and compensation. This finding could result from the effect of the Ghanaian culture where the men are considered as the breadwinners of the house and therefore have higher need for compensation than their women counterparts. The female police officers could spend less and save more of their income and that gives them more satisfaction of their compensation than their male counterparts.

The findings also indicate that there was no significant relationship between opportunities for training and development, career opportunities, supervisor support, and job characteristics on normative commitment. This finding does not support the second hypothesis that opportunities for training and development predict normative commitment. The result does not agree with the findings that there is a positive and significant relationship between commitment and training and development (Courtright & Mackey, 2004). This result may be due to the high unemployment rate in Ghana. It was revealed that there is no significant mean difference between gender and the other organization commitment and retention factors (H3 confirmed). The findings also support the fourth hypothesis that there is a significant difference between gender and the organizational commitment variables. The results could be due to police cultures in Ghana as compared to the police cultures in the Western world.

## Conclusion

The present study suggests that a significant relationship exists between the retention factors and organizational commitment at the GPS and therefore provides a number of implications for managers. The researchers observed that the influence of organizational commitment on outcomes varies across career stages especially with regard to tenure in the service. The study revealed that the police officers who had served 15 years and beyond received the highest scores for normative commitment, affective commitment, and continuance commitment to the service. Thus, the present study infers that the police officer's long service experience in the police service is significantly related to their commitment levels.

The study further observed that women significantly scored higher than their male counterparts on the normative commitment variable. Döckel et al. (2006) reported that strong normative commitment involves being tied to the organization by feelings of obligation and duty while Meyer and Allen (1997) also opined that such feelings would motivate individuals to behave appropriately and do what is right for the organization. Therefore, the present study recommends an increase in the number of female police officers among the personnel at GPS so as to see more appropriate behaviors in the service as they progress through the rank and file of the service.

## References

Bakiev, E. (2013). The influence of integrated trust and organizational commitment on perceived organizational performance. *Journal of Applied Economics and Business Research, 2*(3), 166–180.

Bartlett, J. E., Kotrlik, J. W., & Higgins, C. C. (2001, Spring). Organizational research: Determining appropriate sample size in survey research. *Information Technology, Learning, and Performance Journal, 19*(1), 43–50.

Benligiray, S., & Sonmez, H. (2012, October). Analysis of organizational commitment and work-family conflict in new doctors and nurses. *Journal of Human Resource Management, 23*(18), 3890–3905.

Budihardjo, A. (2013). Job satisfaction, affective commitment, learning climate, and organizational effectiveness: A study on sector managers. *Annual International Conference on Business Strategy & Organizational Behavior*, 196–201.

Chen, V. V., & Kao, R. (2011, July). A multi-study on the relationship between work characteristics, self-efficacy, collective efficacy, and organizational citizenship behavior: The case of Taiwanese police duty-exerting organization. *Journal of Psychology, 145*(4), 361–390.

Chughtai, A. A., & Zafar, S. (2006). Antecedents and consequences of organizational commitment among Pakistani University teachers. *Applied H. R. M. Research, 11*(1), 39–64.

Courtright, K. E., & Mackey, D. A. (2004, Fall). Job desirability among criminal justice majors: Exploring relationship between personal characteristics and occupational attractiveness. *Journal of Criminal Justice Education, 15*(2), 311–326. doi:10:1080/10511250040008600l.

Delle, E. (2013). The influence of perception of organizational politics on employee job involvement and turnover intentions: Empirical evidence from Ghanaian organizations. *European Journal of Business and Management, 5*(9), 151–160.

Dick, G. P. M. (2011, June). The influence of managerial and job variables on organizational commitment in the police. *Public Administration, 89*(2), 557–576.

Döckel, A. (2003). The effect of retention factors on organizational commitment: An investigation of high technology employees (Unpublished Master's Thesis), University of Pretoria, Pretoria, South Africa.

Döckel, A., Basson, J. S., & Coetzee, M. (2006). The effect of retention factors on organizational commitment: An investigation of high technology employees. *SA Journal of Human Resource Management/SA Tydskrif vir Menslikehulpbronbestuur, 4*(2), 20–28.

Essiam, J. O. (2013). Service quality and patients' satisfaction with healthcare delivery: Empirical evidence from patients of the outpatient department of a public university hospital in Ghana. *European Journal of Business and Management, 5*(28), 52–59.

Ford, J. K., & Weissbein, D. A. (2003, March). Distinguishing organizational commitment from strategic commitment: Linking officers' commitment to community policing to job behaviors and satisfaction. *Justice Quarterly, 20*(1), 159–185.

Gonzalez Santa Cruz, F., Lopez-Guzman, T., & Sanchez Canizares, S. M. (2014). Job satisfaction and organizational commitment in human resources in the hotel sector of Cordoba: Influence of the type of contract working day. *Intangible Capital, 10*(1), 189–211.

Green, J. R. (2000). Community policing in America: Changing nature, structure, and function of the police. *Criminal Justice, 3*, 299–363.

Gyamfi, G. D. (2011, January). Assessing the effects of industrial unrest on Ghana health service. *International Journal of Nursing and Midwifery, 3*(1), 1–5.

Gyamfi, G. D. (2012). Evaluating the relationship between selection requirements and performance of police in Ghana. *Human Resource Management Research, 1*(1), 1–5. doi:10. 5923/j. hrmr20110101.01.

Hausknecht, J. P., Rodda, J., & Howard, M. J. (2009, May/June). Targeted employee retention: Performance-based and job-related differences in reported reasons for staying. *Journal of Human Resource Management, 48*(2), 269–288.

Julseth, J., Ruiz, J., & Hummer, D. (2011, Autumn). Municipal police officer job satisfaction in Pennsylvania: A study of organizational development in small police departments. *International Journal of Police Science & Management, 13*(3), 243–254.

Keskes, S. (2014). Relationship between leadership styles and dimensions of employee commitment: A critical review and discussion of future directions. *Omniscience, 10*(1), 26–51.

Kim, B., & Merlo, A. (2010). Policing in Korea: Why women choose law enforcement careers. *Journal of Ethnicity in Criminal Justice, 8*(1), 1–17. doi:10.1080/15377930903583046.

Linden, R. (1983). Women in policing: A study of Lower Mainland RCMP. *Canadian Police Journal, 7*(3), 217–229.

Maanen, J. (1975, June). Police socialization: A longitudinal examination of job attitudes in an urban police department. *Administrative Science Quarterly, 20*(2), 207–228.

Martin, S. E. (1989). Women in policing: The eighties and beyond. *Police & Policing: Contemporary Issues*, 3–16.

Merritt, S. (2012, December). The two-factors solution to Allen and Meyer's (1990) affective commitment scale: Effects of negatively worded items. *Journal of Business & Psychology, 27*(4), 421–436.

Meyer, J. P., & Allen, N. J. (1997). *Commitment in the workplace: Theory, research and application.* London: Sage Publications.

Meyer, J. P, Stanley, D. J., Herscovitch, L., & Topolnytsky, L. (2002). Affective, continuance, and normative commitment to the organization: A meta-analysis of antecedent, correlations, and consequences. *Journal of Vocational Behavior, 61*, 20–52.

Parsons, A. R., Kantt, P., & Coupe, J. (2011, March). Effective policing: Management influence and the commitment of senior police personnel. *Policing & Society, 21*(1), 1–26.

Polatci, S., & Cindiloglu, M. (2013). Effect of person-organization fit on organizational citizenship behavior: Mediating affective commitment. *Demivel University Journal of Faculty of Economics and Administrative Science, 13*(3), 299–313.

Porter, L. W., Steers, R. M., Mowday, R. T., & Boulian, P. V. (1974). Organizational commitment, job satisfaction, and turnover among psychiatric technicians. *Journal of Applied Psychology, 59*(5), 603.

Prenzler, T., Fleming, J., & King, A. L. (2010, Winter). Gender equity in Australia and New Zealand. *International Journal of Police Service Management, 12*(4), 584–595.

Quinet, K., Nunn, S., & Kincaid, N. C. (2003, September). Training police: A case study of differential impacts of problem-oriented police training. *Police Practice & Research, 4*(3), 263–284.

Rees, B., & Smith, J. (2008, Autumn). Breaking the silence: The traumatic circle of policing. *International Journal of Police Science & Management, 10*(3), 207–279.

Rusu, K. (2013). Organizational commitment and job satisfaction. *Buletin Stiintific, 18*(1), 52–55.

Schirmeister, R., & Limongi-França, A. C. (2012, December). The quality of life at work: Relationship with organizational commitment in teams of several forms of employment contract. *Revista Psicologia Organizacoose Trabalho, 12*(3), 283–298.

Shaw, J. D., Delery, J. E., Jenkins, G. D., & Gupta, N. (1998). An organization-level analysis of voluntary and involuntary turnover. *Academy of Management Journal, 41*(5), 511–525.

Shelley, T. O., & Morabito, T. J. (2011). Gendered institutions and gender roles: Understanding the experience of women in policing. *Criminal Justice Studies, 24*(4), 351–367.

Sholihin, M., & Pike, R. (2010). Organizational commitment in the police service: Exploring the effects of performance measures, procedural justice, and interpretational trust. *Financial Accountability & Management, 26*(4), 392–421.

Su, S., Baird, K., & Blair, B. (2009, December). Employee commitment: The influence of cultural and organizational factors in the Australian manufacturing industry. *The International Journal of Human Resource Management, 20*(12), 2494–2516.

Vandenberghe, C., Michon, R., Transbley, M., Bentein, K., Chebat, J. C., & Fils, J. F. (2007). An examination of the role of perceived support and employee commitment in employee-customer encounters. *Journal of Applied Psychology, 92*(4), 1177–1187.

Van Dyk, J., & Coetzee, M. (2012). Retention factors in relation to organisational commitment in medical and information technology services. *SA Journal of Human Resource Management/SA Tydskrif vir Menslikehulpbronbestuur, 10*(2), 433. doi:org/10.4102/sajhrm.v10i2.433.

Walumba, F. O., Orwa, B., Wang, P., & Lawler, J. J. (2005). Transformational leadership, organizational commitment, and job satisfaction: A comparative study of Kenyan and United States financial firms. *Human Resource Development Quarterly, 16*(2), 235–256.

Yasar, M. F., Emhan, A., & Ebere, P. (2014, March). Analysis of organizational justice, supervisor support and organizational commitment: A case of energy sector in Nigeria. *Journal of Business Studies Quarterly, 5*(3), 37–46.

# Safety Management *and* Performance-Based Management – an Excellent Match

# 18

PAUL VAN MUSSCHER AND PETER VERSTEEGH

## Contents

## Abstract

The authors have developed an innovative management model that fits in with the new vision of the Haaglanden Police Service of effective policing. This police service vision especially contains the ingredients of problem-oriented policing that have proven effective, information-driven policing and citizen participation: 'The Best of Three Worlds'. The management model is intended to get from policy to implementation and consists of three connected elements: the police vision, a corresponding management cycle and reputation management. In this model, performance-based management and safety management form an integral whole. The legitimate wishes and expectations of citizens play a central part. One of the main conditions is good leadership. Even though the safety strategy the police have chosen has been proven to be effective, police information is reliable, valid and current, safety intelligence and analyses are of high quality, police chiefs who only aim for measurable performance figures will not prove to be effective police chiefs.

## Introduction

Let's just keep it simple. New York: 8 million residents, one police force. London: 7 million residents, one police force. Tokyo: 13 million residents, one police force. Paris: 9 million residents, one police force. The Netherlands: 17 million residents, 26 police forces. Not even that long ago – before 1993 – the Netherlands with its 16 million residents even had over 60 police forces: one national police force and about 60 municipal police forces. So many different police forces results in very many different information systems, many support services in the field of personnel and finances, many differently trained staff members, many different police cars, and so on and so forth ad infinitum. And, of course, very many coordination and cooperation problems.

A single national police force can therefore be nothing but a big step in the direction of a more efficient as well as effective policing. The transition from 26 police forces to one national police force is an unprecedented reorganization. Such a huge reorganization has never taken place before in the Netherlands and compels a lot of respect. In spite of this, there are concerns about whether the National Police will indeed provide the policing the citizens are waiting for. Will the main safety problems – especially those at local level – be tackled with priority? This is a legitimate question and perhaps a legitimate concern as well. Policing geared to the wishes and expectations of citizens does not only require an adequate structuring of the police organization and a clear view of the performance of duties (KNP, 2012). An appropriate model of management of the police work itself, in which an explicit role is given to the wishes of citizens, is certainly indispensable in such a large police organization. Fortunately, a lot of experience has been gained in recent years in the management of the police – and of other non-profit organizations – at home and abroad. Knowledge that can be used very well in the years to come.

In anticipation of the start of the National Police, the Haaglanden Police Service has already begun to set up an innovative management model in keeping with its new vision of effective policing. This police vision especially contains the ingredients of problem-oriented policing that have proven effective, intelligence-led policing and community-oriented policing (Versteegh et al., 2010, 2012). In this chapter, we reveal our ideas about how this vision can be converted into the actual performance of effective police work, namely by a combination of performance-based management and safety management attuned to the vision, by reputation management and supported by an adequate provision of information.

## Effects of Supervision and Control

The Dutch government frequently experimented in the last decade with forms of management derived from the business world. A better 'product' was expected to be delivered for less money with so-called 'New Public Management', in which the management model of the private sector was applied to the public sector. Meanwhile, a lot has been written about the pros and cons of performance and result-based management. In this chapter, we will deal mainly with three recent studies.

## COMPSTAT

The forerunner in the field of number-based management by local government is undoubtedly New York City in the United States (Eterno and Silverman, 2012). Although COMPSTAT was presumably the best known, there are also numerous other municipal services in New York that, under the heading 'smart governance', manage the performance of work by using statistical number sequences. We, however, limit ourselves here to the New York police, the New York City Police Department (NYPD). COMPSTAT is undoubtedly one of the major police innovations of the past decades (Silverman, 1999). There is no misunderstanding about this. 'Accurate and timely intelligence, effective tactics, rapid deployment, and relentless follow-up and assessment' have undoubtedly made New York City safer in the last few years. The uninterrupted decrease in so-called *index crimes* in the period 1990–2009 by as much as 78 per cent nevertheless gives rise to questions, also about the management of the police force.

Very recent research by Eterno and Silverman (2012) shows that in New York City in the last few years, there were – presumably unintended but – very harmful effects due to very rigorous management by the precinct commanders of the police chiefs ('blaming and shaming') during the weekly COMPSTAT meetings. If the agreed results – namely a decrease in index crimes compared to the year before – were not achieved, the local police chiefs were fired. There were also numerous random arrests and citations in the city without any account being taken of the citizens' wishes. The number of times that searches on suspicion were conducted ('stop-and-frisks') increased from about 100,000 in 1992 to as many as 600,000 in 2009, whereas crime decreased by almost 80 per cent in that period. Stop-and-frisks were conducted mostly in deprived areas. In 85 per cent of the cases, the citizen concerned subsequently proved to be innocent. It also appeared that under pressure from the rigorous number-based management, there was systematic manipulation of crime figures (downgrading and refusing reports of crimes). The huge decrease in crimes such as rape, assault and use of weapons could not be found in other sources of information of, for example, the hospitals. The visible, bad example of police managers led to increased corruption in the workplace. The psychological pressure exerted by management allegedly resulted in a culture of secrecy and cynicism in the workplace. There was also apparently undue influencing of the media by manipulating reports. In conclusion: time and time again, the authors let no misunderstanding exist about this. From its origin, COMPSTAT has been extremely promising and praiseworthy as a safety strategy. The management model of the NYPD, however, was derailed by extremely rigorous management by the senior management whereby local police officers were required to improve the figures year after year. Silverman: 'The name of the game is LOOK GOOD, year after year.'

## Organizing Counterforce

In our own country, the research report '*Tegenkracht organiseren*' (Organizing Counterforce) by the Netherlands Council for Social Development (RMO, 2011) was recently published, in which the flaws in purely number-based performance-based management in social sectors is discussed. Although the report mainly deals with examples from the financial world, education, care and welfare, lessons can also be learned in relation to safety assurance and the police. In performance-based management, good intentions can turn out wrong, according to the RMO. Usually, the initial intention is to improve the performance of one's own organization so it can be used to optimize social output. Over the course of time, productive working methods can, however, transform into working methods with perverse effects. In that case, one loses sight of the original targets. The use of classifications often results in a simplification of the reality on which management is subsequently based. The same pattern reoccurs time after time. The first step is that of *abstraction*. While there are multiple interests in every (large) organization, simplification occurs for the purpose of comparison by looking at quantity instead of quality. In the second step, a selection is then made of targets that *dominate* the others. These are often interests that are the most visible and easily measurable. If one or a few interests dominate, the multiplicity of interests comes under pressure, resulting in a reduction of the available room for opposition and capacity for criticism. The path is then clear for the third step: *strategic action*. People adapt their behaviour to the forces exerted on them by, for example, managers and executives who want to achieve the agreed targets. If financial incentives are linked to the targets, this can strengthen the process. But, remarkably enough, in the practice of performance-based management, most of the pressure comes from co-workers and competitors, who also act strategically. This pattern from abstraction through domination to strategic action is accompanied by *reflectivity*. Reflectivity means that social systems can look at themselves and as a rule respond to new input. According to the RMO, this also means that actors in such systems constantly attribute meaning to reality and adjust their behaviour accordingly. If reality is abstracted to a single interest, the tools and working methods chosen can indeed elicit strategic behaviour.

## The Best of Three Worlds

In conclusion, we briefly discuss the study by the Haaglanden Police of the special development of reported crime in the period 2002–2008: *The Best of Three Worlds* (Versteegh et al., 2010). After a substantial decrease in the number of reports of crime in the first period 2002–2006, there was an increase in the second period 2006–2008. In the study, the possible effects of performance-based management were also examined. It seems plausible that the decrease in crime in the first period can largely be ascribed to the general increase in the chance of being caught through firm performance-based management to increase the number of 'crime suspects sent to the Public Prosecution Service' and the number of times persons are 'stopped and questioned' after a misdemeanor.

The general awareness of this provided in the initial years of the Police Agreement presumably contributed to a higher expected chance of being caught, which may have caused many potential perpetrators to refrain from criminal behaviour. The strong focus on a repressive approach to the usually addicted repeat offenders, with the accompanying custody effects, must have played an important part. According to the authors, the increase in reported crime in the period 2006–2008 could, on the one hand, presumably be ascribed to a change in the problems. While the first group of former repeat offenders returned to society, a stubborn group of 'new' repeat offenders arose in the meantime: young adults, not addicted and usually Moroccan Dutch or from Eastern Europe in particular. The regular approach to repeat offenders was not in keeping with this new target group. In many cases, the new repeat offender did not satisfy the customary definition of repeat offender (a criminal record of more than ten offenses in the past five years) and therefore did not count. On the other hand, the effect of performance-based management seems to have lost its force. A certain 'disappearance of benefits-effect' occurred. The chance of being caught decreased, as well as the clearance rates and the suspect ratios. For the rest – as in the NYPD – researchers did not find any significant perverse effects at the Haaglanden Police. The pressure exerted by the management could therefore presumably not be compared to the pressure exerted on the local police chiefs in America.

The main lessons that can be learned from the above-mentioned reports are:

- Policing should be tuned to the local circumstances and the wishes and expectations of citizens ('Community Partnership').
- The measurable performance indicators should relate to (the approach to) the underlying problems.
- Performance-based management should always deal with quantity and quality.
- Too much pressure to perform has undesired effects.
- There should always be counter-pressure and opposition, in and outside the organization.
- Information on crime and nuisance should be absolutely valid, reliable and as up-to-date as possible.
- Provide for a great degree of transparency.
- Do not only aim for a decrease in unsafety and nuisance compared to the last year.

- Combine performance-based management (*top down*) with safety management (*bottom up*).
- Good leadership is of decisive importance.

## Management Model

Given the experience gained in the past few years, we are of the opinion that the effectiveness of performance-based management will be considerably increased and, at the same time, the chance of perverse effects will be considerably decreased if performance-based management is combined with safety management. The Haaglanden Police Service believes that in tackling crime and danger, there should be a coordinated combination of problem-oriented policing, intelligence-led policing and community-oriented policing.

Practice, however, has taught that converting a convincing and credible strategy into actual performance of police work is not simple and is certainly not a matter of course. To get from policy to performance, we have developed a management model for the police in which we combine our police vision with a corresponding management cycle. Because it is very important for citizens to have realistic expectations of the police, we have included reputation management as the third component in our model. The three elements of the model are interrelated.

The first element – the force vision – is about the police we want to be, now and in the future. A police organization that is equipped to serve society and to effectively tackle the most urgent problems in relation to crime and unsafety. The second element – the management cycle – is about managing policing. It is intended to enable policing to actually tackle the most urgent problems and thereby fulfil the justified wishes and expectations of society. The third element – reputation management – is about really letting society know, see and perceive that the police are doing the right things in the right way. Together, the different aspects of policing summed up in the three elements of our model are also considered a checklist. A police organization that provide for these aspects makes a maximum contribution to safety in society and will also be able to count on the citizens' trust.

## Police Vision: From Policy to Performance

When it comes to the desired performance of police duties – the police vision – we make a distinction between Principles and Orientation. Principles are the starting points that apply to working on Safety & Trust, the general objectives of the police. We make a distinction as well between a substantive side and a procedural side. In Orientation, we distinguish exogenous orientation (from outside to inside) from endogenous orientation (from inside to outside). This forms a quadrant with four dimensions – clockwise: safety policy, performance, management and leadership. See Figure 18.1.

### Safety Policy

In a democracy based on the rule of law, it is not possible for the police to set their own course. The police perform their duties subordinate to the competent authority and within

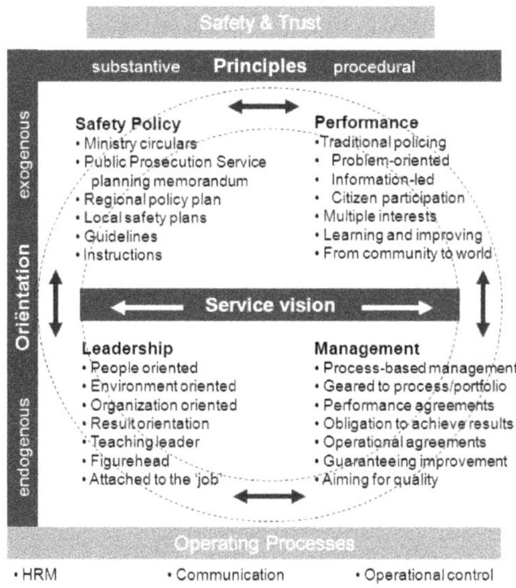


**Figure 18.1** Police Vision: From Policy to Performance.

the agreements set out in various policy plans, guidelines and instructions. That means that the police are not authorized to determine on their own which safety problems will be tackled with priority. A distinction can be made between national, regional and local safety policy. In this context, there are two types of subordination: the lower geographic level is always subordinate to the higher geographic level. For instance, the police have to adhere to various guidelines and agreements set out in the national safety plan, circulars from the Ministry and letters from the Minister. The tackling of national priorities undoubtedly has an effect at regional and local level. The Regional Board determines the long-term policy plan, which contains the regional priorities. The municipalities have a local safety programme in which agreements are made on the tackling of the main local safety problems.

## Performance

With that, we come to the performance by the police of their duties. We want to be very clear about this. The main duties of the police are and will remain to track down criminals and enforce laws, maintain public order and provide emergency assistance. The police are there if a citizen needs the police. This is the traditional police work citizens expect of the police (Berghuis and De Waard, 2011). The difference from before is, however, that the 'remaining' patrol time is no longer filled with unfocused preventive patrolling or more, untargeted 'blue' on the streets. This has proven ineffective, whereas what citizens really want is effective police (Intomart GfK, 2007). That is why we put better blue on the streets. This means that police work will be performed on the basis of 'evidence based policing': safety strategies that have proven effective on the basis of research. The most recent studies show that the tackling of safety problems should always expressly involve the environment of the police. The police are hardly ever able to do it alone. This smoothly creates an exogenous orientation: from outside to inside.

This should focus on the main problems, namely national priorities – insofar as relevant to the geographic area – and local priorities. At the local level, if possible, supralocal or even national if necessary: from the community to the world. Such a problem-oriented approach means that actions are especially focused on concentrations of problems: the hot crimes and hot disorders, hot spots and hot areas, hot shots and hot groups, and those structural improvements are always made in the area where the safety problem originated. The 80–20 rule is followed in this regard: 20 per cent of the causes provide for 80 per cent of the consequences (Koch, 1997). We can find out what the causes are by using tactical problem analyses. In this context, a director's role for the municipalities and cooperation with other organizations, authorities, entrepreneurs and citizens are extremely important conditions.

For the purposes of such a problem-oriented approach, the police are neighbourhood-based with robust base teams, and organized close to the citizens. Precisely because safety problems always arise outside the police organization, in seeking sustainable solutions, the police look beyond the boundaries of their own organization. Problem-oriented policing and networking make it possible to take account of the interests of everyone involved. The intensive involvement of various organizations and organizational units results in continuous alertness to the multiplicity of interests and automatically leads to the desired reflexivity. Safety partners keep one another alert.

## Management

For proper implementation of the adopted safety policy, of course, a police organization is needed that has its affairs in order, which is a matter of good management. This means that important processes – intake, emergency assistance, enforcement, investigation, information and intelligence – are structured according to the nationally agreed upon qualitative standards. Combining problem-oriented policing, intelligence-led policing and community-oriented policing and creating the organizational preconditions needed for this in order to keep the agreed performance and result agreements, are also a matter of good management. Performance (output) means the activities, products and services for which only the police can be held responsible. Results (outcome) refers to the desired effects of the integrated approach in society. All organizations, authorities and persons involved are naturally responsible for the results. If there is an orientation to the most urgent (local) safety problems, this is precisely where performance-based management and safety management come together. Reflexivity can be achieved by aiming to improve quality, guaranteeing desired improvements in the organization as well as improving operational agreements. Aiming at quality results in orientation to the operations, and the manager and those he/she manages will enter into discussions about the professional performance of police work; naturally in light of the desired results. If this does not make things safer – even with the best of intentions – something has nevertheless gone wrong. With this, we automatically come to the issue of leadership.

## Leadership

The management model described here sets high requirements on leadership within the police. These are police managers who implement the adopted policy, and in doing so place themselves at the service of the officers on the beat, and are able to unite the desired approach with their management duties. A police manager takes the lead and – together, with the community police officer, constitutes the so-called 'figurehead role' of the local, area-based police organization. By working together and networking, the police manager continuously seeks a connection with society. By knowing what is going on in his/her own work territory and, of course, across the borders as well, the police manager makes room for professionalism. By taking the lead in operations and showing great interest in what is going on in the community and among the workers, the manager will be outstandingly able to anticipate major developments. He/she must also show courage and respond with alertness. The police manager is always searching for working methods and especially uses innovative (evidence-based) knowledge and experience gained elsewhere and does not try to reinvent the wheel time and time again – to his/her own honour and glory. The police manager also links safety management to performance-based management, with an eye for unintended management effects, and organizes opposition in order to remain connected with the surroundings. Operating processes are geared to the operation. The police manager has an eye for the work environment and wellbeing of the employees as the most important condition for arriving at effective safety assurance. Lastly, the police manager is a role model and manages him/herself.

### Supporting Operating Processes

It is self-evident that effective safety assurance benefits from good support by the operations. This concerns the production of operational products such as a service model, articulation of questions, accommodations and quality assurance. It is clear that each of these products can make their own important contribution – also at local level – to effective policing and to safety and citizens' trust in the police. In spite of this, we will not deal further with these national processes. We will, however, discuss the processes that will be placed with regional and national units: HRM, communications and operational control. Each of these support services will be discussed separately in the following.

## Management Cycle: Performance-Based Management *and* Safety Management

The above-mentioned operational control is intended to keep the day-to-day work of police officers, from management to policing, in line with the agreed upon safety policy, safety programmes and agreed performance and result agreements. Using a management cycle in managing the police organization as a whole connects the different dimensions of the police vision on safety assurance and in that way steers and keeps the organization as a whole in the desired direction. See Figure 18.2 for a schematic representation.

Quantitative performance gets together with qualitative performance-based management if the underlying police vision, the manner in which it is performed, management and leadership are discussed as well. Experience is now being gained with this hybrid management cycle in the Haaglanden region. Because a distinction is made on the one hand between vertical and horizontal management, and on the other (once again) between endogenous and exogenous orientation, the following four related dimensions can be distinguished: police

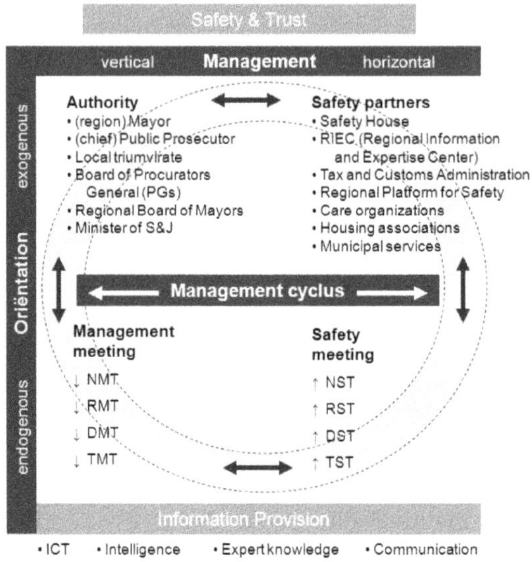


**Figure 18.2** Management Cycle: Performance and Safety Management.

authority and management meetings, safety partners and safety meetings. The two management cycles in this hybrid management model can be distinguished, but not separated. These are, respectively, performance-based management and safety management. They form one cohesive whole. The characteristic distinction is that (traditional) performance-based management takes place from the top down, while safety management runs from the bottom up. In this way, policy and performance are brought together.

## Police Authority

In performance-based management, there is accountability to the police authority for the tackling of crime and unsafety. No guidelines are included for the structure of the management consultations in the new police regions in the bill for the formation of the National Police. The regional mayor has the discretion to give shape to these management consultations, together with the other mayors and the Public Prosecutor. In the bill, there are three organizational levels: (1) the police force as a whole, (2) the national unit and regional units containing (3) territorial units (district and base teams). Each level has his own local triumvirate.

## Management Meetings

Within the police, there is vertical performance-based management by the National Management Team (NMT), Regional Management Team (RMT), District Management Teams (DMTs) and Team Management Teams (TMTs). In performance-based management (*planning and control*), looking back, the performance and result agreements made in the various policy plans took a central place. In our management model, in the management meetings and Management Reports, not only the quantitative targets come up for discussion, but reports are made as well on the (problem-oriented) tackling of the main safety problems, the production and use of intelligence and crime analyses, cooperation with safety partners as well as the way in which citizens and entrepreneurs are involved in tackling these problems. In this way, performance-based management is mixed with aspects of safety management. Each report is accompanied by an appropriate strategic assessment of local crime and safety, the Crime & Safety Area Scan.

## Safety Partners

Performance-based management is about keeping agreements made with others on the basis of a joint analysis of the problems, which is set out in a joint action plan. Performance is managed and accounted for both vertically and horizontally. Account for the tackling of problems and the results are rendered not only to the above-mentioned police authority, but also to the safety partners, including citizens, entrepreneurs and social organizations. This creates a horizontal effect. Safety partners call one another to account for keeping agreements made.

## Safety Consultations

Compared to performance-based management, safety management runs in the opposite direction bottom up, starting with the main safety problems in the districts and neighbourhoods of the region. Safety consultations deal with the safety problems that most seriously impair safety and quality of life, and which citizens expect to be tackled with priority. These are often national priorities as well (such as home burglaries), but they can also be other problems (such as theft from cars or illegal parking). When these local priorities and their tackling are included in the performance indicators, safety management is mixed with performance-based management. The safety strategy chosen in safety management is naturally of fundamental importance. In the Safety Teams problem-oriented tackling of the main *hot crimes, hot disorders, hot spots, hot shots* and *hot groups* takes a central place. Area scans give a view of these *hot problems*. Identification and advice are provided to the police authority through the performance-based management line (TMT or DMT). This creates the desired situation that in problem-oriented tackling, by way of top-down management, the police officers on the beat, e.g. community police officers, come in contact with professionals from other organizations who know in advance that their own organizations will support them. This can close the gap between policy and performance. Policy does not stand in the way of performance, but actually enhances it. Supralocal problems are tackled at district, unit or national level and are brought up for discussion, insofar as relevant, in all Safety Meetings.

In the Safety Meetings the problem-oriented tackling of the main safety problems and the (other) successful operations achieved take a central place. Based on the operations of the police chief concerned, the safety situation and relevant approach are discussed against the background of current developments in crime (last week, last four weeks and since 1 January of this year). This way of monitoring we have copied from the NYPD. The discussion is about policy-related aspects, the safety strategies followed, the (problem-oriented) approach, management and the leadership role. See the questions in Box 18.1 below. It is self-evident that the attainments and results achieved, or not, will also be discussed in the safety meetings. Nevertheless, the safety meetings may expressly not be considered a time for hierarchical management. Hierarchical management takes place along the vertical line of police authority in management meetings. The emphasis in horizontal safety meetings is on cooperation. Police managers are given the professional room to discuss together how the main safety problems are being or can be tackled as effectively as possible on the different geographical levels.

**Box 18.1 Some Relevant Questions in Safety Management**

| | |
|---|---|
| Policy | 1. Has an Area Scan been made? What points for attention were discussed with the police authority? What was agreed upon? What is the relationship between national priorities and local priorities? Has the police authority assumed a director's role in tackling them? Has a project group been formed? |
| Performance | 2. Has a problem analysis been made together with the partners? Why is there a persistent/acute problem? Has attention been paid to offenders, victims, environmental and occasional factors? Who has influence? |
| Management | 3. Has an action plan been made together with the partners in case of a persistent problem? What agreements have been made? What measures will be taken and by whom? What costs will be incurred? Is there a budget? |
| Leadership | 4. How will citizens/entrepreneurs be involved? How will the chance of being caught in the act be increased? Will citizens be used as role models? |
| | 5. What results have meanwhile been achieved? What has fundamentally changed as a result of the approach? Will there be an evaluation? |
| | 6. What kind of internal and external communication is there about the approach? How are the local residents/entrepreneurs informed? |

### Provision of Support

Policing according to the principles of problem-oriented policing, intelligence-led policing and community-oriented policing set high requirements on the operations and the support services and products. It would be going much too far to deal with this in detail. We limit ourselves by stating that the services and products which we believe are decisive in this context, namely those having to do with the provision of supporting information, are: ICT, analysis and communication.

## Reputation Management

For effective police work, the connection the police make with society is of exceptionally great importance. A good relationship between society and the police benefits from

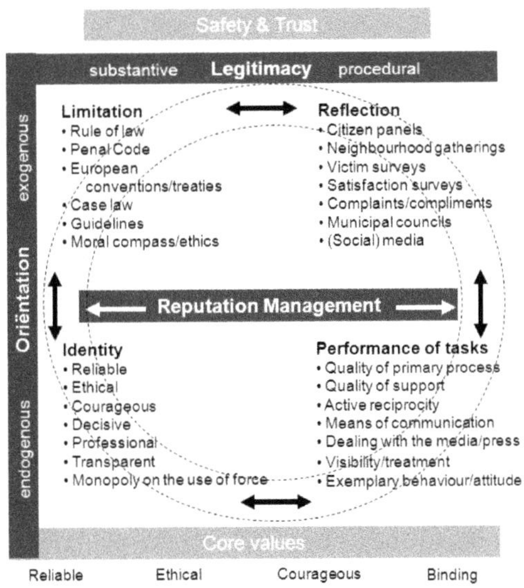


**Figure 18.3** Reputation Management: Performance of Tasks and Reflection.

citizens and other safety partners knowing well what they may and can expect from the police. In this context, we now call this 'reputation management'. It is clear that good reputation management plays an extremely important part in the above-mentioned police vision and in aiming for it. In reputation management, we once again distinguish endogenous and exogenous orientation. In addition, we use the term legitimacy in this context.

Legitimacy is even above authority and is about citizens' trust in police that take sufficient account of their legitimate wishes and expectations. Police who are not adequately able to guarantee safety in society will therefore lose their legitimacy and right to exist (Van Dijk et al., 2011). The police will lose the trust of the citizens if they are not effective enough, whereas citizens trust in the police as a condition for effective policing. In this way safety and trust affect each other and legitimacy is the key concept. By dividing legitimacy into a substantive and procedural side, combined with the two orientations, the four dimensions arise: identity, limitation, reflection and performance of tasks. See Figure 18.3 for a schematic representation. We go through the four dimensions again, starting with identity.

## Identity

Reputation management has everything to do with the manner in which the police are able to bring their appealing qualities to the attention of society. Identity concerns the question of the kind of police the citizens want us to be: reliable, ethical, courageous and binding. Police close to the citizens and who know what is going on decisively help to solve problems. Police who are successful in fighting crime through active cooperation with others. Police who stand up for the interests of well-meaning citizens. Without shortchanging other police officers, the view of the quality of the organization is largely determined by the police officers with the positions that stand out: police managers *and* community police officers. Policy and performance come together in these police officers. In the teaching of leadership programmes and courses for community police officers, a lot of attention needs to be paid to this aspect. Another important characteristic of police identity is transparency. Everyone may see, to the extent the law allows, the way in which the police work and achieve results. This is also allowed in the case of an organization entrusted with a monopoly on the use of force. One reservation needs to be made: we will, of course, never disclose our tactics and methodology particularly in relation to investigation, but we do guarantee that they will always be used within the limits of laws and regulations.

## Performance of Tasks

The stringent requirements set on the identity of the police recur as a matter of course in the performance of the tasks of the police. In both the primary process and support we have to meet stringent quality requirements. For instance, in order to gain trust in performing our tasks, there has to be active reciprocity. In relation to, for example the provision of information after a report of victimization, and reporting back if the citizen has had contact with the police in a different way (e.g. after reporting a criminal caught in the act) a world can still be gained. Lastly, the quality of the communication is, of course, tremendously important. With the present means of communication, including social media and the internet, there are very many possibilities to give citizens custom information about the safety in their own living or working environment, to advise them about what citizens can do on their own to improve their safety situation, and to allow citizens to take an active part in improving their own safety situations. Very recent research has shown that the provision of information to citizens on the internet by using crime maps with information on the local police and crime prevention has had very positive effects on the satisfaction with and trust in the police. A major research finding was that the information did not increase the feelings of a lack of safety, but the reverse. In most criminal districts and among victims, the provision of information gave the citizens concerned more reassurance (Quinton, 2011). Another possibility for communication is to consult citizens about the main safety problems in their district or neighbourhood. With that, we come to the third dimension of reputation management, perhaps the most important: reflection.

## Reflection

In the current police vision, though in close cooperation with other organizations and especially with citizens and entrepreneurs, reflexivity is embedded. Organizing counterforce and opposition is an important characteristic of a police organization that develops along with the society of which it is a part. By way of neighbourhood panels and satisfaction surveys, citizens are periodically offered the opportunity to hold up a mirror to the police regarding the performance of their tasks, the choices made, the problems tackled and the manner in which this is done. Also during the neighbourhood meetings, which are organized according to need, e.g. on hot spots, citizens can indicate whether the police are on the right path. Citizens can, of course, always contact the police for complaints – and compliments. The periodic meetings in which the local administration – in the person of the mayor – account to the municipal council for the performance by the police of their tasks and the choices made, are also important times to find out whether the police are on the right track and meet the wishes and expectations of the citizens and the political administration. Lastly, articles, letters, reports and messages in the (social) media about the police, about policing and about events that affect the police, can be considered important feedback from our main allies – the citizens – on the police organization. From the viewpoint of reflection, it is therefore extremely important for the police to closely follow the reports in the media.

### Limitations

These wishes and expectations of the citizens should, however, be realistic. With that, we come to the last dimension of reputation management, limitation. Citizens may well expect a lot of the police, but the police, as part of a democracy under the rule of law, must indeed adhere to the law, to the Rule of Law. This means that the work of the police is limited by laws and regulations, case law, democratic agreements and human rights. Organizations such as private detective agencies are less bothered by this, although 'bother' might not be the right word. Lastly, there are also such things as a moral compass and ethical limitations. What is allowed does not necessarily have to happen. Policing is balancing time and again between what can and what may be done. That also makes it such a fine, challenging, but also complicated profession (Eterno and Silverman, 2012).

### Core Values

We finally come (once again) to the core values of the police: reliable, ethical, courageous and binding. In reputation management, these core values do not just serve as characteristics of the identity of the police, but also as guiding principles. The expectation is that if these elements are given sufficient substance and attention in the communication with citizens, this will have a positive effect on the legitimacy of trust in the police.

## In Conclusion

'Performance-based management at the police encompasses strategies such as hot spot policing and evidence-based policing and is based on the fundamental conviction that in tackling crime, policing can make a difference and continuous improvement is always possible.' This is how the opening quote reads from O'Connell and Straub (2007) in *The Best of Three Worlds* (Versteegh et al., 2010). Based on the experiences with performance-based management described in this chapter, a decisive condition can be added to this fundamental conviction: good leadership. Even if the safety strategy chosen by the police has proven effective, even if police information is reliable, valid and up-to-date and even if their safety analyses and means of communication are of high quality, police leaders who aim only at measureable performance figures will not prove to be effective police managers.

**Figure 18.4** Cohesive Police Vision, Management Cycle and Reputation Management.

Based on three important aspects of policing – namely the police vision, management cycle and reputation management – we have developed a management model for the police. In conclusion, we discuss the way in which these aspects are connected. See Figure 18.4.

Effective policing starts with effective leadership. High requirements are set on police managers. Police managers are first of all thoroughly aware of the new vision of policing as described in the National Police Organizational Design Plan (KNP, 2012). Policing is problem-oriented and intelligence-led. Safety policy is implemented in close cooperation with other safety partners. The local administration is in charge. Citizens and entrepreneurs are expressly involved in tackling the most important problems. Police managers understand that this safety strategy will require a totally different management style in the future.

Naturally, as usual, the police manager takes the lead if account has to be rendered to the police authority. If in consultation with that authority, the matter is brought up of which acute and persistent safety problems should be tackled with priority, the police leader, as a subordinate WITH authority, gives shape to the identifying and advisory task of the police. As a safety expert, the police manager and his/her organization have evidence-based knowledge at their disposal of what can and may be done and what is effective. The police manager also knows where the possibilities of policing are limited by laws and regulations, treaties, conventions and ethics. The management of his/her own organization is also self-evidently a core task of a good police manager. If the organization is not in order, the desired professional quality cannot be delivered. The police manager's own management team is directed to do so and the police manager is directed by the higher ranking police manager. From the top down with the last word for the police authority, this is how it happens in the Dutch democracy under the rule of law. And then caring for one's own personnel. A good police manager has trust in the skills of the police workers on the beat and gives them the professional space to work together on a safer society.

The main adjustment is, however, that the police manager acts more than before as the visible figurehead of the police. The accent is less on quantitatively measurable achievements and more on providing for quality and satisfaction of the citizens. Police managers are more involved in the actual work than before. This is called 'management by operations'. This automatically provides for more focus on the surroundings of the police. The police manager takes the lead together with the community police officers in cooperating with citizens, entrepreneurs and other safety partners. Also in the (social) media, the police manager, together with the community police officers, is the face of the police. A police manager serves as a role model for both police and citizens through reliability, integrity and transparency; courageous and decisive when necessary, but always ethical and fair. This is performance by the police manager that should definitely benefit the reputation of the police and with that its legitimacy and authority.

The police manager does not only organize opposition in his/her own organization, but also outside it. By entering into discussions with citizens, entrepreneurs and other safety partners the police manager can continuously check whether the police are still on the right path and meet the legitimate wishes and expectations of the citizens. Municipal councils are also periodically informed about local policing, the choices made in it and the results achieved. The proposed model may well offer the local police more opportunities than before to get closer to the citizens. And it will provide the citizens with more possibilities than before to exert influence on the policing in their own neighbourhoods.

As the figurehead, the police manager therefore holds weekly safety meetings with the community police officers, is optimally aware of what is going on in his/her own coverage area and is interested in the solutions thought up from the operation. In addition, the same police manager has safety consultations chaired by the district head with the other heads of the base teams in the district every two weeks. The district head then has safety consultations every two weeks with the other district heads, chaired by the head of the regional unit. Lastly, at national level, the force management has safety meetings every four weeks with the heads of the regional units and the national unit. In this way, from the bottom up, the safety meetings create a focus on the main problems: local, supralocal, regional, national and international. At the same time, the specific tackling of the main problems self-evidently contributes to the national priorities and agreements with the competent authority from the top down. In this way, safety management and performance-based management definitely form an excellent match, but on condition of good leadership.

## References


Berghuis, B. and De Waard, J. (2011). *Effectief optreden van de politie tegen criminaliteit*, Ministry of Safety and Justice, The Hague.

Eterno, J. A. and Silverman, E. B. (2012). *The Crime Numbers Game: Management by Manipulation (Advances in Police Theory and Practice)*, CRC Press, Taylor & Francis Group, New York.

Intomart GfK (2007). *100% Een onderzoek naar het vertrouwen van burgers in de politie*, on commission by the Ministry of the Interior and Kingdom Relations (BZK), The Hague.

Koch, R. (1997). *Het tachtig/twintig principe. Het geheim van meer bereiken met minder moeite*, Academic service, The Hague.

Kwartiermaker Nationale Politie (KNP) (2012). *Ontwerpplan Nationale politie*, January, The Hague.

O'Connell, P. E. and Straub, F. (2007). *Performance-Based Management for Police Organizations*, Waveland Press, Illinois.

Quinton, P. (2011). *The Impact of Information about Crime and Policing on Public Perceptions*, NPIA, UK.

Raad voor de Maatschappelijke Ontwikkeling (RMO) (2011). *Tegenkracht organiseren: lessen uit de kredietcrisis*, The Hague.

Silverman, E. B. (1999). *NYPD Battles Crime, Innovative Strategies in Policing*, Northeastern University Press, Boston.

Van Dijk, A. J., Hoogewoning, F. C. and Welten, B. J. A. M. (2011). *Dienstbaarheid van een rechtsstaat. Biografie van een agora*, Amsterdam-Amstelland Police, Amsterdam, p. 163.

Versteegh, P., Van der Plas, T. and Nieuwstraten, H. (2010). *The Best of Three Worlds. Effectiever politiewerk door een probleemgerichte aanpak van hot crimes, hot spots, hot shots en hot groups*, Politie Haaglanden, The Hague.

Versteegh, P., Van der Plas, T. and Nieuwstraten, H. (2012). The Best of Three Worlds: More effective policing by a problem-oriented approach of hot crimes, hot spots, hot shots, and hot groups. *Police Practice and Research: An International Journal*, *14*(1), 66–81.

**The International Police Executive Symposium was founded in 1994. The aims and objectives of the IPES are to provide a forum to foster closer relationships among police researchers and practitioners globally, to facilitate cross-cultural, international, and interdisciplinary exchanges for the enrichment of the law enforcement profession, and to encourage discussion and published research on challenging and contemporary topics related to the profession.**

One of the most important activities of the IPES is the organization of an annual meeting under the auspices of a police agency or an educational institution. Every year since 1994 annual meetings have been hosted by such agencies and institutions all over the world. Past hosts have included the Canton Police of Geneva, Switzerland; the International Institute of the Sociology of Law, Onati, Spain; Kanagawa University, Yokohama, Japan; the Federal Police, Vienna, Austria; the Dutch Police and Europol, The Hague, The Netherlands; the Andhra Pradesh Police, India; the Center for Public Safety, Northwestern University, USA; the Polish Police Academy, Szczytno, Poland; the Police of Turkey (twice); the Kingdom of Bahrain Police; a group of institutions in Canada (consisting of the University of the Fraser Valley, Abbotsford Police Department, Royal Canadian Mounted Police, the Vancouver Police Department, the Justice Institute of British Columbia, Canadian Police College and the International Centre for Criminal Law Reform and Criminal Justice Policy); the Czech Police Academy, Prague; the Dubai Police; the Ohio Association of Chiefs of Police and the Cincinnati Police Department, Ohio, USA; the Republic of Macedonia and the Police of Malta. The 2011 Annual Meeting on the theme of "Policing Violence, Crime, Disorder and Discontent: International Perspectives" was hosted in Buenos Aires, Argentina on June 26–30, 2011. The 2012 annual meeting was hosted at United Nations in New York on the theme of "Economic Development, Armed Violence and Public Safety" on August 5–10. The 2013 Annual Meeting on the theme of "Global Issues in Contemporary Policing" was hosted by the Ministry of Interior of Hungary and the Hungarian National Police on August 4–9, 2013. In 2014 there were two meetings: the Annual Meeting on the theme "Policing by Consent" was hosted in Trivandrum (Kerala), India on March 16–21, and the other on "Crime Prevention and Community Resilience" was hosted in Bulgaria's capital city Sofia (July 27–31).

There have been also occasional Special Meetings of IPES. A special meeting was cohosted by the Bavarian Police Academy of Continuing Education in Ainring, Germany, University of Passau, Germany and State University of New York, Plattsburgh, USA in 2000. The second Special Meeting was hosted by the police in the Indian state of Kerala. The third Special Meeting on the theme of "Contemporary Issues in Public Safety and Security" was hosted by the Commissioner of Police of the Blekinge Region of Sweden and the President of the University of Technology on August 10–14, 2011.

The majority of participants of the annual meetings are usually directly involved in the police profession. In addition, scholars and researchers in the field also participate.

The meetings comprise both structured and informal sessions to maximize dialogue and exchange of views and information. The executive summary of each meeting is distributed to participants as well as to a wide range of other interested police professionals and scholars. In addition, a book of selected papers from each annual meeting is published through CRC Press/Taylor & Francis Group, Prentice Hall, Lexington Books and other reputed publishers. A Special Issue of *Police Practice and Research: An International Journal* is also published with the most thematically relevant papers after the usual blind review process.

## IPES Institutional Supporters

APCOF, The African Policing Civilian Oversight Forum (contact: Sean Tait), 2nd floor, The Armoury, Buchanan Square, 160 Sir Lowry Road, Woodstock, Cape Town, 8000 South Africa. Tel: 27-21-461-7211; Fax: 27-21-461-7213. Email: sean@apcof.org.za.

Australian Institute of Police Management, Library, 1 Collins Beach Road, Manly, New South Wales 2095, Australia. Tel: 2-9934-4800; Fax: 2-9934-4780. Email: library@aipm.gov.au.

Baker College of Jackson (contact: Blaine Goodrich), 2800 Springport Road, Jackson, MI 49202, USA. Phone: 517-841-4522. Email: blaine.goodrich@baker.edu.

Cliff Roberson, Professor Emeritus, Washburn University, 16307 Sedona Woods, Houston, TX 77082-1665, USA. Tel: 713-703-6639; Fax: 281-596-8483. Email: roberson37@msn.com.

College of Health and Human Services (contact: Mark E. Correia, PhD Dean), Indiana University of Pennsylvania, 216 Zink Hall, Room 105, 1190 Maple Street, Indiana, PA 15705-1059. Tel: 724-357-2555. Email: mcorreia@iup.edu.

Cyber Defense & Research Initiatives, LLC, PO Box 86, Leslie, MI 49251, USA (contact James Lewis). Tel: 517-242-6730. Email: lewisja@cyberdefenseresearch.com.

Defendology Center for Security, Sociology and Criminology Research (Valibor Lalic), Srpska Street 63,78000 Banja Luka, Bosnia and Herzegovina. Tel and Fax: 387-51-308-914. Email: lalicv@teol.net.

De Montfort University, Health and Life Sciences, School of Applied Social Sciences (contact: Dr Perry Stanislas, Hirsh Sethi), Hawthorn Building, The Gateway, Leicester, LE1 9BH, UK. Tel: (0)116-257-7146. Email: pstanislas@dmu.ac.uk, hsethi@dmu.ac.uk.

Department of Criminal Justice (contact: Dr Harvey L. McMurray, Chair), North Carolina Central University, 301 Whiting Criminal Justice Bldg., Durham, NC 27707, USA. Tel: 919-530-5204, 919-530-7909; Fax: 919-530-5195. Email: hmcmurray@nccu.edu.

Department of Psychology (contact: Stephen Perrott), Mount Saint Vincent University, 166 Bedford Highway, Halifax, Nova Scotia, Canada. Email: Stephen.perrott@mvsu.ca.

Edmundo Oliveira, Prof. PhD. 1 Irving Place University Tower Apt. U 7 A 10003.9723 Manhattan–New York, New York. Tel: 407-342-24-73. Email: edmundooliveira@cfl.rr.com.

Fayetteville State University (contact: Dr David E. Barlow, Professor and Dean), College of Basic and Applied Sciences, 130 Chick Building, 1200 Murchison Road, Fayetteville, North Carolina, 28301 USA. Tel: 910-672-1659; Fax: 910-672-1083. Email: dbarlow@uncfsu.edu.

International Council on Security and Development (ICOS) (contact: Andre Souza, Senior Researcher), Visconde de Piraja 577/605, Ipanema, Rio de Janeiro 22410-003, Brazil. Tel: 21-3186-5444. Email: asouza@icosgroup.net.

Kerala Police (contact: Shri Balasubramaniyum, Director General of Police), Police Headquarters, Trivandrum, Kerala, India. Email: manojabraham05@gmail.com.

Law School, John Moores University (contact: David Lowe, LLB Programme Leader), Law School, Redmonds Building, Brownlow Hill, Liverpool, L3 5UG, UK. Tel: (0)151 231 3918. Email: D.Lowe@ljmu.ac.uk.

Molloy College, The Department of Criminal Justice (contact: Dr John A. Eterno, NYPD Captain-Retired), 1000 Hempstead Avenue, PO Box 5002, Rockville Center, NY 11571-5002, USA. Tel: 516-678-5000, Ext. 6135; Fax: 516-256-2289. Email: mailto:jeterno@molloy.edu.

National Institute of Criminology and Forensic Science (contact: Mr Kamalendra Prasad, Inspector General of Police), MHA, Outer Ring Road, Sector 3, Rohini, Delhi 110085, India. Tel: 91-11-275-2-5095; Fax: 91-11-275-1-0586. Email: director.nicfs@nic.in.

National Police Academy, Japan (contact: Naoya Oyaizu, Deputy Director), Police Policy Research Center, Zip 183–8558: 3-12-1 Asahi-cho Fuchu-city, Tokyo, Japan. Tel: 81-42-354-3550; Fax: 81-42-330-3550. Email: PPRC@npa.go.jp.

Royal Canadian Mounted Police (contact: Craig J. Callens), 657 West 37th Avenue, Vancouver, BC V5Z 1K6, Canada. Tel: 604-264-2003; Fax: 604-264-3547. Email: bcrcmp@rcmp-grc.gc.ca.

School of Psychology and Social Science, Head, Social Justice Research Centre (contact: Prof S. Caroline Taylor, Foundation Chair in Social Justice), Edith Cowan University, 270 Joondalup Drive, Joondalup, WA 6027, Australia. Email: c.taylor@ecu.edu.au.

South Australia Police (contact: Commissioner Mal Hyde), Office of the Commissioner, South Australia Police, 30 Flinders Street, Adelaide, SA 5000, Australia. Email: mal.hyde@police.sa.gov.au.

Southeast Missouri State University (contact: Dr Diana Bruns, Dean), Criminal Justice & Sociology, One University Plaza, Cape Girardeau, MO 63701, USA. Tel: 573-651-2178. Email: dbruns@semo.edu.

The Faculty of Criminal Justice and Security (contact: Dr Gorazd Mesko), University of Maribor, Kotnikova 8, 1000 Ljubljana, Slovenia. Tel: 386-1-300-83-39; Fax: 386-1-2302-687. Email: gorazd.mesko@fvv.uni-mb.si.

UNISA, Department of Police Practice (contact: Setlhomamaru Dintwe), Florida Campus, Cnr Christiaan De Wet and Pioneer Avenues, Private Bag X6, Florida, 1710 South Africa. Tel: 011-471-2116; Cell: 083-581-6102; Fax: 011-471-2255. Email: Dintwsi@unisa.ac.za.

University of Maine at Augusta, College of Natural and Social Sciences (contact: Richard Myers, Professor), 46 University Drive, Augusta, ME 04330-9410, USA. Email: rmyers@maine.edu.

University of New Haven (contact: Dr Mario Gaboury, School of Criminal Justice and Forensic Science), 300 Boston Post Road, West Haven, CT 06516, USA. Tel: 203-932-7260. Email: rward@newhaven.edu.

University of South Africa, College of Law (contact: Professor Kris Pillay, School of Criminal Justice, Director), Preller Street, Muckleneuk, Pretoria. Email: cpillay@unisa.ac.za.

University of the Fraser Valley (contact: Dr Darryl Plecas), Department of Criminology & Criminal Justice, 33844 King Road, Abbotsford, British Columbia V2 S7 M9, Canada. Tel: 604-853-7441; Fax: 604-853-9990. Email: Darryl. plecas@ufv.ca.

University of West Georgia (contact: David A. Jenks, PhD), 1601 Maple Street, Pafford Building 2309, Carrollton, GA 30118, USA. Tel: 678-839-6327. Email: djenks@westga.edu.

# Index

Page numbers in *italics* denote tables.

## C



## D

www.ingramcontent.com/pod-product-compliance
Ingram Content Group UK Ltd.
Pitfield, Milton Keynes, MK11 3LW, UK
UKHW050800180926
475701UK00008B/1160
* 9 7 8 0 3 6 7 8 7 5 5 0 3 *